THE ISRAEL BIBLE

BOOK OF

PSALMS

PRAY LIKE DAVID EDITION

With Hebrew, English,
& English Transliteration

A PUBLICATION OF THE ISRAEL BIBLE

The Israel Bible Book of Psalms: Pray Like David Edition
First Edition, 2022

The Israel Bible was produced by Israel365 in cooperation with
Teach for Israel and is used with permission from
Teach for Israel. All rights reserved.

The English translation was adapted by Israel365 from the JPS Tanakh Copyright O
1985 by the Jewish Publication Society. All rights reserved.

Cover design and typesetting: Chana Gordon

ISBN 979-8-218-11750-4, softcover

*The Israel Bible Book of Psalms: Pray Like David Edition is a holy book that contains the name
of God and should be treated with respect.*

Table of Contents

HEBREW ALPHABET CHART

Letter	Name	Sound
א	Aleph	Silent[1]
בּ	Bet	'B'
ב	Vet	'V'
ג	Gimel	'G'
ד	Dalet	'D'
ה	Hay	'H'
ו	Vav	'V'
ז	Zayin	'Z'
ח	Chet	'KH'
ט	Tet	'Tet'
י	Yud	'Y'
כּ	Kaf	'K'
כ	Khaf	'KH'
ך	Final Khaf	'KH'
ל	Lamed	'L'
מ	Mem	'M'
ם	Final Mem	'M'
נ	Nun	'N'
ן	Final Nun	'N'
ס	Samekh	'S'
ע	Ayin	Silent[1]
פּ	Pay	'P'
פ	Fay	'F'
ף	Final Pey	'F'
צ	Tzadi	'TZ'
ץ	Final Tzadi	'TZ'
ק	Kuf	'K'
ר	Raysh	'R'
שׁ	Shin	'SH'
שׂ	Sin	'S'
תּ	Tav	'T'
ת	Sav	'T'

Vowels: The Aleph is silent[1] so we will use it in the example for each sound

Vowel	Name	Sound
אָ	Kamatz	'a' in hurrah
אַ	Patakh	'a' in hurrah
אָ	Kamatz Katan[3]	'o' in host
אֹו / אֹ	Kholam	'o' in host
אִ	Kheerik Khasayr	'i' in igloo
אִי	Kheerik Malay	'ee' in street
אֶ	Segol	'e' in Edward
אֵ	Tzayray	'ay' in day
אֹו / אֻ	Shuruk/Kubutz	'u' in junior
אְ	Sh'va[2]	' (apostrophe)
אַי	Kamatz + Yud	'ai' in aisle
אַי	Patakh + Yud	'ai' in aisle

Above each letter is its numeric value[4]

Notes:

If there is a vowel underneath the letter, the sound of the vowel is pronounced. If there is no vowel underneath, the letter remains silent.

[2] In Hebrew there are 2 types of Sh'vas. A Sh'va na is considered a vowel and is pronounced. This is represented in our transliteration by the apostrophe (') and pronounced like the 'e' in father. The other sh'va, the sh'va nakh, indicates the end of a syllable. It does not have its own sound, and therefore no phonetic representation.

[3] A kamatz katan looks like a regular kamatz but is pronounced like a kholam.

[4] The Hebrew alphabet has a unique feature known as gematriya, in which every letter is assigned a numerical value.

An Introduction to The Book of Psalms

Rabbi Elie Mischel

The late Chief Rabbi of England, Lord Jonathan Sacks, often spoke with great reverence about his father. A poor refugee who arrived in Great Britain as a child, he left school early to help support his family and did not have the opportunity to receive a strong religious education. Yet Rabbi Sacks writes that his father was a man of deep and abiding faith who was fiercely proud of his heritage, for "when he prayed or read the Psalms he felt intensely that God was with him." The Psalms infused his life with faith, giving him great dignity and strength of mind.

All of the books of the Bible are holy, and all are God's word. But the Book of Psalms holds a special place in the hearts of all believers. Its sublime and timeless poetry expresses our deepest emotions, helping us find the words we need to call out to God. No matter how we are feeling at any given moment, we can turn to Psalms for guidance and inspiration.

David, the primary author of Psalms, was neither the greatest scholar of his time nor free of sin. But perhaps more than any other personality in the Bible, David understood that God is always with us, precisely when we feel most alone. Over and over again, David calls out to God in pain:

> *Save me, O God,*
> *for the floodwaters are up to my neck.*
> *Deeper and deeper I sink into the mire;*
> *I can't find a foothold.*
> *I am in deep water,*
> *and the floods overwhelm me.*
>
> **— (Psalms 69:2-3)**

> *From the depths, O Lord,*
> *I call for your help.*
>
> — *(Psalms 130:1)*

From the depths of his soul, David cries out to God. and ultimately feels that God is stretching out His hand to him with love.

Psalms is also a book of extraordinary joy. The very first word of the book, "Ashrei," is one of the Biblical words for happiness. So many of the Psalms are bursting with joy! And even when David spoke of fear and despair, his songs usually end with hope and joy:

> *For His anger lasts only a moment,*
> *but His favor lasts a lifetime;*
> *weeping may stay for the night,*
> *but rejoicing comes in the morning...*
> *You turned my wailing into dancing;*
> *you removed my sackcloth and clothed me with joy,*
> *that my heart may sing your praises and not be silent.*
> *Lord my God, I will praise you forever.*
>
> — *(Psalms 30:6-13)*

In this latest edition of the Book of Psalms, every verse in Psalms is laid out in three columns: in the original Hebrew, transliterated to English, and translated to English. The transliteration of each verse, an exciting new feature, will allow readers who are not fluent in Hebrew to recite Psalms in the holy tongue, just as King David uttered these beautiful words three millennia ago. Readers can also hear the entire Bible read in Hebrew on our website,
WWW.THEISRAELBIBLE.COM.

We pray that this edition of Psalms will bring you strength and joy on your life journey, and that you always feel the presence and love of God, in both good times and bad.

> *The Lord of hosts is with us;*
> *The God of Jacob is our fortress.*
>
> — *(Psalm 46:7)*

1

א

Happy is the man who has not followed the counsel of the wicked, or taken the path of sinners, or joined the company of the insolent;

1

Ashrei-ha'ish asher lo halach ba'atzat resha'im uvederech chatta'im lo amad uvemoshav letzim lo yashav.

אַשְׁרֵי־הָאִישׁ אֲשֶׁר לֹא הָלַךְ בַּעֲצַת רְשָׁעִים וּבְדֶרֶךְ חַטָּאִים לֹא עָמָד וּבְמוֹשַׁב לֵצִים לֹא יָשָׁב: א

rather, the teaching of Hashem is his delight, and he studies that teaching day and night.

2

Ki im betorat Adonai cheftzo uvetorato yehgeh yomam valayla

כִּי אִם בְּתוֹרַת יְהֹוָה חֶפְצוֹ וּבְתוֹרָתוֹ יֶהְגֶּה יוֹמָם וָלָיְלָה: ב

He is like a tree planted beside streams of water, which yields its fruit in season, whose foliage never fades, and whatever it produces thrives.

3

Vehayah ke'etz shatul al-palgei mayim asher piryo yitten be'itto ve'alehu lo-yibbol vechol asher-ya'aseh yatzliach.

וְהָיָה כְּעֵץ שָׁתוּל עַל־פַּלְגֵי מָיִם אֲשֶׁר פִּרְיוֹ יִתֵּן בְּעִתּוֹ וְעָלֵהוּ לֹא־יִבּוֹל וְכֹל אֲשֶׁר־יַעֲשֶׂה יַצְלִיחַ: ג

Not so the wicked; rather, they are like chaff that wind blows away.

4

Lo-chen haresha'im ki im-kammotz asher-tiddefennu ruach.

לֹא־כֵן הָרְשָׁעִים כִּי אִם־כַּמֹּץ אֲשֶׁר־תִּדְּפֶנּוּ רוּחַ: ד

Therefore the wicked will not survive judgment, nor will sinners, in the assembly of the righteous.

5

Al-ken lo-yakumu resha'im bammishpat vechatta'im ba'adat tzaddikim.

עַל־כֵּן לֹא־יָקֻמוּ רְשָׁעִים בַּמִּשְׁפָּט וְחַטָּאִים בַּעֲדַת צַדִּיקִים: ה

6	For Hashem cherishes the way of the righteous, but the way of the wicked is doomed.	*Ki-yodea' Adonai derech tzaddikim vederech resha'im toved.*	כִּי־יוֹדֵעַ יְהֹוָה דֶּרֶךְ צַדִּיקִים וְדֶרֶךְ רְשָׁעִים תֹּאבֵד: ו

2

—⚬◈⚬—

ב

1	Why do nations assemble, and peoples plot vain things;	*Lammah rageshu goyim ule'ummim yehgu-rik.*	לָמָּה רָגְשׁוּ גוֹיִם וּלְאֻמִּים יֶהְגּוּ־רִיק: א
2	kings of the earth take their stand, and regents intrigue together against Hashem and against His anointed?	*Yityatzevu malchei-eretz verozenim nosedu-yachad al-Adonai ve'al-meshicho.*	יִתְיַצְּבוּ מַלְכֵי־אֶרֶץ וְרוֹזְנִים נוֹסְדוּ־יָחַד עַל־יְהֹוָה וְעַל־מְשִׁיחוֹ: ב
3	"Let us break the cords of their yoke, shake off their ropes from us!"	*Nenattekah et-moseroteimo venashlichah mimmennu avoteimo.*	נְנַתְּקָה אֶת־מוֹסְרוֹתֵימוֹ וְנַשְׁלִיכָה מִמֶּנּוּ עֲבֹתֵימוֹ: ג
4	He who is enthroned in heaven laughs; Hashem mocks at them.	*Yoshev bashamayim yischak Adonai yil'ag-lamo.*	יוֹשֵׁב בַּשָּׁמַיִם יִשְׂחָק אֲדֹנָי יִלְעַג־לָמוֹ: ד
5	Then He speaks to them in anger, terrifying them in His rage,	*Az yedabber eleimo ve'appo uvacharono yevahalemo.*	אָז יְדַבֵּר אֵלֵימוֹ בְאַפּוֹ וּבַחֲרוֹנוֹ יְבַהֲלֵמוֹ: ה
6	"But I have installed My king on Tzion, My holy mountain!"	*Va'ani nasachti malki al-tziyyon har-kodshi.*	וַאֲנִי נָסַכְתִּי מַלְכִּי עַל־צִיּוֹן הַר־קָדְשִׁי: ו

7	Let me tell of the decree: Hashem said to me, "You are My son, I have fathered you this day.	*Asapperah el chok Adonai amar elai beni attah ani hayyom yelidticha.*	אֲסַפְּרָה אֶל חֹק יְהֹוָה אָמַר אֵלַי בְּנִי אַתָּה אֲנִי הַיּוֹם יְלִדְתִּיךָ: ז
8	Ask it of Me, and I will make the nations your domain; your estate, the limits of the earth.	*She'al mimmenni ve'ettenah goyim nachalatecha va'achuzzatecha afsei-aretz.*	שְׁאַל מִמֶּנִּי וְאֶתְּנָה גוֹיִם נַחֲלָתֶךָ וַאֲחֻזָּתְךָ אַפְסֵי־אָרֶץ: ח
9	You can smash them with an iron mace, shatter them like potter's ware."	*Tero'em beshevet barzel kichli yotzer tenappetzem.*	תְּרֹעֵם בְּשֵׁבֶט בַּרְזֶל כִּכְלִי יוֹצֵר תְּנַפְּצֵם: ט
10	So now, O kings, be prudent; accept discipline, you rulers of the earth!	*Ve'attah melachim haskilu hivvaseru shofetei aretz.*	וְעַתָּה מְלָכִים הַשְׂכִּילוּ הִוָּסְרוּ שֹׁפְטֵי אָרֶץ: י
11	Serve Hashem in awe; tremble with fright,	*Ivdu et-Adonai beyir'ah vegilu bir'adah.*	עִבְדוּ אֶת־יְהֹוָה בְּיִרְאָה וְגִילוּ בִּרְעָדָה: יא
12	pay homage in good faith, lest He be angered, and your way be doomed in the mere flash of His anger. Happy are all who take refuge in Him.	*Nasheku-var pen-ye'enaf vetovdu derech ki-yiv'ar kim'at appo ashrei kol-chosei vo.*	נַשְּׁקוּ־בַר פֶּן־יֶאֱנַף וְתֹאבְדוּ דֶרֶךְ כִּי־יִבְעַר כִּמְעַט אַפּוֹ אַשְׁרֵי כָּל־חוֹסֵי בוֹ: יב

3

1	A psalm of David when he fled from his son Avshalom.	*Mizmor ledavid bevorcho mippenei avshalom beno.*

מִזְמוֹר לְדָוִד בְּבָרְחוֹ מִפְּנֵי אַבְשָׁלוֹם בְּנוֹ: א

2 Hashem, my foes are so many! Many are those who attack me;

Adonai mah-rabbu tzarai rabbim kamim alai.

יְהֹוָה מָה־רַבּוּ צָרָי רַבִּים קָמִים עָלָי: ב

3 many say of me, "There is no deliverance for him through Hashem." Selah.

Rabbim omerim lenafshi ein yeshu'atah lo velohim selah.

רַבִּים אֹמְרִים לְנַפְשִׁי אֵין יְשׁוּעָתָה לּוֹ בֵאלֹהִים סֶלָה: ג

4 But You, Hashem, are a shield about me, my glory, He who holds my head high.

Ve'attah Adonai magen ba'adi kevodi umerim roshi.

וְאַתָּה יְהֹוָה מָגֵן בַּעֲדִי כְּבוֹדִי וּמֵרִים רֹאשִׁי: ד

5 I cry aloud to Hashem, and He answers me from His holy mountain. Selah.

Koli el-Adonai ekra vayya'aneni mehar kodsho selah.

קוֹלִי אֶל־יְהֹוָה אֶקְרָא וַיַּעֲנֵנִי מֵהַר קָדְשׁוֹ סֶלָה: ה

6 I lie down and sleep and wake again, for Hashem sustains me.

Ani shachavti va'ishanah hekitzoti ki Adonai yismecheni.

אֲנִי שָׁכַבְתִּי וָאִישָׁנָה הֱקִיצוֹתִי כִּי יְהֹוָה יִסְמְכֵנִי: ו

7 I have no fear of the myriad forces arrayed against me on every side.

Lo-ira merivvot am asher saviv shatu alai.

לֹא־אִירָא מֵרִבְבוֹת עָם אֲשֶׁר סָבִיב שָׁתוּ עָלָי: ז

8	Rise, Hashem! Deliver me, O my God! For You slap all my enemies in the face; You break the teeth of the wicked.	*Kumah Adonai hoshi'eni elohai ki-hikkita et-kol-oyevai lechi shinnei resha'im shibbarta.*	קוּמָה יְהֹוָה הוֹשִׁיעֵנִי אֱלֹהַי כִּי־הִכִּיתָ אֶת־כָּל־אֹיְבַי לֶחִי שִׁנֵּי רְשָׁעִים שִׁבַּרְתָּ: ח
9	Deliverance is Hashem's; Your blessing be upon Your people! Selah.	*LAdonai hayyeshu'ah al-ammecha virchatecha selah.*	לַיהֹוָה הַיְשׁוּעָה עַל־עַמְּךָ בִרְכָתֶךָ סֶּלָה: ט

4

——◦◇◇◇◦——

ד

1	For the leader; with instrumental music. A psalm of David.	*Lammenatzeach binginot mizmor ledavid.*	לַמְנַצֵּחַ בִּנְגִינוֹת מִזְמוֹר לְדָוִד: א
2	Answer me when I call, O Hashem, my vindicator! You freed me from distress; have mercy on me and hear my prayer.	*Bekare'i aneni elohei tzidki batzar hirchavta li channeni ushema tefillati.*	בְּקָרְאִי עֲנֵנִי אֱלֹהֵי צִדְקִי בַּצָּר הִרְחַבְתָּ לִּי חָנֵּנִי וּשְׁמַע תְּפִלָּתִי: ב
3	You men, how long will my glory be mocked, will you love illusions, have recourse to frauds? Selah.	*Benei ish ad-meh chevodi lichlimmah te'ehavun rik tevakshu chazav seluh.*	בְּנֵי אִישׁ עַד־מֶה כְבוֹדִי לִכְלִמָּה תֶּאֱהָבוּן רִיק תְּבַקְשׁוּ כָזָב סֶלָה: ג
4	Know that Hashem singles out the faithful for Himself; Hashem hears when I call to Him.	*Ude'u ki-hiflah Adonai chasid lo Adonai yishma bekare'i elav.*	וּדְעוּ כִּי־הִפְלָה יְהֹוָה חָסִיד לוֹ יְהֹוָה יִשְׁמַע בְּקָרְאִי אֵלָיו: ד

5	So tremble, and sin no more; ponder it on your bed, and sigh.	*Rigzu ve'al-techeta'u imru vilvavchem al-mishkavchem vedommu selah.*	רִגְזוּ וְאַל־תֶּחֱטָאוּ אִמְרוּ בִלְבַבְכֶם עַל־מִשְׁכַּבְכֶם וְדֹמּוּ סֶלָה: ה
6	Offer sacrifices in righteousness and trust in Hashem.	*Zivchu zivchei-tzedek uvitchu el-Adonai.*	זִבְחוּ זִבְחֵי־צֶדֶק וּבִטְחוּ אֶל־יְהֹוָה: ו
7	Many say, "O for good days!" Bestow Your favor on us, Hashem.	*Rabbim omerim mi-yar'enu tov nesah-aleinu or panecha Adonai.*	רַבִּים אֹמְרִים מִי־יַרְאֵנוּ טוֹב נְסָה־עָלֵינוּ אוֹר פָּנֶיךָ יְהֹוָה: ז
8	You put joy into my heart when their grain and wine show increase.	*Natattah simchah velibbi me'et deganam vetirosham rabbu.*	נָתַתָּה שִׂמְחָה בְלִבִּי מֵעֵת דְּגָנָם וְתִירוֹשָׁם רָבּוּ: ח
9	Safe and sound, I lie down and sleep, for You alone, Hashem, keep me secure.	*Beshalom yachdav eshkevah ve'ishan ki-attah Adonai levadad lavetach toshiveni.*	בְּשָׁלוֹם יַחְדָּו אֶשְׁכְּבָה וְאִישָׁן כִּי־אַתָּה יְהֹוָה לְבָדָד לָבֶטַח תּוֹשִׁיבֵנִי: ט

5

⸺○⟨⟩○⸺

ה

1	For the leader; on nechiloth. A psalm of David.	*Lammenatzeach el-hannechilot mizmor ledavid.*	לַמְנַצֵּחַ אֶל־הַנְּחִילוֹת מִזְמוֹר לְדָוִד: א
2	Give ear to my speech, Hashem; consider my utterance.	*Amarai ha'azinah Adonai binah hagigi.*	אֲמָרַי הַאֲזִינָה יְהֹוָה בִּינָה הֲגִיגִי: ב

3	Heed the sound of my cry, my king and Hashem, for I pray to You.	*Hakshivah lekol shav'i malki velohai ki-eleicha etpallal*	הַקְשִׁיבָה לְקוֹל שַׁוְעִי מַלְכִּי וֵאלֹהָי כִּי־אֵלֶיךָ אֶתְפַּלָּל:	ג
4	Hear my voice, Hashem, at daybreak; at daybreak I plead before You, and wait.	*Adonai boker tishma koli boker e'erach-lecha va'atzappeh*	יְהֹוָה בֹּקֶר תִּשְׁמַע קוֹלִי בֹּקֶר אֶעֱרָךְ־לְךָ וַאֲצַפֶּה:	ד
5	For You are not a Hashem who desires wickedness; evil cannot abide with You;	*Ki lo el-chafetz resha attah lo yegurcha ra*	כִּי לֹא אֵל־חָפֵץ רֶשַׁע אָתָּה לֹא יְגֻרְךָ רָע:	ה
6	wanton men cannot endure in Your sight. You detest all evildoers;	*Lo-yityatzevu holelim leneged eineicha saneta kol-po'alei aven*	לֹא־יִתְיַצְּבוּ הוֹלְלִים לְנֶגֶד עֵינֶיךָ שָׂנֵאתָ כָּל־פֹּעֲלֵי אָוֶן:	ו
7	You doom those who speak lies; murderous, deceitful men Hashem abhors.	*Te'abbed doverei chazav ish-damim umirmah yeta'ev Adonai*	תְּאַבֵּד דֹּבְרֵי כָזָב אִישׁ־דָּמִים וּמִרְמָה יְתָעֵב יְהֹוָה:	ז
8	But I, through Your abundant love, enter Your house; I bow down in awe at Your holy temple.	*Va'ani berov chasdecha avo veitecha eshtachaveh el-heichal-kodshecha beyir'atecha*	וַאֲנִי בְּרֹב חַסְדְּךָ אָבוֹא בֵיתֶךָ אֶשְׁתַּחֲוֶה אֶל־הֵיכַל־קָדְשְׁךָ בְּיִרְאָתֶךָ:	ח
9	Hashem, lead me along Your righteous [path] because of my watchful foes; make Your way straight before me.	*Adonai necheni vetzidkatecha lema'an shorerai hoshar [hayyeshar] lefanai darkecha*	יְהֹוָה נְחֵנִי בְצִדְקָתֶךָ לְמַעַן שׁוֹרְרָי הוֹשַׁר [הַיְשַׁר] לְפָנַי דַּרְכֶּךָ:	ט

10	For there is no sincerity on their lips; their heart is [filled with] malice; their throat is an open grave; their tongue slippery.	*Ki ein befihu nechonah kirbam havvvot kever-patuach geronam leshonam yachalikun*	כִּי אֵין בְּפִיהוּ נְכוֹנָה קִרְבָּם הַוּוֹת קֶבֶר־פָּתוּחַ גְּרוֹנָם לְשׁוֹנָם יַחֲלִיקוּן:	י
11	Condemn them, O Hashem; let them fall by their own devices; cast them out for their many crimes, for they defy You.	*Ha'ashimem elohim yippelu mimmo'atzoteihem berov pish'eihem haddichemo ki-maru vach*	הַאֲשִׁימֵם אֱלֹהִים יִפְּלוּ מִמֹּעֲצוֹתֵיהֶם בְּרֹב פִּשְׁעֵיהֶם הַדִּיחֵמוֹ כִּי־מָרוּ בָךְ:	יא
12	But let all who take refuge in You rejoice, ever jubilant as You shelter them; and let those who love Your name exult in You.	*Veyismechu chol-chosei vach le'olam yerannenu vetasech aleimo veya'letzu vecha ohavei shemecha*	וְיִשְׂמְחוּ כָל־חוֹסֵי בָךְ לְעוֹלָם יְרַנֵּנוּ וְתָסֵךְ עָלֵימוֹ וְיַעְלְצוּ בְךָ אֹהֲבֵי שְׁמֶךְ:	יב
13	For You surely bless the righteous man, Hashem, encompassing him with favor like a shield.	*Ki-attah tevarech tzaddik Adonai katzinnah ratzon ta'terennu*	כִּי־אַתָּה תְּבָרֵךְ צַדִּיק יְהֹוָה כַּצִּנָּה רָצוֹן תַּעְטְרֶנּוּ:	יג

6

—◦❦◦—

ו

1	For the leader; with instrumental music on the sheminith. A psalm of David.	*Lammenatzeach binginot al-hasheminit mizmor ledavid*	לַמְנַצֵּחַ בִּנְגִינוֹת עַל־הַשְּׁמִינִית מִזְמוֹר לְדָוִד:	א

2	Hashem, do not punish me in anger, do not chastise me in fury.	*Adonai al-be'appecha tochicheni ve'al-bachamatecha teyassereni*

יְהֹוָה אַל־בְּאַפְּךָ תוֹכִיחֵנִי וְאַל־בַּחֲמָתְךָ תְיַסְּרֵנִי: ב

| 3 | Have mercy on me, Hashem, for I languish; heal me, Hashem, for my bones shake with terror. | *Channeni Adonai ki umlal ani refa'eni Adonai ki nivhalu atzamai* |

חָנֵּנִי יְהֹוָה כִּי אֻמְלַל אָנִי רְפָאֵנִי יְהֹוָה כִּי נִבְהֲלוּ עֲצָמָי: ג

| 4 | My whole being is stricken with terror, while You, Hashem—O, how long! | *Venafshi nivhalah me'od v'et [ve'attah] Adonai ad-matai* |

וְנַפְשִׁי נִבְהֲלָה מְאֹד וְאַת [וְאַתָּה] יְהֹוָה עַד־מָתָי: ד

| 5 | Hashem, turn! Rescue me! Deliver me as befits Your faithfulness. | *Shuvah Adonai challetzah nafshi hoshi'eni lema'an chasdecha* |

שׁוּבָה יְהֹוָה חַלְּצָה נַפְשִׁי הוֹשִׁיעֵנִי לְמַעַן חַסְדֶּךָ: ה

| 6 | For there is no praise of You among the dead; in Sheol, who can acclaim You? | *Ki ein bammavet zichrecha bish'ol mi yodeh-lach* |

כִּי אֵין בַּמָּוֶת זִכְרֶךָ בִּשְׁאוֹל מִי יוֹדֶה־לָּךְ: ו

| 7 | I am weary with groaning; every night I drench my bed, I melt my couch in tears. | *Yaga'ti be'anchati ascheh vechol-layyelah mittati bedim'ati arsi amseh* |

יָגַעְתִּי בְּאַנְחָתִי אַשְׂחֶה בְכָל־לַיְלָה מִטָּתִי בְּדִמְעָתִי עַרְשִׂי אַמְסֶה: ז

| 8 | My eyes are wasted by vexation, worn out because of all my foes. | *Asheshah mikka'as eini atekah bechol-tzorerai* |

עָשְׁשָׁה מִכַּעַס עֵינִי עָתְקָה בְּכָל־צוֹרְרָי: ח

| 9 | Away from me, all you evildoers, for Hashem heeds the sound of my weeping. | *suru mimmenni kol-po'alei aven ki-shama Adonai kol bichyi* |

סוּרוּ מִמֶּנִּי כָּל־פֹּעֲלֵי אָוֶן כִּי־שָׁמַע יְהֹוָה קוֹל בִּכְיִי: ט

17

10	Hashem heeds my plea, Hashem accepts my prayer.	*Shama Adonai techinnati Adonai tefillati yikkach*	שָׁמַע יְהֹוָה תְּחִנָּתִי יְהֹוָה תְּפִלָּתִי יִקָּח׃	י
11	All my enemies will be frustrated and stricken with terror; they will turn back in an instant, frustrated.	*Yevoshu veyibbahalu me'od kol-oyevai yashuvu yevoshu raga*	יֵבֹשׁוּ וְיִבָּהֲלוּ מְאֹד כָּל־אֹיְבָי יָשֻׁבוּ יֵבֹשׁוּ רָגַע׃	יא

7

—◦❨❀❩◦—

1	Shiggaion of David, which he sang to Hashem, concerning Cush, a Benjaminite.	*Shiggayon ledavid asher-shar lAdonai al-divrei-chush ben-yemini*	שִׁגָּיוֹן לְדָוִד אֲשֶׁר־שָׁר לַיהֹוָה עַל־דִּבְרֵי־כוּשׁ בֶּן־יְמִינִי׃	א
2	Hashem, my God, in You I seek refuge; deliver me from all my pursuers and save me,	*Adonai elohai becha chasiti hoshi'eni mikkol-rodefai vehatzileni*	יְהֹוָה אֱלֹהַי בְּךָ חָסִיתִי הוֹשִׁיעֵנִי מִכָּל־רֹדְפַי וְהַצִּילֵנִי׃	ב
3	lest, like a lion, they tear me apart, rending in pieces, and no one save me.	*Pen-yitrof ke'aryeh nafshi porek ve'ein matzil*	פֶּן־יִטְרֹף כְּאַרְיֵה נַפְשִׁי פֹּרֵק וְאֵין מַצִּיל׃	ג
4	Hashem, my God, if I have done such things, if my hands bear the guilt of wrongdoing,	*Adonai elohai im-asiti zot im-yesh-avel bechappai*	יְהֹוָה אֱלֹהַי אִם־עָשִׂיתִי זֹאת אִם־יֶשׁ־עָוֶל בְּכַפָּי׃	ד
5	if I have dealt evil to my ally— I who rescued my foe without reward—	*Im-gamalti sholemi ra va'achalletzah tzoreri reikam*	אִם־גָּמַלְתִּי שׁוֹלְמִי רָע וָאֲחַלְּצָה צוֹרְרִי רֵיקָם׃	ה

6 | then let the enemy pursue and overtake me; let him trample my life to the ground, and lay my body in the dust. Selah. | *Yiraddof oyev nafshi veyasseg veyirmos la'aretz chayyai uchevodi le'afar yashken selah* | יִרַדֹּף אוֹיֵב נַפְשִׁי וְיַשֵּׂג וְיִרְמֹס לָאָרֶץ חַיָּי וּכְבוֹדִי לֶעָפָר יַשְׁכֵּן סֶלָה: | ו

7 | Rise, Hashem, in Your anger; assert Yourself against the fury of my foes; bestir Yourself on my behalf; You have ordained judgment. | *Kumah Adonai be'appecha hinnase be'avrot tzorerai ve'urah elai mishpat tzivvita* | קוּמָה יְהֹוָה בְּאַפֶּךָ הִנָּשֵׂא בְּעַבְרוֹת צוֹרְרָי וְעוּרָה אֵלַי מִשְׁפָּט צִוִּיתָ: | ז

8 | Let the assembly of peoples gather about You, with You enthroned above, on high. | *Va'adat le'ummim tesovevekka ve'aleiha lammarom shuvah* | וַעֲדַת לְאֻמִּים תְּסוֹבְבֶךָּ וְעָלֶיהָ לַמָּרוֹם שׁוּבָה: | ח

9 | Hashem judges the peoples; vindicate me, Hashem, for the righteousness and blamelessness that are mine. | *Adonai yadin ammim shafeteni Adonai ketzidki uchetummi alai* | יְהֹוָה יָדִין עַמִּים שָׁפְטֵנִי יְהֹוָה כְּצִדְקִי וּכְתֻמִּי עָלָי: | ט

10 | Let the evil of the wicked come to an end, but establish the righteous; he who probes the mind and conscience is Hashem the righteous. | *Yigmar-na ra resha'im utechonen tzaddik uvochen libbot uchelayot elohim tzaddik* | יִגְמָר נָא רַע רְשָׁעִים וּתְכוֹנֵן צַדִּיק וּבֹחֵן לִבּוֹת וּכְלָיוֹת אֱלֹהִים צַדִּיק: | י

11	I look to Hashem to shield me; the deliverer of the upright.	*Maginni al-elohim moshia' yishrei-lev*	מָגִנִּי עַל־אֱלֹהִים מוֹשִׁיעַ יִשְׁרֵי־לֵב:	יא
12	Hashem vindicates the righteous; Hashem pronounces doom each day.	*Elohim shofet tzaddik ve'el zo'em bechol-yom*	אֱלֹהִים שׁוֹפֵט צַדִּיק וְאֵל זֹעֵם בְּכָל־יוֹם:	יב
13	If one does not turn back, but whets his sword, bends his bow and aims it,	*Im-lo yashuv charbo yiltosh kashto darach vaychoneneha*	אִם־לֹא יָשׁוּב חַרְבּוֹ יִלְטוֹשׁ קַשְׁתּוֹ דָרַךְ וַיְכוֹנְנֶהָ:	יג
14	then against himself he readies deadly weapons, and makes his arrows sharp.	*Velo hechin kelei-mavet chitzav ledolekim yif'al*	וְלוֹ הֵכִין כְּלֵי־מָוֶת חִצָּיו לְדֹלְקִים יִפְעָל:	יד
15	See, he hatches evil, conceives mischief, and gives birth to fraud.	*Hinneh yechabbel-aven veharah amal veyalad shaker*	הִנֵּה יְחַבֶּל־אָוֶן וְהָרָה עָמָל וְיָלַד שָׁקֶר:	טו
16	He has dug a pit and deepened it, and will fall into the trap he made.	*Bor karah vayyachperehu vayyippol beshachat yif'al*	בּוֹר כָּרָה וַיַּחְפְּרֵהוּ וַיִּפֹּל בְּשַׁחַת יִפְעָל:	טז
17	His mischief will recoil upon his own head; his lawlessness will come down upon his skull.	*Yashuv amalo verosho ve'al kadekodo chamaso yered*	יָשׁוּב עֲמָלוֹ בְרֹאשׁוֹ וְעַל קָדְקֳדוֹ חֲמָסוֹ יֵרֵד:	יז
18	I will praise Hashem for His righteousness, and sing a hymn to the name of Hashem Most High.	*Odeh Adonai ketzidko va'azammerah shem-Adonai elyon*	אוֹדֶה יְהוָה כְּצִדְקוֹ וַאֲזַמְּרָה שֵׁם־יְהוָה עֶלְיוֹן:	יח

8   —◦⦉⧓⦊◦—   חח

	English	Transliteration	Hebrew

1 For the leader; on the gittith. A psalm of David.

Lammenatzeach al-haggittit mizmor ledavid

לַמְנַצֵּחַ עַל־הַגִּתִּית מִזְמוֹר לְדָוִד: א

2 Hashem, our Lord, How majestic is Your name throughout the earth, You who have covered the heavens with Your splendor!

Adonai adoneinu mah-addir shimcha bechol-ha'aretz asher tenah hodecha al-hashamayim

יְהֹוָה אֲדֹנֵינוּ מָה־אַדִּיר שִׁמְךָ בְּכָל־הָאָרֶץ אֲשֶׁר תְּנָה הוֹדְךָ עַל־הַשָּׁמָיִם: ב

3 From the mouths of infants and sucklings You have founded strength on account of Your foes, to put an end to enemy and avenger.

Mippi olelim veyonekim yissadta oz lema'an tzorereicha lehashbit oyev umitnakkem

מִפִּי עוֹלְלִים וְיֹנְקִים יִסַּדְתָּ עֹז לְמַעַן צוֹרְרֶיךָ לְהַשְׁבִּית אוֹיֵב וּמִתְנַקֵּם: ג

4 When I behold Your heavens, the work of Your fingers, the moon and stars that You set in place,

Ki-er'eh shameicha ma'asei etzbe'oteicha yareach vechochavim asher konanetah

כִּי־אֶרְאֶה שָׁמֶיךָ מַעֲשֵׂי אֶצְבְּעֹתֶיךָ יָרֵחַ וְכוֹכָבִים אֲשֶׁר כּוֹנָנְתָּה: ד

5 what is man that You have been mindful of him, mortal man that You have taken note of him,

Mah-enosh ki-tizkerennu uven-adam ki tifkedennu

מָה־אֱנוֹשׁ כִּי־תִזְכְּרֶנּוּ וּבֶן־אָדָם כִּי תִפְקְדֶנּוּ: ה

6	that You have made him little less than divine, and adorned him with glory and majesty;	*Vattechasserehu me'at me'elohim vechavod vehadar te'atterehu*	וַתְּחַסְּרֵהוּ מְּעַט מֵאֱלֹהִים וְכָבוֹד וְהָדָר תְּעַטְּרֵהוּ׃
7	You have made him master over Your handiwork, laying the world at his feet,	*Tamshilehu bema'asei yadeicha kol shattah tachat-raglav*	תַּמְשִׁילֵהוּ בְּמַעֲשֵׂי יָדֶיךָ כֹּל שַׁתָּה תַחַת־רַגְלָיו׃
8	sheep and oxen, all of them, and wild beasts, too;	*Tzoneh va'alafim kullam vegam bahamot sadai*	צֹנֶה וַאֲלָפִים כֻּלָּם וְגַם בַּהֲמוֹת שָׂדָי׃
9	the birds of the heavens, the fish of the sea, whatever travels the paths of the seas.	*Tzippor shamayim udegei hayyam over arechot yammim*	צִפּוֹר שָׁמַיִם וּדְגֵי הַיָּם עֹבֵר אָרְחוֹת יַמִּים׃
10	Hashem, our Lord, how majestic is Your name throughout the earth!	*Adonai adoneinu mah-addir shimcha bechol-ha'aretz*	יְהֹוָה אֲדֹנֵינוּ מָה־אַדִּיר שִׁמְךָ בְּכָל־הָאָרֶץ׃

9

—○❈○—

ט

1	For the leader; 'almuth labben. A psalm of David.	*Lammenatzeach almut labben mizmor ledavid*	לַמְנַצֵּחַ עַלְמוּת לַבֵּן מִזְמוֹר לְדָוִד׃

2	I will praise You, Hashem, with all my heart; I will tell all Your wonders.	*Odeh Adonai bechol-libbi asapperah kol-nifle'oteicha*	אוֹדֶה יְהֹוָה בְּכָל־לִבִּי אֲסַפְּרָה כָּל־נִפְלְאוֹתֶיךָ׃
3	I will rejoice and exult in You, singing a hymn to Your name, O Most High.	*Esmechah ve'e'eltzah vach azammerah shimcha elyon*	אֶשְׂמְחָה וְאֶעֶלְצָה בָךְ אֲזַמְּרָה שִׁמְךָ עֶלְיוֹן׃
4	When my enemies retreat, they stumble to their doom at Your presence.	*Beshuv-oyevai achor yikkashelu veyovdu mippanecha*	בְּשׁוּב־אוֹיְבַי אָחוֹר יִכָּשְׁלוּ וְיֹאבְדוּ מִפָּנֶיךָ׃
5	For You uphold my right and claim, enthroned as righteous judge.	*Ki-asita mishpati vedini yashavta lechisse shofet tzedek*	כִּי־עָשִׂיתָ מִשְׁפָּטִי וְדִינִי יָשַׁבְתָּ לְכִסֵּא שׁוֹפֵט צֶדֶק׃
6	You blast the nations; You destroy the wicked; You blot out their name forever.	*Ga'arta goyim ibbadta rasha shemam machita le'olam va'ed*	גָּעַרְתָּ גוֹיִם אִבַּדְתָּ רָשָׁע שְׁמָם מָחִיתָ לְעוֹלָם וָעֶד׃
7	The enemy is no more— ruins everlasting; You have torn down their cities; their very names are lost.	*Ha'oyev tammu choravot lanetzach ve'arim natashta avad zichram hemmah*	הָאוֹיֵב תַּמּוּ חֳרָבוֹת לָנֶצַח וְעָרִים נָתַשְׁתָּ אָבַד זִכְרָם הֵמָּה׃
8	But Hashem abides forever; He has set up His throne for judgment;	*Va'Adonai le'olam yeshev konen lammishpat kis'o*	וַיהֹוָה לְעוֹלָם יֵשֵׁב כּוֹנֵן לַמִּשְׁפָּט כִּסְאוֹ׃

9	it is He who judges the world with righteousness, rules the peoples with equity.	*Vehu yishpot-tevel betzedek yadin le'ummim bemeisharim*	וְהוּא יִשְׁפֹּט־תֵּבֵל בְּצֶדֶק יָדִין לְאֻמִּים בְּמֵישָׁרִים:	ט
10	Hashem is a haven for the oppressed, a haven in times of trouble.	*Vihi Adonai misgav laddach misgav le'ittot batzarah*	וִיהִי יְהֹוָה מִשְׂגָּב לַדָּךְ מִשְׂגָּב לְעִתּוֹת בַּצָּרָה:	י
11	Those who know Your name trust You, for You do not abandon those who turn to You, Hashem.	*Veyivtechu vecha yode'ei shemecha ki lo-azavta doresheicha Adonai*	וְיִבְטְחוּ בְךָ יוֹדְעֵי שְׁמֶךָ כִּי לֹא־עָזַבְתָּ דֹרְשֶׁיךָ יְהֹוָה:	יא
12	Sing a hymn to Hashem, who reigns in Tzion; declare His deeds among the peoples.	*Zammeru lAdonai yoshev tziyyon haggidu va'ammim alilotav*	זַמְּרוּ לַיהֹוָה יֹשֵׁב צִיּוֹן הַגִּידוּ בָעַמִּים עֲלִילוֹתָיו:	יב
13	For He does not ignore the cry of the afflicted; He who requites bloodshed is mindful of them.	*Ki-doresh damim otam zachar lo-shachach tza'akat ani'im [anavim]*	כִּי־דֹרֵשׁ דָּמִים אוֹתָם זָכָר לֹא־שָׁכַח צַעֲקַת עֲנִיִּים [עֲנָוִים]:	יג
14	Have mercy on me, Hashem; see my affliction at the hands of my foes, You who lift me from the gates of death,	*Chaneneni Adonai re'eh aneyi missone'ai meromemi misha'arei mavet*	חָנְנֵנִי יְהֹוָה רְאֵה עָנְיִי מִשֹּׂנְאָי מְרוֹמְמִי מִשַּׁעֲרֵי מָוֶת:	יד
15	so that in the gates of Fair Tzion I might tell all Your praise, I might exult in Your deliverance.	*Lema'an asapperah kol-tehillateicha besha'arei vat-tziyyon agilah bishu'atecha*	לְמַעַן אֲסַפְּרָה כָּל־תְּהִלָּתֶיךָ בְּשַׁעֲרֵי בַת־צִיּוֹן אָגִילָה בִּישׁוּעָתֶךָ:	טו

16	The nations sink in the pit they have made; their own foot is caught in the net they have hidden.	*Tave'u goyim beshachat asu bereshet-zu tamanu nilkedah raglam*	טָבְעוּ גוֹיִם בְּשַׁחַת עָשׂוּ בְּרֶשֶׁת־זוּ טָמָנוּ נִלְכְּדָה רַגְלָם:	טז
17	Hashem has made Himself known: He works judgment; the wicked man is snared by his own devices. Higgaion. Selah.	*Noda Adonai mishpat asah befo'al kappav nokesh rasha higgayon selah*	נוֹדַע יְהֹוָה מִשְׁפָּט עָשָׂה בְּפֹעַל כַּפָּיו נוֹקֵשׁ רָשָׁע הִגָּיוֹן סֶלָה:	יז
18	Let the wicked be in Sheol, all the nations who ignore Hashem!	*Yashuvu resha'im lish'olah kol-goyim shechechei elohim*	יָשׁוּבוּ רְשָׁעִים לִשְׁאוֹלָה כָּל־גּוֹיִם שְׁכֵחֵי אֱלֹהִים:	יח
19	Not always shall the needy be ignored, nor the hope of the afflicted forever lost.	*Ki lo lanetzach yishachach evyon tikvat anavim [aniyyim] tovad la'ad*	כִּי לֹא לָנֶצַח יִשָּׁכַח אֶבְיוֹן תִּקְוַת ענוים [עֲנִיִּים] תֹּאבַד לָעַד:	יט
20	Rise, Hashem! Let not men have power; let the nations be judged in Your presence.	*Kumah Adonai al-ya'oz enosh yishafetu goyim al-panecha*	קוּמָה יְהֹוָה אַל־יָעֹז אֱנוֹשׁ יִשָּׁפְטוּ גוֹיִם עַל־פָּנֶיךָ:	כ
21	Strike fear into them, Hashem; let the nations know they are only men. Selah.	*Shitah Adonai morah lahem yede'u goyim enosh hemmah selah*	שִׁיתָה יְהֹוָה מוֹרָה לָהֶם יֵדְעוּ גוֹיִם אֱנוֹשׁ הֵמָּה סֶּלָה:	כא

10

 י

	English	Transliteration	Hebrew
1	Why, Hashem, do You stand aloof, heedless in times of trouble?	*Lamah Adonai ta'amod berachok ta'lim le'ittot batzarah*	לָמָה יְהֹוָה תַּעֲמֹד בְּרָחוֹק תַּעְלִים לְעִתּוֹת בַּצָּרָה:
2	The wicked in his arrogance hounds the lowly— may they be caught in the schemes they devise!	*Bega'avat rasha yidlak ani yittafesu bimzimmot zu chashavu*	בְּגַאֲוַת רָשָׁע יִדְלַק עָנִי יִתָּפְשׂוּ בִּמְזִמּוֹת זוּ חָשָׁבוּ:
3	The wicked crows about his unbridled lusts; the grasping man reviles and scorns Hashem.	*Ki-hillel rasha al-ta'avat nafsho uvotzea berech ni'etz Adonai*	כִּי־הִלֵּל רָשָׁע עַל־תַּאֲוַת נַפְשׁוֹ וּבֹצֵעַ בֵּרֵךְ נִאֵץ יְהֹוָה:
4	The wicked, arrogant as he is, in all his scheming [thinks], "He does not call to account; Hashem does not care."	*Rasha kegovah appo bal-yidrosh ein elohim kol-mezimmotav*	רָשָׁע כְּגֹבַהּ אַפּוֹ בַּל־יִדְרֹשׁ אֵין אֱלֹהִים כָּל־מְזִמּוֹתָיו:
5	His ways prosper at all times; Your judgments are far beyond him; he snorts at all his foes.	*Yachilu darko [derachav] bechol-et marom mishpateicha minnegdo kol-tzorerav yafiach bahem*	יָחִילוּ דרכו [דְרָכָיו] בְּכָל־עֵת מָרוֹם מִשְׁפָּטֶיךָ מִנֶּגְדּוֹ כָּל־צוֹרְרָיו יָפִיחַ בָּהֶם:
6	He thinks, "I shall not be shaken, through all time never be in trouble."	*Amar belibbo bal-emmot ledor vador asher lo-vera*	אָמַר בְּלִבּוֹ בַּל־אֶמּוֹט לְדֹר וָדֹר אֲשֶׁר לֹא־בְרָע:
7	His mouth is full of oaths, deceit, and fraud; mischief and evil are under his tongue.	*Alah pihu malei umirmot vatoch tachat leshono amal va'aven*	אָלָה פִּיהוּ מָלֵא וּמִרְמוֹת וָתֹךְ תַּחַת לְשׁוֹנוֹ עָמָל וָאָוֶן:

8	He lurks in outlying places; from a covert he slays the innocent; his eyes spy out the hapless.	*Yeshev bema'rav chatzerim bammistarim yaharog naki einav lechelechah yitzponu*	יֵשֵׁב בְּמַאְרַב חֲצֵרִים בַּמִּסְתָּרִים יַהֲרֹג נָקִי עֵינָיו לְחֵלְכָה יִצְפֹּנוּ: ח
9	He waits in a covert like a lion in his lair; waits to seize the lowly; he seizes the lowly as he pulls his net shut;	*Ye'erov bammistar ke'aryeh vesukkoh ye'erov lachatof ani yachtof ani bemoshcho verishto*	יֶאֱרֹב בַּמִּסְתָּר כְּאַרְיֵה בְסֻכֹּה יֶאֱרֹב לַחֲטוֹף עָנִי יַחְטֹף עָנִי בְּמָשְׁכוֹ בְרִשְׁתּוֹ: ט
10	he stoops, he crouches, and the hapless fall prey to his might.	*V'dakah [yidkeh] yashoach venafal ba'atzumav chalka'im [cheil] [ka'im]*	ודכה [וְיִדְכֶּה] יָשֹׁחַ וְנָפַל בַּעֲצוּמָיו חלכאים [חֵיל] [כָּאִים]: י
11	He thinks, "Hashem is not mindful, He hides His face, He never looks."	*Amar belibbo shachach el histir panav bal-ra'ah lanetzach*	אָמַר בְּלִבּוֹ שָׁכַח אֵל הִסְתִּיר פָּנָיו בַּל־רָאָה לָנֶצַח: יא
12	Rise, Hashem! Strike at him, O Hashem! Do not forget the lowly.	*Kumah Adonai el nesa yadecha al-tishkach ani'im [anavim]*	קוּמָה יְהוָה אֵל נְשָׂא יָדֶךָ אַל־תִּשְׁכַּח עניים [עֲנָוִים]: יב
13	Why should the wicked man scorn Hashem, thinking You do not call to account?	*Al-meh ni'etz rasha elohim amar belibbo lo tidrosh*	עַל־מֶה נִאֵץ רָשָׁע אֱלֹהִים אָמַר בְּלִבּוֹ לֹא תִּדְרֹשׁ: יג
14	You do look! You take note of mischief and vexation! To requite is in Your power. To You the hapless can entrust himself; You have ever been the orphan's help.	*Ra'itah ki-attah amal vacha'as tabbit latet beyadecha aleicha ya'azov chelechah yatom attah hayita ozer*	רָאֹתָה כִּי־אַתָּה עָמָל וָכַעַס תַּבִּיט לָתֵת בְּיָדֶךָ עָלֶיךָ יַעֲזֹב חֵלְכָה יָתוֹם אַתָּה הָיִיתָ עוֹזֵר: יד

15	O break the power of the wicked and evil man, so that when You look for his wickedness You will find it no more.	*Shevor zeroa rasha vara tidrosh-rish'o val-timtza*	שְׁבֹר זְרוֹעַ רָשָׁע וָרָע תִּדְרוֹשׁ־רִשְׁעוֹ בַל־תִּמְצָא:	טו
16	Hashem is king for ever and ever; the nations will perish from His land.	*Adonai melech olam va'ed avedu goyim me'artzo*	יְהוָה מֶלֶךְ עוֹלָם וָעֶד אָבְדוּ גוֹיִם מֵאַרְצוֹ:	טז
17	You will listen to the entreaty of the lowly, Hashem, You will make their hearts firm; You will incline Your ear	*Ta'avat anavim shama'ta Adonai tachin libbam takshiv oznecha*	תַּאֲוַת עֲנָוִים שָׁמַעְתָּ יְהוָה תָּכִין לִבָּם תַּקְשִׁיב אָזְנֶךָ:	יז
18	to Champion the orphan and the downtrodden, that men who are of the earth tyrannize no more.	*Lishpot yatom vadach bal-yosif od la'arotz enosh min-ha'aretz*	לִשְׁפֹּט יָתוֹם וָדָךְ בַּל־יוֹסִיף עוֹד לַעֲרֹץ אֱנוֹשׁ מִן־הָאָרֶץ:	יח

11

─○◦◇◦○─

יא

1	For the leader. Of David. In Hashem I take refuge; how can you say to me, "Take to the hills like a bird!	*Lammenatzeach ledavid bAdonai chasiti eich tomru lenafshi nodo [nudi] harchem tzippor*	לַמְנַצֵּחַ לְדָוִד בַּיהוָה חָסִיתִי אֵיךְ תֹּאמְרוּ לְנַפְשִׁי נוּדוּ [נוּדִי] הַרְכֶם צִפּוֹר:	א

2 For see, the wicked bend the bow, they set their arrow on the string to shoot from the shadows at the upright.

Ki hinneh haresha'im yidrechun keshet konenu chitzam al-yeter lirot bemo-ofel leyishrei-lev

כִּי הִנֵּה הָרְשָׁעִים יִדְרְכוּן קֶשֶׁת כּוֹנְנוּ חִצָּם עַל־יֶתֶר לִירוֹת בְּמוֹ־אֹפֶל לְיִשְׁרֵי־לֵב: ב

3 When the foundations are destroyed, what can the righteous man do?"

Ki hashatot yeharesun tzaddik mah-pa'al

כִּי הַשָּׁתוֹת יֵהָרֵסוּן צַדִּיק מַה־פָּעָל: ג

4 Hashem is in His holy palace; Hashem—His throne is in heaven; His eyes behold, His gaze searches mankind.

Adonai beheichal kodsho Adonai bashamayim kis'o einav yechezu af'appav yivchanu benei adam

יְהֹוָה בְּהֵיכַל קָדְשׁוֹ יְהֹוָה בַּשָּׁמַיִם כִּסְאוֹ עֵינָיו יֶחֱזוּ עַפְעַפָּיו יִבְחֲנוּ בְּנֵי אָדָם: ד

5 Hashem seeks out the righteous man, but loathes the wicked one who loves injustice.

Adonai tzaddik yivchan verasha ve'ohev chamas sane'ah nafsho

יְהֹוָה צַדִּיק יִבְחָן וְרָשָׁע וְאֹהֵב חָמָס שָׂנְאָה נַפְשׁוֹ: ה

6 He will rain down upon the wicked blazing coals and sulfur; a scorching wind shall be their lot.

Yamter al-resha'im pachim esh vegaferit veruach zil'afot menat kosam

יַמְטֵר עַל־רְשָׁעִים פַּחִים אֵשׁ וְגָפְרִית וְרוּחַ זִלְעָפוֹת מְנָת כּוֹסָם: ו

7 For Hashem is righteous; He loves righteous deeds; the upright shall behold His face.

Ki-tzaddik Adonai tzedakot ahev yashar yechezu faneimo

כִּי־צַדִּיק יְהֹוָה צְדָקוֹת אָהֵב יָשָׁר יֶחֱזוּ פָנֵימוֹ: ז

12

—◦◦✕◦◦—

יב

1	For the leader; on the sheminith. A psalm of David.	*Lammenatzeach al-hasheminit mizmor ledavid*	לַמְנַצֵּחַ עַל־הַשְּׁמִינִית מִזְמוֹר לְדָוִד: ׀ א
2	Help, Hashem! For the faithful are no more; the loyal have vanished from among men.	*Hoshi'ah Adonai ki-gamar chasid ki-fassu emunim mibbenei adam*	הוֹשִׁיעָה יְהוָה כִּי־גָמַר חָסִיד כִּי־פַסּוּ אֱמוּנִים מִבְּנֵי אָדָם: ׀ ב
3	Men speak lies to one another; their speech is smooth; they talk with duplicity.	*Shave yedabberu ish et-re'ehu sefat chalakot belev valev yedabberu*	שָׁוְא יְדַבְּרוּ אִישׁ אֶת־רֵעֵהוּ שְׂפַת חֲלָקוֹת בְּלֵב וָלֵב יְדַבֵּרוּ: ׀ ג
4	May Hashem cut off all flattering lips, every tongue that speaks arrogance.	*Yachret Adonai kol-siftei chalakot lashon medabberet gedolot*	יַכְרֵת יְהוָה כָּל־שִׂפְתֵי חֲלָקוֹת לָשׁוֹן מְדַבֶּרֶת גְּדֹלוֹת: ׀ ד
5	They say, "By our tongues we shall prevail; with lips such as ours, who can be our master?"	*Asher ameru lilshonenu nagbir sefateinu ittanu mi adon lanu*	אֲשֶׁר אָמְרוּ לִלְשֹׁנֵנוּ נַגְבִּיר שְׂפָתֵינוּ אִתָּנוּ מִי אָדוֹן לָנוּ: ׀ ה
6	"Because of the groans of the plundered poor and needy, I will now act," says Hashem. "I will give help," He affirms to him.	*Mishod aniyyim me'ankat evyonim attah akum yomar Adonai ashit beyesha yafiach lo*	מִשֹּׁד עֲנִיִּים מֵאַנְקַת אֶבְיוֹנִים עַתָּה אָקוּם יֹאמַר יְהוָה אָשִׁית בְּיֵשַׁע יָפִיחַ לוֹ: ׀ ו
7	The words of Hashem are pure words, silver purged in an earthen crucible, refined sevenfold.	*Imarot Adonai amarot tehorot kesef tzaruf ba'alil la'aretz mezukkak shiv'atayim*	אִמְרוֹת יְהוָה אֲמָרוֹת טְהֹרוֹת כֶּסֶף צָרוּף בַּעֲלִיל לָאָרֶץ מְזֻקָּק שִׁבְעָתָיִם: ׀ ז

8	You, Hashem, will keep them, guarding each from this age evermore.	*Attah-Adonai tishmerem titzerennu min-haddor zu le'olam*

אַתָּה־יְהֹוָה תִּשְׁמְרֵם תִּצְּרֶנּוּ מִן־הַדּוֹר זוּ לְעוֹלָם: ח

9	On every side the wicked roam when baseness is exalted among men.	*Saviv resha'im yithallachun kerum zullut livnei adam*

סָבִיב רְשָׁעִים יִתְהַלָּכוּן כְּרֻם זֻלּוּת לִבְנֵי אָדָם: ט

13

—◦◦◦◦◦— יג

1	For the leader. A psalm of David.	*Lammenatzeach mizmor ledavid*

לַמְנַצֵּחַ מִזְמוֹר לְדָוִד: א

2	How long, Hashem; will You ignore me forever? How long will You hide Your face from me?	*Ad-anah Adonai tishkacheni netzach ad-anah tastir et-panecha mimmenni*

עַד־אָנָה יְהֹוָה תִּשְׁכָּחֵנִי נֶצַח עַד־אָנָה תַּסְתִּיר אֶת־פָּנֶיךָ מִמֶּנִּי: ב

3	How long will I have cares on my mind, grief in my heart all day? How long will my enemy have the upper hand?	*Ad-anah ashit etzot benafshi yagon bilvavi yomam ad-anah yarum oyevi alai*

עַד־אָנָה אָשִׁית עֵצוֹת בְּנַפְשִׁי יָגוֹן בִּלְבָבִי יוֹמָם עַד־אָנָה יָרוּם אֹיְבִי עָלָי: ג

4	Look at me, answer me, Hashem, my God! Restore the luster to my eyes, lest I sleep the sleep of death;	*Habbitah aneni Adonai elohai ha'irah einai pen-ishan hammavet*

הַבִּיטָה עֲנֵנִי יְהֹוָה אֱלֹהָי הָאִירָה עֵינַי פֶּן־אִישַׁן הַמָּוֶת: ד

5   lest my enemy say, "I have overcome him," my foes exult when I totter.

Pen-yomar oyevi yechaletiv tzarai yagilu ki emmot

פֶּן־יֹאמַר אֹיְבִי יְכָלְתִּיו צָרַי יָגִילוּ כִּי אֶמּוֹט: ה

6   But I trust in Your faithfulness, my heart will exult in Your deliverance. I will sing to Hashem, for He has been good to me.

Va'ani bechasdecha vatachti yagel libbi bishu'atecha ashirah lAdonai ki gamal alai

וַאֲנִי בְּחַסְדְּךָ בָטַחְתִּי יָגֵל לִבִּי בִּישׁוּעָתֶךָ אָשִׁירָה לַיהוָה כִּי גָמַל עָלָי: ו

14

יד

1   For the leader. Of David. The benighted man thinks, "Hashem does not care." Man's deeds are corrupt and loathsome; no one does good.

Lammenatzeach ledavid amar naval belibbo ein elohim hishchitu hit'ivu alilah ein oseh-tov

לַמְנַצֵּחַ לְדָוִד אָמַר נָבָל בְּלִבּוֹ אֵין אֱלֹהִים הִשְׁחִיתוּ הִתְעִיבוּ עֲלִילָה אֵין עֹשֵׂה־טוֹב: א

2   Hashem looks down from heaven on mankind to find a man of understanding, a man mindful of Hashem.

Adonai mishamayim hishkif al-benei-adam lir'ot hayesh maskil doresh et-elohim

יְהוָה מִשָּׁמַיִם הִשְׁקִיף עַל־בְּנֵי־אָדָם לִרְאוֹת הֲיֵשׁ מַשְׂכִּיל דֹּרֵשׁ אֶת־אֱלֹהִים: ב

3   All have turned bad, altogether foul; there is none who does good, not even one.

Hakkol sar yachdav ne'elachu ein oseh-tov ein gam-echad

הַכֹּל סָר יַחְדָּו נֶאֱלָחוּ אֵין עֹשֵׂה־טוֹב אֵין גַּם־אֶחָד: ג

4	Are they so witless, all those evildoers, who devour my people as they devour food, and do not invoke Hashem?	*Halo yade'u kol-po'alei aven ochelei ammi achelu lechem Adonai lo kara'u*

הֲלֹא יָדְעוּ כָּל־פֹּעֲלֵי אָוֶן אֹכְלֵי עַמִּי אָכְלוּ לֶחֶם יְהֹוָה לֹא קָרָאוּ׃ ד

5	There they will be seized with fright, for Hashem is present in the circle of the righteous.	*Sham pachadu fachad ki-elohim bedor tzaddik*

שָׁם פָּחֲדוּ פָחַד כִּי־אֱלֹהִים בְּדוֹר צַדִּיק׃ ה

6	You may set at naught the counsel of the lowly, but Hashem is his refuge.	*Atzat-ani tavishu ki Adonai machsehu*

עֲצַת־עָנִי תָבִישׁוּ כִּי יְהֹוָה מַחְסֵהוּ׃ ו

7	O that the deliverance of Yisrael might come from Tzion! When Hashem restores the fortunes of His people, Yaakov will exult, Yisrael will rejoice.	*Mi yitten mitziyyon yeshu'at yisra'el beshuv Adonai shevut ammo yagel ya'akov yismach yisra'el*

מִי יִתֵּן מִצִּיּוֹן יְשׁוּעַת יִשְׂרָאֵל בְּשׁוּב יְהֹוָה שְׁבוּת עַמּוֹ יָגֵל יַעֲקֹב יִשְׂמַח יִשְׂרָאֵל׃ ז

15

◦—◦ ⬡⬡⬡ ◦—◦

טו

1	A psalm of David. Hashem, who may sojourn in Your tent, who may dwell on Your holy mountain?	*Mizmor ledavid Adonai mi-yagur be'oholecha mi-yishkon behar kodshecha*

מִזְמוֹר לְדָוִד יְהֹוָה מִי־יָגוּר בְּאׇהֳלֶךָ מִי־יִשְׁכֹּן בְּהַר קׇדְשֶׁךָ׃ א

33

2   He who lives without blame, who does what is right, and in his heart acknowledges the truth;

Holech tamim ufo'el tzedek vedover emet bilvavo

הוֹלֵךְ תָּמִים וּפֹעֵל צֶדֶק וְדֹבֵר אֱמֶת בִּלְבָבוֹ׃   ב

3   whose tongue is not given to evil; who has never done harm to his fellow, or borne reproach for [his acts toward] his neighbor;

Lo-ragal al-leshono lo-asah lere'ehu ra'ah vecherpah lo-nasa al-kerovo

לֹא־רָגַל עַל־לְשֹׁנוֹ לֹא־עָשָׂה לְרֵעֵהוּ רָעָה וְחֶרְפָּה לֹא־נָשָׂא עַל־קְרֹבוֹ׃   ג

4   for whom a contemptible man is abhorrent, but who honors those who fear Hashem; who stands by his oath even to his hurt;

Nivzeh be'einav nim'as ve'et-yir'ei Adonai yechabbed nishba lehara velo yamir

נִבְזֶה בְּעֵינָיו נִמְאָס וְאֶת־יִרְאֵי יְהֹוָה יְכַבֵּד נִשְׁבַּע לְהָרַע וְלֹא יָמִר׃   ד

5   who has never lent money at interest, or accepted a bribe against the innocent. The man who acts thus shall never be shaken.

Kaspo lo-natan beneshech veshochad al-naki lo lakach oseh-elleh lo yimmot le'olam

כַּסְפּוֹ לֹא־נָתַן בְּנֶשֶׁךְ וְשֹׁחַד עַל־נָקִי לֹא לָקָח עֹשֵׂה־אֵלֶּה לֹא יִמּוֹט לְעוֹלָם׃   ה

16

1   A michtam of David. Protect me, O Hashem, for I seek refuge in You.

Michtam ledavid shamereni el ki-chasiti vach

מִכְתָּם לְדָוִד שָׁמְרֵנִי אֵל כִּי־חָסִיתִי בָךְ׃   א

2	I say to Hashem, "You are my Lord, my benefactor; there is none above You."	*Amart lAdonai Adonai attah tovati bal-aleicha*	אָמַרְתְּ לַיהֹוָה אֲדֹנָי אָתָּה טוֹבָתִי בַּל־עָלֶיךָ:	ב
3	As to the holy and mighty ones that are in the land, my whole desire concerning them is that	*Likdoshim asher-ba'aretz hemmah ve'addirei kol-cheftzi-vam*	לִקְדוֹשִׁים אֲשֶׁר־בָּאָרֶץ הֵמָּה וְאַדִּירֵי כָּל־חֶפְצִי־בָם:	ג
4	those who espouse another [god] may have many sorrows! I will have no part of their bloody libations; their names will not pass my lips.	*Yirbu atzevotam acher maharu bal-assich niskeihem middam uval-essa et-shemotam al-sefatai*	יִרְבּוּ עַצְּבוֹתָם אַחֵר מָהָרוּ בַּל־אַסִּיךְ נִסְכֵּיהֶם מִדָּם וּבַל־אֶשָּׂא אֶת־שְׁמוֹתָם עַל־שְׂפָתָי:	ד
5	Hashem is my allotted share and portion; You control my fate.	*Adonai menat-chelki vechosi attah tomich gorali*	יְהֹוָה מְנָת־חֶלְקִי וְכוֹסִי אַתָּה תּוֹמִיךְ גּוֹרָלִי:	ה
6	Delightful country has fallen to my lot; lovely indeed is my estate.	*Chavalim nafelu-li banne'imim af-nachalat shaferah alai*	חֲבָלִים נָפְלוּ־לִי בַּנְּעִמִים אַף־נַחֲלָת שָׁפְרָה עָלָי:	ו
7	I bless Hashem who has guided me; my conscience admonishes me at night.	*Avarech et-Adonai asher ye'atzani af-leilot yisseruni chilyotai*	אֲבָרֵךְ אֶת־יְהֹוָה אֲשֶׁר יְעָצָנִי אַף־לֵילוֹת יִסְּרוּנִי כִלְיוֹתָי:	ז
8	I am ever mindful of Hashem's presence; He is at my right hand; I shall never be shaken.	*Shivviti Adonai lenegdi tamid ki mimini bal-emmot*	שִׁוִּיתִי יְהֹוָה לְנֶגְדִּי תָמִיד כִּי מִימִינִי בַּל־אֶמּוֹט:	ח

9 So my heart rejoices, my whole being exults, and my body rests secure.

Lachen samach libbi vayyagel kevodi af- besari yishkon lavetach

לָכֵן שָׂמַח לִבִּי וַיָּגֶל כְּבוֹדִי אַף־בְּשָׂרִי יִשְׁכֹּן לָבֶטַח׃ ט

10 For You will not abandon me to Sheol, or let Your faithful one see the Pit.

Ki lo-ta'azov nafshi lish'ol lo-titten chasidcha lir'ot shachat

כִּי לֹא־תַעֲזֹב נַפְשִׁי לִשְׁאוֹל לֹא־תִתֵּן חֲסִידְךָ לִרְאוֹת שָׁחַת׃ י

11 You will teach me the path of life. In Your presence is perfect joy; delights are ever in Your right hand.

Todi'eni orach chayyim sova semachot et- panecha ne'imot bimincha netzach

תּוֹדִיעֵנִי אֹרַח חַיִּים שֹׂבַע שְׂמָחוֹת אֶת־פָּנֶיךָ נְעִמוֹת בִּימִינְךָ נֶצַח׃ יא

17

יז

1 A prayer of David. Hear, Hashem, what is just; heed my cry, give ear to my prayer, uttered without guile.

Tefillah ledavid shim'ah Adonai tzedek hakshivah rinnati ha'azinah tefillati belo siftei mirmah

תְּפִלָּה לְדָוִד שִׁמְעָה יְהֹוָה צֶדֶק הַקְשִׁיבָה רִנָּתִי הַאֲזִינָה תְפִלָּתִי בְּלֹא שִׂפְתֵי מִרְמָה׃ א

2 My vindication will come from You; Your eyes will behold what is right.

Millefaneicha mishpati yetze eineicha techezeinah meisharim

מִלְּפָנֶיךָ מִשְׁפָּטִי יֵצֵא עֵינֶיךָ תֶּחֱזֶינָה מֵישָׁרִים׃ ב

3 You have visited me at night, probed my mind, You have tested me and found nothing amiss; I determined that my mouth should not transgress.

Bachanta libbi pakadta layyelah tzeraftani val-timtza zammoti bal- ya'avor-pi

בָּחַנְתָּ לִבִּי פָּקַדְתָּ לַּיְלָה צְרַפְתַּנִי בַל־תִּמְצָא זַמֹּתִי בַּל־יַעֲבָר־פִּי׃ ג

4	As for man's dealings, in accord with the command of Your lips, I have kept in view the fate of the lawless.	*Lif'ullot adam bidvar sefateicha ani shamarti arechot paritz*	לִפְעֻלּוֹת אָדָם בִּדְבַר שְׂפָתֶיךָ אֲנִי שָׁמַרְתִּי אָרְחוֹת פָּרִיץ: ד
5	My feet have held to Your paths; my legs have not given way.	*Tamoch ashurai bema'geloteicha bal-namottu fe'amai*	תָּמֹךְ אֲשֻׁרַי בְּמַעְגְּלוֹתֶיךָ בַּל־נָמוֹטּוּ פְעָמָי: ה
6	I call on You; You will answer me, Hashem; turn Your ear to me, hear what I say.	*Ani-keraticha chi-ta'aneni el hat-oznecha li shema imrati*	אֲנִי־קְרָאתִיךָ כִי־תַעֲנֵנִי אֵל הַט־אָזְנְךָ לִי שְׁמַע אִמְרָתִי: ו
7	Display Your faithfulness in wondrous deeds, You who deliver with Your right hand those who seek refuge from assailants.	*Hafleh chasadeicha moshia chosim mimmitkomemim biminecha*	הַפְלֵה חֲסָדֶיךָ מוֹשִׁיעַ חוֹסִים מִמִּתְקוֹמְמִים בִּימִינֶךָ: ז
8	Guard me like the apple of Your eye; hide me in the shadow of Your wings	*Shamereni ke'ishon bat-ayin betzel kenafeicha tastireni*	שָׁמְרֵנִי כְּאִישׁוֹן בַּת־עָיִן בְּצֵל כְּנָפֶיךָ תַּסְתִּירֵנִי: ח

9	from the wicked who despoil me, my mortal enemies who encircle me.	*Mippenei resha'im zu shadduni oyevai benefesh yakkifu alai*	מִפְּנֵי רְשָׁעִים זוּ שַׁדּוּנִי אֹיְבַי בְּנֶפֶשׁ יַקִּיפוּ עָלָי:	ט
10	Their hearts are closed to pity; they mouth arrogance;	*Chelbamo sageru pimo dibberu vege'ut*	חֶלְבָּמוֹ סָגְרוּ פִּימוֹ דִּבְּרוּ בְגֵאוּת:	י
11	now they hem in our feet on every side; they set their eyes roaming over the land.	*Ashureinu attah sevavuni [sevavunu] eineihem yashitu lintot ba'aretz*	אַשֻּׁרֵינוּ עַתָּה סבבוני [סְבָבוּנוּ] עֵינֵיהֶם יָשִׁיתוּ לִנְטוֹת בָּאָרֶץ:	יא
12	He is like a lion eager for prey, a king of beasts lying in wait.	*Dimyono ke'aryeh yichsof litrof vechichfir yoshev bemistarim*	דִּמְיֹנוֹ כְּאַרְיֵה יִכְסוֹף לִטְרוֹף וְכִכְפִיר יֹשֵׁב בְּמִסְתָּרִים:	יב
13	Rise, Hashem! Go forth to meet him. Bring him down; rescue me from the wicked with Your sword,	*Kumah Adonai kaddemah fanav hachri'ehu palletah nafshi merasha charbecha*	קוּמָה יְהֹוָה קַדְּמָה פָנָיו הַכְרִיעֵהוּ פַּלְּטָה נַפְשִׁי מֵרָשָׁע חַרְבֶּךָ:	יג
14	from men, Hashem, with Your hand, from men whose share in life is fleeting. But as to Your treasured ones, fill their bellies. Their sons too shall be satisfied, and have something to leave over for their young.	*Mimtim yadecha Adonai mimtim mecheled chelkam bachayyim utzefinecha [utzefunecha] temalle vitnam yisbe'u vanim vehinnichu yitram le'oleleihem*	מִמְתִים יָדְךָ יְהֹוָה מִמְתִים מֵחֶלֶד חֶלְקָם בַּחַיִּים וּצְפִינֶךָ [וּצְפוּנְךָ] תְּמַלֵּא בִטְנָם יִשְׂבְּעוּ בָנִים וְהִנִּיחוּ יִתְרָם לְעוֹלְלֵיהֶם:	יד
15	Then I, justified, will behold Your face; awake, I am filled with the vision of You.	*Ani betzedek echezeh faneicha esbe'ah vehakitz temunatecha*	אֲנִי בְּצֶדֶק אֶחֱזֶה פָנֶיךָ אֶשְׂבְּעָה בְהָקִיץ תְּמוּנָתֶךָ:	טו

18

1	For the leader. Of David, the servant of Hashem, who addressed the words of this song to Hashem after Hashem had saved him from the hands of all his enemies and from the clutches of Shaul.	*Lammenatzeach le'eved Adonai ledavid asher dibber lAdonai et-divrei hashirah hazzot beyom hitzil-Adonai oto mikkaf kol-oyevav umiyyad sha'ul*	לַמְנַצֵּחַ לְעֶבֶד יְהֹוָה לְדָוִד אֲשֶׁר דִּבֶּר לַיהֹוָה אֶת־דִּבְרֵי הַשִּׁירָה הַזֹּאת בְּיוֹם הִצִּיל־יְהֹוָה אוֹתוֹ מִכַּף כָּל־אֹיְבָיו וּמִיַּד שָׁאוּל: א
2	He said: I adore you, Hashem, my strength,	*Vayyomar erchamecha Adonai chizki*	וַיֹּאמַר אֶרְחָמְךָ יְהֹוָה חִזְקִי: ב
3	Hashem, my crag, my fortress, my rescuer, my God, my rock in whom I seek refuge, my shield, my mighty Champion, my haven.	*Adonai sal'i umetzudati umefalti eli tzuri echeseh-bo maginni vekeren-yish'i misgabbi*	יְהֹוָה סַלְעִי וּמְצוּדָתִי וּמְפַלְטִי אֵלִי צוּרִי אֶחֱסֶה־בּוֹ מָגִנִּי וְקֶרֶן־יִשְׁעִי מִשְׂגַּבִּי: ג
4	All praise! I called on Hashem and was delivered from my enemies.	*Mehullal ekra Adonai umin-oyevai ivvashea*	מְהֻלָּל אֶקְרָא יְהֹוָה וּמִן־אֹיְבַי אִוָּשֵׁעַ: ד
5	Ropes of Death encompassed me; torrents of Belial terrified me;	*Afafuni chevlei-mavet venachalei veliyya'al yeva'atuni*	אֲפָפוּנִי חֶבְלֵי־מָוֶת וְנַחֲלֵי בְלִיַּעַל יְבַעֲתוּנִי: ה
6	ropes of Sheol encircled me; snares of Death confronted me.	*Chevlei she'ol sevavuni kiddemuni mokeshei mavet*	חֶבְלֵי שְׁאוֹל סְבָבוּנִי קִדְּמוּנִי מוֹקְשֵׁי מָוֶת: ו

7	In my distress I called on Hashem, cried out to my God; in His temple He heard my voice; my cry to Him reached His ears.	*Batzar-li ekra Adonai ve'el-elohai ashavvea yishma meheichalo koli veshav'ati lefanav tavo ve'azenav*	בְּצַר־לִי אֶקְרָא יְהֹוָה וְאֶל־אֱלֹהַי אֲשַׁוֵּעַ יִשְׁמַע מֵהֵיכָלוֹ קוֹלִי וְשַׁוְעָתִי לְפָנָיו תָּבוֹא בְאָזְנָיו:	ז
8	Then the earth rocked and quaked; the foundations of the mountains shook, rocked by His indignation;	*Vattig'ash vattir'ash ha'aretz umosedei harim yirgazu vayyitga'ashu ki-charah lo*	וַתִּגְעַשׁ וַתִּרְעַשׁ הָאָרֶץ וּמוֹסְדֵי הָרִים יִרְגָּזוּ וַיִּתְגָּעֲשׁוּ כִּי־חָרָה לוֹ:	ח
9	smoke went up from His nostrils, from His mouth came devouring fire; live coals blazed forth from Him.	*Alah ashan be'appo ve'esh-mippiv tochel gechalim ba'aru mimmennu*	עָלָה עָשָׁן בְּאַפּוֹ וְאֵשׁ־מִפִּיו תֹּאכֵל גֶּחָלִים בָּעֲרוּ מִמֶּנּוּ:	ט
10	He bent the sky and came down, thick cloud beneath His feet.	*Vayyet shamayim vayyerad va'arafel tachat raglav*	וַיֵּט שָׁמַיִם וַיֵּרַד וַעֲרָפֶל תַּחַת רַגְלָיו:	י
11	He mounted a cherub and flew, gliding on the wings of the wind.	*Vayyirkav al-keruv vayya'of vayyede al-kanfei-ruach*	וַיִּרְכַּב עַל־כְּרוּב וַיָּעֹף וַיֵּדֶא עַל־כַּנְפֵי־רוּחַ:	יא
12	He made darkness His screen; dark thunderheads, dense clouds of the sky were His pavilion round about Him.	*Yashet choshech sitro sevivotav sukkato cheshchat-mayim avei shechakim*	יָשֶׁת חֹשֶׁךְ סִתְרוֹ סְבִיבוֹתָיו סֻכָּתוֹ חֶשְׁכַת־מַיִם עָבֵי שְׁחָקִים:	יב
13	Out of the brilliance before Him, hail and fiery coals pierced His clouds.	*Minnogah negdo avav averu barad vegachalei-esh*	מִנֹּגַהּ נֶגְדּוֹ עָבָיו עָבְרוּ בָּרָד וְגַחֲלֵי־אֵשׁ:	יג

14	Then Hashem thundered from heaven, the Most High gave forth His voice— hail and fiery coals.	*Vayyar'em bashamayim Adonai ve'elyon yitten kolo barad vegachalei-esh*	וַיַּרְעֵם בַּשָּׁמַיִם יְהֹוָה וְעֶלְיוֹן יִתֵּן קֹלוֹ בָּרָד וְגַחֲלֵי־אֵשׁ:	יד
15	He let fly His shafts and scattered them; He discharged lightning and routed them.	*Vayyishlach chitzav vayfitzem uverakim rav vayhummem*	וַיִּשְׁלַח חִצָּיו וַיְפִיצֵם וּבְרָקִים רָב וַיְהֻמֵּם:	טו
16	The ocean bed was exposed; the foundations of the world were laid bare by You mighty roaring, Hashem, at the blast of the breath of Your nostrils.	*Vayyera'u afikei mayim vayyiggalu mosedot tevel migga'aratecha Adonai minnishmat ruach appecha*	וַיֵּרָאוּ אֲפִיקֵי מַיִם וַיִּגָּלוּ מוֹסְדוֹת תֵּבֵל מִגַּעֲרָתְךָ יְהֹוָה מִנִּשְׁמַת רוּחַ אַפֶּךָ:	טז
17	He reached down from on high, He took me; He drew me out of the mighty waters;	*Yishlach mimmarom yikkacheni yamsheni mimmayim rabbim*	יִשְׁלַח מִמָּרוֹם יִקָּחֵנִי יַמְשֵׁנִי מִמַּיִם רַבִּים:	יז
18	He saved me from my fierce enemy, from foes too strong for me.	*Yatzileni me'oyevi az umissone'ai ki-ametzu mimmenni*	יַצִּילֵנִי מֵאֹיְבִי עָז וּמִשֹּׂנְאַי כִּי־אָמְצוּ מִמֶּנִּי:	יח
19	They confronted me on the day of my calamity, but Hashem was my support.	*Yekaddemuni veyom-eidi vayhi-Adonai lemish'an li*	יְקַדְּמוּנִי בְיוֹם־אֵידִי וַיְהִי־ יְהֹוָה לְמִשְׁעָן לִי:	יט
20	He brought me out to freedom; He rescued me because He was pleased with me.	*Vayyotzi'eni lammerchav yechalletzeni ki chafetz bi*	וַיּוֹצִיאֵנִי לַמֶּרְחָב יְחַלְּצֵנִי כִּי חָפֵץ בִּי:	כ

21	Hashem rewarded me according to my merit; He requited the cleanness of my hands;	*Yigmeleni Adonai ketzidki kevor yadai yashiv li*	יִגְמְלֵנִי יְהֹוָה כְּצִדְקִי כְּבֹר יָדַי יָשִׁיב לִי:	כא
22	for I have kept to the ways of Hashem, and have not been guilty before my God;	*Ki-shamarti darchei Adonai velo-rasha'ti me'elohai*	כִּי־שָׁמַרְתִּי דַּרְכֵי יְהֹוָה וְלֹא־רָשַׁעְתִּי מֵאֱלֹהָי:	כב
23	for I am mindful of all His rules; I have not disregarded His laws.	*Ki chol-mishpatav lenegdi vechukkotav lo-asir menni*	כִּי כָל־מִשְׁפָּטָיו לְנֶגְדִּי וְחֻקֹּתָיו לֹא־אָסִיר מֶנִּי:	כג
24	I have been blameless toward Him, and have guarded myself against sinning;	*Va'ehi tamim immo va'eshtammer me'avni*	וָאֱהִי תָמִים עִמּוֹ וָאֶשְׁתַּמֵּר מֵעֲוֹנִי:	כד
25	and Hashem has requited me according to my merit, the cleanness of my hands in His sight.	*Vayyashev-Adonai li chetzidki kevor yadai leneged einav*	וַיָּשֶׁב־יְהֹוָה לִי כְצִדְקִי כְּבֹר יָדַי לְנֶגֶד עֵינָיו:	כה
26	With the loyal, You deal loyally; with the blameless man, blamelessly.	*Im-chasid titchassad im-gevar tamim tittammam*	עִם־חָסִיד תִּתְחַסָּד עִם־גְּבַר תָּמִים תִּתַּמָּם:	כו
27	With the pure, You act purely, and with the perverse, You are wily.	*Im-navar titbarar ve'im-ikkesh titpattal*	עִם־נָבָר תִּתְבָּרָר וְעִם־עִקֵּשׁ תִּתְפַּתָּל:	כז
28	It is You who deliver lowly folk, but haughty eyes You humble.	*Ki-attah am-ani toshia' ve'einayim ramot tashpil*	כִּי־אַתָּה עַם־עָנִי תוֹשִׁיעַ וְעֵינַיִם רָמוֹת תַּשְׁפִּיל:	כח

29	It is You who light my lamp; Hashem, my God, lights up my darkness.	*Ki-attah ta'ir neri Adonai elohai yaggiah chasheki*	כִּי־אַתָּה תָּאִיר נֵרִי יְהֹוָה אֱלֹהַי יַגִּיהַּ חָשְׁכִּי׃	כט
30	With You, I can rush a barrier; with my God I can scale a wall;	*Ki-vecha arutz gedud uvelohai adalleg-shur*	כִּי־בְךָ אָרֻץ גְּדוּד וּבֵאלֹהַי אֲדַלֶּג־שׁוּר׃	ל
31	the way of Hashem is perfect; the word of Hashem is pure; He is a shield to all who seek refuge in Him.	*Ha'el tamim darko imrat-Adonai tzerufah magen hu lechol hachosim bo*	הָאֵל תָּמִים דַּרְכּוֹ אִמְרַת־יְהֹוָה צְרוּפָה מָגֵן הוּא לְכֹל הַחֹסִים בּוֹ׃	לא
32	Truly, who is a god except Hashem, who is a rock but our God?—	*Ki mi eloah mibbal'adei Adonai umi tzur zulati eloheinu*	כִּי מִי אֱלוֹהַּ מִבַּלְעֲדֵי יְהֹוָה וּמִי צוּר זוּלָתִי אֱלֹהֵינוּ׃	לב
33	the God who girded me with might, who made my way perfect;	*Ha'el hamme'azereni chayil vayyitten tamim darki*	הָאֵל הַמְאַזְּרֵנִי חָיִל וַיִּתֵּן תָּמִים דַּרְכִּי׃	לג
34	who made my legs like a deer's, and let me stand firm on the heights;	*Meshavveh raglai ka'ayyalot ve'al bamotai ya'amideni*	מְשַׁוֶּה רַגְלַי כָּאַיָּלוֹת וְעַל בָּמֹתַי יַעֲמִידֵנִי׃	לד
35	who trained my hands for battle; my arms can bend a bow of bronze.	*Melammed yadai lammilchamah venichatah keshet-nechushah zero'otai*	מְלַמֵּד יָדַי לַמִּלְחָמָה וְנִחֲתָה קֶשֶׁת־נְחוּשָׁה זְרוֹעֹתָי׃	לה
36	You have given me the shield of Your protection; Your right hand has sustained me, Your care has made me great.	*Vattitten-li magen yish'echa vimincha tis'adeni ve'anvatcha tarbeni*	וַתִּתֶּן־לִי מָגֵן יִשְׁעֶךָ וִימִינְךָ תִסְעָדֵנִי וְעַנְוַתְךָ תַרְבֵּנִי׃	לו

37	You have let me stride on freely; my feet have not slipped.	*Tarchiv tza'adi tachtai velo ma'adu karsullai*	תַּרְחִיב צַעֲדִי תַחְתָּי וְלֹא מָעֲדוּ קַרְסֻלָּי:	לז
38	I pursued my enemies and overtook them; I did not turn back till I destroyed them.	*Erdof oyevai ve'assigem velo-ashuv ad-kallotam*	אֶרְדּוֹף אוֹיְבַי וְאַשִּׂיגֵם וְלֹא־אָשׁוּב עַד־כַּלּוֹתָם:	לח
39	I struck them down, and they could rise no more; they lay fallen at my feet.	*Emchatzem velo-yuchlu kum yippelu tachat raglai*	אֶמְחָצֵם וְלֹא־יֻכְלוּ קוּם יִפְּלוּ תַּחַת רַגְלָי:	לט
40	You have girded me with strength for battle, brought my adversaries low before me,	*Vatte'azzereni chayil lammilchamah tachria' kamai tachtai*	וַתְּאַזְּרֵנִי חַיִל לַמִּלְחָמָה תַּכְרִיעַ קָמַי תַּחְתָּי:	מ
41	made my enemies turn tail before me; I wiped out my foes.	*Ve'oyevai natattah li oref umesan'ai atzmitem*	וְאֹיְבַי נָתַתָּה לִּי עֹרֶף וּמְשַׂנְאַי אַצְמִיתֵם:	מא
42	They cried out, but there was none to deliver; [cried] to Hashem, but He did not answer them.	*Yeshavve'u ve'ein-moshia' al-Adonai velo anam*	יְשַׁוְּעוּ וְאֵין־מוֹשִׁיעַ עַל־יְהֹוָה וְלֹא עָנָם:	מב
43	I ground them fine as windswept dust; I trod them flat as dirt of the streets.	*Ve'eshchakem ke'afar al-penei-ruach ketit chutzot arikem*	וְאֶשְׁחָקֵם כְּעָפָר עַל־פְּנֵי־רוּחַ כְּטִיט חוּצוֹת אֲרִיקֵם:	מג
44	You have rescued me from the strife of people; You have set me at the head of nations; peoples I knew not must serve me.	*Tefalleteni merivei am tesimeni lerosh goyim am lo-yada'ti ya'avduni*	תְּפַלְּטֵנִי מֵרִיבֵי עָם תְּשִׂימֵנִי לְרֹאשׁ גּוֹיִם עַם לֹא־יָדַעְתִּי יַעַבְדוּנִי:	מד

45	At the mere report of me they are submissive; foreign peoples cower before me;	*Leshema ozen yishame'u li benei-nechar yechachashu-li*	לְשֵׁמַע אֹזֶן יִשָּׁמְעוּ לִי בְּנֵי־נֵכָר יְכַחֲשׁוּ־לִי:	מה
46	foreign peoples lose courage, and come trembling out of their strongholds.	*Benei-nechar yibbolu veyachregu mimmisgeroteihem*	בְּנֵי־נֵכָר יִבֹּלוּ וְיַחְרְגוּ מִמִּסְגְּרוֹתֵיהֶם:	מו
47	Hashem lives! Blessed is my rock! Exalted be Hashem, my deliverer,	*Chai-Adonai uvaruch tzuri veyarum elohei yish'i*	חַי־יְהֹוָה וּבָרוּךְ צוּרִי וְיָרוּם אֱלוֹהֵי יִשְׁעִי:	מז
48	the God who has vindicated me and made peoples subject to me,	*Ha'el hannoten nekamot li vayyadber ammim tachtai*	הָאֵל הַנּוֹתֵן נְקָמוֹת לִי וַיַּדְבֵּר עַמִּים תַּחְתָּי:	מח
49	who rescued me from my enemies, who raised me clear of my adversaries, saved me from lawless men.	*Mefalleti me'oyevai af min-kamai teromemeni me'ish chamas tatzileni*	מְפַלְּטִי מֵאֹיְבָי אַף מִן־קָמַי תְּרוֹמְמֵנִי מֵאִישׁ חָמָס תַּצִּילֵנִי:	מט
50	For this I sing Your praise among the nations, Hashem, and hymn Your name:	*Al-ken odecha vaggoyim Adonai uleshimcha azammerah*	עַל־כֵּן אוֹדְךָ בַגּוֹיִם יְהֹוָה וּלְשִׁמְךָ אֲזַמֵּרָה:	נ
51	He accords great victories to His king, keeps faith with His anointed, with David and his offspring forever.	*Magdal [magdil] yeshu'ot malko ve'oseh chesed limshicho ledavid ulezar'o ad-olam*	מגדל [מַגְדִּיל] יְשׁוּעוֹת מַלְכּוֹ וְעֹשֶׂה חֶסֶד לִמְשִׁיחוֹ לְדָוִד וּלְזַרְעוֹ עַד־עוֹלָם:	נא

19

יט

1	For the leader. A psalm of David.	*Lammenatzeach mizmor ledavid*	לַמְנַצֵּחַ מִזְמוֹר לְדָוִד:
2	The heavens declare the glory of Hashem, the sky proclaims His handiwork.	*Hashamayim mesapperim kevod-el uma'aseh yadav maggid harakia*	הַשָּׁמַיִם מְסַפְּרִים כְּבוֹד־אֵל וּמַעֲשֵׂה יָדָיו מַגִּיד הָרָקִיעַ:
3	Day to day makes utterance, night to night speaks out.	*Yom leyom yabbia omer velayyelah lelaylah yechavveh-da'at*	יוֹם לְיוֹם יַבִּיעַ אֹמֶר וְלַיְלָה לְּלַיְלָה יְחַוֶּה־דָּעַת:
4	There is no utterance, there are no words, whose sound goes unheard.	*Ein-omer ve'ein devarim beli nishma kolam*	אֵין־אֹמֶר וְאֵין דְּבָרִים בְּלִי נִשְׁמָע קוֹלָם:
5	Their voice carries throughout the earth, their words to the end of the world. He placed in them a tent for the sun,	*Bechol-ha'aretz yatza kavvam uviktzeh tevel milleihem lashemesh sam-ohel bahem*	בְּכָל־הָאָרֶץ יָצָא קַוָּם וּבִקְצֵה תֵבֵל מִלֵּיהֶם לַשֶּׁמֶשׁ שָׂם־אֹהֶל בָּהֶם:
6	who is like a groom coming forth from the chamber, like a hero, eager to run his course.	*Vehu kechatan yotze mechuppato yasis kegibbor larutz orach*	וְהוּא כְּחָתָן יֹצֵא מֵחֻפָּתוֹ יָשִׂישׂ כְּגִבּוֹר לָרוּץ אֹרַח:

7	His rising-place is at one end of heaven, and his circuit reaches the other; nothing escapes his heat.	*Miktzeh hashamayim motza'o utekufato al-ketzotam ve'ein nistar mechammato*	מִקְצֵה הַשָּׁמַיִם מוֹצָאוֹ וּתְקוּפָתוֹ עַל־קְצוֹתָם וְאֵין נִסְתָּר מֵחַמָּתוֹ׃	ז
8	The teaching of Hashem is perfect, renewing life; the decrees of Hashem are enduring, making the simple wise;	*Torat Adonai temimah meshivat nafesh edut Adonai ne'emanah machkimat peti*	תּוֹרַת יְהֹוָה תְּמִימָה מְשִׁיבַת נָפֶשׁ עֵדוּת יְהֹוָה נֶאֱמָנָה מַחְכִּימַת פֶּתִי׃	ח
9	The precepts of Hashem are just, rejoicing the heart; the instruction of Hashem is lucid, making the eyes light up.	*Pikkudei Adonai yesharim mesammechei-lev mitzvat Adonai barah me'irat einayim*	פִּקּוּדֵי יְהֹוָה יְשָׁרִים מְשַׂמְּחֵי־לֵב מִצְוַת יְהֹוָה בָּרָה מְאִירַת עֵינָיִם׃	ט
10	The fear of Hashem is pure, abiding forever; the judgments of Hashem are true, righteous altogether,	*Yir'at Adonai tehorah omedet la'ad mishpetei-Adonai emet tzadeku yachdav*	יִרְאַת יְהֹוָה טְהוֹרָה עוֹמֶדֶת לָעַד מִשְׁפְּטֵי־יְהֹוָה אֱמֶת צָדְקוּ יַחְדָּו׃	י
11	more desirable than gold, than much fine gold; sweeter than honey, than drippings of the comb.	*Hannechemadim mizzahav umippaz rav umetukim middevash venofet tzufim*	הַנֶּחֱמָדִים מִזָּהָב וּמִפַּז רָב וּמְתוּקִים מִדְּבַשׁ וְנֹפֶת צוּפִים׃	יא
12	Your servant pays them heed; in obeying them there is much reward.	*Gam-avdecha nizhar bahem beshomram ekev rav*	גַּם־עַבְדְּךָ נִזְהָר בָּהֶם בְּשָׁמְרָם עֵקֶב רָב׃	יב
13	Who can be aware of errors? Clear me of unperceived guilt,	*Shegi'ot mi-yavin minnistarot nakkeni*	שְׁגִיאוֹת מִי־יָבִין מִנִּסְתָּרוֹת נַקֵּנִי׃	יג

14	and from willful sins keep Your servant; let them not dominate me; then shall I be blameless and clear of grave offense.	*Gam mizzedim chasoch avdecha al-yimshelu-vi az eitam venikkeiti mippesha rav*

גַּם מִזֵּדִים חֲשֹׂךְ עַבְדֶּךָ אַל־יִמְשְׁלוּ־בִי אָז אֵיתָם וְנִקֵּיתִי מִפֶּשַׁע רָב: יד

15	May the words of my mouth and the prayer of my heart be acceptable to You, Hashem, my rock and my redeemer.	*Yihyu leratzon imrei-fi vehegyon libbi lefaneicha Adonai tzuri vego'ali*

יִהְיוּ לְרָצוֹן אִמְרֵי־פִי וְהֶגְיוֹן לִבִּי לְפָנֶיךָ יְהֹוָה צוּרִי וְגֹאֲלִי: טו

20

—○⊷⊗⊶○— ⟋

כ

1	For the leader. A psalm of David.	*Lammenatzeach mizmor ledavid*

לַמְנַצֵּחַ מִזְמוֹר לְדָוִד: א

2	May Hashem answer you in time of trouble, the name of Yaakov's Hashem keep you safe.	*Ya'ancha Adonai beyom tzarah yesaggevcha shem elohei ya'akov*

יַעַנְךָ יְהֹוָה בְּיוֹם צָרָה יְשַׂגֶּבְךָ שֵׁם אֱלֹהֵי יַעֲקֹב: ב

3	May He send you help from the sanctuary, and sustain you from Tzion.	*Yishlach-ezrecha mikkodesh umitziyyon yis'adekka*

יִשְׁלַח־עֶזְרְךָ מִקֹּדֶשׁ וּמִצִּיּוֹן יִסְעָדֶךָּ: ג

4	May He receive the tokens of all your meal offerings, and approve your burn offerings. Selah.	*Yizkor kol-minchotecha ve'olatecha yedasheneh selah*	יִזְכֹּר כָּל־מִנְחֹתֶךָ וְעוֹלָתְךָ יְדַשְּׁנֶה סֶלָה:	ד
5	May He grant you your desire, and fulfill your every plan.	*Yitten-lecha chilvavecha vechol-atzatecha yemalle*	יִתֶּן־לְךָ כִלְבָבֶךָ וְכָל־עֲצָתְךָ יְמַלֵּא:	ה
6	May we shout for joy in your victory, arrayed by standards in the name of our God. May Hashem fulfill your every wish.	*Nerannenah bishu'atecha uveshem-eloheinu nidgol yemalle Adonai kol-mish'aloteicha*	נְרַנְּנָה בִּישׁוּעָתֶךָ וּבְשֵׁם־אֱלֹהֵינוּ נִדְגֹּל יְמַלֵּא יְהוָה כָּל־מִשְׁאֲלוֹתֶיךָ:	ו
7	Now I know that Hashem will give victory to His anointed, will answer him from His heavenly sanctuary with the mighty victories of His right arm.	*Attah yada'ti ki hoshia Adonai meshicho ya'anehu mishemei kodsho bigvurot yesha yemino*	עַתָּה יָדַעְתִּי כִּי הוֹשִׁיעַ יְהוָה מְשִׁיחוֹ יַעֲנֵהוּ מִשְּׁמֵי קָדְשׁוֹ בִּגְבֻרוֹת יֵשַׁע יְמִינוֹ:	ז
8	They [call] on chariots, they [call] on horses, but we call on the name of Hashem our God.	*elleh varechev ve'elleh vassusim va'anachnu beshem-Adonai eloheinu nazkir*	אֵלֶּה בָרֶכֶב וְאֵלֶּה בַסּוּסִים וַאֲנַחְנוּ בְּשֵׁם־יְהוָה אֱלֹהֵינוּ נַזְכִּיר:	ח
9	They collapse and lie fallen, but we rally and gather strength.	*hemmah kare'u venafalu va'anachnu kamnu vannit'odad*	הֵמָּה כָּרְעוּ וְנָפָלוּ וַאֲנַחְנוּ קַמְנוּ וַנִּתְעוֹדָד:	ט
10	Hashem, grant victory! May the King answer us when we call.	*Adonai hoshi'ah hammelech ya'anenu veyom-kare'enu*	יְהוָה הוֹשִׁיעָה הַמֶּלֶךְ יַעֲנֵנוּ בְיוֹם־קָרְאֵנוּ:	י

21

—◦○✦○◦—

כא

1	For the leader. A psalm of David.	*Lammenatzeach mizmor ledavid*	לַמְנַצֵּחַ מִזְמוֹר לְדָוִד׃	א
2	Hashem, the king rejoices in Your strength; how greatly he exults in Your victory!	*Adonai be'ozzecha yismach-melech uvishu'atecha mah-yagil [yagel] me'od*	יְהֹוָה בְּעׇזְּךָ יִשְׂמַח־מֶלֶךְ וּבִישׁוּעָתְךָ מַה־יָּגִיל [יָגֶל] מְאֹד׃	ב
3	You have granted him the desire of his heart, have not denied the request of his lips. Selah.	*Ta'avat libbo natattah lo va'areshet sefatav bal-mana'ta selah*	תַּאֲוַת לִבּוֹ נָתַתָּה לּוֹ וַאֲרֶשֶׁת שְׂפָתָיו בַּל־מָנַעְתָּ סֶּלָה׃	ג
4	You have proffered him blessings of good things, have set upon his head a crown of fine gold.	*Ki-tekaddemennu birchot tov tashit lerosho ateret paz*	כִּי־תְקַדְּמֶנּוּ בִּרְכוֹת טוֹב תָּשִׁית לְרֹאשׁוֹ עֲטֶרֶת פָּז׃	ד
5	He asked You for life; You granted it; a long life, everlasting.	*Chayyim sha'al mimmecha natattah lo orech yamim olam va'ed*	חַיִּים שָׁאַל מִמְּךָ נָתַתָּה לּוֹ אֹרֶךְ יָמִים עוֹלָם וָעֶד׃	ה
6	Great is his glory through Your victory; You have endowed him with splendor and majesty.	*Gadol kevodo bishu'atecha hod vehadar teshavveh alav*	גָּדוֹל כְּבוֹדוֹ בִּישׁוּעָתֶךָ הוֹד וְהָדָר תְּשַׁוֶּה עָלָיו׃	ו

7	You have made him blessed forever, gladdened him with the joy of Your presence.	*Ki-teshitehu verachot la'ad techaddehu vesimchah et-panecha*	כִּי־תְשִׁיתֵהוּ בְרָכוֹת לָעַד תְּחַדֵּהוּ בְשִׂמְחָה אֶת־פָּנֶיךָ:	ז
8	For the king trusts in Hashem; Through the faithfulness of the Most High he will not be shaken.	*Ki-hammelech boteach bAdonai uvechesed elyon bal-yimmot*	כִּי־הַמֶּלֶךְ בֹּטֵחַ בַּיהֹוָה וּבְחֶסֶד עֶלְיוֹן בַּל־יִמּוֹט:	ח
9	Your hand is equal to all Your enemies; Your right hand overpowers Your foes.	*Timtza yadecha lechol-oyeveicha yemincha timtza sone'eicha*	תִּמְצָא יָדְךָ לְכָל־אֹיְבֶיךָ יְמִינְךָ תִּמְצָא שֹׂנְאֶיךָ:	ט
10	You set them ablaze like a furnace when You show Your presence. Hashem in anger destroys them; fire consumes them.	*Teshitemo ketannur esh le'et panecha Adonai be'appo yevalle'em vetochlem esh*	תְּשִׁיתֵמוֹ כְּתַנּוּר אֵשׁ לְעֵת פָּנֶיךָ יְהֹוָה בְּאַפּוֹ יְבַלְּעֵם וְתֹאכְלֵם אֵשׁ:	י
11	You wipe their offspring from the earth, their issue from among men.	*Piryamo me'eretz te'abbed vezar'am mibbenei adam*	פִּרְיָמוֹ מֵאֶרֶץ תְּאַבֵּד וְזַרְעָם מִבְּנֵי אָדָם:	יא
12	For they schemed against You; they laid plans, but could not succeed.	*Ki-natu aleicha ra'ah chashevu mezimmah bal-yuchalu*	כִּי־נָטוּ עָלֶיךָ רָעָה חָשְׁבוּ מְזִמָּה בַּל־יוּכָלוּ:	יב
13	For You make them turn back by Your bows aimed at their face.	*Ki teshitemo shechem bemeitareicha techonen al-peneihem*	כִּי תְּשִׁיתֵמוֹ שֶׁכֶם בְּמֵיתָרֶיךָ תְּכוֹנֵן עַל־פְּנֵיהֶם:	יג

14	Be exalted, Hashem, through Your strength; we will sing and chant the praises of Your mighty deeds.	*Rumah Adonai be'uzzecha nashirah unezammerah gevuratecha*	רוּמָה יְהֹוָה בְּעֻזֶּךָ נָשִׁירָה וּנְזַמְּרָה גְּבוּרָתֶךָ׃ יד

22

—◦○⬡○◦—

כב

1	For the leader; on ayyeleth ha-shachar. A psalm of David.	*Lammenatzeach al-ayyelet hashachar mizmor ledavid*	לַמְנַצֵּחַ עַל־אַיֶּלֶת הַשַּׁחַר מִזְמוֹר לְדָוִד׃ א
2	My Hashem, my God, why have You abandoned me; why so far from delivering me and from my anguished roaring?	*Eli eli lamah azavtani rachok mishu'ati divrei sha'agati*	אֵלִי אֵלִי לָמָה עֲזַבְתָּנִי רָחוֹק מִישׁוּעָתִי דִּבְרֵי שַׁאֲגָתִי׃ ב
3	My Hashem, I cry by day—You answer not; by night, and have no respite.	*Elohai ekra yomam velo ta'aneh velayyelah velo-dumiyyah li*	אֱלֹהַי אֶקְרָא יוֹמָם וְלֹא תַעֲנֶה וְלַיְלָה וְלֹא־דֻמִיָּה לִי׃ ג
4	But You are the Holy One, enthroned, the Praise of Yisrael.	*Ve'attah kadosh yoshev tehillot yisra'el*	וְאַתָּה קָדוֹשׁ יוֹשֵׁב תְּהִלּוֹת יִשְׂרָאֵל׃ ד
5	In You our fathers trusted; they trusted, and You rescued them.	*Becha batechu avoteinu batechu vattefalletemo*	בְּךָ בָּטְחוּ אֲבֹתֵינוּ בָּטְחוּ וַתְּפַלְּטֵמוֹ׃ ה
6	To You they cried out and they escaped; in You they trusted and were not disappointed.	*Eleicha za'aku venimlatu becha vatechu velo-voshu*	אֵלֶיךָ זָעֲקוּ וְנִמְלָטוּ בְּךָ בָטְחוּ וְלֹא־בוֹשׁוּ׃ ו

7	But I am a worm, less than human; scorned by men, despised by people.	*Ve'anochi tola'at velo-ish cherpat adam uvezui am*	וְאָנֹכִי תוֹלַעַת וְלֹא־אִישׁ חֶרְפַּת אָדָם וּבְזוּי עָם: ז
8	All who see me mock me; they curl their lips, they shake their heads.	*Kol-ro'ai yal'igu li yaftiru vesafah yani'u rosh*	כָּל־רֹאַי יַלְעִגוּ לִי יַפְטִירוּ בְשָׂפָה יָנִיעוּ רֹאשׁ: ח
9	"Let him commit himself to Hashem; let Him rescue him, let Him save him, for He is pleased with him."	*Gol el-Adonai yefalletehu yatzilehu ki chafetz bo*	גֹּל אֶל־יְהֹוָה יְפַלְּטֵהוּ יַצִּילֵהוּ כִּי חָפֵץ בּוֹ: ט
10	You drew me from the womb, made me secure at my mother's breast.	*Ki-attah gochi mibbaten mavtichi al-shedei immi*	כִּי־אַתָּה גֹחִי מִבָּטֶן מַבְטִיחִי עַל־שְׁדֵי אִמִּי: י
11	I became Your charge at birth; from my mother's womb You have been my God.	*Aleicha hashelachti merachem mibbeten immi eli attah*	עָלֶיךָ הָשְׁלַכְתִּי מֵרָחֶם מִבֶּטֶן אִמִּי אֵלִי אָתָּה: יא
12	Do not be far from me, for trouble is near, and there is none to help.	*Al-tirchak mimmenni ki-tzarah kerovah ki-ein ozer*	אַל־תִּרְחַק מִמֶּנִּי כִּי־צָרָה קְרוֹבָה כִּי־אֵין עוֹזֵר: יב
13	Many bulls surround me, mighty ones of Bashan encircle me.	*Sevavuni parim rabbim abbirei vashan kitteruni*	סְבָבוּנִי פָּרִים רַבִּים אַבִּירֵי בָשָׁן כִּתְּרוּנִי: יג
14	They open their mouths at me like tearing, roaring lions.	*Patzu alai pihem aryeh toref vesho'eg*	פָּצוּ עָלַי פִּיהֶם אַרְיֵה טֹרֵף וְשֹׁאֵג: יד

15 My life ebbs away: all my bones are disjointed; my heart is like wax, melting within me;

Kammayim nishpachti vehitparedu kol-atzmotai hayah libbi kaddonag names betoch me'ai

כַּמַּיִם נִשְׁפַּכְתִּי וְהִתְפָּרְדוּ כָּל־עַצְמוֹתָי הָיָה לִבִּי כַּדּוֹנָג נָמֵס בְּתוֹךְ מֵעָי: טו

16 my vigor dries up like a shard; my tongue cleaves to my palate; You commit me to the dust of death.

Yavesh kacheres kochi uleshoni mudbak malkochai vela'afar-mavet tishpeteni

יָבֵשׁ כַּחֶרֶשׂ כֹּחִי וּלְשׁוֹנִי מֻדְבָּק מַלְקוֹחָי וְלַעֲפַר־מָוֶת תִּשְׁפְּתֵנִי: טז

17 Dogs surround me; a pack of evil ones closes in on me, like lions [they maul] my hands and feet.

Ki sevavuni kelavim adat mere'im hikkifuni ka'ari yadai veraglai

כִּי סְבָבוּנִי כְּלָבִים עֲדַת מְרֵעִים הִקִּיפוּנִי כָּאֲרִי יָדַי וְרַגְלָי: יז

18 I take the count of all my bones while they look on and gloat.

Asapper kol-atzmotai hemmah yabbitu yir'u-vi

אֲסַפֵּר כָּל־עַצְמוֹתָי הֵמָּה יַבִּיטוּ יִרְאוּ־בִי: יח

19 They divide my clothes among themselves, casting lots for my garments.

Yechalleku vegadai lahem ve'al-levushi yappilu goral

יְחַלְּקוּ בְגָדַי לָהֶם וְעַל־לְבוּשִׁי יַפִּילוּ גוֹרָל: יט

20 But You, Hashem, be not far off; my strength, hasten to my aid.

Ve'attah Adonai al-tirchak eyaluti le'ezrati chushah

וְאַתָּה יְהוָה אַל־תִּרְחָק אֱיָלוּתִי לְעֶזְרָתִי חוּשָׁה: כ

21 Save my life from the sword, my precious life from the clutches of a dog.

Hatzilah mecherev nafshi miyyad-kelev yechidati

הַצִּילָה מֵחֶרֶב נַפְשִׁי מִיַּד־כֶּלֶב יְחִידָתִי: כא

22 Deliver me from a lion's mouth; from the horns of wild oxen rescue me.

Hoshi'eni mippi aryeh umikkarnei remim anitani

הוֹשִׁיעֵנִי מִפִּי אַרְיֵה וּמִקַּרְנֵי רֵמִים עֲנִיתָנִי: כב

23	Then will I proclaim Your fame to my brethren, praise You in the congregation.	*Asapperah shimcha le'echai betoch kahal ahallekka*	אֲסַפְּרָה שִׁמְךָ לְאֶחָי בְּתוֹךְ קָהָל אֲהַלְלֶךָּ: כג
24	You who fear Hashem, praise Him! All you offspring of Yaakov, honor Him! Be in dread of Him, all you offspring of Yisrael!	*Yir'ei Adonai halluhu kol-zera ya'akov kabbeduhu veguru mimmennu kol-zera yisra'el*	יִרְאֵי יְהֹוָה הַלְלוּהוּ כָּל־זֶרַע יַעֲקֹב כַּבְּדוּהוּ וְגוּרוּ מִמֶּנּוּ כָּל־זֶרַע יִשְׂרָאֵל: כד
25	For He did not scorn, He did not spurn the plea of the lowly; He did not hide His face from him; when he cried out to Him, He listened.	*Ki lo-vazah velo shikkatz enut ani velo-histir panav mimmennu uveshavve'o elav shomea'*	כִּי לֹא־בָזָה וְלֹא שִׁקַּץ עֱנוּת עָנִי וְלֹא־הִסְתִּיר פָּנָיו מִמֶּנּוּ וּבְשַׁוְּעוֹ אֵלָיו שָׁמֵעַ: כה
26	Because of You I offer praise in the great congregation; I pay my vows in the presence of His worshipers.	*Me'ittecha tehillati bekahal rav nedarai ashallem neged yere'av*	מֵאִתְּךָ תְהִלָּתִי בְּקָהָל רָב נְדָרַי אֲשַׁלֵּם נֶגֶד יְרֵאָיו: כו
27	Let the lowly eat and be satisfied; let all who seek Hashem praise Him. Always be of good cheer!	*Yochlu anavim veyisba'u yehallu Adonai doreshav yechi levavchem la'ad*	יֹאכְלוּ עֲנָוִים וְיִשְׂבָּעוּ יְהַלְלוּ יְהֹוָה דֹּרְשָׁיו יְחִי לְבַבְכֶם לָעַד: כז
28	Let all the ends of the earth pay heed and turn to Hashem, and the peoples of all nations prostrate themselves before You;	*Yizkeru veyashuvu el-Adonai kol-afsei-aretz veyishtachavu lefaneicha kol-mishpechot goyim*	יִזְכְּרוּ וְיָשֻׁבוּ אֶל־יְהֹוָה כָּל־אַפְסֵי־אָרֶץ וְיִשְׁתַּחֲווּ לְפָנֶיךָ כָּל־מִשְׁפְּחוֹת גּוֹיִם: כח

29	for kingship is Hashem's and He rules the nations.	*Ki lAdonai hammeluchah umoshel baggoyim*	כִּי לַיהֹוָה הַמְּלוּכָה וּמֹשֵׁל בַּגּוֹיִם:	כט
30	All those in full vigor shall eat and prostrate themselves; all those at death's door, whose spirits flag, shall bend the knee before Him.	*Achelu vayyishtachavu kol-dishnei-eretz lefanav yichre'u kol-yoredei afar venafsho lo chiyyah*	אָכְלוּ וַיִּשְׁתַּחֲווּ כָּל־דִּשְׁנֵי־אֶרֶץ לְפָנָיו יִכְרְעוּ כָּל־יוֹרְדֵי עָפָר וְנַפְשׁוֹ לֹא חִיָּה:	ל
31	Offspring shall serve Him; Hashem's fame shall be proclaimed to the generation	*Zera ya'avdennu yesuppar lAdonai laddor*	זֶרַע יַעַבְדֶנּוּ יְסֻפַּר לַאדֹנָי לַדּוֹר:	לא
32	to come; they shall tell of His beneficence to people yet to be born, for He has acted.	*Yavo'u veyaggidu tzidkato le'am nolad ki asah*	יָבֹאוּ וְיַגִּידוּ צִדְקָתוֹ לְעַם נוֹלָד כִּי עָשָׂה:	לב

23

—○⟨⟩○—

כג

1	A psalm of David. Hashem is my shepherd; I lack nothing.	*Mizmor ledavid Adonai ro'i lo echsar*	מִזְמוֹר לְדָוִד יְהֹוָה רֹעִי לֹא אֶחְסָר:	א
2	He makes me lie down in green pastures; He leads me to water in places of repose;	*Bin'ot deshe yarbitzeni al-mei menuchot yenahaleni*	בִּנְאוֹת דֶּשֶׁא יַרְבִּיצֵנִי עַל מֵי מְנֻחוֹת יְנַהֲלֵנִי:	ב

3

He renews my life;
He guides me in right
paths as befits His
name.

*Nafshi yeshovev
yancheni vema'gelei-
tzedek lema'an shemo*

נַפְשִׁי יְשׁוֹבֵב יַנְחֵנִי
בְמַעְגְּלֵי־צֶדֶק לְמַעַן שְׁמוֹ:

ג

4

Though I walk through
a valley of deepest
darkness, I fear no
harm, for You are with
me; Your rod and Your
staff—they comfort me.

*Gam ki-elech begei
tzalmavet lo-ira ra ki-
attah immadi shivtecha
umish'antecha hemmah
yenachamuni*

גַּם כִּי־אֵלֵךְ בְּגֵיא צַלְמָוֶת
לֹא־אִירָא רָע כִּי־אַתָּה
עִמָּדִי שִׁבְטְךָ וּמִשְׁעַנְתֶּךָ
הֵמָּה יְנַחֲמֻנִי:

ד

5

You spread a table for
me in full view of my
enemies; You anoint
my head with oil; my
drink is abundant.

*Ta'aroch lefanai
shulchan neged tzorerai
dishanta vashemen
roshi kosi revayah*

תַּעֲרֹךְ לְפָנַי שֻׁלְחָן נֶגֶד
צֹרְרָי דִּשַּׁנְתָּ בַשֶּׁמֶן רֹאשִׁי
כּוֹסִי רְוָיָה:

ה

6

Only goodness and
steadfast love shall
pursue me all the days
of my life, and I shall
dwell in the house of
Hashem for many long
years.

*Ach tov vachesed
yirdefuni kol-yemei
chayyai veshavti beveit-
Adonai le'orech yamim*

אַךְ טוֹב וָחֶסֶד יִרְדְּפוּנִי
כָּל־יְמֵי חַיָּי וְשַׁבְתִּי בְּבֵית־
יְהֹוָה לְאֹרֶךְ יָמִים:

ו

24

כד

1

Of David. A psalm.
The earth is Hashem's
and all that it holds,
the world and its
inhabitants.

*Ledavid mizmor
lAdonai ha'aretz
umelo'ah tevel
veyoshevei vah*

לְדָוִד מִזְמוֹר לַיהֹוָה הָאָרֶץ
וּמְלוֹאָהּ תֵּבֵל וְיֹשְׁבֵי בָהּ:

א

2	For He founded it upon the ocean, set it on the nether-streams.	*Ki-hu al-yammim yesadah ve'al-neharot yechoneneha*	כִּי־הוּא עַל־יַמִּים יְסָדָהּ וְעַל־נְהָרוֹת יְכוֹנְנֶהָ:
3	Who may ascend the mountain of Hashem? Who may stand in His holy place?—	*Mi-ya'aleh vehar-Adonai umi-yakum bimkom kodsho*	מִי־יַעֲלֶה בְהַר־יְהֹוָה וּמִי־יָקוּם בִּמְקוֹם קׇדְשׁוֹ:
4	He who has clean hands and a pure heart, who has not taken a false oath by My life or sworn deceitfully.	*Neki chappayim uvar-levav asher lo-nasa lashave nafshi velo nishba lemirmah*	נְקִי כַפַּיִם וּבַר־לֵבָב אֲשֶׁר לֹא־נָשָׂא לַשָּׁוְא נַפְשִׁי וְלֹא נִשְׁבַּע לְמִרְמָה:
5	He shall carry away a blessing from Hashem, a just reward from Hashem, his deliverer.	*Yissa verachah me'et Adonai utzedakah me'elohei yish'o*	יִשָּׂא בְרָכָה מֵאֵת יְהֹוָה וּצְדָקָה מֵאֱלֹהֵי יִשְׁעוֹ:
6	Such is the circle of those who turn to Him, Yaakov, who seek Your presence. Selah.	*Zeh dor dorshu [doreshav] mevakshei faneicha ya'akov selah*	זֶה דּוֹר דרשו [דֹּרְשָׁיו] מְבַקְשֵׁי פָנֶיךָ יַעֲקֹב סֶלָה:
7	O gates, lift up your heads! Up high, you everlasting doors, so the King of glory may come in!	*Se'u she'arim rasheichem vehinnase'u pitchei olam veyavo melech hakkavod*	שְׂאוּ שְׁעָרִים רָאשֵׁיכֶם וְהִנָּשְׂאוּ פִּתְחֵי עוֹלָם וְיָבוֹא מֶלֶךְ הַכָּבוֹד:
8	Who is the King of glory?— Hashem, mighty and valiant, Hashem, valiant in battle.	*Mi zeh melech hakkavod Adonai izzuz vegibbor Adonai gibbor milchamah*	מִי זֶה מֶלֶךְ הַכָּבוֹד יְהֹוָה עִזּוּז וְגִבּוֹר יְהֹוָה גִּבּוֹר מִלְחָמָה:

9   O gates, lift up your heads! Lift them up, you everlasting doors, so the King of glory may come in!

Se'u she'arim rasheichem use'u pitchei olam veyavo melech hakkavod

שְׂאוּ שְׁעָרִים רָאשֵׁיכֶם וּשְׂאוּ פִּתְחֵי עוֹלָם וְיָבֹא מֶלֶךְ הַכָּבוֹד: ט

10   Who is the King of glory?— the lord of hosts, He is the King of glory! Selah.

Mi hu zeh melech hakkavod Adonai tzeva'ot hu melech hakkavod selah

מִי הוּא זֶה מֶלֶךְ הַכָּבוֹד יְהוָה צְבָאוֹת הוּא מֶלֶךְ הַכָּבוֹד סֶלָה: י

25

—◦❈◦—

כה

1   Of David. Hashem, I set my hope on You;

Ledavid eleicha Adonai nafshi essa

לְדָוִד אֵלֶיךָ יְהוָה נַפְשִׁי אֶשָּׂא: א

2   my God, in You I trust; may I not be disappointed, may my enemies not exult over me.

Elohai becha vatachti al-evoshah al-ya'altzu oyevai li

אֱלֹהַי בְּךָ בָטַחְתִּי אַל-אֵבוֹשָׁה אַל-יַעַלְצוּ אֹיְבַי לִי: ב

3   O let none who look to You be disappointed; let the faithless be disappointed, empty-handed.

Gam kol-koveicha lo yevoshu yevoshu habbogedim reikam

גַּם כָּל-קֹוֶיךָ לֹא יֵבֹשׁוּ יֵבֹשׁוּ הַבּוֹגְדִים רֵיקָם: ג

4   Let me know Your paths, Hashem; teach me Your ways;

Deracheicha Adonai hodi'eni orechoteicha lammedeni

דְּרָכֶיךָ יְהוָה הוֹדִיעֵנִי אֹרְחוֹתֶיךָ לַמְּדֵנִי: ד

5	guide me in Your true way and teach me, for You are Hashem, my deliverer; it is You I look to at all times.	*Hadricheni va'amittecha velammedeni ki-attah elohei yish'i otecha kivviti kol-hayyom*	הַדְרִיכֵנִי בַאֲמִתֶּךָ וְלַמְּדֵנִי כִּי־אַתָּה אֱלֹהֵי יִשְׁעִי אוֹתְךָ קִוִּיתִי כָּל־הַיּוֹם: ה
6	Hashem, be mindful of Your compassion and Your faithfulness; they are old as time.	*Zechor-rachameicha Adonai vachasadeicha ki me'olam hemmah*	זְכֹר־רַחֲמֶיךָ יְהֹוָה וַחֲסָדֶיךָ כִּי מֵעוֹלָם הֵמָּה: ו
7	Be not mindful of my youthful sins and transgressions; in keeping with Your faithfulness consider what is in my favor, as befits Your goodness, Hashem.	*Chattott ne'urai ufesha'ai al-tizkor kechasdecha zechar-li-attah lema'an tuvecha Adonai*	חַטֹּאות נְעוּרַי וּפְשָׁעַי אַל־תִּזְכֹּר כְּחַסְדְּךָ זְכָר־לִי־אַתָּה לְמַעַן טוּבְךָ יְהֹוָה: ז
8	Good and upright is Hashem; therefore He shows sinners the way.	*Tov-veyashar Adonai al-ken yoreh chatta'im baddarech*	טוֹב־וְיָשָׁר יְהֹוָה עַל־כֵּן יוֹרֶה חַטָּאִים בַּדָּרֶךְ: ח
9	He guides the lowly in the right path, and teaches the lowly His way.	*Yadrech anavim bammishpat vilammed anavim darko*	יַדְרֵךְ עֲנָוִים בַּמִּשְׁפָּט וִילַמֵּד עֲנָוִים דַּרְכּוֹ: ט
10	All Hashem's paths are steadfast love for those who keep the decrees of His covenant.	*Kol-arechot Adonai chesed ve'emet lenotzerei verito ve'edotav*	כָּל־אָרְחוֹת יְהֹוָה חֶסֶד וֶאֱמֶת לְנֹצְרֵי בְרִיתוֹ וְעֵדֹתָיו: י
11	As befits Your name, Hashem, pardon my iniquity though it be great.	*Lema'an-shimcha Adonai vesalachta la'avni ki rav-hu*	לְמַעַן־שִׁמְךָ יְהֹוָה וְסָלַחְתָּ לַעֲוֹנִי כִּי רַב־הוּא: יא

12	Whoever fears Hashem, he shall be shown what path to choose.	*Mi-zeh ha'ish yere Adonai yorennu bederech yivchar*	מִי־זֶה הָאִישׁ יְרֵא יְהֹוָה יוֹרֶנּוּ בְּדֶרֶךְ יִבְחָר׃	יב
13	He shall live a happy life, and his children shall inherit the land.	*Nafsho betov talin vezar'o yirash aretz*	נַפְשׁוֹ בְּטוֹב תָּלִין וְזַרְעוֹ יִירַשׁ אָרֶץ׃	יג
14	The counsel of Hashem is for those who fear Him; to them He makes known His covenant.	*Sod Adonai lire'av uverito lehodi'am*	סוֹד יְהֹוָה לִירֵאָיו וּבְרִיתוֹ לְהוֹדִיעָם׃	יד
15	My eyes are ever toward Hashem, for He will loose my feet from the net.	*Einai tamid el-Adonai ki hu-yotzi mereshet raglai*	עֵינַי תָּמִיד אֶל־יְהֹוָה כִּי הוּא־יוֹצִיא מֵרֶשֶׁת רַגְלָי׃	טו
16	Turn to me, have mercy on me, for I am alone and afflicted.	*Peneh-elai vechanneni ki-yachid ve'oni ani*	פְּנֵה־אֵלַי וְחָנֵּנִי כִּי־יָחִיד וְעָנִי אָנִי׃	טז
17	My deep distress increases; deliver me from my straits.	*Tzarot levavi hirchivu mimmetzukotai hotzi'eni*	צָרוֹת לְבָבִי הִרְחִיבוּ מִמְּצוּקוֹתַי הוֹצִיאֵנִי׃	יז
18	Look at my affliction and suffering, and forgive all my sins.	*Re'eh aneyi va'amali vesa lechol-chattotai*	רְאֵה עָנְיִי וַעֲמָלִי וְשָׂא לְכָל־חַטֹּאותָי׃	יח
19	See how numerous my enemies are, and how unjustly they hate me!	*Re'eh-oyevai ki-rabbu vesin'at chamas sene'uni*	רְאֵה־אוֹיְבַי כִּי־רָבּוּ וְשִׂנְאַת חָמָס שְׂנֵאוּנִי׃	יט

20	Protect me and save me; let me not be disappointed, for I have sought refuge in You.	*Shamerah nafshi vehatzileni al-evosh ki-chasiti vach*
21	May integrity and uprightness watch over me, for I look to You.	*Tom-vayosher yitzeruni ki kivviticha*
22	O Hashem, redeem Yisrael from all its distress.	*Pedeh elohim et-yisra'el mikkol tzarotav*

שָׁמְרָה נַפְשִׁי וְהַצִּילֵנִי אַל־אֵבוֹשׁ כִּי־חָסִיתִי בָךְ: כ

תֹּם־וָיֹשֶׁר יִצְּרוּנִי כִּי קִוִּיתִיךָ: כא

פְּדֵה אֱלֹהִים אֶת־יִשְׂרָאֵל מִכֹּל צָרוֹתָיו: כב

26

כו

1	Of David. Vindicate me, Hashem, for I have walked without blame; I have trusted in Hashem; I have not faltered.	*Ledavid shofteini Adonai ki-ani betummi halachti uvaihovah batachti lo em'ad*
2	Probe me, Hashem, and try me, test my heart and mind;	*Bechaneni Adonai venasseni tzerufah [tzarefah] chilyotai velibbi*
3	for my eyes are on Your steadfast love; I have set my course by it.	*Ki-chasdecha leneged einai vehithallachti ba'amittecha*
4	I do not consort with scoundrels, or mix with hypocrites;	*Lo-yashavti im-metei-shave ve'im na'alamim lo avo*

לְדָוִד שָׁפְטֵנִי יְהֹוָה כִּי־אֲנִי בְּתֻמִּי הָלַכְתִּי וּבַיהֹוָה בָּטַחְתִּי לֹא אֶמְעָד: א

בְּחָנֵנִי יְהֹוָה וְנַסֵּנִי צרופה [צָרְפָה] כִלְיוֹתַי וְלִבִּי: ב

כִּי־חַסְדְּךָ לְנֶגֶד עֵינָי וְהִתְהַלַּכְתִּי בַּאֲמִתֶּךָ: ג

לֹא־יָשַׁבְתִּי עִם־מְתֵי־שָׁוְא וְעִם נַעֲלָמִים לֹא אָבוֹא: ד

5	I detest the company of evil men, and do not consort with the wicked;	*Saneti kehal mere'im ve'im-resha'im lo eshev*	שָׂנֵאתִי קְהַל מְרֵעִים וְעִם־רְשָׁעִים לֹא אֵשֵׁב:	ה
6	I wash my hands in innocence, and walk around Your mizbayach, Hashem,	*Erchatz benikkayon kappai va'asovevah et-mizbachacha Adonai*	אֶרְחַץ בְּנִקָּיוֹן כַּפָּי וַאֲסֹבְבָה אֶת־מִזְבַּחֲךָ יְהוָה:	ו
7	raising my voice in thanksgiving, and telling all Your wonders.	*Lashmia' bekol todah ulesapper kol-nifle'oteicha*	לַשְׁמִעַ בְּקוֹל תּוֹדָה וּלְסַפֵּר כָּל־נִפְלְאוֹתֶיךָ:	ז
8	Hashem, I love Your temple abode, the dwelling-place of Your glory.	*Adonai ahavti me'on beitecha umekom mishkan kevodecha*	יְהוָה אָהַבְתִּי מְעוֹן בֵּיתֶךָ וּמְקוֹם מִשְׁכַּן כְּבוֹדֶךָ:	ח
9	Do not sweep me away with sinners, or [snuff out] my life with murderers,	*Al-te'esof im-chatta'im nafshi ve'im-anshei damim chayyai*	אַל־תֶּאֱסֹף עִם־חַטָּאִים נַפְשִׁי וְעִם־אַנְשֵׁי דָמִים חַיָּי:	ט
10	who have schemes at their fingertips, and hands full of bribes.	*Asher-bideihem zimmah viminam male'ah shochad*	אֲשֶׁר־בִּידֵיהֶם זִמָּה וִימִינָם מָלְאָה שֹּׁחַד:	י
11	But I walk without blame; redeem me, have mercy on me!	*Va'ani betummi elech pedeni vechanneni*	וַאֲנִי בְּתֻמִּי אֵלֵךְ פְּדֵנִי וְחָנֵּנִי:	אי
12	My feet are on level ground. In assemblies I will bless Hashem.	*Ragli amedah vemishor bemakhelim avarech Adonai*	רַגְלִי עָמְדָה בְמִישׁוֹר בְּמַקְהֵלִים אֲבָרֵךְ יְהוָה:	יב

27

1	Of David. Hashem is my light and my help; whom should I fear? Hashem is the stronghold of my life, whom should I dread?	*Ledavid Adonai ori veyish'i mimmi ira Adonai ma'oz-chayyai mimmi efchad*

לְדָוִד יְהוָה אוֹרִי וְיִשְׁעִי מִמִּי אִירָא יְהוָה מָעוֹז־חַיַּי מִמִּי אֶפְחָד׃ א

2	When evil men assail me to devour my flesh— it is they, my foes and my enemies, who stumble and fall.	*Bikrov alai mere'im le'echol et-besari tzarai ve'oyevai li hemmah chashelu venafalu*

בִּקְרֹב עָלַי מְרֵעִים לֶאֱכֹל אֶת־בְּשָׂרִי צָרַי וְאֹיְבַי לִי הֵמָּה כָשְׁלוּ וְנָפָלוּ׃ ב

3	Should an army besiege me, my heart would have no fear; should war beset me, still would I be confident.	*Im-tachaneh alai machaneh lo-yira libbi im-takum alai milchamah bezot ani voteach*

אִם־תַּחֲנֶה עָלַי מַחֲנֶה לֹא־יִירָא לִבִּי אִם־תָּקוּם עָלַי מִלְחָמָה בְּזֹאת אֲנִי בוֹטֵחַ׃ ג

4	One thing I ask of Hashem, only that do I seek: to live in the house of Hashem all the days of my life, to gaze upon the beauty of Hashem, to frequent His temple.	*Achat sho'alti me'et-Adonai otah avakkesh shivti beveit-Adonai kol-yemei chayyai lachazot beno'am-Adonai ulevakker beheichalo*

אַחַת שָׁאַלְתִּי מֵאֵת־יְהוָה אוֹתָהּ אֲבַקֵּשׁ שִׁבְתִּי בְּבֵית־יְהוָה כָּל־יְמֵי חַיַּי לַחֲזוֹת בְּנֹעַם־יְהוָה וּלְבַקֵּר בְּהֵיכָלוֹ׃ ד

5	He will shelter me in His pavilion on an evil day, grant me the protection of His tent, raise me high upon a rock.	*Ki yitzpeneni besukkoh beyom ra'ah yastireni beseter oholo betzur yeromemeni*

כִּי יִצְפְּנֵנִי בְּסֻכֹּה בְּיוֹם רָעָה יַסְתִּרֵנִי בְּסֵתֶר אָהֳלוֹ בְּצוּר יְרוֹמְמֵנִי׃ ה

6 Now is my head high over my enemies roundabout; I sacrifice in His tent with shouts of joy, singing and chanting a hymn to Hashem.

Ve'attah yarum roshi al oyevai sevivotai ve'ezbechah ve'oholo zivchei teru'ah ashirah va'azammerah lAdonai

וְעַתָּה יָרוּם רֹאשִׁי עַל אֹיְבַי סְבִיבוֹתַי וְאֶזְבְּחָה בְאָהֳלוֹ זִבְחֵי תְרוּעָה אָשִׁירָה וַאֲזַמְּרָה לַיהֹוָה: ו

7 Hear, Hashem, when I cry aloud; have mercy on me, answer me.

Shema-Adonai koli ekra vechonneni va'aneni

שְׁמַע־יְהֹוָה קוֹלִי אֶקְרָא וְחָנֵּנִי וַעֲנֵנִי: ז

8 In Your behalf my heart says: "Seek My face!" Hashem, I seek Your face.

Lecha amar libbi bakkeshu fanai et-panecha Adonai avakkesh

לְךָ אָמַר לִבִּי בַּקְּשׁוּ פָנָי אֶת־פָּנֶיךָ יְהֹוָה אֲבַקֵּשׁ: ח

9 Do not hide Your face from me; do not thrust aside Your servant in anger; You have ever been my help. Do not forsake me, do not abandon me, O Hashem, my deliverer.

Al-taster panecha mimmenni al-tat-be'af avdecha ezrati hayita al-tittesheni ve'al-ta'azveni elohei yish'i

אַל־תַּסְתֵּר פָּנֶיךָ מִמֶּנִּי אַל־תַּט־בְּאַף עַבְדֶּךָ עֶזְרָתִי הָיִיתָ אַל־תִּטְּשֵׁנִי וְאַל־תַּעַזְבֵנִי אֱלֹהֵי יִשְׁעִי: ט

10 Though my father and mother abandon me, Hashem will take me in.

Ki-avi ve'immi azavuni vaihovah ya'asfeni

כִּי־אָבִי וְאִמִּי עֲזָבוּנִי וַיהֹוָה יַאַסְפֵנִי: י

11 Show me Your way, Hashem, and lead me on a level path because of my watchful foes.

Horeni Adonai darkecha unecheni be'orach mishor lema'an shorerai

הוֹרֵנִי יְהֹוָה דַּרְכֶּךָ וּנְחֵנִי בְּאֹרַח מִישׁוֹר לְמַעַן שׁוֹרְרָי: יא

12	Do not subject me to the will of my foes, for false witnesses and unjust accusers have appeared against me.	*Al-titteneni benefesh tzarai ki kamu-vi edei-sheker vifeach chamas*	אַל־תִּתְּנֵנִי בְּנֶפֶשׁ צָרָי כִּי קָמוּ־בִי עֵדֵי־שֶׁקֶר וִיפֵחַ חָמָס:	יב
13	Had I not the assurance that I would enjoy the goodness of Hashem in the land of the living…	*Lule he'emanti lir'ot betuv-Adonai be'eretz chayyim*	לוּלֵא הֶאֱמַנְתִּי לִרְאוֹת בְּטוּב־יְהֹוָה בְּאֶרֶץ חַיִּים:	יג
14	Look to Hashem; be strong and of good courage! O look to Hashem!	*Kavveh el-Adonai chazak veya'ametz libbecha vekavveh el-Adonai*	קַוֵּה אֶל־יְהֹוָה חֲזַק וְיַאֲמֵץ לִבֶּךָ וְקַוֵּה אֶל־יְהֹוָה:	יד

28 ─◦◎◦─ כח

1	Of David. Hashem, I call to You; my rock, do not disregard me, for if You hold aloof from me, I shall be like those gone down into the Pit.	*Ledavid eleicha Adonai ekra tzuri al-techerash mimmenni pen-techesheh mimmenni venimshalti im-yoredei vor*	לְדָוִד אֵלֶיךָ יְהֹוָה אֶקְרָא צוּרִי אַל־תֶּחֱרַשׁ מִמֶּנִּי פֶּן־תֶּחֱשֶׁה מִמֶּנִּי וְנִמְשַׁלְתִּי עִם־יוֹרְדֵי בוֹר:	א
2	Listen to my plea for mercy when I cry out to You, when I lift my hands toward Your inner sanctuary.	*Shema kol tachanunai beshavve'i eleicha benase'i yadai el-devir kodshecha*	שְׁמַע קוֹל תַּחֲנוּנַי בְּשַׁוְּעִי אֵלֶיךָ בְּנָשְׂאִי יָדַי אֶל־דְּבִיר קָדְשֶׁךָ:	ב

3   Do not count me with the wicked and evildoers who profess goodwill toward their fellows while malice is in their heart.

Al-timshecheni im-resha'im ve'im-po'alei aven doverei shalom im-re'eihem vera'ah bilvavam

אַל־תִּמְשְׁכֵנִי עִם־רְשָׁעִים וְעִם־פֹּעֲלֵי אָוֶן דֹּבְרֵי שָׁלוֹם עִם־רֵעֵיהֶם וְרָעָה בִּלְבָבָם: ג

4   Pay them according to their deeds, their malicious acts; according to their handiwork pay them, give them their deserts.

Ten-lahem kefo'olam ucheroa' ma'alleihem kema'aseh yedeihem ten lahem hashev gemulam lahem

תֶּן־לָהֶם כְּפָעֳלָם וּכְרֹעַ מַעַלְלֵיהֶם כְּמַעֲשֵׂה יְדֵיהֶם תֵּן לָהֶם הָשֵׁב גְּמוּלָם לָהֶם: ד

5   For they do not consider Hashem's deeds, the work of His hands. May He tear them down, never to rebuild them!

Ki lo yavinu el-pe'ullot Adonai ve'el-ma'aseh yadav yehersem velo yivnem

כִּי לֹא יָבִינוּ אֶל־פְּעֻלֹּת יְהֹוָה וְאֶל־מַעֲשֵׂה יָדָיו יֶהֶרְסֵם וְלֹא יִבְנֵם: ה

6   Blessed is Hashem, for He listens to my plea for mercy.

Baruch Adonai ki-shama kol tachanunai

בָּרוּךְ יְהֹוָה כִּי־שָׁמַע קוֹל תַּחֲנוּנָי: ו

7   Hashem is my strength and my shield; my heart trusts in Him. I was helped, and my heart exulted, so I will glorify Him with my song.

Adonai uzzi umaginni bo vatach libbi vene'ezareti vayya'aloz libbi umishiri ahodennu

יְהֹוָה עֻזִּי וּמָגִנִּי בּוֹ בָטַח לִבִּי וְנֶעֱזָרְתִּי וַיַּעֲלֹז לִבִּי וּמִשִּׁירִי אֲהוֹדֶנּוּ: ז

8   Hashem is their strength; He is a stronghold for the deliverance of His anointed.

Adonai oz-lamo uma'oz yeshu'ot meshicho hu

יְהֹוָה עֹז־לָמוֹ וּמָעוֹז יְשׁוּעוֹת מְשִׁיחוֹ הוּא: ח

9 | Deliver and bless Your very own people; tend them and sustain them forever. | *Hoshi'ah et-ammecha uvarech et-nachalatecha ure'em venasse'em ad-ha'olam* | הוֹשִׁיעָה אֶת־עַמֶּךָ וּבָרֵךְ אֶת־נַחֲלָתֶךָ וּרְעֵם וְנַשְּׂאֵם עַד־הָעוֹלָם: | ט

29
—◦⦾⧓⦾◦— **כט**

1 | A psalm of David. Ascribe to Hashem, O divine beings, ascribe to Hashem glory and strength. | *Mizmor ledavid havu lAdonai benei elim havu lAdonai kavod va'oz* | מִזְמוֹר לְדָוִד הָבוּ לַיהֹוָה בְּנֵי אֵלִים הָבוּ לַיהֹוָה כָּבוֹד וָעֹז: | א

2 | Ascribe to Hashem the glory of His name; bow down to Hashem, majestic in holiness. | *Havu lAdonai kevod shemo hishtachavu lAdonai behadrat-kodesh* | הָבוּ לַיהֹוָה כְּבוֹד שְׁמוֹ הִשְׁתַּחֲווּ לַיהֹוָה בְּהַדְרַת־קֹדֶשׁ: | ב

3 | The voice of Hashem is over the waters; the God of glory thunders, Hashem, over the mighty waters. | *Kol Adonai al-hammayim el-hakkavod hir'im Adonai al-mayim rabbim* | קוֹל יְהֹוָה עַל־הַמָּיִם אֵל־הַכָּבוֹד הִרְעִים יְהֹוָה עַל־מַיִם רַבִּים: | ג

4 | The voice of Hashem is power; the voice of Hashem is majesty; | *Kol-Adonai bakkoach kol Adonai behadar* | קוֹל־יְהֹוָה בַּכֹּחַ קוֹל יְהֹוָה בֶּהָדָר: | ד

5 | the voice of Hashem breaks cedars; Hashem shatters the cedars of Lebanon. | *Kol Adonai shover arazim vayshabber Adonai et-arzei hallevanon* | קוֹל יְהֹוָה שֹׁבֵר אֲרָזִים וַיְשַׁבֵּר יְהֹוָה אֶת־אַרְזֵי הַלְּבָנוֹן: | ה

6	He makes Lebanon skip like a calf, Sirion, like a young wild ox.	*Vayyarkidem kemo-egel levanon vesiryon kemo ven-re'emim*	וַיַּרְקִידֵם כְּמוֹ־עֵגֶל לְבָנוֹן וְשִׂרְיֹן כְּמוֹ בֶן־רְאֵמִים:
7	The voice of Hashem kindles flames of fire;	*Kol-Adonai chotzev lahavot esh*	קוֹל־יְהֹוָה חֹצֵב לַהֲבוֹת אֵשׁ:
8	the voice of Hashem convulses the wilderness; Hashem convulses the wilderness of Kadesh;	*Kol Adonai yachil midbar yachil Adonai midbar kadesh*	קוֹל יְהֹוָה יָחִיל מִדְבָּר יָחִיל יְהֹוָה מִדְבַּר קָדֵשׁ:
9	the voice of Hashem causes hinds to calve, and strips forests bare; while in His temple all say "Glory!"	*Kol Adonai yecholel ayyalot vayyechesof ye'arot uveheichalo kullo omer kavod*	קוֹל יְהֹוָה יְחוֹלֵל אַיָּלוֹת וַיֶּחֱשֹׂף יְעָרוֹת וּבְהֵיכָלוֹ כֻּלּוֹ אֹמֵר כָּבוֹד:
10	Hashem sat enthroned at the Flood; Hashem sits enthroned, king forever.	*Adonai lammabbul yashav vayyeshav Adonai melech le'olam*	יְהֹוָה לַמַּבּוּל יָשָׁב וַיֵּשֶׁב יְהֹוָה מֶלֶךְ לְעוֹלָם:
11	May Hashem grant strength to His people; may Hashem bestow on His people wellbeing.	*Adonai oz le'ammo yitten Adonai yevarech et-ammo vashalom*	יְהֹוָה עֹז לְעַמּוֹ יִתֵּן יְהֹוָה יְבָרֵךְ אֶת־עַמּוֹ בַשָּׁלוֹם:

30

ל

1	A psalm of David. A song for the dedication of the House.	*Mizmor shir-chanukkat habbayit ledavid*	מִזְמוֹר שִׁיר־חֲנֻכַּת הַבַּיִת לְדָוִד:

2	I extol You, Hashem, for You have lifted me up, and not let my enemies rejoice over me.	*Aromimcha Adonai ki dillitani velo-simmachta oyevai li*	אֲרוֹמִמְךָ יְהֹוָה כִּי דִלִּיתָנִי וְלֹא־שִׂמַּחְתָּ אֹיְבַי לִי:	ב
3	Hashem, my God, I cried out to You, and You healed me.	*Adonai elohai shivva'ti eleicha vattirpa'eni*	יְהֹוָה אֱלֹהָי שִׁוַּעְתִּי אֵלֶיךָ וַתִּרְפָּאֵנִי:	ג
4	Hashem, You brought me up from Sheol, preserved me from going down into the Pit.	*Adonai he'elita min-she'ol nafshi chiyyitani myvrd[miyyaredi] vor*	יְהֹוָה הֶעֱלִיתָ מִן־שְׁאוֹל נַפְשִׁי חִיִּיתַנִי מִיּוֹרְדִי־ [מִיָּרְדִי־] בוֹר:	ד
5	O you faithful of Hashem, sing to Him, and praise His holy name.	*Zammeru lAdonai chasidav vehodu lezecher kodsho*	זַמְּרוּ לַיהֹוָה חֲסִידָיו וְהוֹדוּ לְזֵכֶר קָדְשׁוֹ:	ה
6	For He is angry but a moment, and when He is pleased there is life. One may lie down weeping at nightfall; but at dawn there are shouts of joy.	*Ki rega be'appo chayyim birtzono ba'erev yalin bechi velabboker rinnah*	כִּי רֶגַע בְּאַפּוֹ חַיִּים בִּרְצוֹנוֹ בָּעֶרֶב יָלִין בֶּכִי וְלַבֹּקֶר רִנָּה:	ו
7	When I was untroubled, I thought, "I shall never be shaken,"	*Va'ani amarti veshalvi bal-emmot le'olam*	וַאֲנִי אָמַרְתִּי בְשַׁלְוִי בַּל־אֶמּוֹט לְעוֹלָם:	ז
8	for You, O Hashem, when You were pleased, made [me] firm as a mighty mountain. When You hid Your face, I was terrified.	*Adonai birtzonecha he'emadtah leharri oz histarta faneicha hayiti nivhal*	יְהֹוָה בִּרְצוֹנְךָ הֶעֱמַדְתָּה לְהַרְרִי עֹז הִסְתַּרְתָּ פָנֶיךָ הָיִיתִי נִבְהָל:	ח

9 I called to You, Hashem; to my Lord I made appeal,

Eleicha Adonai ekra ve'el-Adonai etchannan

אֵלֶיךָ יְהֹוָה אֶקְרָא וְאֶל־אֲדֹנָי אֶתְחַנָּן: ט

10 "What is to be gained from my death, from my descent into the Pit? Can dust praise You? Can it declare Your faithfulness?

Mah-betza bedami beridti el-shachat hayodecha afar hayaggid amittecha

מַה־בֶּצַע בְּדָמִי בְּרִדְתִּי אֶל־שָׁחַת הֲיוֹדְךָ עָפָר הֲיַגִּיד אֲמִתֶּךָ: י

11 Hear, Hashem, and have mercy on me; Hashem, be my help!"

Shema-Adonai vechanneni Adonai heyeh-ozer li

שְׁמַע־יְהֹוָה וְחָנֵּנִי יְהֹוָה הֱיֵה־עֹזֵר לִי: יא

12 You turned my lament into dancing, you undid my sackcloth and girded me with joy,

Hafachta mispedi lemachol li pittachta sakki vatte'azzereni simchah

הָפַכְתָּ מִסְפְּדִי לְמָחוֹל לִי פִּתַּחְתָּ שַׂקִּי וַתְּאַזְּרֵנִי שִׂמְחָה: יב

13 that [my] whole being might sing hymns to You endlessly; Hashem my God, I will praise You forever.

Lema'an yezammercha chavod velo yiddom Adonai elohai le'olam odekka

לְמַעַן יְזַמֶּרְךָ כָבוֹד וְלֹא יִדֹּם יְהֹוָה אֱלֹהַי לְעוֹלָם אוֹדֶךָּ: יג

31

─○◈◈◈○─

לא

1 For the leader. A psalm of David.

Lammenatzeach mizmor ledavid

לַמְנַצֵּחַ מִזְמוֹר לְדָוִד: א

2	I seek refuge in You, Hashem; may I never be disappointed; as You are righteous, rescue me.	*Becha Adonai chasiti al-evoshah le'olam betzidkatecha falleteni*	בְּךָ יְהֹוָה חָסִיתִי אַל־אֵבוֹשָׁה לְעוֹלָם בְּצִדְקָתְךָ פַלְּטֵנִי: ב
3	Incline Your ear to me; be quick to save me; be a rock, a stronghold for me, a citadel, for my deliverance.	*Hatteh elai oznecha meherah hatzileni heyeh li letzur-ma'oz leveit metzudot lehoshi'eni*	הַטֵּה אֵלַי אָזְנְךָ מְהֵרָה הַצִּילֵנִי הֱיֵה לִי לְצוּר־מָעוֹז לְבֵית מְצוּדוֹת לְהוֹשִׁיעֵנִי: ג
4	For You are my rock and my fortress; You lead me and guide me as befits Your name.	*Ki-sal'i umetzudati attah ulema'an shimcha tancheni utenahaleni*	כִּי־סַלְעִי וּמְצוּדָתִי אָתָּה וּלְמַעַן שִׁמְךָ תַּנְחֵנִי וּתְנַהֲלֵנִי: ד
5	You free me from the net laid for me, for You are my stronghold.	*Totzi'eni mereshet zu tamenu li ki-attah ma'uzzi*	תּוֹצִיאֵנִי מֵרֶשֶׁת זוּ טָמְנוּ לִי כִּי־אַתָּה מָעוּזִּי: ה
6	Into Your hand I entrust my spirit; You redeem me, Hashem, faithful Hashem.	*Beyadecha afkid ruchi paditah oti Adonai el emet*	בְּיָדְךָ אַפְקִיד רוּחִי פָּדִיתָה אוֹתִי יְהֹוָה אֵל אֱמֶת: ו
7	I detest those who rely on empty folly, but I trust in Hashem.	*Saneti hashomerim havlei-shave va'ani el-Adonai batacheti*	שָׂנֵאתִי הַשֹּׁמְרִים הַבְלֵי־שָׁוְא וַאֲנִי אֶל־יְהֹוָה בָּטָחְתִּי: ז
8	Let me exult and rejoice in Your faithfulness when You notice my affliction, are mindful of my deep distress,	*Agilah ve'esmechah bechasdecha asher ra'ita et-aneyi yada'ta betzarot nafshi*	אָגִילָה וְאֶשְׂמְחָה בְּחַסְדֶּךָ אֲשֶׁר רָאִיתָ אֶת־עָנְיִי יָדַעְתָּ בְּצָרוֹת נַפְשִׁי: ח

9	and do not hand me over to my enemy, but grant me relief.	*Velo hisgartani beyad-oyev he'emadta vammerchav raglai*	וְלֹא הִסְגַּרְתַּנִי בְּיַד־אוֹיֵב הֶעֱמַדְתָּ בַמֶּרְחָב רַגְלָי:	ט
10	Have mercy on me, Hashem, for I am in distress; my eyes are wasted by vexation, my substance and body too.	*Channeni Adonai ki tzar-li asheshah vecha'as eini nafshi uvitni*	חָנֵּנִי יְהֹוָה כִּי צַר־לִי עָשְׁשָׁה בְכַעַס עֵינִי נַפְשִׁי וּבִטְנִי:	י
11	My life is spent in sorrow, my years in groaning; my strength fails because of my iniquity, my limbs waste away.	*Ki chalu veyagon chayyai ushenotai ba'anachah kashal ba'avni chochi va'atzamai asheshu*	כִּי כָלוּ בְיָגוֹן חַיַּי וּשְׁנוֹתַי בַּאֲנָחָה כָּשַׁל בַּעֲוֹנִי כֹחִי וַעֲצָמַי עָשֵׁשׁוּ:	יא
12	Because of all my foes I am the particular butt of my neighbors, a horror to my friends; those who see me on the street avoid me.	*Mikkol-tzorerai hayiti cherpah velishachenai me'od ufachad limyudda'ai ro'ai bachutz nadedu mimmenni*	מִכָּל־צֹרְרַי הָיִיתִי חֶרְפָּה וְלִשְׁכֵנַי מְאֹד וּפַחַד לִמְיֻדָּעַי רֹאַי בַּחוּץ נָדְדוּ מִמֶּנִּי:	יב
13	I am put out of mind like the dead; I am like an object given up for lost.	*Nishkachti kemet millev hayiti kichli oved*	נִשְׁכַּחְתִּי כְּמֵת מִלֵּב הָיִיתִי כִּכְלִי אֹבֵד:	יג
14	I hear the whisperings of many, intrigue on every side, as they scheme together against me, plotting to take my life.	*Ki shama'ti dibbat rabbim magor missaviv behivvosdam yachad alai lakachat nafshi zamamu*	כִּי שָׁמַעְתִּי דִּבַּת רַבִּים מָגוֹר מִסָּבִיב בְּהִוָּסְדָם יַחַד עָלַי לָקַחַת נַפְשִׁי זָמָמוּ:	יד
15	But I trust in You, Hashem; I say, "You are my God!"	*Va'ani aleicha vatachti Adonai amarti elohai attah*	וַאֲנִי עָלֶיךָ בָטַחְתִּי יְהֹוָה אָמַרְתִּי אֱלֹהַי אָתָּה:	טו

16	My fate is in Your hand; save me from the hand of my enemies and pursuers.	*Beyadecha ittotai hatzileni miyyad-oyevai umerodefai*	בְּיָדְךָ עִתֹּתָי הַצִּילֵנִי מִיַּד־אוֹיְבַי וּמֵרֹדְפָי:
17	Show favor to Your servant; as You are faithful, deliver me.	*Ha'irah faneicha al-avdecha hoshi'eni vechasdecha*	הָאִירָה פָנֶיךָ עַל־עַבְדֶּךָ הוֹשִׁיעֵנִי בְחַסְדֶּךָ:
18	Hashem, let me not be disappointed when I call You; let the wicked be disappointed; let them be silenced in Sheol;	*Adonai al-evoshah ki keraticha yevoshu resha'im yiddemu lish'ol*	יְהוָה אַל־אֵבוֹשָׁה כִּי קְרָאתִיךָ יֵבֹשׁוּ רְשָׁעִים יִדְּמוּ לִשְׁאוֹל:
19	let lying lips be stilled that speak haughtily against the righteous with arrogance and contempt.	*Te'alamnah siftei shaker haddoverot al-tzaddik atak bega'avah vavuz*	תֵּאָלַמְנָה שִׂפְתֵי שָׁקֶר הַדֹּבְרוֹת עַל־צַדִּיק עָתָק בְּגַאֲוָה וָבוּז:
20	How abundant is the good that You have in store for those who fear You, that You do in the full view of men for those who take refuge in You.	*Mah rav-tuvecha asher-tzafanta lire'eicha pa'alta lachosim bach neged benei adam*	מָה רַב־טוּבְךָ אֲשֶׁר־צָפַנְתָּ לִּירֵאֶיךָ פָּעַלְתָּ לַחֹסִים בָּךְ נֶגֶד בְּנֵי אָדָם:
21	You grant them the protection of Your presence against scheming men; You shelter them in Your pavilion from contentious tongues.	*Tastirem beseter panecha meruchsei ish titzpenem besukkah meriv leshonot*	תַּסְתִּירֵם בְּסֵתֶר פָּנֶיךָ מֵרֻכְסֵי אִישׁ תִּצְפְּנֵם בְּסֻכָּה מֵרִיב לְשֹׁנוֹת:

טז	
יז	
יח	
יט	
כ	
כא	

22	Blessed is Hashem, for He has been wondrously faithful to me, a veritable bastion.	*Baruch Adonai ki hifli chasdo li be'ir matzor*

בָּרוּךְ יְהֹוָה כִּי הִפְלִיא
חַסְדּוֹ לִי בְּעִיר מָצוֹר: כב

23	Alarmed, I had thought, "I am thrust out of Your sight"; yet You listened to my plea for mercy when I cried out to You.	*Va'ani amarti vechafezi nigrazti minneged eineicha achen shama'ta kol tachanunai beshavve'i eleicha*

וַאֲנִי אָמַרְתִּי בְחָפְזִי
נִגְרַזְתִּי מִנֶּגֶד עֵינֶיךָ אָכֵן
שָׁמַעְתָּ קוֹל תַּחֲנוּנַי
בְּשַׁוְּעִי אֵלֶיךָ: כג

24	So love Hashem, all you faithful; Hashem guards the loyal, and more than requites him who acts arrogantly.	*Ehevu et-Adonai kol-chasidav emunim notzer Adonai umeshallem al-yeter oseh ga'avah*

אֶהֱבוּ אֶת־יְהֹוָה כָּל־
חֲסִידָיו אֱמוּנִים נֹצֵר
יְהֹוָה וּמְשַׁלֵּם עַל־יֶתֶר
עֹשֵׂה גַאֲוָה: כד

25	Be strong and of good courage, all you who wait for Hashem.	*Chizku veya'ametz levavchem kol-hammeyachalim lAdonai*

חִזְקוּ וְיַאֲמֵץ לְבַבְכֶם כָּל־
הַמְיַחֲלִים לַיהֹוָה: כה

32

—o◦⊰⧓⊱◦o—

לב

1	Of David. A maskil. Happy is he whose transgression is forgiven, whose sin is covered over.	*Ledavid maskil ashrei nesui-pesha kesui chata'ah*

לְדָוִד מַשְׂכִּיל אַשְׁרֵי נְשׂוּי־
פֶּשַׁע כְּסוּי חֲטָאָה: א

2	Happy the man whom Hashem does not hold guilty, and in whose spirit there is no deceit.	*Ashrei adam lo yachshov Adonai lo avn ve'ein berucho remiyyah*

אַשְׁרֵי אָדָם לֹא יַחְשֹׁב
יְהֹוָה לוֹ עָוֹן וְאֵין בְּרוּחוֹ
רְמִיָּה: ב

3	As long as I said nothing, my limbs wasted away from my anguished roaring all day long.	*Ki-hecherashti balu atzamai besha'agati kol-hayyom*	כִּי־הֶחֱרַשְׁתִּי בָּלוּ עֲצָמָי בְּשַׁאֲגָתִי כָּל־הַיּוֹם: ג
4	For night and day Your hand lay heavy on me; my vigor waned as in the summer drought. Selah.	*Ki yomam valaylah tichbad alai yadecha nehpach leshaddi becharvonei kayitz selah*	כִּי יוֹמָם וָלַיְלָה תִּכְבַּד עָלַי יָדֶךָ נֶהְפַּךְ לְשַׁדִּי בְּחַרְבֹנֵי קַיִץ סֶלָה: ד
5	Then I acknowledged my sin to You; I did not cover up my guilt; I resolved, "I will confess my transgressions to Hashem," and You forgave the guilt of my sin. Selah.	*Chattati odi'acha va'avoni lo-chissiti amarti odeh alei fesha'ai lAdonai ve'attah nasata avon chattati selah*	חַטָּאתִי אוֹדִיעֲךָ וַעֲוֺנִי לֹא־כִסִּיתִי אָמַרְתִּי אוֹדֶה עֲלֵי פְשָׁעַי לַיהוָה וְאַתָּה נָשָׂאתָ עֲוֺן חַטָּאתִי סֶלָה: ה
6	Therefore let every faithful man pray to You upon discovering [his sin], that the rushing mighty waters not overtake him.	*Al-zot yitpallel kol-chasid eleicha le'et metzo rak leshetef mayim rabbim elav lo yaggi'u*	עַל־זֹאת יִתְפַּלֵּל כָּל־חָסִיד אֵלֶיךָ לְעֵת מְצֹא רַק לְשֵׁטֶף מַיִם רַבִּים אֵלָיו לֹא יַגִּיעוּ: ו
7	You are my shelter; You preserve me from distress; You surround me with the joyous shouts of deliverance. Selah.	*Attah seter li mitzar titzereni rannei fallet tesoveveni selah*	אַתָּה סֵתֶר לִי מִצַּר תִּצְּרֵנִי רָנֵּי פַלֵּט תְּסוֹבְבֵנִי סֶלָה: ז
8	Let me enlighten you and show you which way to go; let me offer counsel; my eye is on you.	*Askilcha ve'orecha bederech-zu telech i'atzah aleicha eini*	אַשְׂכִּילְךָ וְאוֹרְךָ בְּדֶרֶךְ־זוּ תֵלֵךְ אִיעֲצָה עָלֶיךָ עֵינִי: ח

9
Be not like a senseless horse or mule whose movement must be curbed by bit and bridle; far be it from you!

Al-tihyu kesus kefered ein havin bemeteg-varesen edyo livlom bal kerov eleicha

אַל־תִּהְיוּ כְּסוּס כְּפֶרֶד אֵין הָבִין בְּמֶתֶג־וָרֶסֶן עֶדְיוֹ לִבְלוֹם בַּל קְרֹב אֵלֶיךָ:

ט

10
Many are the torments of the wicked, but he who trusts in Hashem shall be surrounded with favor.

Rabbim mach'ovim larasha vehabboteach bAdonai chesed yesovevennu

רַבִּים מַכְאוֹבִים לָרָשָׁע וְהַבּוֹטֵחַ בַּיהוָה חֶסֶד יְסוֹבְבֶנּוּ:

י

11
Rejoice in Hashem and exult, O you righteous; shout for joy, all upright men!

Simchu bAdonai vegilu tzaddikim veharninu kol-yishrei-lev

שִׂמְחוּ בַיהוָה וְגִילוּ צַדִּיקִים וְהַרְנִינוּ כָּל־יִשְׁרֵי־לֵב:

יא

33

—◦◦◦⬦◦◦◦—

לג

1
Sing forth, O you righteous, to Hashem; it is fit that the upright acclaim Him.

Rannenu tzaddikim bAdonai layyesharim navah tehillah

רַנְּנוּ צַדִּיקִים בַּיהוָה לַיְשָׁרִים נָאוָה תְהִלָּה:

א

2
Praise Hashem with the lyre; with the ten-stringed harp sing to Him;

hodu lAdonai bechinnor benevel asor zammeru-lo

הוֹדוּ לַיהוָה בְּכִנּוֹר בְּנֵבֶל עָשׂוֹר זַמְּרוּ־לוֹ:

ב

3
sing Him a new song; play sweetly with shouts of joy.

shiru-lo shir chadash heitivu naggen bitru'ah

שִׁירוּ־לוֹ שִׁיר חָדָשׁ הֵיטִיבוּ נַגֵּן בִּתְרוּעָה:

ג

4	For the word of Hashem is right; His every deed is faithful.	*Ki-yashar devar-Adonai vechol-ma'asehu be'emunah*	כִּי־יָשָׁר דְּבַר־יְהֹוָה וְכָל־מַעֲשֵׂהוּ בֶּאֱמוּנָה:	ד
5	He loves what is right and just; the earth is full of Hashem's faithful care.	*Ohev tzedakah umishpat chesed Adonai male'ah ha'aretz*	אֹהֵב צְדָקָה וּמִשְׁפָּט חֶסֶד יְהֹוָה מָלְאָה הָאָרֶץ:	ה
6	By the word of Hashem the heavens were made, by the breath of His mouth, all their host.	*Bidvar Adonai shamayim na'asu uveruach piv kol-tzeva'am*	בִּדְבַר יְהֹוָה שָׁמַיִם נַעֲשׂוּ וּבְרוּחַ פִּיו כָּל־צְבָאָם:	ו
7	He heaps up the ocean waters like a mound, stores the deep in vaults.	*Kones kanned mei hayyam noten be'otzarot tehomot*	כֹּנֵס כַּנֵּד מֵי הַיָּם נֹתֵן בְּאֹצָרוֹת תְּהוֹמוֹת:	ז
8	Let all the earth fear Hashem; let all the inhabitants of the world dread Him.	*Yir'u meAdonai kol-ha'aretz mimmennu yaguru kol-yoshevei tevel*	יִירְאוּ מֵיְהֹוָה כָּל־הָאָרֶץ מִמֶּנּוּ יָגוּרוּ כָּל־יֹשְׁבֵי תֵבֵל:	ח
9	For He spoke, and it was; He commanded, and it endured.	*Ki hu amar vayyehi hu-tzivvah vayya'amod*	כִּי הוּא אָמַר וַיֶּהִי הוּא־צִוָּה וַיַּעֲמֹד:	ט
10	Hashem frustrates the plans of nations, brings to naught the designs of peoples.	*Adonai hefir atzat-goyim heni machshevot ammim*	יְהֹוָה הֵפִיר עֲצַת־גּוֹיִם הֵנִיא מַחְשְׁבוֹת עַמִּים:	י
11	What Hashem plans endures forever, what He designs, for ages on end.	*Atzat Adonai le'olam ta'amod machshevot libbo ledor vador*	עֲצַת יְהֹוָה לְעוֹלָם תַּעֲמֹד מַחְשְׁבוֹת לִבּוֹ לְדֹר וָדֹר:	יא

12	Happy the nation whose Hashem is Hashem, the people He has chosen to be His own.	*Ashrei haggoy asher-Adonai elohav ha'am bachar lenachalah lo*	אַשְׁרֵי הַגּוֹי אֲשֶׁר־יְהֹוָה אֱלֹהָיו הָעָם בָּחַר לְנַחֲלָה לוֹ:	יב
13	Hashem looks down from heaven; He sees all mankind.	*Mishamayim hibbit Adonai ra'ah et-kol-benei ha'adam*	מִשָּׁמַיִם הִבִּיט יְהֹוָה רָאָה אֶת־כָּל־בְּנֵי הָאָדָם:	יג
14	From His dwelling-place He gazes on all the inhabitants of the earth—	*Mimmechon-shivto hishgiach el kol-yoshevei ha'aretz*	מִמְּכוֹן־שִׁבְתּוֹ הִשְׁגִּיחַ אֶל כָּל־יֹשְׁבֵי הָאָרֶץ:	יד
15	He who fashions the hearts of them all, who discerns all their doings.	*Hayyotzer yachad libbam hammevin el-kol-ma'aseihem*	הַיֹּצֵר יַחַד לִבָּם הַמֵּבִין אֶל־כָּל־מַעֲשֵׂיהֶם:	טו
16	Kings are not delivered by a large force; warriors are not saved by great strength;	*Ein-hammelech nosha berav-chayil gibbor lo-yinnatzel berav-koach*	אֵין־הַמֶּלֶךְ נוֹשָׁע בְּרָב־חָיִל גִּבּוֹר לֹא־יִנָּצֵל בְּרָב־כֹּחַ:	טז
17	horses are a false hope for deliverance; for all their great power they provide no escape.	*sheker hassus litshu'ah uverov cheilo lo yemallet*	שֶׁקֶר הַסּוּס לִתְשׁוּעָה וּבְרֹב חֵילוֹ לֹא יְמַלֵּט:	יז
18	Truly the eye of Hashem is on those who fear Him, who wait for His faithful care	*Hinneh ein Adonai el-yere'av lammeyachalim lechasdo*	הִנֵּה עֵין יְהֹוָה אֶל־יְרֵאָיו לַמְיַחֲלִים לְחַסְדּוֹ:	יח
19	to save them from death, to sustain them in famine.	*Lehatzil mimmavet nafsham ulechayyotam bara'av*	לְהַצִּיל מִמָּוֶת נַפְשָׁם וּלְחַיּוֹתָם בָּרָעָב:	יט

20	We set our hope on Hashem, He is our help and shield;	*Nafshenu chikketah lAdonai ezrenu umaginnenu hu*	נַפְשֵׁנוּ חִכְּתָה לַיהוָה עֶזְרֵנוּ וּמָגִנֵּנוּ הוּא:	כ
21	in Him our hearts rejoice, for in His holy name we trust.	*Ki-vo yismach libbenu ki veshem kodsho vatachenu*	כִּי־בוֹ יִשְׂמַח לִבֵּנוּ כִּי בְשֵׁם קָדְשׁוֹ בָטָחְנוּ:	כא
22	May we enjoy, Hashem, Your faithful care, as we have put our hope in You.	*Yehi-chasdecha Adonai aleinu ka'asher yichalnu lach*	יְהִי־חַסְדְּךָ יְהוָה עָלֵינוּ כַּאֲשֶׁר יִחַלְנוּ לָךְ:	כב

34 ─o◦✖◦o─ לד

1	Of David, when he feigned madness in the presence of Abimelech, who turned him out, and he left.	*Ledavid beshannoto et-ta'mo lifnei avimelech vaygarashehu vayyelach*	לְדָוִד בְּשַׁנּוֹתוֹ אֶת־טַעְמוֹ לִפְנֵי אֲבִימֶלֶךְ וַיְגָרֲשֵׁהוּ וַיֵּלַךְ:	א
2	I bless Hashem at all times; praise of Him is ever in my mouth.	*Avarachah et-Adonai bechol-et tamid tehillato befi*	אֲבָרֲכָה אֶת־יְהוָה בְּכָל־עֵת תָּמִיד תְּהִלָּתוֹ בְּפִי:	ב
3	I glory in Hashem; let the lowly hear it and rejoice.	*BAdonai tithallel nafshi yishme'u anavim veyismachu*	בַּיהוָה תִּתְהַלֵּל נַפְשִׁי יִשְׁמְעוּ עֲנָוִים וְיִשְׂמָחוּ:	ג
4	Exalt Hashem with me let us extol His name together.	*Gaddelu lAdonai itti uneromemah shemo yachdav*	גַּדְּלוּ לַיהוָה אִתִּי וּנְרוֹמֲמָה שְׁמוֹ יַחְדָּו:	ד

5	I turned to Hashem, and He answered me; He saved me from all my terrors.	*Darashti et-Adonai ve'anani umikkol-megurotai hitzilani*	דָּרַשְׁתִּי אֶת־יְהֹוָה וְעָנָנִי וּמִכׇּל־מְגוּרוֹתַי הִצִּילָנִי: ה
6	Men look to Him and are radiant; let their faces not be downcast.	*Hibbitu elav venaharu ufeneihem al-yechparu*	הִבִּיטוּ אֵלָיו וְנָהָרוּ וּפְנֵיהֶם אַל־יֶחְפָּרוּ: ו
7	Here was a lowly man who called, and Hashem listened, and delivered him from all his troubles.	*Zeh ani kara va'Adonai shamea' umikkol-tzarotav hoshi'o*	זֶה עָנִי קָרָא וַיהֹוָה שָׁמֵעַ וּמִכׇּל־צָרוֹתָיו הוֹשִׁיעוֹ: ז
8	The angel of Hashem camps around those who fear Him and rescues them.	*Choneh mal'ach-Adonai saviv lire'av vaychalletzem*	חֹנֶה מַלְאַךְ־יְהֹוָה סָבִיב לִירֵאָיו וַיְחַלְּצֵם: ח
9	Taste and see how good Hashem is; happy the man who takes refuge in Him!	*Ta'amu ure'u ki-tov Adonai ashrei haggever yecheseh-bo*	טַעֲמוּ וּרְאוּ כִּי־טוֹב יְהֹוָה אַשְׁרֵי הַגֶּבֶר יֶחֱסֶה־בּוֹ: ט
10	Fear Hashem, you His consecrated ones, for those who fear Him lack nothing.	*Yeru et-Adonai kedoshav ki-ein machsor lire'av*	יְראוּ אֶת־יְהֹוָה קְדֹשָׁיו כִּי־אֵין מַחְסוֹר לִירֵאָיו: י
11	Lions have been reduced to starvation, but those who turn to Hashem shall not lack any good.	*Kefirim rashu vera'evu vedoreshei Adonai lo-yachseru chol-tov*	כְּפִירִים רָשׁוּ וְרָעֵבוּ וְדֹרְשֵׁי יְהֹוָה לֹא־יַחְסְרוּ כׇל־טוֹב: יא
12	Come, my sons, listen to me; I will teach you what it is to fear Hashem.	*Lechu-vanim shim'u-li yir'at Adonai alammedchem*	לְכוּ־בָנִים שִׁמְעוּ־לִי יִרְאַת יְהֹוָה אֲלַמֶּדְכֶם: יב

13	Who is the man who is eager for life, who desires years of good fortune?	*Mi-ha'ish hechafetz chayyim ohev yamim lir'ot tov*	מִי־הָאִישׁ הֶחָפֵץ חַיִּים אֹהֵב יָמִים לִרְאוֹת טוֹב:	יג
14	Guard your tongue from evil, your lips from deceitful speech.	*Netzor leshonecha mera usefateicha middabber mirmah*	נְצֹר לְשׁוֹנְךָ מֵרָע וּשְׂפָתֶיךָ מִדַּבֵּר מִרְמָה:	יד
15	Shun evil and do good, seek amity and pursue it.	*Sur mera va'aseh-tov bakkesh shalom veradefehu*	סוּר מֵרָע וַעֲשֵׂה־טוֹב בַּקֵּשׁ שָׁלוֹם וְרָדְפֵהוּ:	טו
16	The eyes of Hashem are on the righteous, His ears attentive to their cry.	*Einei Adonai el-tzaddikim ve'azenav el-shav'atam*	עֵינֵי יְהֹוָה אֶל־צַדִּיקִים וְאָזְנָיו אֶל־שַׁוְעָתָם:	טז
17	The face of Hashem is set against evildoers, to erase their names from the earth.	*Penei Adonai be'osei ra lehachrit me'eretz zichram*	פְּנֵי יְהֹוָה בְּעֹשֵׂי רָע לְהַכְרִית מֵאֶרֶץ זִכְרָם:	יז
18	They cry out, and Hashem hears, and saves them from all their troubles.	*Tza'aku va'Adonai shamea' umikkol-tzarotam hitzilam*	צָעֲקוּ וַיהֹוָה שָׁמֵעַ וּמִכָּל־צָרוֹתָם הִצִּילָם:	יח
19	Hashem is close to the brokenhearted; those crushed in spirit He delivers.	*Karov Adonai lenishberei-lev ve'et-dakke'ei-ruach yoshia'*	קָרוֹב יְהֹוָה לְנִשְׁבְּרֵי־לֵב וְאֶת־דַּכְּאֵי־רוּחַ יוֹשִׁיעַ:	יט
20	Though the misfortunes of the righteous be many, Hashem will save him from them all,	*Rabbot ra'ot tzaddik umikkullam yatzilennu Adonai*	רַבּוֹת רָעוֹת צַדִּיק וּמִכֻּלָּם יַצִּילֶנּוּ יְהֹוָה:	כ

21	Keeping all his bones intact, not one of them being broken.	*Shomer kol-atzmotav achat mehennah lo nishbarah*	שֹׁמֵר כׇּל־עַצְמוֹתָיו אַחַת מֵהֵנָּה לֹא נִשְׁבָּרָה׃	כא

One misfortune is the deathblow of the wicked; the foes of the righteous shall be ruined.

Temotet rasha ra'ah vesone'ei tzaddik ye'shamu

תְּמוֹתֵת רָשָׁע רָעָה וְשֹׂנְאֵי צַדִּיק יֶאְשָׁמוּ׃ כב

22

Hashem redeems the life of His servants; all who take refuge in Him shall not be ruined.

Podeh Adonai nefesh avadav velo ye'shemu kol-hachosim bo

פּוֹדֶה יְהֹוָה נֶפֶשׁ עֲבָדָיו וְלֹא יֶאְשְׁמוּ כׇּל־הַחֹסִים בּוֹ׃ כג

23

35

⎯o◦⧉◦o⎯

לה

Of David. Hashem, strive with my adversaries, give battle to my foes,

Ledavid rivah Adonai et-yerivai lecham et-lochamai

לְדָוִד רִיבָה יְהֹוָה אֶת־יְרִיבַי לְחַם אֶת־לֹחֲמָי׃ א

1

take up shield and buckler, and come to my defense;

Hachazek magen vetzinnah vekumah be'ezrati

הַחֲזֵק מָגֵן וְצִנָּה וְקוּמָה בְּעֶזְרָתִי׃ ב

2

ready the spear and javelin against my pursuers; tell me, "I am your deliverance."

Veharek chanit usegor likrat rodefai emor lenafshi yeshu'atech ani

וְהָרֵק חֲנִית וּסְגֹר לִקְרַאת רֹדְפָי אֱמֹר לְנַפְשִׁי יְשֻׁעָתֵךְ אָנִי׃ ג

3

4	Let those who seek my life be frustrated and put to shame; let those who plan to harm me fall back in disgrace.	*Yevoshu veyikkalemu mevakshei nafshi yissogu achor veyachperu choshevei ra'ati*	יֵבֹשׁוּ וְיִכָּלְמוּ מְבַקְשֵׁי נַפְשִׁי יִסֹּגוּ אָחוֹר וְיַחְפְּרוּ חֹשְׁבֵי רָעָתִי: ד
5	Let them be as chaff in the wind, Hashem's angel driving them on.	*Yihyu kemotz lifnei-ruach umal'ach Adonai docheh*	יִהְיוּ כְּמֹץ לִפְנֵי־רוּחַ וּמַלְאַךְ יְהֹוָה דּוֹחֶה: ה
6	Let their path be dark and slippery, with Hashem's angel in pursuit.	*Yehi-darkam choshech vachalaklakkot umal'ach Adonai rodefam*	יְהִי־דַרְכָּם חֹשֶׁךְ וַחֲלַקְלַקּוֹת וּמַלְאַךְ יְהֹוָה רֹדְפָם: ו
7	For without cause they hid a net to trap me; without cause they dug a pit* for me.	*Ki-chinnam tamenu-li shachat rishtam chinnam chaferu lenafshi*	כִּי־חִנָּם טָמְנוּ־לִי שַׁחַת רִשְׁתָּם חִנָּם חָפְרוּ לְנַפְשִׁי: ז
8	Let disaster overtake them unawares; let the net they hid catch them; let them fall into it when disaster [strikes].	*Tevo'ehu sho'ah lo-yeda verishto asher-taman tilkedo besho'ah yippal-bah*	תְּבוֹאֵהוּ שׁוֹאָה לֹא־יֵדָע וְרִשְׁתּוֹ אֲשֶׁר־טָמַן תִּלְכְּדוֹ בְּשׁוֹאָה יִפָּל־בָּהּ: ח
9	Then shall I exult in Hashem, rejoice in His deliverance.	*Venafshi tagil bAdonai tasis bishu'ato*	וְנַפְשִׁי תָּגִיל בַּיהֹוָה תָּשִׂישׂ בִּישׁוּעָתוֹ: ט
10	All my bones shall say, "Hashem, who is like You? You save the poor from one stronger than he, the poor and needy from his despoiler."	*Kol atzmotai tomarnah Adonai mi chamocha matzil ani mechazak mimmennu ve'ani ve'evyon miggozelo*	כָּל עַצְמוֹתַי תֹּאמַרְנָה יְהֹוָה מִי כָמוֹךָ מַצִּיל עָנִי מֵחָזָק מִמֶּנּוּ וְעָנִי וְאֶבְיוֹן מִגֹּזְלוֹ: י

11	Malicious witnesses appear who question me about things I do not know.	*Yekumun edei chamas asher lo-yada'ti yish'aluni*	יְקוּמוּן עֵדֵי חָמָס אֲשֶׁר לֹא־יָדַעְתִּי יִשְׁאָלוּנִי:	יא
12	They repay me evil for good, [seeking] my bereavement.	*Yeshallemuni ra'ah tachat tovah shechol lenafshi*	יְשַׁלְּמוּנִי רָעָה תַּחַת טוֹבָה שְׁכוֹל לְנַפְשִׁי:	יב
13	Yet, when they were ill, my dress was sackcloth, I kept a fast— may what I prayed for happen to me!	*Va'ani bachalotam levushi sak inneiti vatzom nafshi utefillati al-cheiki tashuv*	וַאֲנִי בַּחֲלוֹתָם לְבוּשִׁי שָׂק עִנֵּיתִי בַצּוֹם נַפְשִׁי וּתְפִלָּתִי עַל־חֵיקִי תָשׁוּב:	יג
14	I walked about as though it were my friend or my brother; I was bowed with gloom, like one mourning for his mother.	*Kerea'-ke'ach li hithallacheti ka'avel-em koder shachoti*	כְּרֵעַ־כְּאָח לִי הִתְהַלָּכְתִּי כַּאֲבֶל־אֵם קֹדֵר שַׁחוֹתִי:	יד
15	But when I stumble, they gleefully gather; wretches gather against me, I know not why; they tear at me without end.	*Uvetzal'i samechu vene'esafu ne'esfu alai nechim velo yada'ti kare'u velo-dammu*	וּבְצַלְעִי שָׂמְחוּ וְנֶאֱסָפוּ נֶאֶסְפוּ עָלַי נֵכִים וְלֹא יָדַעְתִּי קָרְעוּ וְלֹא־דָמּוּ:	טו
16	With impious, mocking grimace they gnash their teeth at me.	*Bechanfei la'agei ma'og charok alai shinneimo*	בְּחַנְפֵי לַעֲגֵי מָעוֹג חָרֹק עָלַי שִׁנֵּימוֹ:	טז
17	O Hashem, how long will You look on? Rescue me from their attacks, my precious life, from the lions,	*Adonai kammah tir'eh hashivah nafshi misho'eihem mikkefirim yechidati*	אֲדֹנָי כַּמָּה תִּרְאֶה הָשִׁיבָה נַפְשִׁי מִשֹּׁאֵיהֶם מִכְּפִירִים יְחִידָתִי:	יז

18	that I may praise You in a great congregation, acclaim You in a mighty throng.	*Odecha bekahal rav be'am atzum ahallekka*	אוֹדְךָ בְּקָהָל רָב בְּעַם עָצוּם אֲהַלְלֶךָּ׃	יח
19	Let not my treacherous enemies rejoice over me, or those who hate me without reason wink their eyes.	*Al-yismechu-li oyevai sheker sone'ai chinnam yikretzu-ayin*	אַל־יִשְׂמְחוּ־לִי אֹיְבַי שֶׁקֶר שֹׂנְאַי חִנָּם יִקְרְצוּ־עָיִן׃	יט
20	For they do not offer amity, but devise fraudulent schemes against harmless folk.	*Ki lo shalom yedabberu ve'al rig'ei-eretz divrei mirmot yachashovun*	כִּי לֹא שָׁלוֹם יְדַבֵּרוּ וְעַל רִגְעֵי־אֶרֶץ דִּבְרֵי מִרְמוֹת יַחֲשֹׁבוּן׃	כ
21	They open wide their mouths at me, saying, "Aha, aha, we have seen it!"	*Vayyarchivu alai pihem ameru he'ach he'ach ra'atah eineinu*	וַיַּרְחִיבוּ עָלַי פִּיהֶם אָמְרוּ הֶאָח הֶאָח רָאֲתָה עֵינֵינוּ׃	כא
22	You have seen it, Hashem; do not hold aloof! O Hashem, be not far from me!	*Ra'itah Adonai al-techerash Adonai al-tirchak mimmenni*	רָאִיתָה יְהֹוָה אַל־תֶּחֱרַשׁ אֲדֹנָי אַל־תִּרְחַק מִמֶּנִּי׃	כב
23	Wake, rouse Yourself for my cause, for my claim, O my God and my Lord!	*Ha'irah vehakitzah lemishpati elohai vAdonai lerivi*	הָעִירָה וְהָקִיצָה לְמִשְׁפָּטִי אֱלֹהַי וַאדֹנָי לְרִיבִי׃	כג
24	Take up my cause, Hashem my God, as You are beneficent, and let them not rejoice over me.	*Shafeteni chetzidkecha Adonai elohai ve'al-yismechu-li*	שָׁפְטֵנִי כְצִדְקְךָ יְהֹוָה אֱלֹהָי וְאַל־יִשְׂמְחוּ־לִי׃	כד

25	Let them not think, "Aha, just what we wished!" Let them not say, "We have destroyed him!"	*Al-yomru velibbam he'ach nafshenu al-yomru billa'anuhu*	אַל־יֹאמְרוּ בְלִבָּם הֶאָח נַפְשֵׁנוּ אַל־יֹאמְרוּ בִּלַּעֲנוּהוּ: כה
26	May those who rejoice at my misfortune be frustrated and utterly disgraced; may those who vaunt themselves over me be clad in frustration and shame.	*Yevoshu veyachperu yachdav semechei ra'ati yilbeshu-voshet uchelimmah hammagdili*	יֵבֹשׁוּ וְיַחְפְּרוּ יַחְדָּו שְׂמֵחֵי רָעָתִי יִלְבְּשׁוּ־בֹשֶׁת וּכְלִמָּה הַמַּגְדִּילִים עָלָי: כו
27	May those who desire my vindication sing forth joyously; may they always say, "Extolled be Hashem who desires the well-being of His servant,"	*Yaronnu veyismechu chafetzei tzidki veyomru tamid yigdal Adonai hechafetz shelom*	יָרֹנּוּ וְיִשְׂמְחוּ חֲפֵצֵי צִדְקִי וְיֹאמְרוּ תָמִיד יִגְדַּל יְהוָה הֶחָפֵץ שְׁלוֹם עַבְדּוֹ: כז
28	while my tongue shall recite Your beneficent acts, Your praises all day long.	*Uleshoni tehgeh tzidkecha kol-hayyom tehillatecha*	וּלְשׁוֹנִי תֶּהְגֶּה צִדְקֶךָ כָּל־הַיּוֹם תְּהִלָּתֶךָ: כח

36

—◦◦⃝◦◦—

לו

1	For the leader. Of the servant of Hashem, of David.	*Lammenatzeach le'eved-Adonai ledavid*	לַמְנַצֵּחַ לְעֶבֶד־יְהוָה לְדָוִד: א

87

2 I know what Transgression says to the wicked; he has no sense of the dread of Hashem,

Ne'um-pesha larasha bekerev libbi ein-pachad elohim leneged einav

נְאֻם־פֶּשַׁע לָרָשָׁע בְּקֶרֶב לִבִּי אֵין־פַּחַד אֱלֹהִים לְנֶגֶד עֵינָיו׃ ב

3 because its speech is seductive to him till his iniquity be found out and he be hated.

Ki-hechelik elav be'einav limtzo avono lisno

כִּי־הֶחֱלִיק אֵלָיו בְּעֵינָיו לִמְצֹא עֲוֹנוֹ לִשְׂנֹא׃ ג

4 His words are evil and deceitful; he will not consider doing good.

Divrei-fiv aven umirmah chadal lehaskil leheitiv

דִּבְרֵי־פִיו אָוֶן וּמִרְמָה חָדַל לְהַשְׂכִּיל לְהֵיטִיב׃ ד

5 In bed he plots mischief; he is set on a path of no good, he does not reject evil.

aven yachshov al-mishkavo yityatzev al-derech lo-tov ra lo yim'as

אָוֶן יַחְשֹׁב עַל־מִשְׁכָּבוֹ יִתְיַצֵּב עַל־דֶּרֶךְ לֹא־טוֹב רָע לֹא יִמְאָס׃ ה

6 Hashem, Your faithfulness reaches to heaven; Your steadfastness to the sky;

Adonai behashamayim chasdecha emunatecha ad-shechakim

יְהֹוָה בְּהַשָּׁמַיִם חַסְדֶּךָ אֱמוּנָתְךָ עַד־שְׁחָקִים׃ ו

7 Your beneficence is like the high mountains; Your justice like the great deep; man and beast You deliver, Hashem.

Tzidkatecha keharrei-el mishpatecha tehom rabbah adam-uvehemah toshia' Adonai

צִדְקָתְךָ כְּהַרְרֵי־אֵל מִשְׁפָּטֶךָ תְּהוֹם רַבָּה אָדָם־וּבְהֵמָה תוֹשִׁיעַ יְהֹוָה׃ ז

8 How precious is Your faithful care, O Hashem! Mankind shelters in the shadow of Your wings.

Mah-yakar chasdecha elohim uvenei adam betzel kenafeicha yechesayun

מַה־יָּקָר חַסְדְּךָ אֱלֹהִים וּבְנֵי אָדָם בְּצֵל כְּנָפֶיךָ יֶחֱסָיוּן׃ ח

9	They feast on the rich fare of Your house; You let them drink at Your refreshing stream.	*Yirveyun middeshen beitecha venachal adaneicha tashkem*	יִרְוְיֻן מִדֶּשֶׁן בֵּיתֶךָ וְנַחַל עֲדָנֶיךָ תַשְׁקֵם:	ט
10	With You is the fountain of life; by Your light do we see light.	*Ki-immecha mekor chayyim be'orecha nir'eh-or*	כִּי־עִמְּךָ מְקוֹר חַיִּים בְּאוֹרְךָ נִרְאֶה־אוֹר:	י
11	Bestow Your faithful care on those devoted to You, and Your beneficence on upright men.	*Meshoch chasdecha leyode'eicha vetzidkatecha leyishrei-lev*	מְשֹׁךְ חַסְדְּךָ לְיֹדְעֶיךָ וְצִדְקָתְךָ לְיִשְׁרֵי־לֵב:	יא
12	Let not the foot of the arrogant tread on me, or the hand of the wicked drive me away.	*Al-tevo'eni regel ga'avah veyad-resha'im al-tenideni*	אַל־תְּבוֹאֵנִי רֶגֶל גַּאֲוָה וְיַד־רְשָׁעִים אַל־תְּנִדֵנִי:	יב
13	There lie the evildoers, fallen, thrust down, unable to rise.	*Sham nafelu po'alei aven dochu velo-yachelu kum*	שָׁם נָפְלוּ פֹּעֲלֵי אָוֶן דֹּחוּ וְלֹא־יָכְלוּ קוּם:	יג

37

⊸○⊰❈⊱○⊶

לֹג

1	Of David. Do not be vexed by evil men; do not be incensed by wrongdoers;	*Ledavid al-titchar bammere'im al-tekanne be'osei avlah*	לְדָוִד אַל־תִּתְחַר בַּמְּרֵעִים אַל־תְּקַנֵּא בְּעֹשֵׂי עַוְלָה:	א
2	for they soon wither like grass, like verdure fade away.	*Ki chechatzir meherah yimmalu ucheyerek deshe yibbolun*	כִּי כֶחָצִיר מְהֵרָה יִמָּלוּ וּכְיֶרֶק דֶּשֶׁא יִבּוֹלוּן:	ב

3	Trust in Hashem and do good, abide in the land and remain loyal.	*Betach bAdonai va'aseh-tov shechan-eretz ure'eh emunah*	בְּטַח בַּיהֹוָה וַעֲשֵׂה־טוֹב שְׁכָן־אֶרֶץ וּרְעֵה אֱמוּנָה:	ג
4	Seek the favor of Hashem, and He will grant you the desires of your heart.	*Vehit'annag al-Adonai veyitten-lecha mish'alot libbecha*	וְהִתְעַנַּג עַל־יְהֹוָה וְיִתֶּן־לְךָ מִשְׁאֲלֹת לִבֶּךָ:	ד
5	Leave all to Hashem; trust in Him; He will do it.	*Gol al-Adonai darkecha uvetach alav vehu ya'aseh*	גּוֹל עַל־יְהֹוָה דַּרְכֶּךָ וּבְטַח עָלָיו וְהוּא יַעֲשֶׂה:	ה
6	He will cause your vindication to shine forth like the light, the justice of your case, like the noonday sun.	*Vehotzi cha'or tzidkecha umishpatecha katzohorayim*	וְהוֹצִיא כָאוֹר צִדְקֶךָ וּמִשְׁפָּטֶךָ כַּצָּהֳרָיִם:	ו
7	Be patient and wait for Hashem, do not be vexed by the prospering man who carries out his schemes.	*Dom lAdonai vehitcholel lo al-titchar bematzliach darko be'ish oseh mezimmot*	דּוֹם לַיהֹוָה וְהִתְחוֹלֵל לוֹ אַל־תִּתְחַר בְּמַצְלִיחַ דַּרְכּוֹ בְּאִישׁ עֹשֶׂה מְזִמּוֹת:	ז
8	Give up anger, abandon fury, do not be vexed; it can only do harm.	*heref me'af va'azov chemah al-titchar ach-leharea'*	הֶרֶף מֵאַף וַעֲזֹב חֵמָה אַל־תִּתְחַר אַךְ־לְהָרֵעַ:	ח
9	For evil men will be cut off, but those who look to Hashem— they shall inherit the land.	*Ki-mere'im yikkaretun vekovei Adonai hemmah yirshu-aretz*	כִּי־מְרֵעִים יִכָּרֵתוּן וְקֹוֵי יְהֹוָה הֵמָּה יִירְשׁוּ־אָרֶץ:	ט
10	A little longer and there will be no wicked man; you will look at where he was— he will be gonc.	*Ve'od me'at ve'ein rasha vehitbonanta al-mekomo ve'einennu*	וְעוֹד מְעַט וְאֵין רָשָׁע וְהִתְבּוֹנַנְתָּ עַל־מְקוֹמוֹ וְאֵינֶנּוּ:	י

11	But the lowly shall inherit the land, and delight in abundant well-being.	*Va'anavim yirshu-aretz vehit'annegu al-rov shalom*	וַעֲנָוִים יִירְשׁוּ־אָרֶץ וְהִתְעַנְּגוּ עַל־רֹב שָׁלוֹם: יא
12	The wicked man schemes against the righteous, and gnashes his teeth at him.	*Zomem rasha latzaddik vechorek alav shinnav*	זֹמֵם רָשָׁע לַצַּדִּיק וְחֹרֵק עָלָיו שִׁנָּיו: יב
13	Hashem laughs at him, for He knows that his day will come.	*Adonai yischak-lo ki-ra'ah ki-yavo yomo*	אֲדֹנָי יִשְׂחַק־לוֹ כִּי־רָאָה כִּי־יָבֹא יוֹמוֹ: יג
14	The wicked draw their swords, bend their bows, to bring down the lowly and needy, to slaughter upright men.	*cherev patechu resha'im vedarechu kashtam lehappil ani ve'evyon litvoach yishrei*	חֶרֶב פָּתְחוּ רְשָׁעִים וְדָרְכוּ קַשְׁתָּם לְהַפִּיל עָנִי וְאֶבְיוֹן לִטְבוֹחַ יִשְׁרֵי־דָרֶךְ: יד
15	Their swords shall pierce their own hearts, and their bows shall be broken.	*Charbam tavo velibbam vekashetotam tishavarnah*	חַרְבָּם תָּבוֹא בְלִבָּם וְקַשְּׁתוֹתָם תִּשָּׁבַרְנָה: טו
16	Better the little that the righteous man has than the great abundance of the wicked.	*Tov-me'at latzaddik mehamon resha'im rabbim*	טוֹב־מְעַט לַצַּדִּיק מֵהֲמוֹן רְשָׁעִים רַבִּים: טז
17	For the arms of the wicked shall be broken, but Hashem is the support of the righteous.	*Ki zero'ot resha'im tishavarnah vesomech tzaddikim Adonai*	כִּי זְרוֹעוֹת רְשָׁעִים תִּשָּׁבַרְנָה וְסוֹמֵךְ צַדִּיקִים יְהוָה: יז
18	Hashem is concerned for the needs of the blameless; their portion lasts forever;	*Yodea' Adonai yemei temimim venachalatam le'olam tihyeh*	יוֹדֵעַ יְהוָה יְמֵי תְמִימִם וְנַחֲלָתָם לְעוֹלָם תִּהְיֶה: יח

19	they shall not come to grief in bad times; in famine, they shall eat their fill.	*Lo-yevoshu be'et ra'ah uvimei re'avon yisba'u*	לֹא־יֵבֹשׁוּ בְּעֵת רָעָה וּבִימֵי רְעָבוֹן יִשְׂבָּעוּ:	יט
20	But the wicked shall perish, and the enemies of Hashem shall be consumed, like meadow grass consumed in smoke.	*Ki resha'im yovedu ve'oyevei Adonai kikar karim kalu ve'ashan kalu*	כִּי רְשָׁעִים יֹאבֵדוּ וְאֹיְבֵי יְהֹוָה כִּיקַר כָּרִים כָּלוּ בֶעָשָׁן כָּלוּ:	כ
21	The wicked man borrows and does not repay; the righteous is generous and keeps giving.	*Loveh rasha velo yeshallem vetzaddik chonen venoten*	לֹוֶה רָשָׁע וְלֹא יְשַׁלֵּם וְצַדִּיק חוֹנֵן וְנוֹתֵן:	כא
22	Those blessed by Him shall inherit the land, but those cursed by Him shall be cut off.	*Ki mevorachav yirshu aretz umekullalav yikkaretu*	כִּי מְבֹרָכָיו יִירְשׁוּ אָרֶץ וּמְקֻלָּלָיו יִכָּרֵתוּ:	כב
23	The steps of a man are made firm by Hashem, when He delights in his way.	*Me'Adonai mitz'adei-gever konanu vedarko yechpatz*	מֵיְהֹוָה מִצְעֲדֵי־גֶבֶר כּוֹנָנוּ וְדַרְכּוֹ יֶחְפָּץ:	כג
24	Though he stumbles, he does not fall down, for Hashem gives him support.	*Ki-yippol lo-yutal ki-Adonai somech yado*	כִּי־יִפֹּל לֹא־יוּטָל כִּי־יְהֹוָה סוֹמֵךְ יָדוֹ:	כד
25	I have been young and am now old, but I have never seen a righteous man abandoned, or his children seeking bread.	*na'ar hayiti gam-zakanti velo-ra'iti tzaddik ne'ezav vezar'o mevakkesh-lachem*	נַעַר הָיִיתִי גַּם־זָקַנְתִּי וְלֹא־רָאִיתִי צַדִּיק נֶעֱזָב וְזַרְעוֹ מְבַקֶּשׁ־לָחֶם:	כה

26	He is always generous, and lends, and his children are held blessed.	*Kol-hayyom chonen umalveh vezar'o livrachah*	כׇּל־הַיּוֹם חוֹנֵן וּמַלְוֶה וְזַרְעוֹ לִבְרָכָה:
27	Shun evil and do good, and you shall abide forever.	*Sur mera va'aseh-tov ushechon le'olam*	סוּר מֵרָע וַעֲשֵׂה־טוֹב וּשְׁכֹן לְעוֹלָם:
28	For Hashem loves what is right, He does not abandon His faithful ones. They are preserved forever, while the children of the wicked will be cut off.	*Ki Adonai ohev mishpat velo-ya'azov et-chasidav le'olam nishmaru vezera resha'im*	כִּי יְהֹוָה אֹהֵב מִשְׁפָּט וְלֹא־יַעֲזֹב אֶת־חֲסִידָיו לְעוֹלָם נִשְׁמָרוּ וְזֶרַע רְשָׁעִים נִכְרָת:
29	The righteous shall inherit the land, and abide forever in it.	*Tzaddikim yirshu-aretz veyishkenu la'ad aleiha*	צַדִּיקִים יִירְשׁוּ־אָרֶץ וְיִשְׁכְּנוּ לָעַד עָלֶיהָ:
30	The mouth of the righteous utters wisdom, and his tongue speaks what is right.	*Pi-tzaddik yehgeh chochmah uleshono tedabber mishpat*	פִּי־צַדִּיק יֶהְגֶּה חׇכְמָה וּלְשׁוֹנוֹ תְּדַבֵּר מִשְׁפָּט:
31	The teaching of his God is in his heart; his feet do not slip.	*Torat elohav belibbo lo tim'ad ashurav*	תּוֹרַת אֱלֹהָיו בְּלִבּוֹ לֹא תִמְעַד אֲשֻׁרָיו:
32	The wicked watches for the righteous, seeking to put him to death;	*Tzofeh rasha latzaddik umevakkesh lahamito*	צוֹפֶה רָשָׁע לַצַּדִּיק וּמְבַקֵּשׁ לַהֲמִיתוֹ:
33	Hashem will not abandon him to his power; He will not let him be condemned in judgment.	*Adonai lo-ya'azvennu veyado velo yarshi'ennu behishofto*	יְהֹוָה לֹא־יַעַזְבֶנּוּ בְיָדוֹ וְלֹא יַרְשִׁיעֶנּוּ בְּהִשָּׁפְטוֹ:

34	Look to Hashem and keep to His way, and He will raise you high that you may inherit the land; when the wicked are cut off, you shall see it.	*Kavveh el-Adonai ushemor darko viromimcha lareshet aretz behikkaret resha'im tir*	קַוֵּה אֶל־יְהֹוָה וּשְׁמֹר דַּרְכּוֹ וִירוֹמִמְךָ לָרֶשֶׁת אָרֶץ בְּהִכָּרֵת רְשָׁעִים תִּרְאֶה:	לד
35	I saw a wicked man, powerful, well-rooted like a robust native tree.	*Ra'iti rasha aritz umit'areh ke'ezrach ra'anan*	רָאִיתִי רָשָׁע עָרִיץ וּמִתְעָרֶה כְּאֶזְרָח רַעֲנָן:	לה
36	Suddenly he vanished and was gone; I sought him, but he was not to be found.	*Vayya'avor vehinneh einennu va'avakshehu velo nimtza*	וַיַּעֲבֹר וְהִנֵּה אֵינֶנּוּ וָאֲבַקְשֵׁהוּ וְלֹא נִמְצָא:	לו
37	Mark the blameless, note the upright, for there is a future for the man of integrity.	*Shemar-tam ure'eh yashar ki-acharit le'ish shalom*	שְׁמָר־תָּם וּרְאֵה יָשָׁר כִּי־אַחֲרִית לְאִישׁ שָׁלוֹם:	לז
38	But transgressors shall be utterly destroyed, the future of the wicked shall be cut off.	*Ufoshe'im nishmedu yachdav acharit resha'im nichratah*	וּפֹשְׁעִים נִשְׁמְדוּ יַחְדָּו אַחֲרִית רְשָׁעִים נִכְרָתָה:	לח
39	The deliverance of the righteous comes from Hashem, their stronghold in time of trouble.	*Uteshu'at tzaddikim me'Adonai ma'uzzam be'et tzarah*	וּתְשׁוּעַת צַדִּיקִים מֵיְהֹוָה מָעוּזָּם בְּעֵת צָרָה:	לט
40	Hashem helps them and rescues them, rescues them from the wicked and delivers them, for they seek refuge in Him.	*Vayya'zerem Adonai vayfalletem yefalletem meresha'im veyoshi'em ki-chasu vo*	וַיַּעְזְרֵם יְהֹוָה וַיְפַלְּטֵם יְפַלְּטֵם מֵרְשָׁעִים וְיוֹשִׁיעֵם כִּי־חָסוּ בוֹ:	מ

38

1	A psalm of David. Lehazkir.	*Mizmor ledavid lehazkir*	מִזְמוֹר לְדָוִד לְהַזְכִּיר: א
2	Hashem, do not punish me in wrath; do not chastise me in fury.	*Adonai al-beketzpecha tochicheni uvachamatecha teyassereni*	יְהֹוָה אַל־בְּקֶצְפְּךָ תוֹכִיחֵנִי וּבַחֲמָתְךָ תְיַסְּרֵנִי: ב
3	For Your arrows have struck me; Your blows have fallen upon me.	*Ki-chitzeicha nichatu vi vattinchat alai yadecha*	כִּי־חִצֶּיךָ נִחֲתוּ בִי וַתִּנְחַת עָלַי יָדֶךָ: ג
4	There is no soundness in my flesh because of Your rage, no wholeness in my bones because of my sin.	*Ein-metom bivsari mippenei za'mecha ein-shalom ba'atzamai mippenei chattati*	אֵין־מְתֹם בִּבְשָׂרִי מִפְּנֵי זַעְמֶךָ אֵין־שָׁלוֹם בַּעֲצָמַי מִפְּנֵי חַטָּאתִי: ד
5	For my iniquities have overwhelmed me; they are like a heavy burden, more than I can bear.	*Ki avnotai averu roshi kemassa chaved yichbedu mimmenni*	כִּי עֲוֹנֹתַי עָבְרוּ רֹאשִׁי כְּמַשָּׂא כָבֵד יִכְבְּדוּ מִמֶּנִּי: ה
6	My wounds stink and fester because of my folly.	*Hiv'ishu namakku chabburotai mippenei ivvalti*	הִבְאִישׁוּ נָמַקּוּ חַבּוּרֹתָי מִפְּנֵי אִוַּלְתִּי: ו
7	I am all bent and bowed; I walk about in gloom all day long.	*Na'aveiti shachoti ad-me'od kol-hayyom koder hillacheti*	נַעֲוֵיתִי שַׁחֹתִי עַד־מְאֹד כָּל־הַיּוֹם קֹדֵר הִלָּכְתִּי: ז

8	For my sinews are full of fever; there is no soundness in my flesh.	*Ki-chesalai male'u nikleh ve'ein metom bivsari*	כִּי־כְסָלַי מָלְאוּ נִקְלֶה וְאֵין מְתֹם בִּבְשָׂרִי:	ח
9	I am all benumbed and crushed; I roar because of the turmoil in my mind.	*Nefugoti venidkeiti ad-me'od sha'agti minnahamat libbi*	נְפוּגוֹתִי וְנִדְכֵּיתִי עַד־מְאֹד שָׁאַגְתִּי מִנַּהֲמַת לִבִּי:	ט
10	O Hashem, You are aware of all my entreaties; my groaning is not hidden from You.	*Adonai negdecha chol-ta'avati ve'anchati mimmecha lo-nistarah*	אֲדֹנָי נֶגְדְּךָ כָל־תַּאֲוָתִי וְאַנְחָתִי מִמְּךָ לֹא־נִסְתָּרָה:	י
11	My mind reels; my strength fails me; my eyes too have lost their luster.	*Libbi secharchar azavani chochi ve'or-einai gam-hem ein itti*	לִבִּי סְחַרְחַר עֲזָבַנִי כֹחִי וְאוֹר־עֵינַי גַּם־הֵם אֵין אִתִּי:	יא
12	My friends and companions stand back from my affliction; my kinsmen stand far off.	*Ohavai vere'ai minneged nig'i ya'amodu ukerovai merachok amadu*	אֹהֲבַי וְרֵעַי מִנֶּגֶד נִגְעִי יַעֲמֹדוּ וּקְרוֹבַי מֵרָחֹק עָמָדוּ:	יב
13	Those who seek my life lay traps; those who wish me harm speak malice; they utter deceit all the time.	*Vaynakshu mevakshei nafshi vedoreshei ra'ati dibberu havvvot umirmot kol-hayyom*	וַיְנַקְשׁוּ מְבַקְשֵׁי נַפְשִׁי וְדֹרְשֵׁי רָעָתִי דִּבְּרוּ הַוּוֹת וּמִרְמוֹת כָּל־הַיּוֹם יֶהְגּוּ:	יג
14	But I am like a deaf man, unhearing, like a dumb man who cannot speak up;	*Va'ani checheresh lo eshma uche'illem lo yiftach-piv*	וַאֲנִי כְחֵרֵשׁ לֹא אֶשְׁמָע וּכְאִלֵּם לֹא יִפְתַּח־פִּיו:	יד
15	I am like one who does not hear, who has no retort on his lips.	*Va'ehi ke'ish asher lo-shomea' ve'ein befiv tochachot*	וָאֱהִי כְּאִישׁ אֲשֶׁר לֹא־שֹׁמֵעַ וְאֵין בְּפִיו תּוֹכָחוֹת:	טו

16	But I wait for You, Hashem; You will answer, O Hashem, my God.	*Ki-lecha Adonai hochaleti attah ta'aneh Adonai elohai*	כִּי־לְךָ יְהֹוָה הוֹחָלְתִּי אַתָּה תַעֲנֶה אֲדֹנָי אֱלֹהָי:	טז
17	For I fear they will rejoice over me; when my foot gives way they will vaunt themselves against me.	*Ki-amarti pen-yismechu-li bemot ragli alai higdilu*	כִּי־אָמַרְתִּי פֶּן־יִשְׂמְחוּ־לִי בְּמוֹט רַגְלִי עָלַי הִגְדִּילוּ:	יז
18	For I am on the verge of collapse; my pain is always with me.	*Ki-ani letzela nachon umach'ovi negdi tamid*	כִּי־אֲנִי לְצֶלַע נָכוֹן וּמַכְאוֹבִי נֶגְדִּי תָמִיד:	יח
19	I acknowledge my iniquity; I am fearful over my sin;	*Ki-avni aggid ed'ag mechattati*	כִּי־עֲוֹנִי אַגִּיד אֶדְאַג מֵחַטָּאתִי:	יט
20	for my mortal enemies are numerous; my treacherous foes are many.	*Ve'oyevai chayyim atzemu verabbu sone'ai shaker*	וְאֹיְבַי חַיִּים עָצֵמוּ וְרַבּוּ שֹׂנְאַי שָׁקֶר:	כ
21	Those who repay evil for good harass me for pursuing good.	*Umeshallemei ra'ah tachat tovah yistenuni tachat radufi[radefi] tov*	וּמְשַׁלְּמֵי רָעָה תַּחַת טוֹבָה יִשְׂטְנוּנִי תַּחַת רדופי־ [רָדְפִי־] טוֹב:	כא
22	Do not abandon me, Hashem; my God, be not far from me;	*Al-ta'azveni Adonai elohai al-tirchak mimmenni*	אַל־תַּעַזְבֵנִי יְהֹוָה אֱלֹהָי אַל־תִּרְחַק מִמֶּנִּי:	כב
23	hasten to my aid, O Hashem, my deliverance.	*Chushah le'ezrati Adonai teshu'ati*	חוּשָׁה לְעֶזְרָתִי אֲדֹנָי תְּשׁוּעָתִי:	כג

39

1	For the leader; for Yedutun. A psalm of David.	*Lammenatzeach liditun [lidutun] mizmor ledavid*	לַמְנַצֵּחַ לִידִיתוּן [לִידוּתוּן] מִזְמוֹר לְדָוִד:	א

I resolved I would watch my step lest I offend by my speech; I would keep my mouth muzzled while the wicked man was in my presence.

Amarti eshmerah derachai mechato vilshoni eshmerah lefi machsom be'od rasha lenegdi

אָמַרְתִּי אֶשְׁמְרָה דְרָכַי מֵחֲטוֹא בִלְשׁוֹנִי אֶשְׁמְרָה לְפִי מַחְסוֹם בְּעֹד רָשָׁע לְנֶגְדִּי: ב

I was dumb, silent; I was very still while my pain was intense.

Ne'elamti dumiyyah hechesheiti mittov uche'evi ne'kar

נֶאֱלַמְתִּי דוּמִיָּה הֶחֱשֵׁיתִי מִטּוֹב וּכְאֵבִי נֶעְכָּר: ג

My mind was in a rage, my thoughts were all aflame; I spoke out:

Cham-libbi bekirbi bahagigi tiv'ar-esh dibbarti bilshoni

חַם־לִבִּי בְּקִרְבִּי בַּהֲגִיגִי תִבְעַר־אֵשׁ דִּבַּרְתִּי בִּלְשׁוֹנִי: ד

Tell me, Hashem, what my term is, what is the measure of my days; I would know how fleeting my life is.

Hodi'eni Adonai kitzi umiddat yamai mah-hi ede'ah meh-chadel ani

הוֹדִיעֵנִי יְהֹוָה קִצִּי וּמִדַּת יָמַי מַה־הִיא אֵדְעָה מֶה־חָדֵל אָנִי: ה

You have made my life just handbreadths long; its span is as nothing in Your sight; no man endures any longer than a breath. Selah.

Hinneh tefachot natattah yamai vecheldi che'ayin negdecha ach kol-hevel kol-adam

הִנֵּה טְפָחוֹת נָתַתָּה יָמַי וְחֶלְדִּי כְאַיִן נֶגְדֶּךָ אַךְ כָּל־הֶבֶל כָּל־אָדָם נִצָּב סֶלָה: ו

7	Man walks about as a mere shadow; mere futility is his hustle and bustle, amassing and not knowing who will gather in.	*Ach-betzelem yithallech-ish ach-hevel yehemayun yitzbor velo-yeda mi-osefam*	אַךְ־בְּצֶלֶם יִתְהַלֶּךְ־אִישׁ אַךְ־הֶבֶל יֶהֱמָיוּן יִצְבֹּר וְלֹא־יֵדַע מִי־אֹסְפָם:	ז
8	What, then, can I count on, O Hashem? In You my hope lies.	*Ve'attah mah-kivviti Adonai tochalti lecha hi*	וְעַתָּה מַה־קִּוִּיתִי אֲדֹנָי תּוֹחַלְתִּי לְךָ הִיא:	ח
9	Deliver me from all my transgressions; make me not the butt of the benighted.	*Mikkol-pesha'ai hatzileni cherpat naval al-tesimeni*	מִכָּל־פְּשָׁעַי הַצִּילֵנִי חֶרְפַּת נָבָל אַל־תְּשִׂימֵנִי:	ט
10	I am dumb, I do not speak up, for it is Your doing.	*Ne'elamti lo eftach-pi ki attah asita*	נֶאֱלַמְתִּי לֹא אֶפְתַּח־פִּי כִּי אַתָּה עָשִׂיתָ:	י
11	Take away Your plague from me; I perish from Your blows.	*Haser me'alai nig'echa mittigrat yadecha ani chaliti*	הָסֵר מֵעָלַי נִגְעֶךָ מִתִּגְרַת יָדְךָ אֲנִי כָלִיתִי:	יא
12	You chastise a man in punishment for his sin, consuming like a moth what he treasures. No man is more than a breath. Selah.	*Betochachot al-avon yissarta ish vattemes ka'ash chamudo ach hevel kol-adam selah*	בְּתוֹכָחוֹת עַל־עָוֹן יִסַּרְתָּ אִישׁ וַתֶּמֶס כָּעָשׁ חֲמוּדוֹ אַךְ הֶבֶל כָּל־אָדָם סֶלָה:	יב
13	Hear my prayer, Hashem; give ear to my cry; do not disregard my tears; for like all my forebears I am an alien, resident with You.	*Shim'ah-tefillati Adonai veshav'ati ha'azinah el-dim'ati al-techerash ki ger ano*	שִׁמְעָה־תְפִלָּתִי יְהוָה וְשַׁוְעָתִי הַאֲזִינָה אֶל־דִּמְעָתִי אַל־תֶּחֱרַשׁ כִּי גֵר אָנֹכִי עִמָּךְ תּוֹשָׁב כְּכָל־אֲבוֹתָי:	יג

99

14	Look away from me, that I may recover, before I pass away and am gone.	*Hasha mimmenni ve'avligah beterem elech ve'einenni*	הָשַׁע מִמֶּנִּי וְאַבְלִיגָה בְּטֶרֶם אֵלֵךְ וְאֵינֶנִּי: יד

40

—◦○◇○◦— מ

1	For the leader. A psalm of David.	*Lammenatzeach ledavid mizmor*	לַמְנַצֵּחַ לְדָוִד מִזְמוֹר: א
2	I put my hope in Hashem; He inclined toward me, and heeded my cry.	*Kavvh kivviti Adonai vayyet elai vayyishma shav'ati*	קַוֹּה קִוִּיתִי יְהֹוָה וַיֵּט אֵלַי וַיִּשְׁמַע שַׁוְעָתִי: ב
3	He lifted me out of the miry pit, the slimy clay, and set my feet on a rock, steadied my legs.	*Vayya'aleni mibbor sha'on mittit hayyaven vayyakem al-sela raglai konen ashurai*	וַיַּעֲלֵנִי מִבּוֹר שָׁאוֹן מִטִּיט הַיָּוֵן וַיָּקֶם עַל־סֶלַע רַגְלַי כּוֹנֵן אֲשֻׁרָי: ג
4	He put a new song into my mouth, a hymn to our God. May many see it and stand in awe, and trust in Hashem.	*Vayyitten befi shir chadash tehillah leloheinu yir'u rabbim veyira'u veyivtechu ba'Adonai*	וַיִּתֵּן בְּפִי שִׁיר חָדָשׁ תְּהִלָּה לֵאלֹהֵינוּ יִרְאוּ רַבִּים וְיִירָאוּ וְיִבְטְחוּ בַּיהֹוָה: ד
5	Happy is the man who makes Hashem his trust, who turns not to the arrogant or to followers of falsehood.	*Ashrei haggever asher-sam Adonai mivtacho velo-fanah el-rehavim vesatei chazav*	אַשְׁרֵי הַגֶּבֶר אֲשֶׁר־שָׂם יְהֹוָה מִבְטַחוֹ וְלֹא־פָנָה אֶל־רְהָבִים וְשָׂטֵי כָזָב: ה

6 | You, Hashem my God, have done many things; the wonders You have devised for us cannot be set out before You; I would rehearse the tale of them, but they are more than can be told. | *Rabbot asita attah Adonai elohai nifle'oteicha umachshevotecha eleinu ein aroch eilecha agidah va'adabarah atzemo misaper.* | רַבּוֹת עָשִׂיתָ אַתָּה יְהֹוָה אֱלֹהַי נִפְלְאֹתֶיךָ וּמַחְשְׁבֹתֶיךָ אֵלֵינוּ אֵין עֲרֹךְ אֵלֶיךָ אַגִּידָה וַאֲדַבֵּרָה עָצְמוּ מִסַּפֵּר: | ו

7 | You gave me to understand that You do not desire sacrifice and meal offering; You do not ask for burnt offering and sin offering. | *zevach uminchah lo-chafatzta oznayim karita li olah vachata'ah lo sha'alta* | זֶבַח וּמִנְחָה לֹא־חָפַצְתָּ אָזְנַיִם כָּרִיתָ לִי עוֹלָה וַחֲטָאָה לֹא שָׁאָלְתָּ: | ז

8 | Then I said, "See, I will bring a scroll recounting what befell me." | *Az amarti hinneh-vati bimgillat-sefer katuv alai* | אָז אָמַרְתִּי הִנֵּה־בָאתִי בִּמְגִלַּת־סֵפֶר כָּתוּב עָלָי: | ח

9 | To do what pleases You, my God, is my desire; Your teaching is in my inmost parts. | *La'asot-retzonecha elohai chafatzeti vetoratecha betoch me'ai* | לַעֲשׂוֹת־רְצוֹנְךָ אֱלֹהַי חָפָצְתִּי וְתוֹרָתְךָ בְּתוֹךְ מֵעָי: | ט

10 | I proclaimed [Your] righteousness in a great congregation; see, I did not withhold my words; Hashem, You must know it. | *Bissarti tzedek bekahal rav hinneh sefatai lo echla Adonai attah yadata* | בִּשַּׂרְתִּי צֶדֶק בְּקָהָל רָב הִנֵּה שְׂפָתַי לֹא אֶכְלָא יְהֹוָה אַתָּה יָדָעְתָּ: | י

11 | I did not keep Your beneficence to myself; I declared Your faithful deliverance; I did not fail to speak of Your steadfast love in a great congregation. | *Tzidkatecha lo-chissiti betoch libbi emunatecha uteshu'atecha amareti lo-chichadti chasdecha va'amitcha lekahal rav* | צִדְקָתְךָ לֹא־כִסִּיתִי בְּתוֹךְ לִבִּי אֱמוּנָתְךָ וּתְשׁוּעָתְךָ אָמַרְתִּי לֹא־כִחַדְתִּי חַסְדְּךָ וַאֲמִתְּךָ לְקָהָל רָב: | יא

12	Hashem, You will not withhold from me Your compassion; Your steadfast love will protect me always.	*Attah Adonai lo-tichla rachameicha mimmenni chasdecha va'amittecha tamid yitzruni*	אַתָּה יְהֹוָה לֹא־תִכְלָא רַחֲמֶיךָ מִמֶּנִּי חַסְדְּךָ וַאֲמִתְּךָ תָּמִיד יִצְּרוּנִי: יב
13	For misfortunes without number envelop me; my iniquities have caught up with me; I cannot see; they are more than the hairs of my head; I am at my wits' end.	*Ki afefu-alai ra'ot ad-ein mispar hissiguni avnotai velo-yacholeti lir'ot atzemu*	כִּי אָפְפוּ־עָלַי רָעוֹת עַד־אֵין מִסְפָּר הִשִּׂיגוּנִי עֲוֺנֹתַי וְלֹא־יָכֹלְתִּי לִרְאוֹת עָצְמוּ מִשַּׂעֲרוֹת רֹאשִׁי וְלִבִּי עֲזָבָנִי: יג
14	O favor me, Hashem, and save me; Hashem, hasten to my aid.	*Retzeh Adonai lehatzileni Adonai le'ezrati chushah*	רְצֵה יְהֹוָה לְהַצִּילֵנִי יְהֹוָה לְעֶזְרָתִי חוּשָׁה: יד
15	Let those who seek to destroy my life be frustrated and disgraced; let those who wish me harm fall back in shame.	*Yevoshu veyachperu yachad mevakshei nafshi lispotah yissogu achor veyikkalemu chafetzei ra'ati*	יֵבֹשׁוּ וְיַחְפְּרוּ יַחַד מְבַקְשֵׁי נַפְשִׁי לִסְפּוֹתָהּ יִסֹּגוּ אָחוֹר וְיִכָּלְמוּ חֲפֵצֵי רָעָתִי: טו
16	Let those who say "Aha! Aha!" over me be desolate because of their frustration.	*Yashommu al-ekev bashetam ha'omerim li he'ach he'ach*	יָשֹׁמּוּ עַל־עֵקֶב בָּשְׁתָּם הָאֹמְרִים לִי הֶאָח הֶאָח: טז
17	But let all who seek You be glad and rejoice in You; let those who are eager for Your deliverance always say, "Extolled be Hashem!"	*Yasisu veyismechu becha kol-mevaksheicha yomru tamid yigdal Adonai ohavei teshuatecha*	יָשִׂישׂוּ וְיִשְׂמְחוּ בְּךָ כָּל־מְבַקְשֶׁיךָ יֹאמְרוּ תָמִיד יִגְדַּל יְהֹוָה אֹהֲבֵי תְּשׁוּעָתֶךָ: יז

18	But I am poor and needy; may Hashem devise [deliverance] for me. You are my help and my rescuer; my God, do not delay.	*Va'ani ani ve'evyon Adonai yachashav li ezrati umefalti attah elohai al-te'achar*

וַאֲנִי עָנִי וְאֶבְיוֹן אֲדֹנָי
יַחֲשָׁב לִי עֶזְרָתִי וּמְפַלְטִי
אַתָּה אֱלֹהַי אַל-תְּאַחַר: יח

41

—◦❂◦—

מא

1	For the leader. A psalm of David.	*Lammenatzeach mizmor ledavid*

לַמְנַצֵּחַ מִזְמוֹר לְדָוִד: א

2	Happy is he who is thoughtful of the wretched; in bad times may Hashem keep him from harm.	*Ashrei maskil el-dal beyom ra'ah yemalletehu Adonai*

אַשְׁרֵי מַשְׂכִּיל אֶל-דָּל
בְּיוֹם רָעָה יְמַלְּטֵהוּ יְהֹוָה: ב

3	May Hashem guard him and preserve him; and may he be thought happy in the land. Do not subject him to the will of his enemies.	*Adonai yishmerehu vichayyehu yashar [ve'ushar] ba'aretz ve'al-tittenehu benefesh oyevav*

יְהֹוָה יִשְׁמְרֵהוּ וִיחַיֵּהוּ
יֻאַשַּׁר [וְאֻשַּׁר] בָּאָרֶץ וְאַל-
תִּתְּנֵהוּ בְּנֶפֶשׁ אֹיְבָיו: ג

4	Hashem will sustain him on his sickbed; You shall wholly transform his bed of suffering.	*Adonai yis'adennu al-eres devai kol-mishkavo hafachta vecholyo*

יְהֹוָה יִסְעָדֶנּוּ עַל-עֶרֶשׂ דְּוָי
כָּל-מִשְׁכָּבוֹ הָפַכְתָּ בְחָלְיוֹ: ד

5	I said, "Hashem, have mercy on me, heal me, for I have sinned against You."	*Ani-amarti Adonai channeni refa'ah nafshi ki-chatati lach*

אֲנִי-אָמַרְתִּי יְהֹוָה חָנֵּנִי
רְפָאָה נַפְשִׁי כִּי-חָטָאתִי
לָךְ: ה

6	My enemies speak evilly of me, "When will he die and his name perish?"	*Oyevai yomru ra li matai yamut ve'avad shemo*	אוֹיְבַי יֹאמְרוּ רַע לִי מָתַי יָמוּת וְאָבַד שְׁמוֹ: ו
7	If one comes to visit, he speaks falsely; his mind stores up evil thoughts; once outside, he speaks them.	*Ve'im-ba lir'ot shave yedabber libbo yikbatz-aven lo yetze lachutz yedabber*	וְאִם־בָּא לִרְאוֹת שָׁוְא יְדַבֵּר לִבּוֹ יִקְבָּץ־אָוֶן לוֹ יֵצֵא לַחוּץ יְדַבֵּר: ז
8	All my enemies whisper together against me, imagining the worst for me.	*yachad alai yitlachashu kol-sone'ai alai yachshevu ra'ah li*	יַחַד עָלַי יִתְלַחֲשׁוּ כָּל־שֹׂנְאָי עָלַי יַחְשְׁבוּ רָעָה לִי: ח
9	"Something baneful has settled in him; he'll not rise from his bed again."	*Devar-beliyya'al yatzuk bo va'asher shachav lo-yosif lakum*	דְּבַר־בְּלִיַּעַל יָצוּק בּוֹ וַאֲשֶׁר שָׁכַב לֹא־יוֹסִיף לָקוּם: ט
10	My ally in whom I trusted, even he who shares my bread, has been utterly false to me.	*Gam-ish shelomi asher-batachti vo ochel lachmi higdil alai akev*	גַּם־אִישׁ שְׁלוֹמִי אֲשֶׁר בָּטַחְתִּי בוֹ אוֹכֵל לַחְמִי הִגְדִּיל עָלַי עָקֵב: י
11	But You, Hashem, have mercy on me; let me rise again and repay them.	*Ve'attah Adonai channeni vahakimeni va'ashallemah lahem*	וְאַתָּה יְהוָה חָנֵּנִי וַהֲקִימֵנִי וַאֲשַׁלְּמָה לָהֶם: יא
12	Then shall I know that You are pleased with me: when my enemy cannot shout in triumph over me.	*Bezot yada'ti ki-chafatzta bi ki lo-yaria' oyevi alai*	בְּזֹאת יָדַעְתִּי כִּי־חָפַצְתָּ בִּי כִּי לֹא־יָרִיעַ אֹיְבִי עָלָי: יב

| 13 | You will support me because of my integrity, and let me abide in Your presence forever. | *Va'ani betummi tamachta bi vattatziveni lefaneicha le'olam* | וַאֲנִי בְּתֻמִּי תָּמַכְתָּ בִּי וַתַּצִּיבֵנִי לְפָנֶיךָ לְעוֹלָם: | יג |
| 14 | Blessed is Hashem, God of Yisrael, from eternity to eternity. Amen and Amen. | *Baruch Adonai elohei yisra'el meha'olam ve'ad ha'olam amen ve'amen* | בָּרוּךְ יְהוָה אֱלֹהֵי יִשְׂרָאֵל מֵהָעוֹלָם וְעַד הָעוֹלָם אָמֵן וְאָמֵן: | יד |

42

⟶◦❈◦⟵

מב

1	For the leader. A maskil of the Korahites.	*Lammenatzeach maskil livnei-korach*	לַמְנַצֵּחַ מַשְׂכִּיל לִבְנֵי־קֹרַח:	א
2	Like a hind crying for water, my soul cries for You, O Hashem;	*Ke'ayyal ta'arog al-afikei-mayim ken nafshi ta'arog eleicha elohim*	כְּאַיָּל תַּעֲרֹג עַל־אֲפִיקֵי־מָיִם כֵּן נַפְשִׁי תַעֲרֹג אֵלֶיךָ אֱלֹהִים:	ב
3	my soul thirsts for Hashem, the living Hashem; O when will I come to appear before Hashem!	*Tzame'ah nafshi lelohim le'el chai matai avo ve'era'eh penei elohim*	צָמְאָה נַפְשִׁי לֵאלֹהִים לְאֵל חָי מָתַי אָבוֹא וְאֵרָאֶה פְּנֵי אֱלֹהִים:	ג
4	My tears have been my food day and night; I am ever taunted with, "Where is your God?"	*Hayetah-li dim'ati lechem yomam valayelah be'emor elai kol-hayyom ayyeh elohecha*	הָיְתָה־לִּי דִמְעָתִי לֶחֶם יוֹמָם וָלַיְלָה בֶּאֱמֹר אֵלַי כָּל־הַיּוֹם אַיֵּה אֱלֹהֶיךָ:	ד

5

When I think of this,
I pour out my soul:
how I walked with
the crowd, moved
with them, the festive
throng, to the House
of Hashem with joyous
shouts of praise.

*elleh ezkerah
ve'eshpechah alai
nafshi ki e'evor bassach
eddaddam ad-beit
elohim bekol-rinah
vetodah hamon chogeg*

אֵלֶּה אֶזְכְּרָה וְאֶשְׁפְּכָה
עָלַי נַפְשִׁי כִּי אֶעֱבֹר בַּסָּךְ
אֶדַּדֵּם עַד־בֵּית אֱלֹהִים
בְּקוֹל־רִנָּה וְתוֹדָה הָמוֹן
חוֹגֵג:

ה

6

Why so downcast, my
soul, why disquieted
within me? Have hope
in Hashem; I will yet
praise Him for His
saving presence.

*Mah-tishtochachi nafshi
vattehemi alai hochili
lelohim ki-od odennu
yeshu'ot panav*

מַה־תִּשְׁתּוֹחֲחִי נַפְשִׁי
וַתֶּהֱמִי עָלַי הוֹחִילִי
לֵאלֹהִים כִּי־עוֹד אוֹדֶנּוּ
יְשׁוּעוֹת פָּנָיו:

ו

7

O my God, my soul is
downcast; therefore
I think of You in this
land of Yarden and
Chermon, in Mount
Mizar,

*Elohai alai nafshi
tishtochach al-ken
ezkarecha me'eretz
yarden vechermonim
maher mitz'ar*

אֱלֹהַי עָלַי נַפְשִׁי
תִשְׁתּוֹחָח עַל־כֵּן אֶזְכָּרְךָ
מֵאֶרֶץ יַרְדֵּן וְחֶרְמוֹנִים
מֵהַר מִצְעָר:

ז

8

where deep calls to
deep in the roar of
Your cataracts; all Your
breakers and billows
have swept over me.

*Tehom-el-tehom kore
lekol tzinnoreicha
kol-mishbareicha
vegalleicha alai avaru*

תְּהוֹם־אֶל־תְּהוֹם קוֹרֵא
לְקוֹל צִנּוֹרֶיךָ כָּל־מִשְׁבָּרֶיךָ
וְגַלֶּיךָ עָלַי עָבָרוּ:

ח

9

By day may Hashem
vouchsafe His faithful
care, so that at night
a song to Him may be
with me, a prayer to the
God of my life.

*Yomam yetzavveh
Adonai chasdo
uvallaylah shirah
[shiro] immi tefillah
le'el chayyai*

יוֹמָם יְצַוֶּה יְהֹוָה חַסְדּוֹ
וּבַלַּיְלָה שִׁירָה [שִׁירֹו] עִמִּי
תְּפִלָּה לְאֵל חַיָּי:

ט

10 I say to Hashem, my rock, "Why have You forgotten me, why must I walk in gloom, oppressed by my enemy?"

Omerah le'el sal'i lamah shechachtani lammah-koder elech belachatz oyev

אוֹמְרָה לְאֵל סַלְעִי לָמָה שְׁכַחְתָּנִי לָמָה־קֹדֵר אֵלֵךְ בְּלַחַץ אוֹיֵב:

י

11 Crushing my bones, my foes revile me, taunting me always with, "Where is your God?"

Beretzach be'atzmotai cherefuni tzorerai be'omram elai kol-hayyom ayyeh eloheicha

בְּרֶצַח בְּעַצְמוֹתַי חֵרְפוּנִי צוֹרְרָי בְּאָמְרָם אֵלַי כָּל־הַיּוֹם אַיֵּה אֱלֹהֶיךָ:

יא

12 Why so downcast, my soul, why disquieted within me? Have hope in Hashem; I will yet praise Him, my ever-present help, my God.

Mah-tishtochachi nafshi umah-tehemi alai hochili lelohim ki-od odennu yeshu'ot panai velohai

מַה־תִּשְׁתּוֹחֲחִי נַפְשִׁי וּמַה־תֶּהֱמִי עָלָי הוֹחִילִי לֵאלֹהִים כִּי־עוֹד אוֹדֶנּוּ יְשׁוּעֹת פָּנַי וֵאלֹהָי:

יב

43

בג

1 Vindicate me, O Hashem, Champion my cause against faithless people; rescue me from the treacherous, dishonest man.

Shafeteni elohim verivah rivi miggoy lo-chasid me'ish-mirmah ve'avlah tefalleteni

שָׁפְטֵנִי אֱלֹהִים וְרִיבָה רִיבִי מִגּוֹי לֹא־חָסִיד מֵאִישׁ־מִרְמָה וְעַוְלָה תְפַלְּטֵנִי:

א

2 For You are my God, my stronghold; why have You rejected me? Why must I walk in gloom, oppressed by the enemy?

Ki-attah elohei ma'uzzi lamah zenachtani lammah-koder ethallech belachatz oyev

כִּי־אַתָּה אֱלֹהֵי מָעוּזִּי לָמָה זְנַחְתָּנִי לָמָה־קֹדֵר אֶתְהַלֵּךְ בְּלַחַץ אוֹיֵב:

ב

3	Send forth Your light and Your truth; they will lead me; they will bring me to Your holy mountain, to Your dwelling-place,	*Shelach-orecha va'amittecha hemmah yanchuni yevi'uni el-har-kodshecha ve'el-mishkenoteicha*	שְׁלַח־אוֹרְךָ וַאֲמִתְּךָ הֵמָּה יַנְחוּנִי יְבִיאוּנִי אֶל־הַר־ קָדְשְׁךָ וְאֶל־מִשְׁכְּנוֹתֶיךָ: ג
4	that I may come to the mizbayach of Hashem, Hashem, my delight, my joy; that I may praise You with the lyre, O Hashem, my God.	*Ve'avo'ah el-mizbach elohim el-el simchat gili ve'odecha vechinnor elohim elohai*	וְאָבוֹאָה אֶל־מִזְבַּח אֱלֹהִים אֶל־אֵל שִׂמְחַת גִּילִי וְאוֹדְךָ בְכִנּוֹר אֱלֹהִים אֱלֹהָי: ד
5	Why so downcast, my soul, why disquieted within me? Have hope in Hashem; I will yet praise Him, my ever-present help, my God.	*Mah-tishtochachi nafshi umah-tehemi alai hochili lelohim ki-od odennu yeshu'ot panai velohai*	מַה־תִּשְׁתּוֹחֲחִי נַפְשִׁי וּמַה־תֶּהֱמִי עָלַי הוֹחִילִי לֵאלֹהִים כִּי־עוֹד אוֹדֶנּוּ יְשׁוּעֹת פָּנַי וֵאלֹהָי: ה

44

—◦⬡◦—

מד

1	For the leader. Of the Korahites. A maskil.	*Lammenatzeach livnei-korach maskil*	לַמְנַצֵּחַ לִבְנֵי־קֹרַח מַשְׂכִּיל: א
2	We have heard, O Hashem, our fathers have told us the deeds You performed in their time, in days of old.	*Elohim be'azeneinu shama'nu avoteinu sipperu-lanu po'al pa'alta vimeihem bimei kedem*	אֱלֹהִים בְּאָזְנֵינוּ שָׁמַעְנוּ אֲבוֹתֵינוּ סִפְּרוּ־לָנוּ פֹּעַל פָּעַלְתָּ בִימֵיהֶם בִּימֵי קֶדֶם: ב

3	With Your hand You planted them, displacing nations; You brought misfortune on peoples, and drove them out.	*Attah yadecha goyim horashta vattitta'em tara le'ummim vatteshallechem*	אַתָּה יָדְךָ גּוֹיִם הוֹרַשְׁתָּ וַתִּטָּעֵם תָּרַע לְאֻמִּים וַתְּשַׁלְּחֵם: ג
4	It was not by their sword that they took the land, their arm did not give them victory, but Your right hand, Your arm, and Your goodwill, for You favored them.	*Ki lo vecharbam yareshu aretz uzero'am lo-hoshi'ah lamo ki-yemincha uzero'acha ve'or panecha ki retzitam*	כִּי לֹא בְחַרְבָּם יָרְשׁוּ אֶרֶץ וּזְרוֹעָם לֹא-הוֹשִׁיעָה לָּמוֹ כִּי-יְמִינְךָ וּזְרוֹעֲךָ וְאוֹר פָּנֶיךָ כִּי רְצִיתָם: ד
5	You are my king, O Hashem; decree victories for Yaakov!	*Attah-hu malki elohim tzavveh yeshu'ot ya'akov*	אַתָּה-הוּא מַלְכִּי אֱלֹהִים צַוֵּה יְשׁוּעוֹת יַעֲקֹב: ה
6	Through You we gore our foes; by Your name we trample our adversaries;	*Becha tzareinu nenaggeach beshimcha navus kameinu*	בְּךָ צָרֵינוּ נְנַגֵּחַ בְּשִׁמְךָ נָבוּס קָמֵינוּ: ו
7	I do not trust in my bow; it is not my sword that gives me victory;	*Ki lo vekashti evtach vecharbi lo toshi'eni*	כִּי לֹא בְקַשְׁתִּי אֶבְטָח וְחַרְבִּי לֹא תוֹשִׁיעֵנִי: ז
8	You give us victory over our foes; You thwart those who hate us.	*Ki hosha'tanu mitzareinu umesan'einu hevishota*	כִּי הוֹשַׁעְתָּנוּ מִצָּרֵינוּ וּמְשַׂנְאֵינוּ הֱבִישׁוֹתָ: ח
9	In Hashem we glory at all times, and praise Your name unceasingly. Selah.	*Belohim hillalnu chol-hayyom veshimcha le'olam nodeh selah*	בֵּאלֹהִים הִלַּלְנוּ כָל-הַיּוֹם וְשִׁמְךָ לְעוֹלָם נוֹדֶה סֶלָה: ט

10	Yet You have rejected and disgraced us; You do not go with our armies.	*Af-zanachta vattachlimenu velo-tetze betziv'oteinu*	אַף־זָנַחְתָּ וַתַּכְלִימֵנוּ וְלֹא־תֵצֵא בְּצִבְאוֹתֵינוּ:	י
11	You make us retreat before our foe; our enemies plunder us at will.	*Teshivenu achor minni-tzar umesan'einu shasu lamo*	תְּשִׁיבֵנוּ אָחוֹר מִנִּי־צָר וּמְשַׂנְאֵינוּ שָׁסוּ לָמוֹ:	יא
12	You let them devour us like sheep; You disperse us among the nations.	*Tittenenu ketzon ma'achal uvaggoyim zeritanu*	תִּתְּנֵנוּ כְּצֹאן מַאֲכָל וּבַגּוֹיִם זֵרִיתָנוּ:	יב
13	You sell Your people for no fortune, You set no high price on them.	*Timkor-ammecha velo-hon velo-ribbita bimchireihem*	תִּמְכֹּר־עַמְּךָ בְלֹא־הוֹן וְלֹא־רִבִּיתָ בִּמְחִירֵיהֶם:	יג
14	You make us the butt of our neighbors the scorn and derision of those around us.	*Tesimenu cherpah lishcheneinu la'ag vakeles lisvivoteinu*	תְּשִׂימֵנוּ חֶרְפָּה לִשְׁכֵנֵינוּ לַעַג וָקֶלֶס לִסְבִיבוֹתֵינוּ:	יד
15	You make us a byword among the nations, a laughingstock among the peoples.	*Tesimenu mashal baggoyim menod-rosh bal-ummim*	תְּשִׂימֵנוּ מָשָׁל בַּגּוֹיִם מְנוֹד־רֹאשׁ בַּל־אֻמִּים:	טו
16	I am always aware of my disgrace; I am wholly covered with shame	*Kol-hayyom kelimmati negdi uvoshet panai kissateni*	כָּל־הַיּוֹם כְּלִמָּתִי נֶגְדִּי וּבֹשֶׁת פָּנַי כִּסָּתְנִי:	טז
17	at the sound of taunting revilers, in the presence of the vengeful foe.	*Mikkol mecharef umegaddef mippenei oyev umitnakkem*	מִקּוֹל מְחָרֵף וּמְגַדֵּף מִפְּנֵי אוֹיֵב וּמִתְנַקֵּם:	יז

18	All this has come upon us, yet we have not forgotten You, or been false to Your covenant.	*Kol-zot ba'atnu velo shechachanucha velo-shikkarnu bivritecha*	כָּל־זֹאת בָּאַתְנוּ וְלֹא שְׁכַחֲנוּךָ וְלֹא־שִׁקַּרְנוּ בִּבְרִיתֶךָ׃	יח
19	Our hearts have not gone astray, nor have our feet swerved from Your path,	*Lo-nasog achor libbenu vattet ashureinu minni orchecha*	לֹא־נָסוֹג אָחוֹר לִבֵּנוּ וַתֵּט אֲשֻׁרֵינוּ מִנִּי אָרְחֶךָ׃	יט
20	though You cast us, crushed, to where the sea monster is, and covered us over with deepest darkness.	*Ki dikkitanu bimkom tannim vattechas aleinu vetzalmavet*	כִּי דִכִּיתָנוּ בִּמְקוֹם תַּנִּים וַתְּכַס עָלֵינוּ בְצַלְמָוֶת׃	כ
21	If we forgot the name of our God and spread forth our hands to a foreign god,	*Im-shachachnu shem eloheinu vannifros kappeinu le'el zar*	אִם־שָׁכַחְנוּ שֵׁם אֱלֹהֵינוּ וַנִּפְרֹשׂ כַּפֵּינוּ לְאֵל זָר׃	כא
22	Hashem would surely search it out, for He knows the secrets of the heart.	*Halo elohim yachakar-zot ki-hu yodea' ta'alumot lev*	הֲלֹא אֱלֹהִים יַחֲקָר־זֹאת כִּי־הוּא יֹדֵעַ תַּעֲלֻמוֹת לֵב׃	כב
23	It is for Your sake that we are slain all day long, that we are regarded as sheep to be slaughtered.	*Ki-aleicha horagnu chol-hayyom nechshavnu ketzon tivchah*	כִּי־עָלֶיךָ הֹרַגְנוּ כָל־הַיּוֹם נֶחְשַׁבְנוּ כְּצֹאן טִבְחָה׃	כג
24	Rouse Yourself; why do You sleep, O Hashem? Awaken, do not reject us forever!	*Urah lammah tishan Adonai hakitzah al-tiznach lanetzach*	עוּרָה לָמָּה תִישַׁן אֲדֹנָי הָקִיצָה אַל־תִּזְנַח לָנֶצַח׃	כד
25	Why do You hide Your face, ignoring our affliction and distress?	*lammah-faneicha tastir tishkach aneyenu velachatzenu*	לָמָּה־פָנֶיךָ תַסְתִּיר תִּשְׁכַּח עָנְיֵנוּ וְלַחֲצֵנוּ׃	כה

26	We lie prostrate in the dust; our body clings to the ground.	*Ki shachah le'afar nafshenu davekah la'aretz bitnenu*	כִּי שָׁחָה לֶעָפָר נַפְשֵׁנוּ דָּבְקָה לָאָרֶץ בִּטְנֵנוּ: כו
27	Arise and help us, redeem us, as befits Your faithfulness.	*Kumah ezratah lanu ufedenu lema'an chasdecha*	קוּמָה עֶזְרָתָה לָּנוּ וּפְדֵנוּ לְמַעַן חַסְדֶּךָ: כז

45

מה

1	For the leader; on shoshannim. Of the Korahites. A maskil. A love song.	*Lammenatzeach al-shoshannim livnei-korach maskil shir yedidot*	לַמְנַצֵּחַ עַל־שֹׁשַׁנִּים לִבְנֵי־קֹרַח מַשְׂכִּיל שִׁיר יְדִידֹת: א
2	My heart is astir with gracious words; I speak my poem to a king; my tongue is the pen of an expert scribe.	*Rachash libbi davar tov omer ani ma'asai lemelech leshoni et sofer mahir*	רָחַשׁ לִבִּי דָּבָר טוֹב אֹמֵר אָנִי מַעֲשַׂי לְמֶלֶךְ לְשׁוֹנִי עֵט סוֹפֵר מָהִיר: ב
3	You are fairer than all men; your speech is endowed with grace; rightly has Hashem given you an eternal blessing.	*Yafeyafita mibbenei adam hutzak chen besefetoteicha al-ken berachcha elohim le'olam*	יָפְיָפִיתָ מִבְּנֵי אָדָם הוּצַק חֵן בְּשְׂפְתוֹתֶיךָ עַל־כֵּן בֵּרַכְךָ אֱלֹהִים לְעוֹלָם: ג
4	Gird your sword upon your thigh, O hero, in your splendor and glory;	*Chagor-charbecha al-yarech gibbor hodecha vahadarecha*	חֲגוֹר־חַרְבְּךָ עַל־יָרֵךְ גִּבּוֹר הוֹדְךָ וַהֲדָרֶךָ: ד

5	in your glory, win success; ride on in the cause of truth and meekness and right; and let your right hand lead you to awesome deeds.	*Vahadarecha tzelach rechav al-devar-emet ve'anvah-tzedek vetorecha nora'ot yeminecha*	וַהֲדָרְךָ צְלַח רְכַב עַל־דְּבַר־ אֱמֶת וְעַנְוָה־צֶּדֶק וְתוֹרְךָ נוֹרָאוֹת יְמִינֶךָ׃	ה
6	Your arrows, sharpened, [pierce] the breast of the king's enemies; peoples fall at your feet.*	*Chitzeicha shenunim ammim tachteicha yippelu belev oyevei hammelech*	חִצֶּיךָ שְׁנוּנִים עַמִּים תַּחְתֶּיךָ יִפְּלוּ בְּלֵב אוֹיְבֵי הַמֶּלֶךְ׃	ו
7	Your divine throne is everlasting; your royal scepter is a scepter of equity.	*Kis'acha elohim olam va'ed shevet mishor shevet malchutecha*	כִּסְאֲךָ אֱלֹהִים עוֹלָם וָעֶד שֵׁבֶט מִישֹׁר שֵׁבֶט מַלְכוּתֶךָ׃	ז
8	You love righteousness and hate wickedness; rightly has Hashem, your God, chosen to anoint you with oil of gladness over all your peers.	*Ahavta tzedek vattisna resha al-ken meshachacha elohim eloheicha shemen sason mechavereicha*	אָהַבְתָּ צֶּדֶק וַתִּשְׂנָא רֶשַׁע עַל־כֵּן מְשָׁחֲךָ אֱלֹהִים אֱלֹהֶיךָ שֶׁמֶן שָׂשׂוֹן מֵחֲבֵרֶיךָ׃	ח
9	All your robes [are fragrant] with myrrh and aloes and cassia; from ivoried palaces lutes entertain you.	*Mor-va'ahalot ketzi'ot kol-bigdoteicha min- heichlei shen minni simmechucha*	מֹר־וַאֲהָלוֹת קְצִיעוֹת כָּל־ בִּגְדֹתֶיךָ מִן־הֵיכְלֵי שֵׁן מִנִּי שִׂמְּחוּךָ׃	ט
10	Royal princesses are your favorites; the consort stands at your right hand, decked in gold of Ophir.	*Benot melachim beyikkeroteicha nitzevah shegal liminicha bechetem ofir*	בְּנוֹת מְלָכִים בְּיִקְּרוֹתֶיךָ נִצְּבָה שֵׁגַל לִימִינְךָ בְּכֶתֶם אוֹפִיר׃	י

11	Take heed, lass, and note, incline your ear: forget your people and your father's house,	*Shim'i-vat ure'i vehatti azenech veshichchi ammech uveit avich*	שִׁמְעִי־בַת וּרְאִי וְהַטִּי אָזְנֵךְ וְשִׁכְחִי עַמֵּךְ וּבֵית אָבִיךְ:
12	and let the king be aroused by your beauty; since he is your lord, bow to him.	*Veyit'av hammelech yafeyech ki-hu adonayich vehishtachavi-lo*	וְיִתְאָו הַמֶּלֶךְ יָפְיֵךְ כִּי־הוּא אֲדֹנַיִךְ וְהִשְׁתַּחֲוִי־לוֹ:
13	O Tyrian lass, the wealthiest people will court your favor with gifts,	*Uvat-tzor beminchah panayich yechallu ashirei am*	וּבַת־צֹר בְּמִנְחָה פָּנַיִךְ יְחַלּוּ עֲשִׁירֵי עָם:
14	goods of all sorts. The royal princess, her dress embroidered with golden mountings,	*Kol-kevuddah vat-melech penimah mimmishbetzot zahav levushah*	כָּל־כְּבוּדָּה בַת־מֶלֶךְ פְּנִימָה מִמִּשְׁבְּצוֹת זָהָב לְבוּשָׁהּ:
15	is led inside to the king; maidens in her train, her companions, are presented to you.	*Lirkamot tuval lammelech betulot achareiha re'oteiha muva'ot lach*	לִרְקָמוֹת תּוּבַל לַמֶּלֶךְ בְּתוּלוֹת אַחֲרֶיהָ רֵעוֹתֶיהָ מוּבָאוֹת לָךְ:
16	They are led in with joy and gladness; they enter the palace of the king.	*Tuvalnah bismachot vagil tevo'einah beheichal melech*	תּוּבַלְנָה בִּשְׂמָחֹת וָגִיל תְּבֹאֶינָה בְּהֵיכַל מֶלֶךְ:
17	Your sons will succeed your ancestors; you will appoint them princes throughout the land.	*tachat avoteicha yihyu vaneicha teshitemo lesarim bechol-ha'aretz*	תַּחַת אֲבֹתֶיךָ יִהְיוּ בָנֶיךָ תְּשִׁיתֵמוֹ לְשָׂרִים בְּכָל־הָאָרֶץ:

18	I commemorate your fame for all generations, so peoples will praise you forever and ever.	*Azkirah shimcha bechol-dor vador al-ken ammim yehoducha le'olam va'ed*	אַזְכִּירָה שִׁמְךָ בְּכָל־דֹּר וָדֹר עַל־כֵּן עַמִּים יְהוֹדֻךָ לְעֹלָם וָעֶד:	יח

46

—◦◦⬡◦◦— **מו**

1	For the leader. Of the Korahites; on alamoth. A song.	*Lammenatzeach livnei-korach al-alamot shir*	לַמְנַצֵּחַ לִבְנֵי־קֹרַח עַל־עֲלָמוֹת שִׁיר:	א
2	Hashem is our refuge and stronghold, a help in trouble, very near.	*Elohim lanu machaseh va'oz ezrah vetzarot nimtza me'od*	אֱלֹהִים לָנוּ מַחֲסֶה וָעֹז עֶזְרָה בְצָרוֹת נִמְצָא מְאֹד:	ב
3	Therefore we are not afraid though the earth reels, though mountains topple into the sea—	*Al-ken lo-nira behamir aretz uvemot harim belev yammim*	עַל־כֵּן לֹא־נִירָא בְּהָמִיר אָרֶץ וּבְמוֹט הָרִים בְּלֵב יַמִּים:	ג
4	its waters rage and foam; in its swell mountains quake. Selah.	*Yehemu yechmeru meimav yir'ashu-harim bega'avato selah*	יֶהֱמוּ יֶחְמְרוּ מֵימָיו יִרְעֲשׁוּ־הָרִים בְּגַאֲוָתוֹ סֶלָה:	ד
5	There is a river whose streams gladden Hashem's city, the holy dwelling-place of the Most High.	*Nahar pelagav yesammechu ir-elohim kedosh mishkenei elyon*	נָהָר פְּלָגָיו יְשַׂמְּחוּ עִיר־אֱלֹהִים קְדֹשׁ מִשְׁכְּנֵי עֶלְיוֹן:	ה

6	Hashem is in its midst, it will not be toppled; by daybreak Hashem will come to its aid.	*Elohim bekirbah bal-timmot ya'zereha elohim lifnot boker*	אֱלֹהִים בְּקִרְבָּהּ בַּל-תִּמּוֹט יַעְזְרֶהָ אֱלֹהִים לִפְנוֹת בֹּקֶר:	ו
7	Nations rage, kingdoms topple; at the sound of His thunder the earth dissolves.	*Hamu goyim matu mamlachot natan bekolo tamug aretz*	הָמוּ גוֹיִם מָטוּ מַמְלָכוֹת נָתַן בְּקוֹלוֹ תָּמוּג אָרֶץ:	ז
8	The lord of hosts is with us; the God of Yaakov is our haven. Selah.	*Adonai tzeva'ot immanu misgav-lanu elohei ya'akov selah*	יְהֹוָה צְבָאוֹת עִמָּנוּ מִשְׂגָּב-לָנוּ אֱלֹהֵי יַעֲקֹב סֶלָה:	ח
9	Come and see what Hashem has done, how He has wrought desolation on the earth.	*Lechu-chazu mif'alot Adonai asher-sam shammot ba'aretz*	לְכוּ-חֲזוּ מִפְעֲלוֹת יְהֹוָה אֲשֶׁר-שָׂם שַׁמּוֹת בָּאָרֶץ:	ט
10	He puts a stop to wars throughout the earth, breaking the bow, snapping the spear, consigning wagons to the flames.	*Mashbit milchamot ad-ketzeh ha'aretz keshet yeshabber vekitzetz chanit agalot yisrof ba'esh*	מַשְׁבִּית מִלְחָמוֹת עַד-קְצֵה הָאָרֶץ קֶשֶׁת יְשַׁבֵּר וְקִצֵּץ חֲנִית עֲגָלוֹת יִשְׂרֹף בָּאֵשׁ:	י
11	"Desist! Realize that I am Hashem! I dominate the nations; I dominate the earth."	*Harpu ude'u ki-anochi elohim arum baggoyim arum ba'aretz*	הַרְפּוּ וּדְעוּ כִּי-אָנֹכִי אֱלֹהִים אָרוּם בַּגּוֹיִם אָרוּם בָּאָרֶץ:	יא
12	The lord of hosts is with us; the God of Yaakov is our haven. Selah.	*Adonai tzeva'ot immanu misgav-lanu elohei ya'akov selah*	יְהֹוָה צְבָאוֹת עִמָּנוּ מִשְׂגָּב-לָנוּ אֱלֹהֵי יַעֲקֹב סֶלָה:	יב

47

1	For the leader. Of the Korahites. A psalm.	*Lammenatzeach livnei-korach mizmor*	לַמְנַצֵּחַ לִבְנֵי־קֹרַח מִזְמוֹר׃	א

2 All you peoples, clap your hands, raise a joyous shout for Hashem.

Kol-ha'ammim tik'u-chaf hari'u lelohim bekol rinnah

כָּל־הָעַמִּים תִּקְעוּ־כָף הָרִיעוּ לֵאלֹהִים בְּקוֹל רִנָּה׃ ב

3 For Hashem Most High is awesome, great king over all the earth;

Ki-Adonai elyon nora melech gadol al-kol-ha'aretz

כִּי־יְהֹוָה עֶלְיוֹן נוֹרָא מֶלֶךְ גָּדוֹל עַל־כָּל־הָאָרֶץ׃ ג

4 He subjects peoples to us, sets nations at our feet.

Yadber ammim tachteinu ule'ummim tachat ragleinu

יַדְבֵּר עַמִּים תַּחְתֵּינוּ וּלְאֻמִּים תַּחַת רַגְלֵינוּ׃ ד

5 He chose our heritage for us, the pride of Yaakov whom He loved. Selah.

Yivchar-lanu et-nachalatenu et ge'on ya'akov asher-ahev selah

יִבְחַר־לָנוּ אֶת־נַחֲלָתֵנוּ אֶת גְּאוֹן יַעֲקֹב אֲשֶׁר־אָהֵב סֶלָה׃ ה

6 Hashem ascends midst acclamation; Hashem, to the blasts of the shofar.

Alah elohim bitru'ah Adonai bekol shofar

עָלָה אֱלֹהִים בִּתְרוּעָה יְהֹוָה בְּקוֹל שׁוֹפָר׃ ו

7 Sing, O sing to Hashem; sing, O sing to our king;

Zammeru elohim zammeru zammeru lemalkenu zammeru

זַמְּרוּ אֱלֹהִים זַמֵּרוּ זַמְּרוּ לְמַלְכֵּנוּ זַמֵּרוּ׃ ז

8	for Hashem is king over all the earth; sing a hymn.	*Ki melech kol-ha'aretz elohim zammeru maskil*	כִּי מֶלֶךְ כָּל־הָאָרֶץ אֱלֹהִים זַמְּרוּ מַשְׂכִּיל: ח
9	Hashem reigns over the nations; Hashem is seated on His holy throne.	*Malach elohim al-goyim elohim yashav al-kisse kodsho*	מָלַךְ אֱלֹהִים עַל־גּוֹיִם אֱלֹהִים יָשַׁב עַל־כִּסֵּא קָדְשׁוֹ: ט
10	The great of the peoples are gathered together, the retinue of Avraham's Hashem; for the guardians of the earth belong to Hashem; He is greatly exalted.	*Nedivei ammim ne'esafu am elohei avraham ki lelohim maginnei-eretz me'od na'alah*	נְדִיבֵי עַמִּים נֶאֱסָפוּ עַם אֱלֹהֵי אַבְרָהָם כִּי לֵאלֹהִים מָגִנֵּי־אֶרֶץ מְאֹד נַעֲלָה: י

48   —◦◦❋◦◦—   מזח

1	A song. A psalm of the Korahites.	*Shir mizmor livnei-korach*	שִׁיר מִזְמוֹר לִבְנֵי־קֹרַח: א
2	Hashem is great and much acclaimed in the city of our God, His holy mountain—	*Gadol Adonai umehullal me'od be'ir eloheinu har-kodsho*	גָּדוֹל יְהֹוָה וּמְהֻלָּל מְאֹד בְּעִיר אֱלֹהֵינוּ הַר־קָדְשׁוֹ: ב
3	fair-crested, joy of all the earth, Mount Tzion, summit of Zaphon, city of the great king.	*Yefeh nof mesos kol-ha'aretz har-tziyyon yarketei tzafon kiryat melech rav*	יְפֵה נוֹף מְשׂוֹשׂ כָּל־הָאָרֶץ הַר־צִיּוֹן יַרְכְּתֵי צָפוֹן קִרְיַת מֶלֶךְ רָב: ג

4	Through its citadels, Hashem has made Himself known as a haven.	*Elohim be'armenoteiha noda lemisgav*	אֱלֹהִים בְּאַרְמְנוֹתֶיהָ נוֹדַע לְמִשְׂגָּב:	ד
5	See, the kings joined forces; they advanced together.	*Ki-hinneh hammelachim no'adu averu yachdav*	כִּי־הִנֵּה הַמְּלָכִים נוֹעֲדוּ עָבְרוּ יַחְדָּו:	ה
6	At the mere sight of it they were stunned, they were terrified, they panicked;	*hemmah ra'u ken tamahu nivhalu nechpazu*	הֵמָּה רָאוּ כֵּן תָּמָהוּ נִבְהֲלוּ נֶחְפָּזוּ:	ו
7	they were seized there with a trembling, like a woman in the throes of labor,	*Re'adah achazatam sham chil kayyoledah*	רְעָדָה אֲחָזָתַם שָׁם חִיל כַּיּוֹלֵדָה:	ז
8	as the Tarshish fleet was wrecked in an easterly gale.	*Beruach kadim teshabber oniyyot tarshish*	בְּרוּחַ קָדִים תְּשַׁבֵּר אֳנִיּוֹת תַּרְשִׁישׁ:	ח
9	The likes of what we heard we have now witnessed in the city of the lord of hosts, in the city of our God— may Hashem preserve it forever! Selah.	*Ka'asher shama'nu ken ra'inu be'ir-Adonai tzeva'ot be'ir eloheinu elohim yechoneneha ad-olam selah*	כַּאֲשֶׁר שָׁמַעְנוּ כֵּן רָאִינוּ בְּעִיר־יְהוָה צְבָאוֹת בְּעִיר אֱלֹהֵינוּ אֱלֹהִים יְכוֹנְנֶהָ עַד־עוֹלָם סֶלָה:	ט
10	In Your temple, Hashem, we meditate upon Your faithful care.	*Dimminu elohim chasdecha bekerev heichalecha*	דִּמִּינוּ אֱלֹהִים חַסְדֶּךָ בְּקֶרֶב הֵיכָלֶךָ:	י

11	The praise of You, Hashem, like Your name, reaches to the ends of the earth; Your right hand is filled with beneficence.	*Keshimcha elohim ken tehillatecha al-katzvei-eretz tzedek male'ah yeminecha*

כְּשִׁמְךָ אֱלֹהִים כֵּן תְּהִלָּתְךָ עַל־קַצְוֵי־אֶרֶץ צֶדֶק מָלְאָה יְמִינֶךָ: יא

12	Let Mount Tzion rejoice! Let the towns of Yehuda exult, because of Your judgments.	*Yismach har-tziyyon tagelenah benot yehudah lema'an mishpateicha*

יִשְׂמַח הַר־צִיּוֹן תָּגֵלְנָה בְּנוֹת יְהוּדָה לְמַעַן מִשְׁפָּטֶיךָ: יב

13	Walk around Tzion, circle it; count its towers,	*Sobbu tziyyon vehakkifuha sifru migdaleiha*

סֹבּוּ צִיּוֹן וְהַקִּיפוּהָ סִפְרוּ מִגְדָּלֶיהָ: יג

14	take note of its ramparts; go through its citadels, that you may recount it to a future age.	*shitu libbechem lecheilah passegu armenoteiha lema'an tesapperu ledor acharon*

שִׁיתוּ לִבְּכֶם לְחֵילָה פַּסְּגוּ אַרְמְנוֹתֶיהָ לְמַעַן תְּסַפְּרוּ לְדוֹר אַחֲרוֹן: יד

15	For Hashem—He is our God forever; He will lead us evermore.	*Ki zeh elohim eloheinu olam va'ed hu yenahagenu al-mut*

כִּי זֶה אֱלֹהִים אֱלֹהֵינוּ עוֹלָם וָעֶד הוּא יְנַהֲגֵנוּ עַל־מוּת: טו

49

—◦◦◦◦—

מט

1	For the leader. Of the Korahites. A psalm.	*Lammenatzeach livnei-korach mizmor*

לַמְנַצֵּחַ לִבְנֵי־קֹרַח מִזְמוֹר: א

2	Hear this, all you peoples; give ear, all inhabitants of the world,	*Shim'u-zot kol-ha'ammim ha'azinu kol-yoshevei chaled*	שִׁמְעוּ־זֹאת כָּל־הָעַמִּים הַאֲזִינוּ כָּל־יֹשְׁבֵי חָלֶד׃ ב
3	men of all estates, rich and poor alike.	*Gam-benei adam gam-benei-ish yachad ashir ve'evyon*	גַּם־בְּנֵי אָדָם גַּם־בְּנֵי־אִישׁ יַחַד עָשִׁיר וְאֶבְיוֹן׃ ג
4	My mouth utters wisdom, my speech is full of insight.	*Pi yedabber chachemot vehagut libbi tevunot*	פִּי יְדַבֵּר חָכְמוֹת וְהָגוּת לִבִּי תְבוּנוֹת׃ ד
5	I will turn my attention to a theme, set forth my lesson to the music of a lyre.	*Atteh lemashal azeni eftach bechinnor chidati*	אַטֶּה לְמָשָׁל אָזְנִי אֶפְתַּח בְּכִנּוֹר חִידָתִי׃ ה
6	In time of trouble, why should I fear the encompassing evil of those who would supplant me—	*lammah ira bimei ra avon akevai yesubbeni*	לָמָּה אִירָא בִּימֵי רָע עֲוֺן עֲקֵבַי יְסוּבֵּנִי׃ ו
7	men who trust in their riches, who glory in their great wealth?	*Habbotechim al-cheilam uverov oshram yithallalu*	הַבֹּטְחִים עַל־חֵילָם וּבְרֹב עָשְׁרָם יִתְהַלָּלוּ׃ ז
8	Ah, it cannot redeem a man, or pay his ransom to Hashem;	*Ach lo-fadoh yifdeh ish lo-yitten lelohim kofro*	אָח לֹא־פָדֹה יִפְדֶּה אִישׁ לֹא־יִתֵּן לֵאלֹהִים כָּפְרוֹ׃ ח
9	the price of life is too high; and so one ceases to be, forever.	*Veyekar pidyon nafsham vechadal le'olam*	וְיֵקַר פִּדְיוֹן נַפְשָׁם וְחָדַל לְעוֹלָם׃ ט
10	Shall he live eternally, and never see the grave?	*Vichi-od lanetzach lo yir'eh hashachat*	וִיחִי־עוֹד לָנֶצַח לֹא יִרְאֶה הַשָּׁחַת׃ י

11	For one sees that the wise die, that the foolish and ignorant both perish, leaving their wealth to others.	*Ki yir'eh chachamim yamutu yachad kesil vava'ar yovedu ve'azevu la'acherim cheilam*	כִּי יִרְאֶה חֲכָמִים יָמוּתוּ יַחַד כְּסִיל וָבַעַר יֹאבֵדוּ וְעָזְבוּ לַאֲחֵרִים חֵילָם:	יא
12	Their grave is their eternal home, the dwelling-place for all generations of those once famous on earth.	*Kirbam batteimo le'olam mishkenotam ledor vador kare'u vishmotam alei adamot*	קִרְבָּם בָּתֵּימוֹ לְעוֹלָם מִשְׁכְּנֹתָם לְדֹר וָדֹר קָרְאוּ בִשְׁמוֹתָם עֲלֵי אֲדָמוֹת:	יב
13	Man does not abide in honor; he is like the beasts that perish.	*Ve'adam bikar bal-yalin nimshal kabbehemot nidmu*	וְאָדָם בִּיקָר בַּל־יָלִין נִמְשַׁל כַּבְּהֵמוֹת נִדְמוּ:	יג
14	Such is the fate of those who are self-confident, the end of those pleased with their own talk. Selah.	*Zeh darkam kesel lamo ve'achareihem befihem yirtzu selah*	זֶה דַרְכָּם כֵּסֶל לָמוֹ וְאַחֲרֵיהֶם בְּפִיהֶם יִרְצוּ סֶלָה:	יד
15	Sheeplike they head for Sheol, with Death as their shepherd. The upright shall rule over them at daybreak, and their form shall waste away in Sheol till its nobility be gone.	*Katzon lish'ol shattu mavet yir'em vayyirdu vam yesharim labboker vitziram [vetzuram] levallot she'ol mizzevul lo*	כַּצֹּאן לִשְׁאוֹל שַׁתּוּ מָוֶת יִרְעֵם וַיִּרְדּוּ בָם יְשָׁרִים לַבֹּקֶר וצירם [וְצוּרָם] לְבַלּוֹת שְׁאוֹל מִזְּבֻל לוֹ:	טו
16	But Hashem will redeem my life from the clutches of Sheol, for He will take me. Selah.	*Ach-elohim yifdeh nafshi miyyad-she'ol ki yikkacheni selah*	אַךְ־אֱלֹהִים יִפְדֶּה נַפְשִׁי מִיַּד־שְׁאוֹל כִּי יִקָּחֵנִי סֶלָה:	טז

17 Do not be afraid when a man becomes rich, when his household goods increase;

Al-tira ki-ya'ashir ish ki-yirbeh kevod beito

אַל־תִּירָא כִּי־יַעֲשִׁר אִישׁ כִּי־יִרְבֶּה כְּבוֹד בֵּיתוֹ: יז

18 for when he dies he can take none of it along; his goods cannot follow him down.

Ki lo vemoto yikkach hakkol lo-yered acharav kevodo

כִּי לֹא בְמוֹתוֹ יִקַּח הַכֹּל לֹא־יֵרֵד אַחֲרָיו כְּבוֹדוֹ: יח

19 Though he congratulates himself in his lifetime —"They must admit that you did well by yourself"—

Ki-nafsho bechayyav yevarech veyoducha ki-teitiv lach

כִּי־נַפְשׁוֹ בְּחַיָּיו יְבָרֵךְ וְיוֹדֻךָ כִּי־תֵיטִיב לָךְ: יט

20 yet he must join the company of his ancestors, who will never see daylight again.

Tavo ad-dor avotav ad-netzach lo yir'u-or

תָּבוֹא עַד־דּוֹר אֲבוֹתָיו עַד־נֵצַח לֹא יִרְאוּ־אוֹר: כ

21 Man does not understand honor; he is like the beasts that perish.

Adam bikar velo yavin nimshal kabbehemot nidmu

אָדָם בִּיקָר וְלֹא יָבִין נִמְשַׁל כַּבְּהֵמוֹת נִדְמוּ: כא

50

—∘⟨⟨⊗⟩⟩∘—

נ

1 A psalm of Asaf. Hashem, Hashem spoke and summoned the world from east to west.

Mizmor le'asaf el elohim Adonai dibber vayyikra-aretz mimmizrach-shemesh ad-mevo'o

מִזְמוֹר לְאָסָף אֵל אֱלֹהִים יְהֹוָה דִּבֶּר וַיִּקְרָא־אָרֶץ מִמִּזְרַח־שֶׁמֶשׁ עַד־מְבֹאוֹ: א

2	From Tzion, perfect in beauty, Hashem appeared	*Mitziyyon michlal-yofi elohim hofia'*	מִצִּיּוֹן מִכְלַל־יֹפִי אֱלֹהִים הוֹפִיעַ:	ב
3	—let our God come and not fail to act! Devouring fire preceded Him; it stormed around Him fiercely.	*Yavo eloheinu ve'al-yecherash esh-lefanav tochel usevivav nis'arah me'od*	יָבֹא אֱלֹהֵינוּ וְאַל־יֶחֱרַשׁ אֵשׁ־לְפָנָיו תֹּאכֵל וּסְבִיבָיו נִשְׂעֲרָה מְאֹד:	ג
4	He summoned the heavens above, and the earth, for the trial of His people.	*Yikra el-hashamayim me'al ve'el-ha'aretz ladin ammo*	יִקְרָא אֶל־הַשָּׁמַיִם מֵעָל וְאֶל־הָאָרֶץ לָדִין עַמּוֹ:	ד
5	"Bring in My devotees, who made a covenant with Me over sacrifice!"	*Isfu-li chasidai koretei veriti alei-zavach*	אִסְפוּ־לִי חֲסִידָי כֹּרְתֵי בְרִיתִי עֲלֵי־זָבַח:	ה
6	Then the heavens proclaimed His righteousness, for He is a Hashem who judges. Selah.	*Vayyaggidu shamayim tzidko ki-elohim shofet hu selah*	וַיַּגִּידוּ שָׁמַיִם צִדְקוֹ כִּי־אֱלֹהִים שֹׁפֵט הוּא סֶלָה:	ו
7	"Pay heed, My people, and I will speak, O Yisrael, and I will arraign you. I am Hashem, your God.	*Shim'ah ammi va'adabberah yisra'el ve'a'idah bach elohim eloheicha anochi*	שִׁמְעָה עַמִּי וַאֲדַבֵּרָה יִשְׂרָאֵל וְאָעִידָה בָּךְ אֱלֹהִים אֱלֹהֶיךָ אָנֹכִי:	ז
8	I censure you not for your sacrifices, and your burnt offerings, made to Me daily;	*Lo al-zevacheicha ochichecha ve'oloteicha lenegdi tamid*	לֹא עַל־זְבָחֶיךָ אוֹכִיחֶךָ וְעוֹלֹתֶיךָ לְנֶגְדִּי תָמִיד:	ח
9	I claim no bull from your estate, no he-goats from your pens.	*Lo-ekkach mibbeitcha far mimmichle'oteicha attudim*	לֹא־אֶקַּח מִבֵּיתְךָ פָר מִמִּכְלְאֹתֶיךָ עַתּוּדִים:	ט

10	For Mine is every animal of the forest, the beasts on a thousand mountains.	*Ki-li chol-chayto-ya'ar behemot beharrei-alef*	כִּי־לִי כָל־חַיְתוֹ־יָ֑עַר בְּהֵמ֗וֹת בְּהַרְרֵי־אָֽלֶף׃	י
11	I know every bird of the mountains, the creatures of the field are subject to Me.	*Yada'ti kol-of harim veziz sadai immadi*	יָדַעְתִּי כָּל־ע֣וֹף הָרִ֑ים וְזִ֥יז שָׂ֝דַ֗י עִמָּדִֽי׃	יא
12	Were I hungry, I would not tell you, for Mine is the world and all it holds.	*Im-er'av lo-omar lach ki-li tevel umelo'ah*	אִם־אֶ֭רְעַב לֹא־אֹ֣מַר לָ֑ךְ כִּי־לִ֥י תֵ֝בֵ֗ל וּמְלֹאָֽהּ׃	יב
13	Do I eat the flesh of bulls, or drink the blood of he-goats?	*Ha'ochal besar abbirim vedam attudim eshteh*	הַֽ֭אוֹכַל בְּשַׂ֣ר אַבִּירִ֑ים וְדַ֖ם עַתּוּדִ֣ים אֶשְׁתֶּֽה׃	יג
14	Sacrifice a thank offering to Hashem, and pay your vows to the Most High.	*Zevach lelohim todah veshallem le'elyon nedareicha*	זְבַ֣ח לֵאלֹהִ֣ים תּוֹדָ֑ה וְשַׁלֵּ֖ם לְעֶלְי֣וֹן נְדָרֶֽיךָ׃	יד
15	Call upon Me in time of trouble; I will rescue you, and you shall honor Me."	*Ukera'eni beyom tzarah achalletzcha utechabbedeni*	וּ֭קְרָאֵנִי בְּי֣וֹם צָרָ֑ה אֲ֝חַלֶּצְךָ֗ וּֽתְכַבְּדֵֽנִי׃	טו
16	And to the wicked, Hashem said: "Who are you to recite My laws, and mouth the terms of My covenant,	*Velarasha amar elohim mah-lecha lesapper chukkai vattissa veriti alei-ficha*	וְלָ֤רָשָׁ֨ע ׀ אָ֘מַ֤ר אֱלֹהִ֗ים מַה־לְּ֭ךָ לְסַפֵּ֣ר חֻקָּ֑י וַתִּשָּׂ֖א בְרִיתִ֣י עֲלֵי־פִֽיךָ׃	טז
17	seeing that you spurn My discipline, and brush My words aside?	*Ve'attah saneta musar vattashlech devarai achareicha*	וְ֭אַתָּה שָׂנֵ֣אתָ מוּסָ֑ר וַתַּשְׁלֵ֖ךְ דְּבָרַ֣י אַחֲרֶֽיךָ׃	יז

18	When you see a thief, you fall in with him, and throw in your lot with adulterers;	*Im-ra'ita gannav vattiretz immo ve'im mena'afim chelkecha*

אִם־רָאִיתָ גַנָּב וַתִּרֶץ עִמּוֹ וְעִם מְנָאֲפִים חֶלְקֶךָ: יח

19	you devote your mouth to evil, and yoke your tongue to deceit;	*picha shalachta vera'ah uleshonecha tatzmid mirmah*

פִּיךָ שָׁלַחְתָּ בְרָעָה וּלְשׁוֹנְךָ תַּצְמִיד מִרְמָה: יט

20	you are busy maligning your brother, defaming the son of your mother.	*Teshev be'achicha tedabber beven-immecha titten-dofi*

תֵּשֵׁב בְּאָחִיךָ תְדַבֵּר בְּבֶן אִמְּךָ תִּתֶּן־דֹּפִי: כ

21	If I failed to act when you did these things, you would fancy that I was like you; so I censure you and confront you with charges.	*elleh asita vehecherashti dimmita heyot-ehyeh chamocha ochichacha ve'e'erchah le'eineicha*

אֵלֶּה עָשִׂיתָ וְהֶחֱרַשְׁתִּי דִּמִּיתָ הֱיוֹת־אֶהְיֶה כָמוֹךָ אוֹכִיחֲךָ וְאֶעֶרְכָה לְעֵינֶיךָ: כא

22	Mark this, you who are unmindful of Hashem, lest I tear you apart and no one save you.	*binu-na zot shochechei eloah pen-etrof ve'ein matzil*

בִּינוּ־נָא זֹאת שֹׁכְחֵי אֱלוֹהַּ פֶּן־אֶטְרֹף וְאֵין מַצִּיל: כב

23	He who sacrifices a thank offering honors Me, and to him who improves his way I will show the salvation of Hashem."	*Zoveach todah yechabbedaneni vesam derech ar'ennu beyesha elohim*

זֹבֵחַ תּוֹדָה יְכַבְּדָנְנִי וְשָׂם דֶּרֶךְ אַרְאֶנּוּ בְּיֵשַׁע אֱלֹהִים: כג

51

1	For the leader. A psalm of David,	*Lammenatzeach mizmor ledavid*	לַמְנַצֵּחַ מִזְמוֹר לְדָוִד: א
2	when Natan the Navi came to him after he had come to Batsheva.	*Bevo-eilav natan hannavi ka'asher-ba el-bat-shava*	בְּבוֹא־אֵלָיו נָתָן הַנָּבִיא כַּאֲשֶׁר־בָּא אֶל־בַּת־שָׁבַע: ב
3	Have mercy upon me, O Hashem, as befits Your faithfulness; in keeping with Your abundant compassion, blot out my transgressions.	*Channeni elohim kechasdecha kerov rachamecha mecheh fesha'ai*	חָנֵּנִי אֱלֹהִים כְּחַסְדֶּךָ כְּרֹב רַחֲמֶיךָ מְחֵה פְשָׁעָי: ג
4	Wash me thoroughly of my iniquity, and purify me of my sin;	*Herev kabbeseni me'avoni umechattati tahareini*	הרבה [הֶרֶב] כַּבְּסֵנִי מֵעֲוֹנִי וּמֵחַטָּאתִי טַהֲרֵנִי: ד
5	for I recognize my transgressions, and am ever conscious of my sin.	*Ki-fesha'ai ani eida vechattati negdi tamid*	כִּי־פְשָׁעַי אֲנִי אֵדָע וְחַטָּאתִי נֶגְדִּי תָמִיד: ה
6	Against You alone have I sinned, and done what is evil in Your sight; so You are just in Your sentence, and right in Your judgment.	*Lecha levaddecha chatati vehara be'eineicha asiti lema'an titzdak bedovrecha tizkeh veshoftecha*	לְךָ לְבַדְּךָ חָטָאתִי וְהָרַע בְּעֵינֶיךָ עָשִׂיתִי לְמַעַן תִּצְדַּק בְּדָבְרֶךָ תִּזְכֶּה בְשָׁפְטֶךָ: ו

7	Indeed I was born with iniquity; with sin my mother conceived me.	*Hen-be'avon cholaleti uvechet yechematni immi*	הֵן־בְּעָווֹן חוֹלָלְתִּי וּבְחֵטְא יֶחֱמַתְנִי אִמִּי׃	ז
8	Indeed You desire truth about that which is hidden; teach me wisdom about secret things.	*Hen-emet chafatzta vattuchot uvesatum chochmah todi'eni*	הֵן־אֱמֶת חָפַצְתָּ בַטֻּחוֹת וּבְסָתֻם חָכְמָה תוֹדִיעֵנִי׃	ח
9	Purge me with hyssop till I am pure; wash me till I am whiter than snow.	*Techatte'eni ve'ezov ve'ethar techabbeseni umisheleg albin*	תְּחַטְּאֵנִי בְאֵזוֹב וְאֶטְהָר תְּכַבְּסֵנִי וּמִשֶּׁלֶג אַלְבִּין׃	ט
10	Let me hear tidings of joy and gladness; let the bones You have crushed exult.	*Tashmi'eni sason vesimchah tagelenah atzamot dikkita*	תַּשְׁמִיעֵנִי שָׂשׂוֹן וְשִׂמְחָה תָּגֵלְנָה עֲצָמוֹת דִּכִּיתָ׃	י
11	Hide Your face from my sins; blot out all my iniquities.	*Haster panecha mechata'ai vechol-avonotai mecheh*	הַסְתֵּר פָּנֶיךָ מֵחֲטָאָי וְכָל־עֲוֺנֹתַי מְחֵה׃	יא
12	Fashion a pure heart for me, O Hashem; create in me a steadfast spirit.	*Lev tahor bera-li elohim veruach nachon chaddesh bekirbi*	לֵב טָהוֹר בְּרָא־לִי אֱלֹהִים וְרוּחַ נָכוֹן חַדֵּשׁ בְּקִרְבִּי׃	יב
13	Do not cast me out of Your presence, or take Your holy spirit away from me.	*Al-tashlicheni millefanecha veruach kodshecha al-tikkach mimmenni*	אַל־תַּשְׁלִיכֵנִי מִלְּפָנֶיךָ וְרוּחַ קָדְשְׁךָ אַל־תִּקַּח מִמֶּנִּי׃	יג
14	Let me again rejoice in Your help; let a vigorous spirit sustain me.	*Hashivah li seson yish'echa veruach nedivah tismecheni*	הָשִׁיבָה לִּי שְׂשׂוֹן יִשְׁעֶךָ וְרוּחַ נְדִיבָה תִסְמְכֵנִי׃	יד

15	I will teach transgressors Your ways, that sinners may return to You.	*Alammedah foshe'im deracheicha vechatta'im eleicha yashuvu*	אֲלַמְּדָה פֹשְׁעִים דְּרָכֶיךָ וְחַטָּאִים אֵלֶיךָ יָשׁוּבוּ:	טו
16	Save me from bloodguilt, O Hashem, Hashem, my deliverer, that I may sing forth Your beneficence.	*Hatzileni middamim elohim elohei teshu'ati terannen leshoni tzidkatecha*	הַצִּילֵנִי מִדָּמִים אֱלֹהִים אֱלֹהֵי תְּשׁוּעָתִי תְּרַנֵּן לְשׁוֹנִי צִדְקָתֶךָ:	טז
17	O Hashem, open my lips, and let my mouth declare Your praise.	*Adonai sefatai tiftach ufi yaggid tehillatecha*	אֲדֹנָי שְׂפָתַי תִּפְתָּח וּפִי יַגִּיד תְּהִלָּתֶךָ:	יז
18	You do not want me to bring sacrifices; You do not desire burnt offerings;	*Ki lo-tachpotz zevach ve'ettenah olah lo tirtzeh*	כִּי לֹא־תַחְפֹּץ זֶבַח וְאֶתֵּנָה עוֹלָה לֹא תִרְצֶה:	יח
19	True sacrifice to Hashem is a contrite spirit; Hashem, You will not despise a contrite and crushed heart.	*Zivchei elohim ruach nishbarah lev-nishbar venidkeh elohim lo tivzeh*	זִבְחֵי אֱלֹהִים רוּחַ נִשְׁבָּרָה לֵב־נִשְׁבָּר וְנִדְכֶּה אֱלֹהִים לֹא תִבְזֶה:	יט
20	May it please You to make Tzion prosper; rebuild the walls of Yerushalayim.	*Heitivah virtzonecha et-tziyyon tivneh chomot yerushalayim*	הֵיטִיבָה בִרְצוֹנְךָ אֶת־צִיּוֹן תִּבְנֶה חוֹמוֹת יְרוּשָׁלָ‍ִם:	כ
21	Then You will want sacrifices offered in righteousness, burnt and whole offerings; then bulls will be offered on Your mizbayach.	*Az tachpotz zivchei-tzedek olah vechalil az ya'alu al-mizbachacha farim*	אָז תַּחְפֹּץ זִבְחֵי־צֶדֶק עוֹלָה וְכָלִיל אָז יַעֲלוּ עַל־מִזְבַּחֲךָ פָרִים:	כא

52

1	For the leader. A maskil of David,	*Lammenatzayach maskil ledavid*	לַמְנַצֵּחַ מַשְׂכִּיל לְדָוִד: א
2	when Doeg Ha'adomi came and informed Shaul, telling him, "David came to Achimelech's house."	*Bevo do'eg ha'adomi vayyagged lesha'ul vayyomer lo ba david el-beit achimelech*	בְּבוֹא דּוֹאֵג הָאֲדֹמִי וַיַּגֵּד לְשָׁאוּל וַיֹּאמֶר לוֹ בָּא דָוִד אֶל־בֵּית אֲחִימֶלֶךְ: ב
3	Why do you boast of your evil, brave fellow? Hashem's faithfulness never ceases.	*Mah-tithallel bera'ah haggibbor chesed el kol-hayyom*	מַה־תִּתְהַלֵּל בְּרָעָה הַגִּבּוֹר חֶסֶד אֵל כָּל־הַיּוֹם: ג
4	Your tongue devises mischief, like a sharpened razor that works treacherously.	*Havvvot tachshov leshonecha keta'ar meluttash oseh remiyyah*	הַוּוֹת תַּחְשֹׁב לְשׁוֹנֶךָ כְּתַעַר מְלֻטָּשׁ עֹשֵׂה רְמִיָּה: ד
5	You prefer evil to good, the lie, to speaking truthfully. Selah.	*Ahavta ra mittov sheker middabber tzedek selah*	אָהַבְתָּ רָּע מִטּוֹב שֶׁקֶר מִדַּבֵּר צֶדֶק סֶלָה: ה
6	You love all pernicious words, treacherous speech.	*Ahavta chol-divrei-vala leshon mirmah*	אָהַבְתָּ כָל־דִּבְרֵי־בָלַע לְשׁוֹן מִרְמָה: ו
7	So Hashem will tear you down for good, will break you and pluck you from your tent, and root you out of the land of the living. Selah.	*Gam-el yittatzecha lanetzach yachtecha veyissachacha me'ohel vesheshcha me'eretz chayyim selah*	גַּם־אֵל יִתָּצְךָ לָנֶצַח יַחְתְּךָ וְיִסָּחֲךָ מֵאֹהֶל וְשֵׁרֶשְׁךָ מֵאֶרֶץ חַיִּים סֶלָה: ז

8	The righteous, seeing it, will be awestruck; they will jibe at him, saying,	*Veyir'u tzaddikim veyira'u ve'alav yischaku*	וְיִרְאוּ צַדִּיקִים וְיִירָאוּ וְעָלָיו יִשְׂחָקוּ: ח
9	"Here was a fellow who did not make Hashem his refuge, but trusted in his great wealth, relied upon his mischief."	*Hinneh haggever lo yasim elohim ma'uzzo vayyivtach berov oshro ya'oz behavvato*	הִנֵּה הַגֶּבֶר לֹא יָשִׂים אֱלֹהִים מָעוּזּוֹ וַיִּבְטַח בְּרֹב עָשְׁרוֹ יָעֹז בְּהַוָּתוֹ: ט
10	But I am like a thriving olive tree in Hashem's house; I trust in the faithfulness of Hashem forever and ever.	*Va'ani kezayit ra'anan beveit elohim batachti vechesed-elohim olam va'ed*	וַאֲנִי כְּזַיִת רַעֲנָן בְּבֵית אֱלֹהִים בָּטַחְתִּי בְחֶסֶד־אֱלֹהִים עוֹלָם וָעֶד: י
11	I praise You forever, for You have acted; I declare that Your name is good in the presence of Your faithful ones.	*Odecha le'olam ki asita va'akavveh shimcha chi-tov neged chasideicha*	אוֹדְךָ לְעוֹלָם כִּי עָשִׂיתָ וַאֲקַוֶּה שִׁמְךָ כִי־טוֹב נֶגֶד חֲסִידֶיךָ: יא

53

━━○◈◈◈○━━

נג

1	For the leader; on mahalath. A maskil of David.	*Lammenatzeach al-machalat maskil ledavid*	לַמְנַצֵּחַ עַל־מָחֲלַת מַשְׂכִּיל לְדָוִד: א
2	The benighted man thinks, "Hashem does not care." Man's wrongdoing is corrupt and loathsome; no one does good.	*Amar naval belibbo ein elohim hishchitu vehit'ivu avel ein oseh-tov*	אָמַר נָבָל בְּלִבּוֹ אֵין אֱלֹהִים הִשְׁחִיתוּ וְהִתְעִיבוּ עָוֶל אֵין עֹשֵׂה־טוֹב: ב

3

Hashem looks down from heaven on mankind to find a man of understanding, a man mindful of Hashem.

Elohim mishamayim hishkif al-benei adam lir'ot hayesh maskil doresh et-elohim

אֱלֹהִים מִשָּׁמַיִם הִשְׁקִיף עַל־בְּנֵי אָדָם לִרְאוֹת הֲיֵשׁ מַשְׂכִּיל דֹּרֵשׁ אֶת־אֱלֹהִים:

ג

4

Everyone is dross, altogether foul; there is none who does good, not even one.

Kullo sag yachdav ne'elachu ein oseh-tov ein gam-echad

כֻּלּוֹ סָג יַחְדָּו נֶאֱלָחוּ אֵין עֹשֵׂה־טוֹב אֵין גַּם־אֶחָד:

ד

5

Are they so witless, those evildoers, who devour my people as they devour food, and do not invoke Hashem?

Halo yade'u po'alei aven ochelei ammi achelu lechem elohim lo kara'u

הֲלֹא יָדְעוּ פֹּעֲלֵי אָוֶן אֹכְלֵי עַמִּי אָכְלוּ לֶחֶם אֱלֹהִים לֹא קָרָאוּ:

ה

6

There they will be seized with fright — never was there such a fright— for Hashem has scattered the bones of your besiegers; you have put them to shame, for Hashem has rejected them.

Sham pachadu-fachad lo-hayah fachad ki-elohim pizzar atzmot chonach hevishotah ki-elohim me'asam

שָׁם פָּחֲדוּ־פַחַד לֹא־הָיָה פָחַד כִּי־אֱלֹהִים פִּזַּר עַצְמוֹת חֹנָךְ הֱבִשֹׁתָה כִּי־אֱלֹהִים מְאָסָם:

ו

7

O that the deliverance of Yisrael might come from Tzion! When Hashem restores the fortunes of His people, Yaakov will exult, Yisrael will rejoice.

Mi yitten mitziyyon yeshu'ot yisra'el beshuv elohim shevut ammo yagel ya'akov yismach yisra'el

מִי יִתֵּן מִצִּיּוֹן יְשֻׁעוֹת יִשְׂרָאֵל בְּשׁוּב אֱלֹהִים שְׁבוּת עַמּוֹ יָגֵל יַעֲקֹב יִשְׂמַח יִשְׂרָאֵל:

ז

54

1	For the leader; with instrumental music. A maskil of David,	*Lammenatzeach binginot maskil ledavid*	לַמְנַצֵּחַ בִּנְגִינֹת מַשְׂכִּיל לְדָוִד:	א

2	when the Ziphites came and told Shaul, "Know, David is in hiding among us."	*Bevo hazzifim vayyomru lesha'ul halo david mistatter immanu*	בְּבוֹא הַזִּיפִים וַיֹּאמְרוּ לְשָׁאוּל הֲלֹא דָוִד מִסְתַּתֵּר עִמָּנוּ:	ב

3	O Hashem, deliver me by Your name; by Your power vindicate me.	*Elohim beshimcha hoshi'eni uvigvuratecha tedineni*	אֱלֹהִים בְּשִׁמְךָ הוֹשִׁיעֵנִי וּבִגְבוּרָתְךָ תְדִינֵנִי:	ג

4	O Hashem, hear my prayer; give ear to the words of my mouth.	*Elohim shema tefillati ha'azinah le'imrei-fi*	אֱלֹהִים שְׁמַע תְּפִלָּתִי הַאֲזִינָה לְאִמְרֵי־פִי:	ד

5	For strangers have risen against me, and ruthless men seek my life; they are unmindful of Hashem. Selah.	*Ki zarim kamu alai ve'aritzim bikshu nafshi lo samu elohim lenegdam selah*	כִּי זָרִים קָמוּ עָלַי וְעָרִיצִים בִּקְשׁוּ נַפְשִׁי לֹא שָׂמוּ אֱלֹהִים לְנֶגְדָּם סֶלָה:	ה

6	See, Hashem is my helper; Hashem is my support.	*Hinneh elohim ozer li Adonai besomechei nafshi*	הִנֵּה אֱלֹהִים עֹזֵר לִי אֲדֹנָי בְּסֹמְכֵי נַפְשִׁי:	ו

7	He will repay the evil of my watchful foes; by Your faithfulness, destroy them!	*Yshvv [yashiv] hara leshorerai ba'amittecha hatzmitem*	יָשׁוּב [יָשִׁיב] הָרַע לְשֹׁרְרָי בַּאֲמִתְּךָ הַצְמִיתֵם:	ז

8

Then I will offer You a freewill sacrifice; I will praise Your name, Hashem, for it is good,

Bindavah ezbechah-lach odeh shimcha Adonai ki-tov

בְּנְדָבָה אֶזְבְּחָה־לָּךְ אוֹדֶה שִׁמְךָ יְהֹוָה כִּי־טוֹב: ח

9

for it has saved me from my foes, and let me gaze triumphant upon my enemies.

Ki mikkol-tzarah hitzilani uve'oyevai ra'atah eini

כִּי מִכָּל־צָרָה הִצִּילָנִי וּבְאֹיְבַי רָאֲתָה עֵינִי: ט

55

—◦⊛◦—

נה

1

For the leader; with instrumental music. A maskil of David.

Lammenatzeach binginot maskil ledavid

לַמְנַצֵּחַ בִּנְגִינֹת מַשְׂכִּיל לְדָוִד: א

2

Give ear, O Hashem, to my prayer; do not ignore my plea;

Ha'azinah elohim tefillati ve'al-tit'allam mittechinnati

הַאֲזִינָה אֱלֹהִים תְּפִלָּתִי וְאַל־תִּתְעַלַּם מִתְּחִנָּתִי: ב

3

pay heed to me and answer me. I am tossed about, complaining and moaning

Hakshivah li va'aneni arid besichi ve'ahimah

הַקְשִׁיבָה לִּי וַעֲנֵנִי אָרִיד בְּשִׂיחִי וְאָהִימָה: ג

4

at the clamor of the enemy, because of the oppression of the wicked; for they bring evil upon me and furiously harass me.

Mikkol oyev mippenei akat rasha ki-yamitu alai aven uve'af yistemuni

מִקּוֹל אוֹיֵב מִפְּנֵי עָקַת רָשָׁע כִּי־יָמִיטוּ עָלַי אָוֶן וּבְאַף יִשְׂטְמוּנִי: ד

5

My heart is convulsed within me; terrors of death assail me.

Libbi yachil bekirbi ve'eimot mavet nafelu alai

לִבִּי יָחִיל בְּקִרְבִּי וְאֵימוֹת מָוֶת נָפְלוּ עָלָי: ה

6	Fear and trembling invade me; I am clothed with horror.	*Yir'ah vara'ad yavo vi vattechasseni pallatzut*	יִרְאָה וָרַעַד יָבֹא בִי וַתְּכַסֵּנִי פַּלָּצוּת:
7	I said, "O that I had the wings of a dove I would fly away and find rest;	*Va'omar mi-yitten-li ever kayyonah a'ufah ve'eshkonah*	וָאֹמַר מִי־יִתֶּן־לִי אֵבֶר כַּיּוֹנָה אָעוּפָה וְאֶשְׁכֹּנָה:
8	surely, I would flee far off; I would lodge in the wilderness; Selah	*Hinneh archik nedod alin bammidbar selah*	הִנֵּה אַרְחִיק נְדֹד אָלִין בַּמִּדְבָּר סֶלָה:
9	I would soon find me a refuge from the sweeping wind, from the tempest."	*Achishah miflat li meruach so'ah missa'ar*	אָחִישָׁה מִפְלָט לִי מֵרוּחַ סֹעָה מִסָּעַר:
10	O Hashem, confound their speech, confuse it! For I see lawlessness and strife in the city;	*Balla Adonai pallag leshonam ki-ra'iti chamas veriv ba'ir*	בַּלַּע אֲדֹנָי פַּלַּג לְשׁוֹנָם כִּי־רָאִיתִי חָמָס וְרִיב בָּעִיר:
11	day and night they make their rounds on its walls; evil and mischief are inside it.	*Yomam valaylah yesovevuha al-chomoteiha ve'aven ve'amal bekirbah*	יוֹמָם וָלַיְלָה יְסוֹבְבֻהָ עַל־חוֹמֹתֶיהָ וְאָוֶן וְעָמָל בְּקִרְבָּהּ:
12	Malice is within it; fraud and deceit never leave its square.	*Havvvot bekirbah velo-yamish merechovah toch umirmah*	הַוּוֹת בְּקִרְבָּהּ וְלֹא־יָמִישׁ מֵרְחֹבָהּ תֹּךְ וּמִרְמָה:
13	It is not an enemy who reviles me —I could bear that; it is not my foe who vaunts himself against me —I could hide from him	*Ki lo-oyev yecharefeni ve'essa lo-mesan'i alai higdil ve'essater mimmennu*	כִּי לֹא־אוֹיֵב יְחָרְפֵנִי וְאֶשָּׂא לֹא־מְשַׂנְאִי עָלַי הִגְדִּיל וְאֶסָּתֵר מִמֶּנּוּ:

14	but it is you, my equal, my companion, my friend;	*Ve'attah enosh ke'erki allufi umeyudda'i*	וְאַתָּה אֱנוֹשׁ כְּעֶרְכִּי אַלּוּפִי וּמְיֻדָּעִי׃	יד
15	sweet was our fellowship; we walked together in Hashem's house.	*Asher yachdav namtik sod beveit elohim nehallech beragesh*	אֲשֶׁר יַחְדָּו נַמְתִּיק סוֹד בְּבֵית אֱלֹהִים נְהַלֵּךְ בְּרָגֶשׁ׃	טו
16	Let Him incite death against them; may they go down alive into Sheol! For where they dwell, there evil is.	*Yshmvt [yashi] [mavet] aleimo yeredu she'ol chayyim ki-ra'ot bimguram bekirbam*	יַשִּׁימָוֶת [יַשִּׁי] [מָוֶת] עָלֵימוֹ יֵרְדוּ שְׁאוֹל חַיִּים כִּי־רָעוֹת בִּמְגוּרָם בְּקִרְבָּם׃	טז
17	As for me, I call to Hashem; Hashem will deliver me.	*Ani el-elohim ekra vaihovah yoshi'eni*	אֲנִי אֶל־אֱלֹהִים אֶקְרָא וַיהֹוָה יוֹשִׁיעֵנִי׃	יז
18	Evening, morning, and noon, I complain and moan, and He hears my voice.	*erev vavoker vetzohorayim asichah ve'ehemeh vayyishma koli*	עֶרֶב וָבֹקֶר וְצָהֳרַיִם אָשִׂיחָה וְאֶהֱמֶה וַיִּשְׁמַע קוֹלִי׃	יח
19	He redeems me unharmed from the battle against me; it is as though many are on my side.	*Padah veshalom nafshi mikkarav-li ki-verabbim hayu immadi*	פָּדָה בְשָׁלוֹם נַפְשִׁי מִקְּרָב־לִי כִּי־בְרַבִּים הָיוּ עִמָּדִי׃	יט
20	Hashem who has reigned from the first, who will have no successor, hears and humbles those who have no fear of Hashem. Selah.	*Yishma el veya'anem veyoshev kedem selah asher ein chalifot lamo velo yaru elohim*	יִשְׁמַע אֵל וְיַעֲנֵם וְיֹשֵׁב קֶדֶם סֶלָה אֲשֶׁר אֵין חֲלִיפוֹת לָמוֹ וְלֹא יָרְאוּ אֱלֹהִים׃	כ

21	He harmed his ally, he broke his pact;	*Shalach yadav bishlomav chillel brito*	שָׁלַח יָדָיו בִּשְׁלֹמָיו חִלֵּל בְּרִיתוֹ:

כא

22	his talk was smoother than butter, yet his mind was on war; his words were more soothing than oil, yet they were drawn swords.	*Chalku machma'ot piv ukarav-libbo rakku devarav mishemen vehemmah fetichot*	חָלְקוּ מַחְמָאֹת פִּיו וּקְרָב־לִבּוֹ רַכּוּ דְבָרָיו מִשֶּׁמֶן וְהֵמָּה פְתִחוֹת:

כב

23	Cast your burden on Hashem and He will sustain you; He will never let the righteous man collapse.	*Hashlech al-Adonai yehavecha vehu yechalkelecha lo-yitten le'olam mot latzaddik*	הַשְׁלֵךְ עַל־יְהֹוָה יְהָבְךָ וְהוּא יְכַלְכְּלֶךָ לֹא־יִתֵּן לְעוֹלָם מוֹט לַצַּדִּיק:

כג

24	For You, O Hashem, will bring them down to the nethermost Pit— those murderous, treacherous men; they shall not live out half their days; but I trust in You.	*Ve'attah elohim toridem liv'er shachat anshei damim umirmah lo-yechetzu yemeihem va'ani evtach-bach*	וְאַתָּה אֱלֹהִים תּוֹרִדֵם לִבְאֵר שַׁחַת אַנְשֵׁי דָמִים וּמִרְמָה לֹא־יֶחֱצוּ יְמֵיהֶם וַאֲנִי אֶבְטַח־בָּךְ:

כד

56

—◦⟨⊗⟩◦—

נ֖ו

1	For the leader; on yonath elem rechokim. Of David. A michtam; when the Philistines seized him in Gath.	*Lammenatzeach al-yonat aylem rechokim ledavid michtam be'echoz oto felishtim begat*	לַמְנַצֵּחַ עַל־יוֹנַת אֵלֶם רְחֹקִים לְדָוִד מִכְתָּם בֶּאֱחֹז אֹתוֹ פְלִשְׁתִּים בְּגַת:

א

2	Have mercy on me, O Hashem, for men persecute me; all day long my adversary oppresses me.	*Channeni elohim ki-she'afani enosh kol-hayyom lochem yilchatzeni*	חָנֵּנִי אֱלֹהִים כִּי־שְׁאָפַנִי אֱנוֹשׁ כָּל־הַיּוֹם לֹחֵם יִלְחָצֵנִי: ב
3	My watchful foes persecute me all day long; many are my adversaries, O Exalted One.	*Sha'afu shorerai kol-hayyom ki-rabbim lochamim li marom*	שָׁאֲפוּ שׁוֹרְרַי כָּל־הַיּוֹם כִּי־רַבִּים לֹחֲמִים לִי מָרוֹם: ג
4	When I am afraid, I trust in You,	*Yom ira ani eleicha evtach*	יוֹם אִירָא אֲנִי אֵלֶיךָ אֶבְטָח: ד
5	in Hashem, whose word I praise, in Hashem I trust; I am not afraid; what can mortals do to me?	*Belohim ahallel devaro belohim batachti lo ira mah-ya'aseh vasar li*	בֵּאלֹהִים אֲהַלֵּל דְּבָרוֹ בֵּאלֹהִים בָּטַחְתִּי לֹא אִירָא מַה־יַּעֲשֶׂה בָשָׂר לִי: ה
6	All day long they cause me grief in my affairs, they plan only evil against me.	*Kol-hayyom devarai ye'atzayvu alai kol-machshevotam lara*	כָּל־הַיּוֹם דְּבָרַי יְעַצֵּבוּ עָלַי כָּל־מַחְשְׁבֹתָם לָרָע: ו
7	They plot, they lie in ambush; they watch my every move, hoping for my death.	*Yaguru [yitzponu] hemmah akevai yishmoru ka'asher kivoo nafshi*	יָגוּרוּ יצפינו [יִצְפֹּנוּ] הֵמָּה עֲקֵבַי יִשְׁמֹרוּ כַּאֲשֶׁר קִוּוּ נַפְשִׁי: ז
8	Cast them out for their evil; subdue peoples in Your anger, O Hashem.	*Al-aven pallet-lamo be'af ammim hored elohim*	עַל־אָוֶן פַּלֶּט־לָמוֹ בְּאַף עַמִּים הוֹרֵד אֱלֹהִים: ח
9	You keep count of my wanderings; put my tears into Your flask, into Your record.	*Nodi safartah attah simah dim'ati venodecha halo besifratecha*	נֹדִי סָפַרְתָּה אַתָּה שִׂימָה דִמְעָתִי בְנֹאדֶךָ הֲלֹא בְּסִפְרָתֶךָ: ט

10	Then my enemies will retreat when I call on You; this I know, that Hashem is for me.	*Az yashuvu oyevai achor beyom ekra zeh-yada'ti ki-elohim li*	אָז יָשׁוּבוּ אוֹיְבַי אָחוֹר בְּיוֹם אֶקְרָא זֶה־יָדַעְתִּי כִּי־אֱלֹהִים לִי:	י
11	In Hashem, whose word I praise, in Hashem, whose word I praise,	*Belohim ahallel davar bAdonai ahallel davar*	בֵּאלֹהִים אֲהַלֵּל דָּבָר בַּיהוָה אֲהַלֵּל דָּבָר:	יא
12	in Hashem I trust; I am not afraid; what can man do to me?	*Belohim batachti lo ira mah-ya'aseh adam li*	בֵּאלֹהִים בָּטַחְתִּי לֹא אִירָא מַה־יַּעֲשֶׂה אָדָם לִי:	יב
13	I must pay my vows to You, O Hashem; I will render thank offerings to You.	*Alai elohim nedareicha ashallem todot lach*	עָלַי אֱלֹהִים נְדָרֶיךָ אֲשַׁלֵּם תּוֹדֹת לָךְ:	יג
14	For You have saved me from death, my foot from stumbling, that I may walk before Hashem in the light of life.	*Ki hitzalta nafshi mimmavet halo ragley middechi lehithallech lifnei elohim be'or hachayyim*	כִּי הִצַּלְתָּ נַפְשִׁי מִמָּוֶת הֲלֹא רַגְלַי מִדֶּחִי לְהִתְהַלֵּךְ לִפְנֵי אֱלֹהִים בְּאוֹר הַחַיִּים:	יד

57

—◦◦◦—

נז

1	For the leader; al tashcheth. Of David. A michtam; when he fled from Shaul into a cave.	*Lammenatzeach al-tashchet ledavid michtam bevorcho mippenei-sha'ul bamme'arah*	לַמְנַצֵּחַ אַל־תַּשְׁחֵת לְדָוִד מִכְתָּם בְּבָרְחוֹ מִפְּנֵי־שָׁאוּל בַּמְּעָרָה:	א

2 | Have mercy on me, O Hashem, have mercy on me, for I seek refuge in You, I seek refuge in the shadow of Your wings, until danger passes. | *Channeni elohim channeni ki vecha chasayah nafshi uvetzel-kenafeicha echseh ad ya'avor havvvot* | חָנֵּנִי אֱלֹהִים חָנֵּנִי כִּי בְךָ חָסָיָה נַפְשִׁי וּבְצֵל־כְּנָפֶיךָ אֶחְסֶה עַד יַעֲבֹר הַוּוֹת: | ב

3 | I call to Hashem Most High, to Hashem who is good to me. | *Ekra lelohim elyon la'el gomer alai* | אֶקְרָא לֵאלֹהִים עֶלְיוֹן לָאֵל גֹּמֵר עָלָי: | ג

4 | He will reach down from heaven and deliver me: Hashem will send down His steadfast love; my persecutor reviles. Selah. | *Yishlach mishamayim veyoshi'eni cheref sho'afi selah yishlach elohim chasdo va'amitto* | יִשְׁלַח מִשָּׁמַיִם וְיוֹשִׁיעֵנִי חֵרֵף שֹׁאֲפִי סֶלָה יִשְׁלַח אֱלֹהִים חַסְדּוֹ וַאֲמִתּוֹ: | ד

5 | As for me, I lie down among man-eating lions whose teeth are spears and arrows, whose tongue is a sharp sword. | *Nafshi betoch leva'im eshkevah lohatim benei-adam shinneihem chanit vechitzim uleshonam cherev chaddah* | נַפְשִׁי בְּתוֹךְ לְבָאִם אֶשְׁכְּבָה לֹהֲטִים בְּנֵי־אָדָם שִׁנֵּיהֶם חֲנִית וְחִצִּים וּלְשׁוֹנָם חֶרֶב חַדָּה: | ה

6 | Exalt Yourself over the heavens, O Hashem, let Your glory be over all the earth! | *Rumah al-hashamayim elohim al kol-ha'aretz kevodecha* | רוּמָה עַל־הַשָּׁמַיִם אֱלֹהִים עַל כָּל־הָאָרֶץ כְּבוֹדֶךָ: | ו

7 | They prepared a net for my feet to ensnare me; they dug a pit for me, but they fell into it. Selah. | *reshet hechinu lif'amai kafaf nafshi karu lefanai shichah naflu vetochah selah* | רֶשֶׁת הֵכִינוּ לִפְעָמַי כָּפַף נַפְשִׁי כָּרוּ לְפָנַי שִׁיחָה נָפְלוּ בְתוֹכָהּ סֶלָה: | ז

140

8	My heart is firm, O Hashem; my heart is firm; I will sing, I will chant a hymn.	*Nachon libbi elohim nachon libbi ashirah va'azammayrah*

נָכוֹן לִבִּי אֱלֹהִים נָכוֹן לִבִּי אָשִׁירָה וַאֲזַמֵּרָה: ח

9	Awake, O my soul! Awake, O harp and lyre! I will wake the dawn.	*Urah chevodi urah hannevel vechinnor a'irah shachar*

עוּרָה כְבוֹדִי עוּרָה הַנֵּבֶל וְכִנּוֹר אָעִירָה שָּׁחַר: ט

10	I will praise You among the peoples, O Hashem; I will sing a hymn to You among the nations;	*Odecha va'ammim Adonai azammercha bal-ummim*

אוֹדְךָ בָעַמִּים אֲדֹנָי אֲזַמֶּרְךָ בַּל־אֻמִּים: י

11	for Your faithfulness is as high as heaven; Your steadfastness reaches to the sky.	*Ki-gadol ad-shamayim chasdecha ve'ad-shechakim amittecha*

כִּי־גָדֹל עַד־שָׁמַיִם חַסְדֶּךָ וְעַד־שְׁחָקִים אֲמִתֶּךָ: יא

12	Exalt Yourself over the heavens, O Hashem, let Your glory be over all the earth!	*Rumah al-shamayim elohim al kol-ha'aretz kevodecha*

רוּמָה עַל־שָׁמַיִם אֱלֹהִים עַל כָּל־הָאָרֶץ כְּבוֹדֶךָ: יב

58

—○⦿⧀⧁⦿○—

נֵ֯ח

1	For the leader; al tashcheth. Of David. A michtam.	*Lammenatzeach al-tashchet ledavid michtam*

לַמְנַצֵּחַ אַל־תַּשְׁחֵת לְדָוִד מִכְתָּם: א

2	O mighty ones, do you really decree what is just? Do you judge mankind with equity?	*Ha'umnam elem tzedek tedabberun meisharim tishpetu benei adam*

הַאֻמְנָם אֵלֶם צֶדֶק תְּדַבֵּרוּן מֵישָׁרִים תִּשְׁפְּטוּ בְּנֵי אָדָם: ב

3
In your minds you devise wrongdoing in the land; with your hands you deal out lawlessness.

Af-belev olot tif'alun ba'aretz chamas yedeichem tefallesun

אַף־בְּלֵב עוֹלֹת תִּפְעָלוּן בָּאָרֶץ חֲמַס יְדֵיכֶם תְּפַלֵּסוּן:
ג

4
The wicked are defiant from birth; the liars go astray from the womb.

Zoru resha'im merachem ta'u mibbeten dovrei chazav

זֹרוּ רְשָׁעִים מֵרָחֶם תָּעוּ מִבֶּטֶן דֹּבְרֵי כָזָב:
ד

5
Their venom is like that of a snake, a deaf viper that stops its ears

Chamat-lamo kidmut chamat-nachash kemo-feten cheresh ya'tem ozno

חֲמַת־לָמוֹ כִּדְמוּת חֲמַת־נָחָשׁ כְּמוֹ־פֶתֶן חֵרֵשׁ יַאְטֵם אָזְנוֹ:
ה

6
so as not to hear the voice of charmers or the expert mutterer of spells.

Asher lo-yishma lekol melachashim chover chavarim mechukkam

אֲשֶׁר לֹא־יִשְׁמַע לְקוֹל מְלַחֲשִׁים חוֹבֵר חֲבָרִים מְחֻכָּם:
ו

7
O Hashem, smash their teeth in their mouth; shatter the fangs of lions, Hashem;

Elohim haras-shinneimo befimo malte'ot kefirim netotz Adonai

אֱלֹהִים הֲרָס־שִׁנֵּימוֹ בְּפִימוֹ מַלְתְּעוֹת כְּפִירִים נְתֹץ יְהֹוָה:
ז

8
let them melt, let them vanish like water; let Him aim His arrows that they be cut down;

Yimma'asu chemo-mayim yithallchu-lamo yidroch chitzav kemo yitmolalu

יִמָּאֲסוּ כְמוֹ־מַיִם יִתְהַלְּכוּ־לָמוֹ יִדְרֹךְ חִצּוֹ [חִצָּיו] כְּמוֹ יִתְמֹלָלוּ:
ח

9
like a snail that melts away as it moves; like a woman's stillbirth, may they never see the sun!

Kemo shabbelul temes yahaloch nefel eshet bal-chazu shamesh

כְּמוֹ שַׁבְּלוּל תֶּמֶס יַהֲלֹךְ נֵפֶל אֵשֶׁת בַּל־חָזוּ שָׁמֶשׁ:
ט

10
Before the thorns grow into a bramble, may He whirl them away alive in fury.

Beterem yavinu siroteichem atad kemo-chai kemo-charon yis'arennu

בְּטֶרֶם יָבִינוּ סִירֹתֵיכֶם אָטָד כְּמוֹ־חַי כְּמוֹ־חָרוֹן יִשְׂעָרֶנּוּ:
י

11	The righteous man will rejoice when he sees revenge; he will bathe his feet in the blood of the wicked.	*Yismach tzaddik ki-chazah nakam pe'amav yirchatz bedam harasha*	יִשְׂמַח צַדִּיק כִּי־חָזָה נָקָם פְּעָמָיו יִרְחַץ בְּדַם הָרָשָׁע:	יא
12	Men will say, "There is, then, a reward for the righteous; there is, indeed, divine justice on earth."	*Veyomar adam ach-peri latzaddik ach yesh-elohim shofetim ba'aretz*	וְיֹאמַר אָדָם אַךְ־פְּרִי לַצַּדִּיק אַךְ יֵשׁ־אֱלֹהִים שֹׁפְטִים בָּאָרֶץ:	יב

59

—○◦◦❈◦◦○—

נט

1	For the leader; al tashcheth. Of David. A michtam; when Shaul sent men to watch his house in order to put him to death.	*Lammenatzeach al-tashchet ledavid michtam bishloach sha'ul vayyishmeru et-habbayit lahamito*	לַמְנַצֵּחַ אַל־תַּשְׁחֵת לְדָוִד מִכְתָּם בִּשְׁלֹחַ שָׁאוּל וַיִּשְׁמְרוּ אֶת־הַבַּיִת לַהֲמִיתוֹ:	א
2	Save me from my enemies, O my God; secure me against my assailants.	*Hatzileni me'oyevai elohai mimitkomemai tesaggeveni*	הַצִּילֵנִי מֵאֹיְבַי אֱלֹהָי מִמִּתְקוֹמְמַי תְּשַׂגְּבֵנִי:	ב
3	Save me from evildoers; deliver me from murderers.	*Hatzileni mippo'alei aven ume'anshei damim hoshi'eni*	הַצִּילֵנִי מִפֹּעֲלֵי אָוֶן וּמֵאַנְשֵׁי דָמִים הוֹשִׁיעֵנִי:	ג
4	For see, they lie in wait for me; fierce men plot against me for no offense of mine, for no transgression, Hashem;	*Ki hinnay arvu lenafshi yaguru alai azim lo-fish'i velo-chattati Adonai*	כִּי הִנֵּה אָרְבוּ לְנַפְשִׁי יָגוּרוּ עָלַי עַזִים לֹא־פִשְׁעִי וְלֹא־חַטָּאתִי יְהוָה:	ד

5	for no guilt of mine, do they rush to array themselves against me. Look, rouse Yourself on my behalf!	*Beli-avon yerutzun veyikkonanu urah likrati ure'eh*	בְּלִי־עָוֺן יְרוּצוּן וְיִכּוֹנָנוּ עוּרָה לִקְרָאתִי וּרְאֵה:	ה
6	You, O lord God of hosts, God of Yisrael, bestir Yourself to bring all nations to account; have no mercy on any treacherous villain. Selah.	*Ve'attah Adonai-elohim tzeva'ot elohei yisra'el hakitzah lifkod kol-haggoyim al-tachon kol-bogedei aven selah*	וְאַתָּה יְהֹוָה־אֱלֹהִים צְבָאוֹת אֱלֹהֵי יִשְׂרָאֵל הָקִיצָה לִפְקֹד כָּל־הַגּוֹיִם אַל־תָּחֹן כָּל־בֹּגְדֵי אָוֶן סֶלָה:	ו
7	They come each evening growling like dogs, roaming the city.	*Yashuvu la'erev yehemu chakkalev visovevu ir*	יָשׁוּבוּ לָעֶרֶב יֶהֱמוּ כַכָּלֶב וִיסוֹבְבוּ עִיר:	ז
8	They rave with their mouths, sharp words are on their lips; [they think,] "Who hears?"	*Hinneh yabbi'un befihem charavot besiftoteihem ki-mi shomea'*	הִנֵּה יַבִּיעוּן בְּפִיהֶם חֲרָבוֹת בְּשִׂפְתוֹתֵיהֶם כִּי־מִי שֹׁמֵעַ:	ח
9	But You, Hashem, laugh at them; You mock all the nations.	*Ve'attah Adonai tischak-lamo til'ag lechol-goyim*	וְאַתָּה יְהֹוָה תִּשְׂחַק־לָמוֹ תִּלְעַג לְכָל־גּוֹיִם:	ט
10	O my strength, I wait for You; for Hashem is my haven.	*Uzzo eleicha eshmorah ki-elohim misgabbi*	עֻזּוֹ אֵלֶיךָ אֶשְׁמֹרָה כִּי־אֱלֹהִים מִשְׂגַּבִּי:	י
11	My faithful God will come to aid me; Hashem will let me gloat over my watchful foes.	*Elohei chasdi yekaddemeni elohim yar'eni veshorerai*	אֱלֹהֵי חסדו [חַסְדִּי] יְקַדְּמֵנִי אֱלֹהִים יַרְאֵנִי בְּשֹׁרְרָי:	יא

12	Do not kill them lest my people be unmindful; with Your power make wanderers of them; bring them low, O our shield, Hashem,	*Al-tahargem pen-yishkechu ammi hani'emo vecheilcha vehoridemo maginnenu Adonai*

אַל־תַּהַרְגֵם פֶּן־יִשְׁכְּחוּ עַמִּי הֲנִיעֵמוֹ בְחֵילְךָ וְהוֹרִידֵמוֹ מָגִנֵּנוּ אֲדֹנָי: יב

13	because of their sinful mouths, the words on their lips. Let them be trapped by their pride, and by the imprecations and lies they utter.	*Chattat-pimo devar-sefateimo veyillachedu vig'onam ume'alah umikkachash yesapperu*

חַטַּאת־פִּימוֹ דְּבַר־שְׂפָתֵימוֹ וְיִלָּכְדוּ בִגְאוֹנָם וּמֵאָלָה וּמִכַּחַשׁ יְסַפֵּרוּ: יג

14	In Your fury put an end to them; put an end to them that they be no more; that it may be known to the ends of the earth that Hashem does rule over Yaakov. Selah.	*Kalleh vechemah kalleh ve'einemo veyede'u ki-elohim moshel beya'akov le'afsei ha'aretz selah*

כַּלֵּה בְחֵמָה כַּלֵּה וְאֵינֵמוֹ וְיֵדְעוּ כִּי־אֱלֹהִים מֹשֵׁל בְּיַעֲקֹב לְאַפְסֵי הָאָרֶץ סֶלָה: יד

15	They come each evening growling like dogs, roaming the city.	*Veyashuvu la'erev yehemu chakkalev visovevu ir*

וְיָשׁוּבוּ לָעֶרֶב יֶהֱמוּ כַכָּלֶב וִיסוֹבְבוּ עִיר: טו

16	They wander in search of food; and whine if they are not satisfied.	*hemmah yeni'un le'echol im-lo yisbe'u vayyalinu*

הֵמָּה ינועון [יְנִיעוּן] לֶאֱכֹל אִם־לֹא יִשְׂבְּעוּ וַיָּלִינוּ: טז

17	But I will sing of Your strength, extol each morning Your faithfulness; for You have been my haven, a refuge in time of trouble.	*Va'ani ashir uzzecha va'arannen labboker chasdecha ki-hayita misgav li umanos beyom tzar-li*

וַאֲנִי אָשִׁיר עֻזֶּךָ וַאֲרַנֵּן לַבֹּקֶר חַסְדֶּךָ כִּי־הָיִיתָ מִשְׂגָּב לִי וּמָנוֹס בְּיוֹם צַר־לִי: יז

18	O my strength, to You I sing hymns; for Hashem is my haven, my faithful Hashem.	*Uzzi eleicha azammerah ki-elohim misgabbi elohei chasdi*	עֻזִּי אֵלֶיךָ אֲזַמֵּרָה כִּי־אֱלֹהִים מִשְׂגַּבִּי אֱלֹהֵי חַסְדִּי: יח

60 —o⟨⟩o— ס

1	For the leader; on shushan eduth. A michtam of David (to be taught),	*Lammenatzeach al-shushan edut michtam ledavid lelammed*	לַמְנַצֵּחַ עַל־שׁוּשַׁן עֵדוּת מִכְתָּם לְדָוִד לְלַמֵּד: א
2	when he fought with Aram-Naharaim and Aram-Zobah, and Yoav returned and defeated Edom—[an army] of twelve thousand men—in the Valley of Salt.	*Behatzoto et aram naharayim ve'et-aram tzovah vayyashov yo'av vayyach et-edom begei-melach sheneim asar alef*	בְּהַצּוֹתוֹ אֶת אֲרַם נַהֲרַיִם וְאֶת־אֲרַם צוֹבָה וַיָּשָׁב יוֹאָב וַיַּךְ אֶת־אֱדוֹם בְּגֵיא־מֶלַח שְׁנֵים עָשָׂר אָלֶף: ב
3	O Hashem, You have rejected us, You have made a breach in us; You have been angry; restore us!	*Elohim zenachtanu feratztanu anafta teshovev lanu*	אֱלֹהִים זְנַחְתָּנוּ פְרַצְתָּנוּ אָנַפְתָּ תְּשׁוֹבֵב לָנוּ: ג
4	You have made the land quake; You have torn it open. Mend its fissures, for it is collapsing.	*Hir'ashtah eretz petzamtah refah shevareiha chi-matah*	הִרְעַשְׁתָּה אֶרֶץ פְּצַמְתָּהּ רְפָה שְׁבָרֶיהָ כִי־מָטָה: ד
5	You have made Your people suffer hardship; You have given us wine that makes us reel.	*Hir'itah amcha kashah hishketanu yayin tar'elah*	הִרְאִיתָה עַמְּךָ קָשָׁה הִשְׁקִיתָנוּ יַיִן תַּרְעֵלָה: ה

6	Give those who fear You because of Your truth a banner for rallying. Selah.	*Natattah lire'eicha nes lehitnoses mippenei koshet selah*	נָתַתָּה לִּירֵאֶיךָ נֵּס לְהִתְנוֹסֵס מִפְּנֵי קֹשֶׁט סֶלָה:
7	That those whom You love might be rescued, deliver with Your right hand and answer me.	*Lema'an yechaletzun yedideicha hoshi'ah yemincha va'aneni*	לְמַעַן יֵחָלְצוּן יְדִידֶיךָ הוֹשִׁיעָה יְמִינְךָ וַעֲנֵנוּ [וַעֲנֵנִי:]
8	Hashem promised in His sanctuary that I would exultingly divide up Shechem, and measure the Valley of Sukkoth;	*elohim dibber bekodsho e'lozah achallekah shechem ve'emek sukkot amadded*	אֱלֹהִים דִּבֶּר בְּקָדְשׁוֹ אֶעְלֹזָה אֲחַלְּקָה שְׁכֶם וְעֵמֶק סֻכּוֹת אֲמַדֵּד:
9	Gilad and Menashe would be mine, Efraim my chief stronghold, Yehuda my scepter;	*Li gil'ad veli menasheh ve'efrayim ma'oz roshi yehudah mechokeki*	לִי גִלְעָד וְלִי מְנַשֶּׁה וְאֶפְרַיִם מָעוֹז רֹאשִׁי יְהוּדָה מְחֹקְקִי:
10	Moab would be my washbasin; on Edom I would cast my shoe; acclaim me, O Philistia!	*Mo'av sir rachtzi al-edom ashlich na'ali alai peleshet hitro'a'i*	מוֹאָב סִיר רַחְצִי עַל־אֱדוֹם אַשְׁלִיךְ נַעֲלִי עָלַי פְּלֶשֶׁת הִתְרֹעָעִי:
11	Would that I were brought to the bastion! Would that I were led to Edom!	*Mi yovileni ir matzor mi nachani ad-edom*	מִי יֹבִלֵנִי עִיר מָצוֹר מִי נָחַנִי עַד־אֱדוֹם:
12	But You have rejected us, O Hashem; Hashem, You do not march with our armies.	*Halo-attah elohim zenachtanu velo-tetze elohim betziv'oteinu*	הֲלֹא־אַתָּה אֱלֹהִים זְנַחְתָּנוּ וְלֹא־תֵצֵא אֱלֹהִים בְּצִבְאוֹתֵינוּ:

| 13 | Grant us Your aid against the foe, for the help of man is worthless. | *Havah-lanu ezrat mitzar veshave teshu'at adam* | הָבָה־לָּנוּ עֶזְרָת מִצָּר וְשָׁוְא תְּשׁוּעַת אָדָם: | יג |

| 14 | With Hashem we shall triumph; He will trample our foes. | *Belohim na'aseh-chayil vehu yavus tzareinu* | בֵּאלֹהִים נַעֲשֶׂה־חָיִל וְהוּא יָבוּס צָרֵינוּ: | יד |

61 —◦⟨❈⟩◦— סא

| 1 | For the leader; with instrumental music. Of David. | *Lammenatzeach al-neginat ledavid* | לַמְנַצֵּחַ עַל־נְגִינַת לְדָוִד: | א |

| 2 | Hear my cry, O Hashem, heed my prayer. | *Shim'ah elohim rinnati hakshivah tefillati* | שִׁמְעָה אֱלֹהִים רִנָּתִי הַקְשִׁיבָה תְּפִלָּתִי: | ב |

| 3 | From the end of the earth I call to You; when my heart is faint, You lead me to a rock that is high above me. | *Miktzeh ha'aretz eleicha ekra ba'atof libbi betzur-yarum mimmenni tancheni* | מִקְצֵה הָאָרֶץ אֵלֶיךָ אֶקְרָא בַּעֲטֹף לִבִּי בְּצוּר־יָרוּם מִמֶּנִּי תַנְחֵנִי: | ג |

| 4 | For You have been my refuge, a tower of strength against the enemy. | *Ki-hayita machseh li migdal-oz mippenei oyev* | כִּי־הָיִיתָ מַחְסֶה לִי מִגְדַּל־עֹז מִפְּנֵי אוֹיֵב: | ד |

| 5 | O that I might dwell in Your tent forever, take refuge under Your protecting wings. Selah. | *Agurah ve'ahalecha olamim echeseh veseter kenafeicha selah* | אָגוּרָה בְאָהָלְךָ עוֹלָמִים אֶחֱסֶה בְסֵתֶר כְּנָפֶיךָ סֶּלָה: | ה |

6	O Hashem, You have heard my vows; grant the request of those who fear Your name.	*Ki-attah elohim shama'ta lindarai natatta yerushat yir'ei shemecha*

כִּי־אַתָּה אֱלֹהִים שָׁמַעְתָּ לִנְדָרָי נָתַתָּ יְרֻשַּׁת יִרְאֵי שְׁמֶךָ: ו

7	Add days to the days of the king; may his years extend through generations;	*Yamim al-yemei-melech tosif shenotav kemo-dor vador*

יָמִים עַל־יְמֵי־מֶלֶךְ תּוֹסִיף שְׁנוֹתָיו כְּמוֹ־דֹר וָדֹר: ז

8	may he dwell in Hashem's presence forever; appoint steadfast love to guard him.	*Yeshev olam lifnei elohim chesed ve'emet man yintzeruhu*

יֵשֵׁב עוֹלָם לִפְנֵי אֱלֹהִים חֶסֶד וֶאֱמֶת מַן יִנְצְרֻהוּ: ח

9	So I will sing hymns to Your name forever, as I fulfill my vows day after day.	*Ken azammerah shimcha la'ad leshallemi nedarai yom yom*

כֵּן אֲזַמְּרָה שִׁמְךָ לָעַד לְשַׁלְּמִי נְדָרַי יוֹם יוֹם: ט

62

—◦○✸○◦—

סב

1	For the leader; on Yedutun. A psalm of David.	*Lammenatzeach al-yedutun mizmor ledavid*

לַמְנַצֵּחַ עַל־יְדוּתוּן מִזְמוֹר לְדָוִד: א

2	Truly my soul waits quietly for Hashem; my deliverance comes from Him.	*Ach el-elohim dumiyyah nafshi mimmennu yeshu'ati*

אַךְ אֶל־אֱלֹהִים דּוּמִיָּה נַפְשִׁי מִמֶּנּוּ יְשׁוּעָתִי: ב

3	Truly He is my rock and deliverance, my haven; I shall never be shaken.	*Ach-hu tzuri vishu'ati misgabbi lo-emmot rabbah*	אַךְ־הוּא צוּרִי וִישׁוּעָתִי מִשְׂגַּבִּי לֹא־אֶמּוֹט רַבָּה:	ג
4	How long will all of you attack a man, to crush him, as though he were a leaning wall, a tottering fence?	*Ad-anah tehotetu al ish teratzechu chullechem kekir natui gader haddechuyah*	עַד־אָנָה תְּהוֹתְתוּ עַל אִישׁ תְּרָצְּחוּ כֻלְּכֶם כְּקִיר נָטוּי גָּדֵר הַדְּחוּיָה:	ד
5	They lay plans to topple him from his rank; they delight in falsehood; they bless with their mouths, while inwardly they curse. Selah.	*Ach misse'eto ya'atzu lehaddiach yirtzu chazav befiv yevarechu uvekirbam yekallu-selah*	אַךְ מִשְּׂאֵתוֹ יָעֲצוּ לְהַדִּיחַ יִרְצוּ כָזָב בְּפִיו יְבָרֵכוּ וּבְקִרְבָּם יְקַלְלוּ־סֶלָה:	ה
6	Truly, wait quietly for Hashem, O my soul, for my hope comes from Him.	*Ach lelohim dommi nafshi ki-mimmennu tikvati*	אַךְ לֵאלֹהִים דּוֹמִּי נַפְשִׁי כִּי־מִמֶּנּוּ תִּקְוָתִי:	ו
7	He is my rock and deliverance, my haven; I shall not be shaken.	*Ach-hu tzuri vishu'ati misgabbi lo emmot*	אַךְ־הוּא צוּרִי וִישׁוּעָתִי מִשְׂגַּבִּי לֹא אֶמּוֹט:	ז
8	I rely on Hashem, my deliverance and glory, my rock of strength; in Hashem is my refuge.	*Al-elohim yish'i uchevodi tzur-uzzi machsi belohim*	עַל־אֱלֹהִים יִשְׁעִי וּכְבוֹדִי צוּר־עֻזִּי מַחְסִי בֵּאלֹהִים:	ח
9	Trust in Him at all times, O people; pour out your hearts before Him; Hashem is our refuge. Selah.	*Bitchu vo vechol-et am shifchu-lefanav levavchem elohim machaseh-lanu selah*	בִּטְחוּ בוֹ בְכָל־עֵת עָם שִׁפְכוּ־לְפָנָיו לְבַבְכֶם אֱלֹהִים מַחֲסֶה־לָּנוּ סֶלָה:	ט

10 Men are mere breath; mortals, illusion; placed on a scale all together, they weigh even less than a breath.

Ach hevel benei-adam kazav benei ish bemoznayim la'alot heymah mehevel yachad

אַךְ הֶבֶל בְּנֵי־אָדָם כָּזָב בְּנֵי אִישׁ בְּמֹאזְנַיִם לַעֲלוֹת הֵמָּה מֵהֶבֶל יָחַד׃ י

11 Do not trust in violence, or put false hopes in robbery; if force bears fruit pay it no mind.

Al-tivtechu ve'oshek uvegazel al-tehbalu chayil ki-yanuv al-tashitu lev

אַל־תִּבְטְחוּ בְעֹשֶׁק וּבְגָזֵל אַל־תֶּהְבָּלוּ חַיִל כִּי־יָנוּב אַל־תָּשִׁיתוּ לֵב׃ יא

12 One thing Hashem has spoken; two things have I heard: that might belongs to Hashem,

Achat dibber elohim shetayim-zu shama'eti ki oz lelohim

אַחַת דִּבֶּר אֱלֹהִים שְׁתַּיִם־זוּ שָׁמָעְתִּי כִּי עֹז לֵאלֹהִים׃ יב

13 and faithfulness is Yours, O Hashem, to reward each man according to his deeds.

Ulecha-Adonai chasad ki-attah teshallem le'ish kema'asehu

וּלְךָ־אֲדֹנָי חָסֶד כִּי־אַתָּה תְשַׁלֵּם לְאִישׁ כְּמַעֲשֵׂהוּ׃ יג

63

─○─✕✕✕─○─

סג

1 A psalm of David, when he was in the Wilderness of Yehuda.

Mizmor ledavid bihyoto bemidbar yehudah

מִזְמוֹר לְדָוִד בִּהְיוֹתוֹ בְּמִדְבַּר יְהוּדָה׃ א

2 Hashem, You are my God; I search for You, my soul thirsts for You, my body yearns for You, as a parched and thirsty land that has no water.

Elohim eli attah ashacharekka tzame'ah lecha nafshi kamah lecha vesari be'eretz-tziyyah ve'ayef beli-mayim

אֱלֹהִים אֵלִי אַתָּה אֲשַׁחֲרֶךָּ צָמְאָה לְךָ נַפְשִׁי כָּמַהּ לְךָ בְשָׂרִי בְּאֶרֶץ־צִיָּה וְעָיֵף בְּלִי־מָיִם׃ ב

3	I shall behold You in the sanctuary, and see Your might and glory,	*Ken bakkodesh chaziticha lir'ot uzzecha uchevodecha*	כֵּן בַּקֹּדֶשׁ חֲזִיתִיךָ לִרְאוֹת עֻזְּךָ וּכְבוֹדֶךָ:	ג
4	Truly Your faithfulness is better than life; my lips declare Your praise.	*Ki-tov chasdecha mechayyim sefatai yeshabbechunecha*	כִּי־טוֹב חַסְדְּךָ מֵחַיִּים שְׂפָתַי יְשַׁבְּחוּנֶךָ:	ד
5	I bless You all my life; I lift up my hands, invoking Your name.	*Ken avarechcha vechayyai beshimcha essa chappai*	כֵּן אֲבָרֶכְךָ בְחַיָּי בְּשִׁמְךָ אֶשָּׂא כַפָּי:	ה
6	I am sated as with a rich feast, I sing praises with joyful lips	*Kemo chelev vadeshen tisba nafshi vesiftei renanot yehallel-pi*	כְּמוֹ חֵלֶב וָדֶשֶׁן תִּשְׂבַּע נַפְשִׁי וְשִׂפְתֵי רְנָנוֹת יְהַלֶּל־פִּי:	ו
7	when I call You to mind upon my bed, when I think of You in the watches of the night;	*Im-zecharticha al-yetzu'ai be'ashmurot ehgeh-bach*	אִם־זְכַרְתִּיךָ עַל־יְצוּעָי בְּאַשְׁמֻרוֹת אֶהְגֶּה־בָּךְ:	ז
8	for You are my help, and in the shadow of Your wings I shout for joy.	*Ki-hayita ezratah li uvetzel kenafeicha arannen*	כִּי־הָיִיתָ עֶזְרָתָה לִּי וּבְצֵל כְּנָפֶיךָ אֲרַנֵּן:	ח
9	My soul is attached to You; Your right hand supports me.	*Davekah nafshi achareicha bi tamechah yeminecha*	דָּבְקָה נַפְשִׁי אַחֲרֶיךָ בִּי תָּמְכָה יְמִינֶךָ:	ט
10	May those who seek to destroy my life enter the depths of the earth.	*Vehemmah lesho'ah yevakshu nafshi yavo'u betachtiyyot ha'aretz*	וְהֵמָּה לְשׁוֹאָה יְבַקְשׁוּ נַפְשִׁי יָבֹאוּ בְּתַחְתִּיּוֹת הָאָרֶץ:	י

11	May they be gutted by the sword; may they be prey to jackals.	*Yaggiruhu al-yedei-charev menat shu'alim yihyu*	יַגִּירֻהוּ עַל־יְדֵי־חָרֶב מְנָת שֻׁעָלִים יִהְיוּ:	יא
12	But the king shall rejoice in Hashem; all who swear by Him shall exult, when the mouth of liars is stopped.	*Vehammelech yismach belohim yithallel kol-hannishba bo ki yissacher pi doverei-shaker*	וְהַמֶּלֶךְ יִשְׂמַח בֵּאלֹהִים יִתְהַלֵּל כָּל־הַנִּשְׁבָּע בּוֹ כִּי יִסָּכֵר פִּי דוֹבְרֵי־שָׁקֶר:	יב

64

—◦⬡◦—

סד

1	For the leader. A psalm of David.	*Lammenatzeach mizmor ledavid*	לַמְנַצֵּחַ מִזְמוֹר לְדָוִד:	א
2	Hear my voice, O Hashem, when I plead; guard my life from the enemy's terror.	*Shema-elohim koli vesichi mippachad oyev titzor chayyai*	שְׁמַע־אֱלֹהִים קוֹלִי בְשִׂיחִי מִפַּחַד אוֹיֵב תִּצֹּר חַיָּי:	ב
3	Hide me from a band of evil men, from a crowd of evildoers,	*Tastireni missod mere'im merigshat po'alei aven*	תַּסְתִּירֵנִי מִסּוֹד מְרֵעִים מֵרִגְשַׁת פֹּעֲלֵי אָוֶן:	ג
4	who whet their tongues like swords; they aim their arrows—cruel words—	*Asher shanenu chacherev leshonam darechu chitzam davar mar*	אֲשֶׁר שָׁנְנוּ כַחֶרֶב לְשׁוֹנָם דָּרְכוּ חִצָּם דָּבָר מָר:	ד

5	to shoot from hiding at the blameless man; they shoot him suddenly and without fear.	*Lirot bammistarim tam pit'om yoruhu velo yira'u*	לִירוֹת בַּמִּסְתָּרִים תָּם פִּתְאֹם יֹרֻהוּ וְלֹא יִירָאוּ: ה
6	They arm themselves with an evil word; when they speak, it is to conceal traps; they think, "Who will see them?"	*Yechazzeku-lamo davar ra yesapperu litmon mokeshim ameru mi yir'eh-lamo*	יְחַזְּקוּ־לָמוֹ דָּבָר רָע יְסַפְּרוּ לִטְמוֹן מוֹקְשִׁים אָמְרוּ מִי יִרְאֶה־לָּמוֹ: ו
7	Let the wrongdoings they have concealed, each one inside him, his secret thoughts, be wholly exposed.	*Yachpesu-olot tamnu chefes mechuppas vekerev ish velev amok*	יַחְפְּשׂוּ־עוֹלֹת תַּמְנוּ חֵפֶשׂ מְחֻפָּשׂ וְקֶרֶב אִישׁ וְלֵב עָמֹק: ז
8	Hashem shall shoot them with arrows; they shall be struck down suddenly.	*Vayyorem elohim chetz pit'om hayu makkotam*	וַיֹּרֵם אֱלֹהִים חֵץ פִּתְאוֹם הָיוּ מַכּוֹתָם: ח
9	Their tongue shall be their downfall; all who see them shall recoil in horror;	*Vayyachshiluhu aleimo leshonam yitnodadu kol-ro'ay vam*	וַיַּכְשִׁילוּהוּ עָלֵימוֹ לְשׁוֹנָם יִתְנֹדְדוּ כָּל־רֹאֵה בָם: ט
10	all men shall stand in awe; they shall proclaim the work of Hashem and His deed which they perceived.	*Vayyir'u kol-adam vayyaggidu po'al elohim uma'asehu hiskilu*	וַיִּירְאוּ כָּל־אָדָם וַיַּגִּידוּ פֹּעַל אֱלֹהִים וּמַעֲשֵׂהוּ הִשְׂכִּילוּ: י
11	The righteous shall rejoice in Hashem, and take refuge in Him; all the upright shall exult.	*Yismach tzaddik bAdonai vechasah vo veyithallu kol-yishrei-lev*	יִשְׂמַח צַדִּיק בַּיהוָה וְחָסָה בוֹ וְיִתְהַלְלוּ כָּל־יִשְׁרֵי־לֵב: יא

65

—◦❈◦—

סה

1	For the leader. A psalm of David. A song.	*Lammenatzeach mizmor ledavid shir*	לַמְנַצֵּחַ מִזְמוֹר לְדָוִד שִׁיר: א
2	Praise befits You in Tzion, O Hashem; vows are paid to You;	*Lecha dumiyyah tehillah elohim betziyyon ulecha yeshullam-neder*	לְךָ דֻמִיָּה תְהִלָּה אֱלֹהִים בְּצִיּוֹן וּלְךָ יְשֻׁלַּם־נֶדֶר: ב
3	all mankind comes to You, You who hear prayer.	*Shomea' tefillah adeicha kol-basar yavo'u*	שֹׁמֵעַ תְּפִלָּה עָדֶיךָ כָּל־ בָּשָׂר יָבֹאוּ: ג
4	When all manner of sins overwhelm me, it is You who forgive our iniquities.	*Divrei avnot gavru menni pesha'einu attah techapperem*	דִּבְרֵי עֲוֹנֹת גָּבְרוּ מֶנִּי פְּשָׁעֵינוּ אַתָּה תְכַפְּרֵם: ד
5	Happy is the man You choose and bring near to dwell in Your courts; may we be sated with the blessings of Your house, Your holy temple.	*Ashrei tivchar utekarev yishkon chatzereicha nisbe'ah betuv beitecha kedosh heichalecha*	אַשְׁרֵי תִּבְחַר וּתְקָרֵב יִשְׁכֹּן חֲצֵרֶיךָ נִשְׂבְּעָה בְּטוּב בֵּיתֶךָ קְדֹשׁ הֵיכָלֶךָ: ה
6	Answer us with victory through awesome deeds, O Hashem, our deliverer, in whom all the ends of the earth and the distant seas put their trust;	*Nora'ot betzedek ta'anenu elohei yish'enu mivtach kol-katzvei-eretz veyam rechokim*	נוֹרָאוֹת בְּצֶדֶק תַּעֲנֵנוּ אֱלֹהֵי יִשְׁעֵנוּ מִבְטָח כָּל־ קַצְוֵי־אֶרֶץ וְיָם רְחֹקִים: ו

7	who by His power fixed the mountains firmly, who is girded with might,	*Mechin harim bechocho ne'zar bigvurah*	מֵכִין הָרִים בְּכֹחוֹ נֶאְזָר בִּגְבוּרָה: ז
8	who stills the raging seas, the raging waves, and tumultuous peoples.	*Mashbiach she'on yammim she'on galleihem vahamon le'ummim*	מַשְׁבִּיחַ שְׁאוֹן יַמִּים שְׁאוֹן גַּלֵּיהֶם וַהֲמוֹן לְאֻמִּים: ח
9	Those who live at the ends of the earth are awed by Your signs; You make the lands of sunrise and sunset shout for joy.	*Vayyir'u yoshevei ketzavot me'ototeicha motza'ei-voker va'erev tarnin*	וַיִּירְאוּ יֹשְׁבֵי קְצָוֹת מֵאוֹתֹתֶיךָ מוֹצָאֵי-בֹקֶר וָעֶרֶב תַּרְנִין: ט
10	You take care of the earth and irrigate it; You enrich it greatly, with the channel of Hashem full of water; You provide grain for men; for so do You prepare it.	*Pakadta ha'aretz vatteshokekeha rabbat ta'sherennah peleg elohim malay mayim tachin deganam ki-chen techineha*	פָּקַדְתָּ הָאָרֶץ וַתְּשֹׁקְקֶהָ רַבַּת תַּעְשְׁרֶנָּה פֶּלֶג אֱלֹהִים מָלֵא מָיִם תָּכִין דְּגָנָם כִּי-כֵן תְּכִינֶהָ: י
11	Saturating its furrows, leveling its ridges, You soften it with showers, You bless its growth.	*Telameiha ravveh nachet gedudeiha birvivim temogegennah tzimchah tevarech*	תְּלָמֶיהָ רַוֵּה נַחֵת גְּדוּדֶיהָ בִּרְבִיבִים תְּמֹגְגֶנָּה צִמְחָהּ תְּבָרֵךְ: יא
12	You crown the year with Your bounty; fatness is distilled in Your paths;	*Ittarta shenat tovatecha uma'galeicha yir'afun dashen*	עִטַּרְתָּ שְׁנַת טוֹבָתֶךָ וּמַעְגָּלֶיךָ יִרְעֲפוּן דָּשֶׁן: יב
13	the pasturelands distill it; the hills are girded with joy.	*Yir'afu ne'ot midbar vegil geva'ot tachgornah*	יִרְעֲפוּ נְאוֹת מִדְבָּר וְגִיל גְּבָעוֹת תַּחְגֹּרְנָה: יג

14 The meadows are clothed with flocks, the valleys mantled with grain; they raise a shout, they break into song.

Lavshu charim hatzon va'amakim ya'atfu-var yitro'a'u af-yashiru

לָבְשׁוּ כָרִים הַצֹּאן וַעֲמָקִים יַעַטְפוּ־בָר יִתְרוֹעֲעוּ אַף־יָשִׁירוּ: יד

66

—◦⊂⬡⬡⊃◦—

סו

1 For the leader. A song. A psalm. Raise a shout for Hashem, all the earth;

Lammenatzeach shir mizmor hari'u lelohim kol-ha'aretz

לַמְנַצֵּחַ שִׁיר מִזְמוֹר הָרִיעוּ לֵאלֹהִים כָּל־הָאָרֶץ: א

2 sing the glory of His name, make glorious His praise.

Zammeru chevod-shemo simu chavod tehillato

זַמְּרוּ כְבוֹד־שְׁמוֹ שִׂימוּ כָבוֹד תְּהִלָּתוֹ: ב

3 Say to Hashem, "How awesome are Your deeds, Your enemies cower before Your great strength;

Imru lelohim mah-nora ma'aseicha berov uzzecha yechachashu lecha oyeveicha

אִמְרוּ לֵאלֹהִים מַה־נּוֹרָא מַעֲשֶׂיךָ בְּרֹב עֻזְּךָ יְכַחֲשׁוּ לְךָ אֹיְבֶיךָ: ג

4 all the earth bows to You, and sings hymns to You; all sing hymns to Your name." Selah.

Kol-ha'aretz yishtachavu lecha vizammeru-lach yezammeru shimcha selah

כָּל־הָאָרֶץ יִשְׁתַּחֲווּ לְךָ וִיזַמְּרוּ־לָךְ יְזַמְּרוּ שִׁמְךָ סֶלָה: ד

5 Come and see the works of Hashem, who is held in awe by men for His acts.

Lechu ure'u mif'alot elohim nora alilah al-benei adam

לְכוּ וּרְאוּ מִפְעֲלוֹת אֱלֹהִים נוֹרָא עֲלִילָה עַל־בְּנֵי אָדָם: ה

6	He turned the sea into dry land; they crossed the river on foot; we therefore rejoice in Him.	*Hafach yam leyabbashah bannahar ya'avru veragel sham nismechah-bo*	הָפַךְ יָם לְיַבָּשָׁה בַּנָּהָר יַעַבְרוּ בְרָגֶל שָׁם נִשְׂמְחָה־בּוֹ׃	ו
7	He rules forever in His might; His eyes scan the nations; let the rebellious not assert themselves. Selah.	*Moshel bigvurato olam einav baggoyim titzpeinah hassorerim al-yarumu lamo selah*	מֹשֵׁל בִּגְבוּרָתוֹ עוֹלָם עֵינָיו בַּגּוֹיִם תִּצְפֶּינָה הַסּוֹרְרִים אַל־יָרִימוּ [יָרוּמוּ] לָמוֹ סֶלָה׃	ז
8	O peoples, bless our God, celebrate His praises;	*Barechu ammim eloheinu vehashmi'u kol tehillato*	בָּרְכוּ עַמִּים אֱלֹהֵינוּ וְהַשְׁמִיעוּ קוֹל תְּהִלָּתוֹ׃	ח
9	who has granted us life, and has not let our feet slip.	*Hassam nafshaynu bachayyim velo-natan lammot raglaynu*	הַשָּׂם נַפְשֵׁנוּ בַּחַיִּים וְלֹא־נָתַן לַמּוֹט רַגְלֵנוּ׃	ט
10	You have tried us, O Hashem, refining us, as one refines silver.	*Ki-vechantanu elohim tzeraftanu kitzraf-kasef*	כִּי־בְחַנְתָּנוּ אֱלֹהִים צְרַפְתָּנוּ כִּצְרָף־כָּסֶף׃	י
11	You have caught us in a net, caught us in trammels.	*Havetanu vammetzudah samta mu'akah vematneinu*	הֲבֵאתָנוּ בַמְּצוּדָה שַׂמְתָּ מוּעָקָה בְמָתְנֵינוּ׃	יא
12	You have let men ride over us; we have endured fire and water, and You have brought us through to prosperity.	*Hirkavta enosh leroshenu banu-va'esh uvammayim vattotzi'enu larevayah*	הִרְכַּבְתָּ אֱנוֹשׁ לְרֹאשֵׁנוּ בָּאנוּ־בָאֵשׁ וּבַמַּיִם וַתּוֹצִיאֵנוּ לָרְוָיָה׃	יב
13	I enter Your house with burnt offerings, I pay my vows to You,	*Avo veitcha ve'olot ashallem lecha nedarai*	אָבוֹא בֵיתְךָ בְעוֹלוֹת אֲשַׁלֵּם לְךָ נְדָרָי׃	יג

14	[vows] that my lips pronounced, that my mouth uttered in my distress.	*Asher-patzu sefatai vedeber-pi batzar-li*	אֲשֶׁר־פָּצוּ שְׂפָתָי וְדִבֶּר־פִּי בַּצַּר־לִי: יד
15	I offer up fatlings to You, with the odor of burning rams; I sacrifice bulls and he-goats. Selah.	*Olot mechim a'aleh-lach im-ketoret eilim e'eseh vakar im-attudim selah*	עֹלוֹת מֵחִים אַעֲלֶה־לָּךְ עִם־קְטֹרֶת אֵילִים אֶעֱשֶׂה בָקָר עִם־עַתּוּדִים סֶלָה: טו
16	Come and hear, all Hashem-fearing men, as I tell what He did for me.	*Lechu-shim'u va'asapperah kol-yir'ei elohim asher asah lenafshi*	לְכוּ־שִׁמְעוּ וַאֲסַפְּרָה כָּל־יִרְאֵי אֱלֹהִים אֲשֶׁר עָשָׂה לְנַפְשִׁי: טז
17	I called aloud to Him, glorification on my tongue.	*Aylav pi-karati veromam tachat leshoni*	אֵלָיו פִּי־קָרָאתִי וְרוֹמַם תַּחַת לְשׁוֹנִי: יז
18	Had I an evil thought in my mind, Hashem would not have listened.	*aven im-ra'iti velibbi lo yishma Adonai*	אָוֶן אִם־רָאִיתִי בְלִבִּי לֹא יִשְׁמַע אֲדֹנָי: יח
19	But Hashem did listen; He paid heed to my prayer.	*Achen shama elohim hikshiv bekol tefillati*	אָכֵן שָׁמַע אֱלֹהִים הִקְשִׁיב בְּקוֹל תְּפִלָּתִי: יט
20	Blessed is Hashem who has not turned away my prayer, or His faithful care from me.	*Baruch elohim asher lo-hayesir tefillati vechasdo me'itti*	בָּרוּךְ אֱלֹהִים אֲשֶׁר לֹא־הֵסִיר תְּפִלָּתִי וְחַסְדּוֹ מֵאִתִּי: כ

67

א

1	For the leader; with instrumental music. A psalm. A song.	*Lammenatzech binginot mizmor shir*	לַמְנַצֵּחַ בִּנְגִינֹת מִזְמוֹר שִׁיר:

ב

| 2 | May Hashem be gracious to us and bless us; may He show us favor, selah | *Elohim yechonnenu vivarechenu ya'er panav ittanu selah* | אֱלֹהִים יְחָנֵּנוּ וִיבָרְכֵנוּ יָאֵר פָּנָיו אִתָּנוּ סֶלָה: |

ג

| 3 | that Your way be known on earth, Your deliverance among all nations. | *Lada'at ba'aretz darkecha bechol-goyim yeshu'atecha* | לָדַעַת בָּאָרֶץ דַּרְכֶּךָ בְּכָל־גּוֹיִם יְשׁוּעָתֶךָ: |

ד

| 4 | Peoples will praise You, O Hashem; all peoples will praise You. | *Yoducha ammim elohim yoducha ammim kullam* | יוֹדוּךָ עַמִּים אֱלֹהִים יוֹדוּךָ עַמִּים כֻּלָּם: |

ה

| 5 | Nations will exult and shout for joy, for You rule the peoples with equity, You guide the nations of the earth. Selah. | *Yismechu virannenu le'ummim ki-tishpot ammim mishor ule'ummim ba'aretz tanchem selah* | יִשְׂמְחוּ וִירַנְּנוּ לְאֻמִּים כִּי־תִשְׁפֹּט עַמִּים מִישׁוֹר וּלְאֻמִּים בָּאָרֶץ תַּנְחֵם סֶלָה: |

ו

| 6 | The peoples will praise You, O Hashem; all peoples will praise You. | *Yoducha ammim elohim yoducha ammim kullam* | יוֹדוּךָ עַמִּים אֱלֹהִים יוֹדוּךָ עַמִּים כֻּלָּם: |

ז

| 7 | May the earth yield its produce; may Hashem, our God, bless us. | *eretz natnah yevulah yevarechenu elohim eloheinu* | אֶרֶץ נָתְנָה יְבוּלָהּ יְבָרְכֵנוּ אֱלֹהִים אֱלֹהֵינוּ: |

ח

8 May Hashem bless us, and be revered to the ends of the earth.

Yevarchenu elohim veyir'u oto kol-afsei-aretz

יְבָרְכֵנוּ אֱלֹהִים וְיִירְאוּ אֹתוֹ כָּל־אַפְסֵי־אָרֶץ: ט

68

⎯○⦅✸⦆○⎯

סח

1 For the leader. Of David. A psalm. A song.

Lammenatzeach ledavid mizmor shir

לַמְנַצֵּחַ לְדָוִד מִזְמוֹר שִׁיר: א

2 Hashem will arise, His enemies shall be scattered, His foes shall flee before Him.

Yakum elohim yafutzu oyevav veyanusu mesan'av mippanav

יָקוּם אֱלֹהִים יָפוּצוּ אוֹיְבָיו וְיָנוּסוּ מְשַׂנְאָיו מִפָּנָיו: ב

3 Disperse them as smoke is dispersed; as wax melts at fire, so the wicked shall perish before Hashem.

Kehindof ashan tindof kehimmes donag mippenei-esh yovdu resha'im mippenei elohim

כְּהִנְדֹּף עָשָׁן תִּנְדֹּף כְּהִמֵּס דּוֹנַג מִפְּנֵי־אֵשׁ יֹאבְדוּ רְשָׁעִים מִפְּנֵי אֱלֹהִים: ג

4 But the righteous shall rejoice; they shall exult in the presence of Hashem; they shall be exceedingly joyful.

Vetzaddikim yismechu ya'altzu lifnei elohim veyasisu vesimchah

וְצַדִּיקִים יִשְׂמְחוּ יַעַלְצוּ לִפְנֵי אֱלֹהִים וְיָשִׂישׂוּ בְשִׂמְחָה: ד

5 Sing to Hashem, chant hymns to His name; extol Him who rides the clouds; Hashem is His name. Exult in His presence—

shiru lelohim zammeru shemo sollu larochev ba'aravot beyah shemo ve'ilzu lefanav

שִׁירוּ לֵאלֹהִים זַמְּרוּ שְׁמוֹ סֹלּוּ לָרֹכֵב בָּעֲרָבוֹת בְּיָהּ שְׁמוֹ וְעִלְזוּ לְפָנָיו: ה

6	the father of orphans, the Champion of widows, Hashem, in His holy habitation.	*Avi yetomim vedayyan almanot elohim bim'on kodsho*	אֲבִי יְתוֹמִים וְדַיַּן אַלְמָנוֹת אֱלֹהִים בִּמְעוֹן קׇדְשׁוֹ:	ו
7	Hashem restores the lonely to their homes, sets free the imprisoned, safe and sound, while the rebellious must live in a parched land.	*Elohim moshiv yechidim bayyetah motzi asirim bakkosharot ach sorarim shachenu tzechichah*	אֱלֹהִים מוֹשִׁיב יְחִידִים בַּיְתָה מוֹצִיא אֲסִירִים בַּכּוֹשָׁרוֹת אַךְ סוֹרֲרִים שָׁכְנוּ צְחִיחָה:	ז
8	O Hashem, when You went at the head of Your army, when You marched through the desert, selah	*Elohim betzetcha lifnei ammecha betza'decha vishimon selah*	אֱלֹהִים בְּצֵאתְךָ לִפְנֵי עַמֶּךָ בְּצַעְדְּךָ בִישִׁימוֹן סֶלָה:	ח
9	the earth trembled, the sky rained because of Hashem, yon Sinai, because of Hashem, the God of Yisrael.	*Eretz ra'ashah af-shamayim natfu mippenei elohim zeh sinai mippenei elohim elohei yisra'el*	אֶרֶץ רָעָשָׁה אַף־שָׁמַיִם נָטְפוּ מִפְּנֵי אֱלֹהִים זֶה סִינַי מִפְּנֵי אֱלֹהִים אֱלֹהֵי יִשְׂרָאֵל:	ט
10	You released a bountiful rain, O Hashem; when Your own land languished, You sustained it.	*Geshem nedavot tanif elohim nachalatcha venil'ah attah chonantah*	גֶּשֶׁם נְדָבוֹת תָּנִיף אֱלֹהִים נַחֲלָתְךָ וְנִלְאָה אַתָּה כוֹנַנְתָּהּ:	י
11	Your tribe dwells there; O Hashem, in Your goodness You provide for the needy.	*Chayyatcha yashevu-vah tachin betovatcha le'ani Elohim*	חַיָּתְךָ יָשְׁבוּ־בָהּ תָּכִין בְּטוֹבָתְךָ לֶעָנִי אֱלֹהִים:	יא
12	Hashem gives a command; the women who bring the news are a great host:	*Adonai yitten-omer hammevasserot tzava rav*	אֲדֹנָי יִתֶּן־אֹמֶר הַמְבַשְּׂרוֹת צָבָא רָב:	יב

13	"The kings and their armies are in headlong flight; housewives are sharing in the spoils;	*Malchei tzeva'ot yiddodun yiddodun unevat bayit techallek shalal*	מַלְכֵי צְבָאוֹת יִדֹּדוּן יִדֹּדוּן וּנְוַת בַּיִת תְּחַלֵּק שָׁלָל: יג
14	even for those of you who lie among the sheepfolds there are wings of a dove sheathed in silver, its pinions in fine gold."	*Im-tishkevun bein shefattayim kanfei yonah nechpah vakkesef ve'evroteiha birakrak charutz*	אִם־תִּשְׁכְּבוּן בֵּין שְׁפַתָּיִם כַּנְפֵי יוֹנָה נֶחְפָּה בַכֶּסֶף וְאֶבְרוֹתֶיהָ בִּירַקְרַק חָרוּץ: יד
15	When Shaddai scattered the kings, it seemed like a snowstorm in Zalmon.	*Befares shaddai melachim bah tashleg betzalmon*	בְּפָרֵשׂ שַׁדַּי מְלָכִים בָּהּ תַּשְׁלֵג בְּצַלְמוֹן: טו
16	O majestic mountain, Mount Bashan; O jagged mountain, Mount Bashan;	*Har-elohim har-bashan har gavnunnim har-bashan*	הַר־אֱלֹהִים הַר־בָּשָׁן הַר גַּבְנֻנִּים הַר־בָּשָׁן: טז
17	why so hostile, O jagged mountains, toward the mountain Hashem desired as His dwelling? Hashem shall abide there forever.	*Lammah teratzdun harim gavnunnim hahar chamad Elohim leshivto af-Adonai yishkon lanetzach*	לָמָּה תְּרַצְּדוּן הָרִים גַּבְנֻנִּים הָהָר חָמַד אֱלֹהִים לְשִׁבְתּוֹ אַף־יְהֹוָה יִשְׁכֹּן לָנֶצַח: יז
18	Hashem's chariots are myriads upon myriads, thousands upon thousands; Hashem is among them as in Sinai in holiness.	*Rechev Elohim ribbotayim alfei shin'an Adonai vam sinai bakkodesh*	רֶכֶב אֱלֹהִים רִבֹּתַיִם אַלְפֵי שִׁנְאָן אֲדֹנָי בָם סִינַי בַּקֹּדֶשׁ: יח

19	You went up to the heights, having taken captives, having received tribute of men, even of those who rebel against Hashem's abiding there.	*Alita lammarom shavita shevi lakachta mattanot ba'adam ve'af sorerim lishkon yah elohim*	עָלִיתָ לַמָּרוֹם שָׁבִיתָ שֶּׁבִי לָקַחְתָּ מַתָּנוֹת בָּאָדָם וְאַף סוֹרְרִים לִשְׁכֹּן יָהּ אֱלֹהִים:	יט
20	Blessed is Hashem. Day by day He supports us, Hashem, our deliverance. Selah.	*Baruch Adonai yom yom ya'amas-lanu ha'el yeshu'atenu selah*	בָּרוּךְ אֲדֹנָי יוֹם יוֹם יַעֲמָס־לָנוּ הָאֵל יְשׁוּעָתֵנוּ סֶלָה:	כ
21	Hashem is for us a God of deliverance; Hashem the Lord provides an escape from death.	*Ha'el lanu el lemosha'ot vel'Elohim Adonai lammavet totza'ot*	הָאֵל לָנוּ אֵל לְמוֹשָׁעוֹת וְלֵיהוָה אֲדֹנָי לַמָּוֶת תּוֹצָאוֹת:	כא
22	Hashem will smash the heads of His enemies, the hairy crown of him who walks about in his guilt.	*Ach-Elohim yimchatz rosh oyevav kadekod se'ar mithallech ba'ashamav*	אַךְ־אֱלֹהִים יִמְחַץ רֹאשׁ אֹיְבָיו קָדְקֹד שֵׂעָר מִתְהַלֵּךְ בַּאֲשָׁמָיו:	כב
23	Hashem said, "I will retrieve from Bashan, I will retrieve from the depths of the sea;	*Amar Adonai mibbashan ashiv ashiv mimmetzulot yam*	אָמַר אֲדֹנָי מִבָּשָׁן אָשִׁיב אָשִׁיב מִמְּצֻלוֹת יָם:	כג
24	that your feet may wade through blood; that the tongue of your dogs may have its portion of your enemies."	*Lema'an timchatz raglecha bedam leshon kelavecha me'oyevim minnehu*	לְמַעַן תִּמְחַץ רַגְלְךָ בְּדָם לְשׁוֹן כְּלָבֶיךָ מֵאֹיְבִים מִנֵּהוּ:	כד
25	Men see Your processions, O Hashem, the processions of my God, my king, into the sanctuary.	*Ra'u halichoteicha Elohim halichotay eli malki vakkodesh*	רָאוּ הֲלִיכוֹתֶיךָ אֱלֹהִים הֲלִיכוֹת אֵלִי מַלְכִּי בַקֹּדֶשׁ:	כה

26	First come singers, then musicians, amidst maidens playing timbrels.	*Kiddmu sharim achar nogenim betoch alamot tofefot*	קִדְּמוּ שָׁרִים אַחַר נֹגְנִים בְּתוֹךְ עֲלָמוֹת תּוֹפֵפוֹת:	כו
27	In assemblies bless Hashem, Hashem, O you who are from the fountain of Yisrael.	*Bemakhaylot bar'echu Elohim Adonai mimmekor yisra'el*	בְּמַקְהֵלוֹת בָּרְכוּ אֱלֹהִים יְהֹוָה מִמְּקוֹר יִשְׂרָאֵל:	כז
28	There is little Binyamin who rules them, the princes of Yehuda who command them, the princes of Zevulun and Naftali.	*Sham binyamin tza'ir rodem sarei yehudah rigmatam sarei zevulun sarei naftali*	שָׁם בִּנְיָמִן צָעִיר רֹדֵם שָׂרֵי יְהוּדָה רִגְמָתָם שָׂרֵי זְבֻלוּן שָׂרֵי נַפְתָּלִי:	כח
29	Your God has ordained strength for you, the strength, O Hashem, which You displayed for us	*Tzivvah Eloheicha uzzecha uzzah elohim zu pa'alta lanu*	צִוָּה אֱלֹהֶיךָ עֻזֶּךָ עוּזָּה אֱלֹהִים זוּ פָּעַלְתָּ לָּנוּ:	כט
30	from Your temple above Yerushalayim. The kings bring You tribute.	*Meheichalecha al-yerushalayim lecha yovilu melachim shai*	מֵהֵיכָלֶךָ עַל־יְרוּשָׁלָ͏ִם לְךָ יוֹבִילוּ מְלָכִים שָׁי:	ל
31	Blast the beast of the marsh, the herd of bulls among the peoples, the calves, till they come cringing with pieces of silver. Scatter the peoples who delight in wars!	*Ge'ar chayyat kaneh adat abbirim be'eglei ammim mitrappes beratzei-chasef bizzar ammim keravot yechpatzu*	גְּעַר חַיַּת קָנֶה עֲדַת אַבִּירִים בְּעֶגְלֵי עַמִּים מִתְרַפֵּס בְּרַצֵּי־כָסֶף בִּזַּר עַמִּים קְרָבוֹת יֶחְפָּצוּ:	לא
32	Tribute-bearers shall come from Egypt; Cush shall hasten its gifts to Hashem.	*Ye'etayu chashmannim minni mitzrayim kush taritz yadav lelohim*	יֶאֱתָיוּ חַשְׁמַנִּים מִנִּי מִצְרָיִם כּוּשׁ תָּרִיץ יָדָיו לֵאלֹהִים:	לב

33	O kingdoms of the earth, sing to Hashem; chant hymns to Hashem, selah	*Mamlechot ha'aretz shiru lElohim zammeru Adonai selah*	מַמְלְכוֹת הָאָרֶץ שִׁירוּ לֵאלֹהִים זַמְּרוּ אֲדֹנָי סֶלָה:	לג
34	to Him who rides the ancient highest heavens, who thunders forth with His mighty voice.	*Larochev bishmei shemei-kedem hen yitten bekolo kol oz*	לָרֹכֵב בִּשְׁמֵי שְׁמֵי־קֶדֶם הֵן יִתֵּן בְּקוֹלוֹ קוֹל עֹז:	לד
35	Ascribe might to Hashem, whose majesty is over Yisrael, whose might is in the skies.	*Tenu oz lElohim al-yisra'el ga'avato ve'uzzo bashechakim*	תְּנוּ עֹז לֵאלֹהִים עַל־יִשְׂרָאֵל גַּאֲוָתוֹ וְעֻזּוֹ בַּשְּׁחָקִים:	לה
36	You are awesome, O Hashem, in Your holy places; it is the God of Yisrael who gives might and power to the people. Blessed is Hashem.	*Nora Elohim mimmikdasheicha el yisra'el hu noten oz veta'atzumot la'am baruch Elohim*	נוֹרָא אֱלֹהִים מִמִּקְדָּשֶׁיךָ אֵל יִשְׂרָאֵל הוּא נֹתֵן עֹז וְתַעֲצֻמוֹת לָעָם בָּרוּךְ אֱלֹהִים:	לו

69

—○⬡○—

סט

1	For the leader. On shoshannim. Of David.	*Lammenatzeach al-shoshannim ledavid*	לַמְנַצֵּחַ עַל־שׁוֹשַׁנִּים לְדָוִד:	א
2	Deliver me, O Hashem, for the waters have reached my neck;	*Hoshi'eni elohim ki va'u mayim ad-nafesh*	הוֹשִׁיעֵנִי אֱלֹהִים כִּי בָאוּ מַיִם עַד־נָפֶשׁ:	ב

3 I am sinking into the slimy deep and find no foothold; I have come into the watery depths; the flood sweeps me away.

Tava'ti biven metzulah ve'ein mo'omad bati vema'amakkei-mayim veshibbolet shetafatni

טָבַעְתִּי בִּיוֵן מְצוּלָה וְאֵין מָעֳמָד בָּאתִי בְמַעֲמַקֵּי־מַיִם וְשִׁבֹּלֶת שְׁטָפָתְנִי׃ ג

4 I am weary with calling; my throat is dry; my eyes fail while I wait for Hashem.

Yaga'ti vekare'i nichar geroni kalu einai meyachel lElohai

יָגַעְתִּי בְקָרְאִי נִחַר גְּרוֹנִי כָּלוּ עֵינַי מְיַחֵל לֵאלֹהָי׃ ד

5 More numerous than the hairs of my head are those who hate me without reason; many are those who would destroy me, my treacherous enemies. Must I restore what I have not stolen?

Rabbu missa'arot roshi sone'ai chinnam atzemu matzmitai oyevai sheker asher lo-gazalti az ashiv

רַבּוּ מִשַּׂעֲרוֹת רֹאשִׁי שֹׂנְאַי חִנָּם עָצְמוּ מַצְמִיתַי אֹיְבַי שֶׁקֶר אֲשֶׁר לֹא־גָזַלְתִּי אָז אָשִׁיב׃ ה

6 Hashem, You know my folly; my guilty deeds are not hidden from You.

Elohim attah yada'ta le'ivvalti ve'ashmotai mimmecha lo-nichchadu

אֱלֹהִים אַתָּה יָדַעְתָּ לְאִוַּלְתִּי וְאַשְׁמוֹתַי מִמְּךָ לֹא־נִכְחָדוּ׃ ו

7 Let those who look to You, O Hashem, God of hosts, not be disappointed on my account; let those who seek You, O God of Yisra'el, not be shamed because of me.

Al-yevoshu vi koveicha Adonai Elohim tzeva'ot al-yikkalemu vi mevaksheicha elohei Yisra'el

אַל־יֵבֹשׁוּ בִי קֹוֶיךָ אֲדֹנָי יְהֹוִה צְבָאוֹת אַל־יִכָּלְמוּ בִי מְבַקְשֶׁיךָ אֱלֹהֵי יִשְׂרָאֵל׃ ז

8 It is for Your sake that I have been reviled, that shame covers my face;

Ki-aleicha nasati cherpah kissetah chelimmah fanai

כִּי־עָלֶיךָ נָשָׂאתִי חֶרְפָּה כִּסְּתָה כְלִמָּה פָנָי׃ ח

9 | I am a stranger to my brothers, an alien to my kin. | *Muzar hayiti le'echai venacheri livnei immi* | מוּזָר הָיִיתִי לְאֶחָי וְנׇכְרִי לִבְנֵי אִמִּי: | ט

10 | My zeal for Your house has been my undoing; the reproaches of those who revile You have fallen upon me. | *Ki-kin'at beitcha achalatni vecherpot chorefeicha naflu alai* | כִּי־קִנְאַת בֵּיתְךָ אֲכָלָתְנִי וְחֶרְפּוֹת חוֹרְפֶיךָ נָפְלוּ עָלָי: | י

11 | When I wept and fasted, I was reviled for it. | *Va'evkeh vatzom nafshi vattehi lacharafot li* | וָאֶבְכֶּה בַצּוֹם נַפְשִׁי וַתְּהִי לַחֲרָפוֹת לִי: | יא

12 | I made sackcloth my garment; I became a byword among them. | *Va'ettenah levushi sak va'ehi lahem lemashal* | וָאֶתְּנָה לְבוּשִׁי שָׂק וָאֱהִי לָהֶם לְמָשָׁל: | יב

13 | Those who sit in the gate talk about me; I am the taunt of drunkards. | *Yasichu vi yoshevei sha'ar uneginot shotei shechar* | יָשִׂיחוּ בִי יֹשְׁבֵי שָׁעַר וּנְגִינוֹת שׁוֹתֵי שֵׁכָר: | יג

14 | As for me, may my prayer come to You, Hashem, at a favorable moment; O Hashem, in Your abundant faithfulness, answer me with Your sure deliverance. | *Va'ani tefillati-lecha Adonai et ratzon Elohim berav-chasdecha aneni be'emet yish'echa* | וַאֲנִי תְפִלָּתִי־לְךָ יְהֹוָה עֵת רָצוֹן אֱלֹהִים בְּרׇב־חַסְדֶּךָ עֲנֵנִי בֶּאֱמֶת יִשְׁעֶךָ: | יד

15 | Rescue me from the mire; let me not sink; let me be rescued from my enemies, and from the watery depths. | *Hatzileni mittit ve'al-etba'ah innatzelh misson'ai umimma'amakkei-mayim* | הַצִּילֵנִי מִטִּיט וְאַל־אֶטְבָּעָה אִנָּצְלָה מִשֹּׂנְאַי וּמִמַּעֲמַקֵּי־מָיִם: | טו

16	Let the floodwaters not sweep me away; let the deep not swallow me; let the mouth of the Pit not close over me.	*Al-tishtefeni shibbolet mayim ve'al-tivla'eni metzulah ve'al-te'tar-alai be'er piha*	אַל־תִּשְׁטְפֵנִי שִׁבֹּלֶת מַיִם וְאַל־תִּבְלָעֵנִי מְצוּלָה וְאַל־תֶּאְטַר־עָלַי בְּאֵר פִּיהָ:	טז
17	Answer me, Hashem, according to Your great steadfastness; in accordance with Your abundant mercy turn to me;	*Aneni Adonai ki-tov chasdecha kerov rachameicha peneh elai*	עֲנֵנִי יְהֹוָה כִּי־טוֹב חַסְדֶּךָ כְּרֹב רַחֲמֶיךָ פְּנֵה אֵלָי:	יז
18	do not hide Your face from Your servant, for I am in distress; answer me quickly.	*Ve'al-taster panecha me'avdecha ki-tzar-li maher aneni*	וְאַל־תַּסְתֵּר פָּנֶיךָ מֵעַבְדֶּךָ כִּי־צַר־לִי מַהֵר עֲנֵנִי:	יח
19	Come near to me and redeem me; free me from my enemies.	*Karevah el-nafshi ge'alah lema'an oyevai pedayni*	קָרְבָה אֶל־נַפְשִׁי גְאָלָה לְמַעַן אֹיְבַי פְּדֵנִי:	יט
20	You know my reproach, my shame, my disgrace; You are aware of all my foes.	*Attah yada'ta cherpati uvasheti uchelimmati negdecha kol-tzorerai*	אַתָּה יָדַעְתָּ חֶרְפָּתִי וּבָשְׁתִּי וּכְלִמָּתִי נֶגְדְּךָ כָּל־צוֹרְרָי:	כ
21	Reproach breaks my heart, I am in despair; I hope for consolation, but there is none, for comforters, but find none.	*Cherpah shaverah libbi va'anushah va'akavveh lanud va'ayin velammenachamim velo matzati*	חֶרְפָּה שָׁבְרָה לִבִּי וָאָנוּשָׁה וָאֲקַוֶּה לָנוּד וָאַיִן וְלַמְנַחֲמִים וְלֹא מָצָאתִי:	כא
22	They give me gall for food, vinegar to quench my thirst.	*Vayyittenu bevaruti rosh velitzma'i yashkuni chometz*	וַיִּתְּנוּ בְּבָרוּתִי רֹאשׁ וְלִצְמָאִי יַשְׁקוּנִי חֹמֶץ:	כב

23	May their table be a trap for them, a snare for their allies.	*Yehi-shulchanam lifneihem lefach velishlomim lemokesh*	יְהִי־שֻׁלְחָנָם לִפְנֵיהֶם לְפָח וְלִשְׁלוֹמִים לְמוֹקֵשׁ׃	כג
24	May their eyes grow dim so that they cannot see; may their loins collapse continually.	*Techshachnah eineihem mere'ot umateneihem tamid hamme'ad*	תֶּחְשַׁכְנָה עֵינֵיהֶם מֵרְאוֹת וּמָתְנֵיהֶם תָּמִיד הַמְעַד׃	כד
25	Pour out Your wrath on them; may Your blazing anger overtake them;	*Shefach-aleihem za'mecha vacharon appecha yassigem*	שְׁפׇךְ־עֲלֵיהֶם זַעְמֶךָ וַחֲרוֹן אַפְּךָ יַשִּׂיגֵם׃	כה
26	may their encampments be desolate; may their tents stand empty.	*Tehi-tiratam neshammah be'oholeihem al-yehi yoshev*	תְּהִי־טִירָתָם נְשַׁמָּה בְּאׇהֳלֵיהֶם אַל־יְהִי יֹשֵׁב׃	כו
27	For they persecute those You have struck; they talk about the pain of those You have felled.	*Ki-attah asher-hikkita radafu ve'el-mach'ov chalaleicha yesapperu*	כִּי־אַתָּה אֲשֶׁר־הִכִּיתָ רָדָפוּ וְאֶל־מַכְאוֹב חֲלָלֶיךָ יְסַפֵּרוּ׃	כז
28	Add that to their guilt; let them have no share of Your beneficence;	*Tenah-avon al-avonam ve'al-yavo'u betzidkatecha*	תְּנָה־עָוֺן עַל־עֲוֺנָם וְאַל־יָבֹאוּ בְּצִדְקָתֶךָ׃	כח
29	may they be erased from the book of life, and not be inscribed with the righteous.	*Yimmachu missefer chayyim ve'im tzaddikim al-yikkatayvu*	יִמָּחוּ מִסֵּפֶר חַיִּים וְעִם צַדִּיקִים אַל־יִכָּתֵבוּ׃	כט

30	But I am lowly and in pain; Your help, O Hashem, keeps me safe.	*Va'ani ani vecho'ev yeshu'atecha Elohim tesaggeveni*	וַאֲנִי עָנִי וְכוֹאֵב יְשׁוּעָתְךָ אֱלֹהִים תְּשַׂגְּבֵנִי:	ל
31	I will extol Hashem's name with song, and exalt Him with praise.	*Ahallah shem-elohim beshir va'agaddelennu vetodah*	אֲהַלְלָה שֵׁם־אֱלֹהִים בְּשִׁיר וַאֲגַדְּלֶנּוּ בְתוֹדָה:	לא
32	That will please Hashem more than oxen, than bulls with horns and hooves.	*Vetitav lAdonai mishor par makrin mafris*	וְתִיטַב לַיהוָה מִשּׁוֹר פָּר מַקְרִן מַפְרִיס:	לב
33	The lowly will see and rejoice; you who are mindful of Hashem, take heart!	*Ra'u anavim yismachu doreshei Elohim vichi levavchem*	רָאוּ עֲנָוִים יִשְׂמָחוּ דֹּרְשֵׁי אֱלֹהִים וִיחִי לְבַבְכֶם:	לג
34	For Hashem listens to the needy, and does not spurn His captives.	*Ki-shomea' el-evyonim Adonai ve'et-asirav lo vazah*	כִּי־שֹׁמֵעַ אֶל־אֶבְיוֹנִים יְהוָה וְאֶת־אֲסִירָיו לֹא בָזָה:	לד
35	Heaven and earth shall extol Him, the seas, and all that moves in them.	*Yehalluhu shamayim va'aretz yammim vechol-romes bam*	יְהַלְלוּהוּ שָׁמַיִם וָאָרֶץ יַמִּים וְכָל־רֹמֵשׂ בָּם:	לה
36	For Hashem will deliver Tzion and rebuild the cities of Yehuda; they shall live there and inherit it;	*Ki Elohim yoshia' tziyyon veyivneh arei yehudah veyashvu sham virayshuha*	כִּי אֱלֹהִים יוֹשִׁיעַ צִיּוֹן וְיִבְנֶה עָרֵי יְהוּדָה וְיָשְׁבוּ שָׁם וִירֵשׁוּהָ:	לו
37	the offspring of His servants shall possess it; those who cherish His name shall dwell there.	*Vezera avadav yinchaluha ve'ohavei shemo yishkenu-vah*	וְזֶרַע עֲבָדָיו יִנְחָלוּהָ וְאֹהֲבֵי שְׁמוֹ יִשְׁכְּנוּ־בָהּ:	לז

70

1	For the leader. Of David. Lehazkir.	*Lammenatzeach ledavid lehazkir*	לַמְנַצֵּחַ לְדָוִד לְהַזְכִּיר:	א
2	Hasten, O Hashem, to save me; Hashem, to aid me!	*Elohim lehatzileni Adonai le'ezrati chushah*	אֱלֹהִים לְהַצִּילֵנִי יְהֹוָה לְעֶזְרָתִי חוּשָׁה:	ב
3	Let those who seek my life be frustrated and disgraced; let those who wish me harm, fall back in shame.	*Yevoshu veyachperu mevakshei nafshi yissogu achor veyikkalemu chafetzei ra'ati*	יֵבֹשׁוּ וְיַחְפְּרוּ מְבַקְשֵׁי נַפְשִׁי יִסֹּגוּ אָחוֹר וְיִכָּלְמוּ חֲפֵצֵי רָעָתִי:	ג
4	Let those who say, "Aha! Aha!" turn back because of their frustration.	*Yashuvu al-ekev bashtam ha'omerim he'ach he'ach*	יָשׁוּבוּ עַל־עֵקֶב בָּשְׁתָּם הָאֹמְרִים הֶאָח הֶאָח:	ד
5	But let all who seek You be glad and rejoice in You; let those who are eager for Your deliverance always say, "Extolled be Hashem!"	*Yasisu veyismechu becha kol-mevaksheicha veyomru tamid yigdal Elohim ohavei yeshu'atecha*	יָשִׂישׂוּ וְיִשְׂמְחוּ בְּךָ כָּל־מְבַקְשֶׁיךָ וְיֹאמְרוּ תָמִיד יִגְדַּל אֱלֹהִים אֹהֲבֵי יְשׁוּעָתֶךָ:	ה
6	But I am poor and needy; O Hashem, hasten to me! You are my help and my rescuer; Hashem, do not delay.	*Va'ani ani ve'evyon Elohim chushah-li ezri umefalti attah Adonai al-te'achar*	וַאֲנִי עָנִי וְאֶבְיוֹן אֱלֹהִים חוּשָׁה־לִּי עֶזְרִי וּמְפַלְטִי אַתָּה יְהֹוָה אַל־תְּאַחַר:	ו

71

1	I seek refuge in You, Hashem; may I never be disappointed.	*Becha-Adonai chasiti al-evoshah le'olam*	בְּךָ־יְהֹוָה חָסִיתִי אַל־אֵבוֹשָׁה לְעוֹלָם:	א
2	As You are beneficent, save me and rescue me; incline Your ear to me and deliver me.	*Betzidkatecha tatzileni utefalleteni hattay-aylai oznecha vehoshi'eni*	בְּצִדְקָתְךָ תַּצִּילֵנִי וּתְפַלְּטֵנִי הַטֵּה־אֵלַי אָזְנְךָ וְהוֹשִׁיעֵנִי:	ב
3	Be a sheltering rock for me to which I may always repair; decree my deliverance, for You are my rock and my fortress.	*Heyeh li letzur ma'on lavo tamid tzivvita lehoshi'eni ki-sal'i umetzudati attah*	הֱיֵה לִי לְצוּר מָעוֹן לָבוֹא תָּמִיד צִוִּיתָ לְהוֹשִׁיעֵנִי כִּי־סַלְעִי וּמְצוּדָתִי אָתָּה:	ג
4	My Hashem, rescue me from the hand of the wicked, from the grasp of the unjust and the lawless.	*Elohai palleteni miyyad rasha mikkaf me'avvel vechometz*	אֱלֹהַי פַּלְּטֵנִי מִיַּד רָשָׁע מִכַּף מְעַוֵּל וְחוֹמֵץ:	ד
5	For You are my hope, O Hashem, my trust from my youth.	*Ki-attah tikvati Adonai Elohim mivtachi minne'urai*	כִּי־אַתָּה תִקְוָתִי אֲדֹנָי יְהוִה מִבְטַחִי מִנְּעוּרָי:	ה
6	While yet unborn, I depended on You; in the womb of my mother, You were my support; I sing Your praises always.	*Aleicha nismachti mibbeten mimme'ei immi attah gozi becha tehillati tamid*	עָלֶיךָ נִסְמַכְתִּי מִבֶּטֶן מִמְּעֵי אִמִּי אַתָּה גוֹזִי בְּךָ תְהִלָּתִי תָמִיד:	ו

7	I have become an example for many, since You are my mighty refuge.	*Kemofet hayiti lerabbim ve'attah machasi-oz*	כְּמוֹפֵת הָיִיתִי לְרַבִּים וְאַתָּה מַחֲסִי־עֹז:	ז
8	My mouth is full of praise to You, glorifying You all day long.	*Yimmale fi tehillatecha kol-hayyom tif'artecha*	יִמָּלֵא פִי תְּהִלָּתֶךָ כָּל־הַיּוֹם תִּפְאַרְתֶּךָ:	ח
9	Do not cast me off in old age; when my strength fails, do not forsake me!	*Al-tashlicheni le'et ziknah kichlot kochi al-ta'azveni*	אַל־תַּשְׁלִיכֵנִי לְעֵת זִקְנָה כִּכְלוֹת כֹּחִי אַל־תַּעַזְבֵנִי:	ט
10	For my enemies talk against me; those who wait for me are of one mind,	*Ki-ameru oyevai li veshomerei nafshi no'atzu yachdav*	כִּי־אָמְרוּ אוֹיְבַי לִי וְשֹׁמְרֵי נַפְשִׁי נוֹעֲצוּ יַחְדָּו:	י
11	saying, "Hashem has forsaken him; chase him and catch him, for no one will save him!"	*Laymor Elohim azavo ridfu vetifsuhu ki-ein matzil*	לֵאמֹר אֱלֹהִים עֲזָבוֹ רִדְפוּ וְתִפְשׂוּהוּ כִּי־אֵין מַצִּיל:	יא
12	O Hashem, be not far from me; my God, hasten to my aid!	*Elohim al-tirchak mimmenni Elohai le'ezrati chushah*	אֱלֹהִים אַל־תִּרְחַק מִמֶּנִּי אֱלֹהַי לְעֶזְרָתִי חִישָׁה [חוּשָׁה:]	יב
13	Let my accusers perish in frustration; let those who seek my ruin be clothed in reproach and disgrace!	*Yevoshu yichlu sotnay nafshi ya'atu cherpah uchelimmah mevakshei ra'ati*	יֵבֹשׁוּ יִכְלוּ שֹׂטְנֵי נַפְשִׁי יַעֲטוּ חֶרְפָּה וּכְלִמָּה מְבַקְשֵׁי רָעָתִי:	יג
14	As for me, I will hope always, and add to the many praises of You.	*Va'ani tamid ayachel vehosafti al-kol-tehillatecha*	וַאֲנִי תָּמִיד אֲיַחֵל וְהוֹסַפְתִּי עַל־כָּל־תְּהִלָּתֶךָ:	יד

15	My mouth tells of Your beneficence, of Your deliverance all day long, though I know not how to tell it.	*Pi yesapper tzidkatecha kol-hayyom teshu'atecha ki lo yada'ti seforot*	פִּי יְסַפֵּר צִדְקָתֶךָ כָּל־הַיּוֹם תְּשׁוּעָתֶךָ כִּי לֹא יָדַעְתִּי סְפֹרוֹת: טו
16	I come with praise of Your mighty acts, O Hashem; I celebrate Your beneficence, Yours alone.	*Avo bigvurot Adonai Elohim azkir tzidkatecha levaddecha*	אָבוֹא בִּגְבֻרוֹת אֲדֹנָי יְהוִה אַזְכִּיר צִדְקָתְךָ לְבַדֶּךָ: טז
17	You have let me experience it, Hashem, from my youth; until now I have proclaimed Your wondrous deeds,	*Elohim limmadtani minne'urai ve'ad-hennah aggid nifle'oteicha*	אֱלֹהִים לִמַּדְתַּנִי מִנְּעוּרָי וְעַד־הֵנָּה אַגִּיד נִפְלְאוֹתֶיךָ: יז
18	and even in hoary old age do not forsake me, Hashem, until I proclaim Your strength to the next generation, Your mighty acts, to all who are to come,	*Vegam ad-ziknah veseivah Elohim al-ta'azveni ad-aggid zero'acha ledor lechol-yavo gevuratecha*	וְגַם עַד־זִקְנָה וְשֵׂיבָה אֱלֹהִים אַל־תַּעַזְבֵנִי עַד־אַגִּיד זְרוֹעֲךָ לְדוֹר לְכָל־יָבוֹא גְּבוּרָתֶךָ: יח
19	Your beneficence, high as the heavens, O Hashem, You who have done great things; O Hashem, who is Your peer!	*Vetzidkatecha Elohim ad-marom asher-asita gedolot Elohim mi chamocha*	וְצִדְקָתְךָ אֱלֹהִים עַד־מָרוֹם אֲשֶׁר־עָשִׂיתָ גְדֹלוֹת אֱלֹהִים מִי כָמוֹךָ: יט
20	You who have made me undergo many troubles and misfortunes will revive me again, and raise me up from the depths of the earth.	*Asher hir'itani tzarot rabbot vera'ot tashuv techayyeini umittehomot ha'aretz tashuv ta'aleni*	אֲשֶׁר הראיתנו [הִרְאִיתַנִי] צָרוֹת רַבּוֹת וְרָעוֹת תָּשׁוּב תחיינו [תְּחַיֵּינִי] וּמִתְּהֹמוֹת הָאָרֶץ תָּשׁוּב תַּעֲלֵנִי: כ

21 You will grant me much greatness, You will turn and comfort me.

Terev gedullati vetissov tenachameni

תֶּרֶב גְּדֻלָּתִי וְתִסֹּב תְּנַחֲמֵנִי:

כא

22 Then I will acclaim You to the music of the lyre for Your faithfulness, O my God; I will sing a hymn to You with a harp, O Holy One of Yisrael.

Gam-ani odecha vichli-nevel amittecha Elohai azammerah lecha vechinnor kedosh yisra'el

גַּם־אֲנִי אוֹדְךָ בִכְלִי־נֶבֶל אֲמִתְּךָ אֱלֹהָי אֲזַמְּרָה לְּךָ בְּכִנּוֹר קְדוֹשׁ יִשְׂרָאֵל:

כב

23 My lips shall be jubilant, as I sing a hymn to You, my whole being, which You have redeemed.

Terannennah sefatai ki azammerah-lach venafshi asher padita

תְּרַנֵּנָּה שְׂפָתַי כִּי אֲזַמְּרָה־לָּךְ וְנַפְשִׁי אֲשֶׁר פָּדִיתָ:

כג

24 All day long my tongue shall recite Your beneficent acts, how those who sought my ruin were frustrated and disgraced.

Gam-leshoni kol-hayyom tehgeh tzidkatecha ki-voshu chi-chaferu mevakshei ra'ati

גַּם־לְשׁוֹנִי כָּל־הַיּוֹם תֶּהְגֶּה צִדְקָתֶךָ כִּי־בֹשׁוּ כִי־חָפְרוּ מְבַקְשֵׁי רָעָתִי:

כד

72

⎯○⦿○⎯

עב

1 Of Shlomo. O Hashem, endow the king with Your judgments, the king's son with Your righteousness;

Lishlomoh elohim mishpateicha lemelech ten vetzidkatecha leven-melech

לִשְׁלֹמֹה אֱלֹהִים מִשְׁפָּטֶיךָ לְמֶלֶךְ תֵּן וְצִדְקָתְךָ לְבֶן־מֶלֶךְ:

א

2 that he may judge Your people rightly, Your lowly ones, justly.

Yadin ammecha vetzedek va'aniyyeicha vemishpat

יָדִין עַמְּךָ בְצֶדֶק וַעֲנִיֶּיךָ בְמִשְׁפָּט:

ב

3	Let the mountains produce well-being for the people, the hills, the reward of justice.	*Yis'u harim shalom la'am ugeva'ot bitzdakah*	יִשְׂאוּ הָרִים שָׁלוֹם לָעָם וּגְבָעוֹת בִּצְדָקָה: ג
4	Let him Champion the lowly among the people, deliver the needy folk, and crush those who wrong them.	*Yishpot aniyyei-am yoshia' livnei evyon vidakke oshek*	יִשְׁפֹּט עֲנִיֵּי־עָם יוֹשִׁיעַ לִבְנֵי אֶבְיוֹן וִידַכֵּא עוֹשֵׁק: ד
5	Let them fear You as long as the sun shines, while the moon lasts, generations on end.	*Yira'ucha im-shamesh velifnei yareach dor dorim*	יִירָאוּךָ עִם־שָׁמֶשׁ וְלִפְנֵי יָרֵחַ דּוֹר דּוֹרִים: ה
6	Let him be like rain that falls on a mown field, like a downpour of rain on the ground,	*Yered kematar al-gez kirvivim zarzif aretz*	יֵרֵד כְּמָטָר עַל־גֵּז כִּרְבִיבִים זַרְזִיף אָרֶץ: ו
7	that the righteous may flourish in his time, and well-being abound, till the moon is no more.	*Yifrach-beyamav tzaddik verov shalom ad-beli yareach*	יִפְרַח־בְּיָמָיו צַדִּיק וְרֹב שָׁלוֹם עַד־בְּלִי יָרֵחַ: ז
8	Let him rule from sea to sea, from the river to the ends of the earth.	*Veyered miyyam ad-yam uminnahar ad-afsei-aretz*	וְיֵרְדְּ מִיָּם עַד־יָם וּמִנָּהָר עַד־אַפְסֵי־אָרֶץ: ח
9	Let desert-dwellers kneel before him, and his enemies lick the dust.	*Lefanav yichre'u tziyyim ve'oyevav afar yelachaychu*	לְפָנָיו יִכְרְעוּ צִיִּים וְאֹיְבָיו עָפָר יְלַחֵכוּ: ט
10	Let kings of Tarshish and the islands pay tribute, kings of Sheba and Seba offer gifts.	*Malchei tarshish ve'iyyim minchah yashivu malchei sheva useva eshkar yakrivu*	מַלְכֵי תַרְשִׁישׁ וְאִיִּים מִנְחָה יָשִׁיבוּ מַלְכֵי שְׁבָא וּסְבָא אֶשְׁכָּר יַקְרִיבוּ: י

11	Let all kings bow to him, and all nations serve him.	*Veyishtachavu-lo chol-melachim kol-goyim ya'avduhu*	וְיִשְׁתַּחֲווּ־לוֹ כָל־מְלָכִים כָּל־גּוֹיִם יַעַבְדוּהוּ:	יא
12	For he saves the needy who cry out, the lowly who have no helper.	*Ki-yatzil evyon meshavvea' ve'ani ve'ein-ozer lo*	כִּי־יַצִּיל אֶבְיוֹן מְשַׁוֵּעַ וְעָנִי וְאֵין־עֹזֵר לוֹ:	יב
13	He cares about the poor and the needy; He brings the needy deliverance.	*Yachos al-dal ve'evyon venafshot evyonim yoshia'*	יָחֹס עַל־דַּל וְאֶבְיוֹן וְנַפְשׁוֹת אֶבְיוֹנִים יוֹשִׁיעַ:	יג
14	He redeems them from fraud and lawlessness; the shedding of their blood weighs heavily upon him.	*Mittoch umechamas yig'al nafsham veyeikar damam be'einav*	מִתּוֹךְ וּמֵחָמָס יִגְאַל נַפְשָׁם וְיֵיקַר דָּמָם בְּעֵינָיו:	יד
15	So let him live, and receive gold of Sheba; let prayers for him be said always, blessings on him invoked at all times.	*Vichi veyitten-lo mizzehav sheva veyitpallel ba'ado tamid kol-hayyom yevarachenhu*	וִיחִי וְיִתֶּן־לוֹ מִזְּהַב שְׁבָא וְיִתְפַּלֵּל בַּעֲדוֹ תָמִיד כָּל־הַיּוֹם יְבָרֲכֶנְהוּ:	טו
16	Let abundant grain be in the land, to the tops of the mountains; let his crops thrive like the forest of Lebanon; and let men sprout up in towns like country grass.	*Yehi fissat-bar ba'aretz berosh harim yir'ash kallevanon piryo veyatzitzu me'ir ke'esev ha'aretz*	יְהִי פִסַּת־בַּר בָּאָרֶץ בְּרֹאשׁ הָרִים יִרְעַשׁ כַּלְּבָנוֹן פִּרְיוֹ וְיָצִיצוּ מֵעִיר כְּעֵשֶׂב הָאָרֶץ:	טז

17	May his name be eternal; while the sun lasts, may his name endure; let men invoke his blessedness upon themselves; let all nations count him happy.	*Yehi shemo le'olam lifnei-shemesh yinnon shemo veyitbarechu vo kol-goyim ye'asheruhu*

יְהִי שְׁמוֹ לְעוֹלָם לִפְנֵי־שֶׁמֶשׁ יִנִּין [יִנּוֹן] שְׁמוֹ וְיִתְבָּרְכוּ בוֹ כָּל־גּוֹיִם יְאַשְּׁרוּהוּ: יז

18	Blessed is Hashem, God of Yisrael, who alone does wondrous things;	*Baruch Adonai Elohim Elohei yisra'el oseh nifla'ot levaddo*

בָּרוּךְ יְהֹוָה אֱלֹהִים אֱלֹהֵי יִשְׂרָאֵל עֹשֵׂה נִפְלָאוֹת לְבַדּוֹ: יח

19	Blessed is His glorious name forever; His glory fills the whole world. Amen and Amen.	*Uvaruch shem kevodo le'olam veyimmale chevodo et-kol ha'aretz amen ve'amen*

וּבָרוּךְ שֵׁם כְּבוֹדוֹ לְעוֹלָם וְיִמָּלֵא כְבוֹדוֹ אֶת־כֹּל הָאָרֶץ אָמֵן וְאָמֵן: יט

20	End of the prayers of David son of Yishai.	*Kallu tefillot david ben-yishai*

כָּלּוּ תְפִלּוֹת דָּוִד בֶּן־יִשָׁי: כ

73

—०◦⬗⬗◦०—

עג

1	A psalm of Asaf. Hashem is truly good to Yisrael, to those whose heart is pure.	*Mizmor le'asaf ach tov leyisra'el elohim levarei levav*

מִזְמוֹר לְאָסָף אַךְ טוֹב לְיִשְׂרָאֵל אֱלֹהִים לְבָרֵי לֵבָב: א

2	As for me, my feet had almost strayed, my steps were nearly led off course,	*Va'ani kim'at [natayu] raglai ke'ayin [shuppechu] ashurai*

וַאֲנִי כִּמְעַט נטוי [נָטָיוּ] רַגְלָי כְּאַיִן שפכה [שֻׁפְּכוּ] אֲשֻׁרָי: ב

3	for I envied the wanton; I saw the wicked at ease.	*Ki-kinneti baholelim shelom resha'im er'eh*	כִּי־קִנֵּאתִי בַּהוֹלְלִים שְׁלוֹם רְשָׁעִים אֶרְאֶה:	ג
4	Death has no pangs for them; their body is healthy.	*Ki ein chartzubbot lemotam uvari ulam*	כִּי אֵין חַרְצֻבּוֹת לְמוֹתָם וּבָרִיא אוּלָם:	ד
5	They have no part in the travail of men; they are not afflicted like the rest of mankind.	*Ba'amal enosh einemo ve'im-adam lo yenugga'u*	בַּעֲמַל אֱנוֹשׁ אֵינֵמוֹ וְעִם־אָדָם לֹא יְנֻגָּעוּ:	ה
6	So pride adorns their necks, lawlessness enwraps them as a mantle.	*Lachen anakatmo ga'avah ya'ataf-sheet chamas lamo*	לָכֵן עֲנָקַתְמוֹ גַאֲוָה יַעֲטָף־שִׁית חָמָס לָמוֹ:	ו
7	Fat shuts out their eyes; their fancies are extravagant.	*Yatza mechelev einemo averu maskiyyot levav*	יָצָא מֵחֵלֶב עֵינֵמוֹ עָבְרוּ מַשְׂכִּיּוֹת לֵבָב:	ז
8	They scoff and plan evil; from their eminence they plan wrongdoing.	*Yamiku vidabberu vera oshek mimmarom yedabberu*	יָמִיקוּ וִידַבְּרוּ בְרָע עֹשֶׁק מִמָּרוֹם יְדַבֵּרוּ:	ח
9	They set their mouths against heaven, and their tongues range over the earth.	*Shattu vashamayim pihem uleshonam tihalach ba'aretz*	שַׁתּוּ בַשָּׁמַיִם פִּיהֶם וּלְשׁוֹנָם תִּהֲלַךְ בָּאָרֶץ:	ט
10	So they pound His people again and again, until they are drained of their very last tear.	*Lachen [yashuv] ammo halom umei malei yimmatzu lamo*	לָכֵן ישיב [יָשׁוּב] עַמּוֹ הֲלֹם וּמֵי מָלֵא יִמָּצוּ לָמוֹ:	י

11	Then they say, "How could Hashem know? Is there knowledge with the Most High?"	*Ve'ameru eichah yada-el veyesh de'ah ve'elyon*	וְאָמְרוּ אֵיכָה יָדַע־אֵל וְיֵשׁ דֵּעָה בְעֶלְיוֹן:	יא
12	Such are the wicked; ever tranquil, they amass wealth.	*Hinneh-eilleh resha'im veshalvei olam hisgu-chayil*	הִנֵּה־אֵלֶּה רְשָׁעִים וְשַׁלְוֵי עוֹלָם הִשְׂגּוּ־חָיִל:	יב
13	It was for nothing that I kept my heart pure and washed my hands in innocence,	*Ach-rik zikkiti levavi va'erchatz benikkayon kappai*	אַךְ־רִיק זִכִּיתִי לְבָבִי וָאֶרְחַץ בְּנִקָּיוֹן כַּפָּי:	יג
14	seeing that I have been constantly afflicted, that each morning brings new punishments.	*Va'ehi nagua' kol-hayyom vetochachti labbekarim*	וָאֱהִי נָגוּעַ כָּל־הַיּוֹם וְתוֹכַחְתִּי לַבְּקָרִים:	יד
15	Had I decided to say these things, I should have been false to the circle of Your disciples.	*Im-amarti asapperah chemo hinneh dor banecha vagadeti*	אִם־אָמַרְתִּי אֲסַפְּרָה כְמוֹ הִנֵּה דוֹר בָּנֶיךָ בָגָדְתִּי:	טו
16	So I applied myself to understand this, but it seemed a hopeless task	*Va'achashevah lada'at zot amal [hu] ve'einai*	וָאֲחַשְּׁבָה לָדַעַת זֹאת עָמָל הִיא [הוּא] בְעֵינָי:	טז
17	till I entered Hashem's sanctuary and reflected on their fate.	*Ad-avo el-mikdeshei-el avinah le'acharitam*	עַד־אָבוֹא אֶל־מִקְדְּשֵׁי־אֵל אָבִינָה לְאַחֲרִיתָם:	יז
18	You surround them with flattery; You make them fall through blandishments.	*Ach bachalakot tashit lamo hippaltam lemashu'ot*	אַךְ בַּחֲלָקוֹת תָּשִׁית לָמוֹ הִפַּלְתָּם לְמַשּׁוּאוֹת:	יח

19	How suddenly are they ruined, wholly swept away by terrors.	*Eich hayu leshammah cheraga safu tammu min-ballahot*	אֵיךְ הָיוּ לְשַׁמָּה כְרָגַע סָפוּ תַמּוּ מִן־בַּלָּהוֹת:	יט
20	When You are aroused You despise their image, as one does a dream after waking, O Hashem.	*Kachalom mehakitz Adonai ba'ir tzalmam tivzeh*	כַּחֲלוֹם מֵהָקִיץ אֲדֹנָי בָּעִיר צַלְמָם תִּבְזֶה:	כ
21	My mind was stripped of its reason, my feelings were numbed.	*Ki yitchammetz levavi vechilyotai eshtonan*	כִּי יִתְחַמֵּץ לְבָבִי וְכִלְיוֹתַי אֶשְׁתּוֹנָן:	כא
22	I was a dolt, without knowledge; I was brutish toward You.	*Va'ani-va'ar velo eda behemot hayiti immach*	וַאֲנִי־בַעַר וְלֹא אֵדָע בְּהֵמוֹת הָיִיתִי עִמָּךְ:	כב
23	Yet I was always with You, You held my right hand;	*Va'ani tamid immach achazta beyad-yemini*	וַאֲנִי תָמִיד עִמָּךְ אָחַזְתָּ בְּיַד־יְמִינִי:	כג
24	You guided me by Your counsel and led me toward honor.	*Ba'atzatecha tancheni ve'achar kavod tikkacheni*	בַּעֲצָתְךָ תַנְחֵנִי וְאַחַר כָּבוֹד תִּקָּחֵנִי:	כד
25	Whom else have I in heaven? And having You, I want no one on earth.	*Mi-li vashamayim ve'immecha lo-chafatzti va'aretz*	מִי־לִי בַשָּׁמַיִם וְעִמְּךָ לֹא־ חָפַצְתִּי בָאָרֶץ:	כה
26	My body and mind fail; but Hashem is the stay of my mind, my portion forever.	*Kalah she'eri ulevavi tzur-levavi vechelki elohim le'olam*	כָּלָה שְׁאֵרִי וּלְבָבִי צוּר־ לְבָבִי וְחֶלְקִי אֱלֹהִים לְעוֹלָם:	כו

27	Those who keep far from You perish; You annihilate all who are untrue to You.	*Ki-hinneh rechekecha yovedu hitzmattah kol-zoneh mimmekka*

כִּי־הִנֵּה רְחֵקֶיךָ יֹאבֵדוּ הִצְמַתָּה כָּל־זוֹנֶה מִמֶּךָּ: כז

28	As for me, nearness to Hashem is good; I have made Hashem my refuge, that I may recount all Your works.	*Va'ani kiravat elohim li-tov shatti bAdonai Adonai machsi lesapper kol-mal'achotecha*

וַאֲנִי קִרֲבַת אֱלֹהִים לִי־טוֹב שַׁתִּי בַּאדֹנָי יְהֹוָה מַחְסִי לְסַפֵּר כָּל־מַלְאֲכוֹתֶיךָ: כח

74

עד

1	A maskil of Asaf. Why, O Hashem, do You forever reject us, do You fume in anger at the flock that You tend?	*Maskil le'asaf lamah elohim zanachta lanetzach ye'shan appecha betzon mar'itecha*

מַשְׂכִּיל לְאָסָף לָמָה אֱלֹהִים זָנַחְתָּ לָנֶצַח יֶעְשַׁן אַפְּךָ בְּצֹאן מַרְעִיתֶךָ: א

2	Remember the community You made Yours long ago, Your very own tribe that You redeemed, Mount Tzion, where You dwell.	*Zechor adatecha kanita kedem ga'alta shevet nachalatecha har-tziyyon zeh shachanta bo*

זְכֹר עֲדָתְךָ קָנִיתָ קֶּדֶם גָּאַלְתָּ שֵׁבֶט נַחֲלָתֶךָ הַר־צִיּוֹן זֶה שָׁכַנְתָּ בּוֹ: ב

3	Bestir Yourself because of the perpetual tumult, all the outrages of the enemy in the sanctuary.	*Harimah fe'amecha lemashu'ot netzach kol-heira oyev bakkodesh*

הָרִימָה פְעָמֶיךָ לְמַשֻּׁאוֹת נֶצַח כָּל־הֵרַע אוֹיֵב בַּקֹּדֶשׁ: ג

4	Your foes roar inside Your meeting-place; they take their signs for true signs.	*Sha'agu tzorerecha bekerev mo'adecha samu ototam otot*	שָׁאֲגוּ צֹרְרֶיךָ בְּקֶרֶב מוֹעֲדֶךָ שָׂמוּ אוֹתֹתָם אֹתוֹת:	ד
5	It is like men wielding axes against a gnarled tree;	*Yivvada kemevi lemalah bisavach-etz kardummot*	יִוָּדַע כְּמֵבִיא לְמָעְלָה בִּסֲבָךְ־עֵץ קַרְדֻּמּוֹת:	ה
6	with hatchet and pike they hacked away at its carved work.	*[ve'attah] pittucheiha yachad bechashil vecheilappot yahalomun*	ועת [וְעַתָּה] פִּתּוּחֶיהָ יָּחַד בְּכַשִּׁיל וְכֵילַפֹּת יַהֲלֹמוּן:	ו
7	They made Your sanctuary go up in flames; they brought low in dishonor the dwelling-place of Your presence.	*Shilchu va'esh mikdashecha la'aretz chillelu mishkan-shemecha*	שִׁלְחוּ בָאֵשׁ מִקְדָּשֶׁךָ לָאָרֶץ חִלְּלוּ מִשְׁכַּן־שְׁמֶךָ:	ז
8	They resolved, "Let us destroy them altogether!" They burned all Hashem's Mishkans in the land.	*Ameru velibbam ninam yachad sarefu chol-mo'adei-el ba'aretz*	אָמְרוּ בְלִבָּם נִינָם יָחַד שָׂרְפוּ כָל־מוֹעֲדֵי־אֵל בָּאָרֶץ:	ח
9	No signs appear for us; there is no longer any Navi; no one among us knows for how long.	*Ototeinu lo ra'inu ein-od navi velo-ittanu yodea' ad-mah*	אוֹתֹתֵינוּ לֹא רָאִינוּ אֵין־ עוֹד נָבִיא וְלֹא־אִתָּנוּ יֹדֵעַ עַד־מָה:	ט
10	Till when, O Hashem, will the foe blaspheme, will the enemy forever revile Your name?	*Ad-matai elohim yecharef tzar yena'etz oyev shimcha lanetzach*	עַד־מָתַי אֱלֹהִים יְחָרֶף צָר יְנָאֵץ אוֹיֵב שִׁמְךָ לָנֶצַח:	י
11	Why do You hold back Your hand, Your right hand? Draw it out of Your bosom!	*lammah tashiv yadecha viminecha mikkerev [cheikcha] challei*	לָמָּה תָשִׁיב יָדְךָ וִימִינֶךָ מִקֶּרֶב חוקך [חֵיקְךָ] כַלֵּה:	יא

12	O Hashem, my King from of old, who brings deliverance throughout the land;	*Veilohim malki mikkedem po'el yeshu'ot bekerev ha'aretz*	וֵאלֹהִים מַלְכִּי מִקֶּדֶם פֹּעֵל יְשׁוּעוֹת בְּקֶרֶב הָאָרֶץ:	יב
13	it was You who drove back the sea with Your might, who smashed the heads of the monsters in the waters;	*Attah forarta ve'azzecha yam shibbarta rashei tanninim al-ha'mayim*	אַתָּה פוֹרַרְתָּ בְעָזְּךָ יָם שִׁבַּרְתָּ רָאשֵׁי תַנִּינִים עַל־הַמָּיִם:	יג
14	it was You who crushed the heads of Leviathan, who left him as food for the denizens of the desert;	*Attah ritzatzta rashei livyatan tittenennu ma'achal le'am letziyyim*	אַתָּה רִצַּצְתָּ רָאשֵׁי לִוְיָתָן תִּתְּנֶנּוּ מַאֲכָל לְעָם לְצִיִּים:	יד
15	it was You who released springs and torrents, who made mighty rivers run dry;	*Attah vaka'ta ma'yan vanachal attah hovashta naharot eitan*	אַתָּה בָקַעְתָּ מַעְיָן וָנָחַל אַתָּה הוֹבַשְׁתָּ נַהֲרוֹת אֵיתָן:	טו
16	the day is Yours, the night also; it was You who set in place the orb of the sun;	*Lecha yom af-lecha layelah attah hachinota ma'or vashamesh*	לְךָ יוֹם אַף־לְךָ לָיְלָה אַתָּה הֲכִינוֹתָ מָאוֹר וָשָׁמֶשׁ:	טז
17	You fixed all the boundaries of the earth; summer and winter—You made them.	*Attah hitzavta kol-gevulot aretz kayitz vachoref attah yetzartam*	אַתָּה הִצַּבְתָּ כָּל־גְּבוּלוֹת אָרֶץ קַיִץ וָחֹרֶף אַתָּה יְצַרְתָּם:	יז
18	Be mindful of how the enemy blasphemes Hashem, how base people revile Your name.	*Zechar-zot oyev cheref Adonai ve'am naval ni'atzu shemecha*	זְכָר־זֹאת אוֹיֵב חֵרֵף יְהוָה וְעַם נָבָל נִאֲצוּ שְׁמֶךָ:	יח

19	Do not deliver Your dove to the wild beast; do not ignore forever the band of Your lowly ones.	*Al-titten lechayyat nefesh torecha chayyat aniyyeicha al-tishkach lanetzach*	אַל־תִּתֵּן לְחַיַּת נֶפֶשׁ תּוֹרֶךָ חַיַּת עֲנִיֶּיךָ אַל־תִּשְׁכַּח לָנֶצַח:	יט
20	Look to the covenant! For the dark places of the land are full of the haunts of lawlessness.	*Habbet labberit ki male'u machashakkei-eretz ne'ot chamas*	הַבֵּט לַבְּרִית כִּי מָלְאוּ מַחֲשַׁכֵּי־אֶרֶץ נְאוֹת חָמָס:	כ
21	Let not the downtrodden turn away disappointed; let the poor and needy praise Your name.	*Al-yashov dach nichlam ani ve'evyon yehallelu shemecha*	אַל־יָשֹׁב דַּךְ נִכְלָם עָנִי וְאֶבְיוֹן יְהַלְלוּ שְׁמֶךָ:	כא
22	Rise, O Hashem, Champion Your cause; be mindful that You are blasphemed by base men all day long.	*Kumah elohim rivah rivecha zechor cherpatecha minni-naval kol-hayyom*	קוּמָה אֱלֹהִים רִיבָה רִיבֶךָ זְכֹר חֶרְפָּתְךָ מִנִּי־נָבָל כָּל־הַיּוֹם:	כב
23	Do not ignore the shouts of Your foes, the din of Your adversaries that ascends all the time.	*Al-tishkach kol tzorerecha she'on kamecha oleh tamid*	אַל־תִּשְׁכַּח קוֹל צֹרְרֶיךָ שְׁאוֹן קָמֶיךָ עֹלֶה תָמִיד:	כג

75

—◦✦◦— עה

1	For the leader; al tashcheth. A psalm of Asaf, a song.	*Lammenatzeach al-tashcheit mizmor le'asaf shir*	לַמְנַצֵּחַ אַל־תַּשְׁחֵת מִזְמוֹר לְאָסָף שִׁיר:	א

2 We praise You, O Hashem; we praise You; Your presence is near; men tell of Your wondrous deeds.

Hodinu lecha elohim hodinu vekarov shemecha sipperu nifle'otecha

הוֹדִינוּ לְּךָ אֱלֹהִים הוֹדִינוּ וְקָרוֹב שְׁמֶךָ סִפְּרוּ נִפְלְאוֹתֶיךָ׃ ב

3 "At the time I choose, I will give judgment equitably.

Ki ekkach mo'ed ani meisharim eshpot

כִּי אֶקַּח מוֹעֵד אֲנִי מֵישָׁרִים אֶשְׁפֹּט׃ ג

4 Earth and all its inhabitants dissolve; it is I who keep its pillars firm. Selah.

Nemogim eretz vechol-yoshveha anochi tikkanti ammudeha selah

נְמֹגִים אֶרֶץ וְכָל־יֹשְׁבֶיהָ אָנֹכִי תִכַּנְתִּי עַמּוּדֶיהָ סֶלָה׃ ד

5 To wanton men I say, 'Do not be wanton!' to the wicked, 'Do not lift up your horns!'"

Amarti laholelim al-tahollu velaresha'im al-tarimu karen

אָמַרְתִּי לַהוֹלְלִים אַל־תָּהֹלּוּ וְלָרְשָׁעִים אַל־תָּרִימוּ קָרֶן׃ ה

6 Do not lift your horns up high in vainglorious bluster.

Al-tarimu lammarom karnechem tedabberu vetzavvar atak

אַל־תָּרִימוּ לַמָּרוֹם קַרְנְכֶם תְּדַבְּרוּ בְצַוָּאר עָתָק׃ ו

7 For what lifts a man comes not from the east or the west or the wilderness;

Ki lo mimmotza umimma'arav velo mimmidbar harim

כִּי לֹא מִמּוֹצָא וּמִמַּעֲרָב וְלֹא מִמִּדְבַּר הָרִים׃ ז

8 for Hashem it is who gives judgment; He brings down one man, He lifts up another.

Ki-elohim shofet zeh yashpil vezeh yarim

כִּי־אֱלֹהִים שֹׁפֵט זֶה יַשְׁפִּיל וְזֶה יָרִים׃ ח

9 There is a cup in Hashem's hand with foaming wine fully mixed; from this He pours; all the wicked of the earth drink, draining it to the very dregs.

Ki chos beyad-Adonai veyayin chamar malei mesech vayyagger mizzeh ach-shemareha yimtzu yishtu kol rish'ei-aretz

כִּי כוֹס בְּיַד־יְהֹוָה וְיַיִן חָמַר מָלֵא מֶסֶךְ וַיַּגֵּר מִזֶּה אַךְ־שְׁמָרֶיהָ יִמְצוּ יִשְׁתּוּ כֹּל רִשְׁעֵי־אָרֶץ: ט

10 As for me, I will declare forever, I will sing a hymn to the God of Yaakov.

Va'ani aggid le'olam azammerah lei'lohei ya'akov

וַאֲנִי אַגִּיד לְעֹלָם אֲזַמְּרָה לֵאלֹהֵי יַעֲקֹב: י

11 "All the horns of the wicked I will cut; but the horns of the righteous shall be lifted up."

Vechol-karnei resha'im agaddea teromamnah karnot tzaddik

וְכָל־קַרְנֵי רְשָׁעִים אֲגַדֵּעַ תְּרוֹמַמְנָה קַרְנוֹת צַדִּיק: יא

76

עו

1 For the leader; with instrumental music. A psalm of Asaf, a song.

Lam'natzeach binginot mizmor le'asaf shir

לַמְנַצֵּחַ בִּנְגִינֹת מִזְמוֹר לְאָסָף שִׁיר: א

2 Hashem has made Himself known in Yehuda, His name is great in Yisrael;

Noda bihudah elohim beyisra'el gadol shemo

נוֹדָע בִּיהוּדָה אֱלֹהִים בְּיִשְׂרָאֵל גָּדוֹל שְׁמוֹ: ב

3 Shalem became His abode; Tzion, His den.

Vayhi veshalem sukko ume'onato vetziyyon

וַיְהִי בְשָׁלֵם סֻכּוֹ וּמְעוֹנָתוֹ בְצִיּוֹן: ג

4	There He broke the fiery arrows of the bow, the shield and the sword of war. Selah.	*shammah shibbar rishfei-kashet magen vecherev umilchamah selah*

שָׁמָּה שִׁבַּר רִשְׁפֵי־קָשֶׁת מָגֵן וְחֶרֶב וּמִלְחָמָה סֶלָה׃ ד

5	You were resplendent, glorious, on the mountains of prey.	*Na'or attah addir me'harerei-taref*

נָאוֹר אַתָּה אַדִּיר מֵהַרְרֵי־טָרֶף׃ ה

6	The stout-hearted were despoiled; they were in a stupor; the bravest of men could not lift a hand.	*Eshtolelu abbirei lev namu shenatam velo-matze'u chol-anshei-chayil yedeihem*

אֶשְׁתּוֹלְלוּ אַבִּירֵי לֵב נָמוּ שְׁנָתָם וְלֹא־מָצְאוּ כָל־אַנְשֵׁי־חַיִל יְדֵיהֶם׃ ו

7	At Your blast, O God of Yaakov, horse and chariot lay stunned.	*Migga'aratecha elohei ya'akov nirdam verechev vasus*

מִגַּעֲרָתְךָ אֱלֹהֵי יַעֲקֹב נִרְדָּם וְרֶכֶב וָסוּס׃ ז

8	O You! You are awesome! Who can withstand You when You are enraged?	*Attah nora attah umi-ya'amod lefanecha me'az appecha*

אַתָּה נוֹרָא אַתָּה וּמִי־יַעֲמֹד לְפָנֶיךָ מֵאָז אַפֶּךָ׃ ח

9	In heaven You pronounced sentence; the earth was numbed with fright	*Mishamayim hishma'ta din eretz yare'ah veshakatah*

מִשָּׁמַיִם הִשְׁמַעְתָּ דִּין אֶרֶץ יָרְאָה וְשָׁקָטָה׃ ט

10	as Hashem rose to execute judgment, to deliver all the lowly of the earth. Selah.	*Bekum-lammishpat elohim lehoshia kol-anvei-eretz selah*

בְּקוּם־לַמִּשְׁפָּט אֱלֹהִים לְהוֹשִׁיעַ כָּל־עַנְוֵי־אֶרֶץ סֶלָה׃ י

11	The fiercest of men shall acknowledge You, when You gird on the last bit of fury.	*Ki-chamat adam todekka she'erit cheimot tachgor*

כִּי־חֲמַת אָדָם תּוֹדֶךָּ שְׁאֵרִית חֵמֹת תַּחְגֹּר׃ יא

12	Make vows and pay them to Hashem your God; all who are around Him shall bring tribute to the Awesome One.	*Nidaru veshallemu lAdonai eloheichem kol-sevivav yovilu shai lammora*	נִדְרוּ וְשַׁלְּמוּ לַיהֹוָה אֱלֹהֵיכֶם כָּל־סְבִיבָיו יוֹבִילוּ שַׁי לַמּוֹרָא:	יב
13	He curbs the spirit of princes, inspires awe in the kings of the earth.	*Yivtzor ruach negidim nora lemalchei-aretz*	יִבְצֹר רוּחַ נְגִידִים נוֹרָא לְמַלְכֵי־אָרֶץ:	יג

77

⸺◦◦◯◈◈◯◦◦⸺

עז

1	For the leader; on Yedutun. Of Asaf. A psalm.	*Lammenatzeach al-[yedutun] le'asaf mizmor*	לַמְנַצֵּחַ עַל־יְדִיתוּן [יְדוּתוּן] לְאָסָף מִזְמוֹר:	א
2	I cry aloud to Hashem; I cry to Hashem that He may give ear to me.	*Koli el-elohim ve'etz'akah koli el-elohim veha'azin eilai*	קוֹלִי אֶל־אֱלֹהִים וְאֶצְעָקָה קוֹלִי אֶל־אֱלֹהִים וְהַאֲזִין אֵלָי:	ב
3	In my time of distress I turn to Hashem, with my hand [uplifted]; [my eyes] flow all night without respite; I will not be comforted.	*Beyom tzarati Adonai darasheti yadi layyelah niggerah velo tafug mei'anah hinnacheim nafshi*	בְּיוֹם צָרָתִי אֲדֹנָי דָּרָשְׁתִּי יָדִי לַיְלָה נִגְּרָה וְלֹא תָפוּג מֵאֲנָה הִנָּחֵם נַפְשִׁי:	ג
4	I call Hashem to mind, I moan, I complain, my spirit fails. Selah.	*Ezkerah elohim ve'ehemayah asichah vetit'attef ruchi selah*	אֶזְכְּרָה אֱלֹהִים וְאֶהֱמָיָה אָשִׂיחָה וְתִתְעַטֵּף רוּחִי סֶלָה:	ד

5	You have held my eyelids open; I am overwrought, I cannot speak.	*Achazta shemurot einai nif'amti velo adabber*	אָחַזְתָּ שְׁמֻרוֹת עֵינָי נִפְעַמְתִּי וְלֹא אֲדַבֵּר: ה
6	My thoughts turn to days of old, to years long past.	*Chishavti yamim mikkedem shenot olamim*	חִשַּׁבְתִּי יָמִים מִקֶּדֶם שְׁנוֹת עוֹלָמִים: ו
7	I recall at night their jibes at me; I commune with myself; my spirit inquires,	*Ezkerah neginati ballayelah im-levavi asichah vaychappeis ruchi*	אֶזְכְּרָה נְגִינָתִי בַּלַּיְלָה עִם־לְבָבִי אָשִׂיחָה וַיְחַפֵּשׂ רוּחִי: ז
8	"Will Hashem reject forever and never again show favor?	*Hal'olamim yiznach Adonai velo-yosif lirtzot od*	הַלְעוֹלָמִים יִזְנַח אֲדֹנָי וְלֹא־יֹסִיף לִרְצוֹת עוֹד: ח
9	Has His faithfulness disappeared forever? Will His promise be unfulfilled for all time?	*He'afeis lanetzach chasdo gamar omer ledor vador*	הֶאָפֵס לָנֶצַח חַסְדּוֹ גָּמַר אֹמֶר לְדֹר וָדֹר: ט
10	Has Hashem forgotten how to pity? Has He in anger stifled His compassion?" Selah.	*Hashachach channot el im-kafatz be'af rachamav selah*	הֲשָׁכַח חַנּוֹת אֵל אִם־קָפַץ בְּאַף רַחֲמָיו סֶלָה: י
11	And I said, "It is my fault that the right hand of the Most High has changed."	*Va'omar challoti hi shenot yemin elyon*	וָאֹמַר חַלּוֹתִי הִיא שְׁנוֹת יְמִין עֶלְיוֹן: יא
12	I recall the deeds of Hashem; yes, I recall Your wonders of old;	*[Ezkor] ma'allelei-yah ki-ezkerah mikkedem pil'echa*	אזכיר [אֶזְכּוֹר] מַעַלְלֵי־יָהּ כִּי־אֶזְכְּרָה מִקֶּדֶם פִּלְאֶךָ: יב

13	I recount all Your works; I speak of Your acts.	*Vehagiti vechol-po'olecha uva'alilotecha asichah*	וְהָגִיתִי בְכָל־פָּעֳלֶךָ וּבַעֲלִילוֹתֶיךָ אָשִׂיחָה:	יג
14	O Hashem, Your ways are holiness; what god is as great as Hashem?	*Elohim bakkodesh darkecha mi-el gadol keilohim*	אֱלֹהִים בַּקֹּדֶשׁ דַּרְכֶּךָ מִי־אֵל גָּדוֹל כֵּאלֹהִים:	יד
15	You are the God who works wonders; You have manifested Your strength among the peoples.	*Attah ha'el oseih fele hoda'ta va'ammim uzzecha*	אַתָּה הָאֵל עֹשֵׂה פֶלֶא הוֹדַעְתָּ בָעַמִּים עֻזֶּךָ:	טו
16	By Your arm You redeemed Your people, the children of Yaakov and Yosef. Selah.	*Ga'alta bizroa' ammecha benei-ya'akov veyosef selah*	גָּאַלְתָּ בִּזְרוֹעַ עַמֶּךָ בְּנֵי־יַעֲקֹב וְיוֹסֵף סֶלָה:	טז
17	The waters saw You, O Hashem, the waters saw You and were convulsed; the very deep quaked as well.	*Ra'ucha mayim elohim ra'ucha mayim yachilu af yirgezu tehomot*	רָאוּךָ מַּיִם אֱלֹהִים רָאוּךָ מַּיִם יָחִילוּ אַף יִרְגְּזוּ תְהֹמוֹת:	יז
18	Clouds streamed water; the heavens rumbled; Your arrows flew about;	*Zoremu mayim avot kol natenu shechakim af-chatzatzecha yithallachu*	זֹרְמוּ מַיִם עָבוֹת קוֹל נָתְנוּ שְׁחָקִים אַף־חֲצָצֶיךָ יִתְהַלָּכוּ:	יח
19	Your thunder rumbled like wheels; lightning lit up the world; the earth quaked and trembled.	*Kol ra'amcha baggalgal he'iru verakim teivel ragezah vattir'ash ha'aretz*	קוֹל רַעַמְךָ בַּגַּלְגַּל הֵאִירוּ בְרָקִים תֵּבֵל רָגְזָה וַתִּרְעַשׁ הָאָרֶץ:	יט

20	Your way was through the sea, Your path, through the mighty waters; Your tracks could not be seen.	*Bayyam darkecha [ushevilcha] bemayim rabbim ve'ikkevotecha lo noda'u*

בַּיָּם דַּרְכֶּךָ וּשְׁבִילְךָ [וּשְׁבִילְךָ] בְּמַיִם רַבִּים וְעִקְּבוֹתֶיךָ לֹא נֹדָעוּ׃ כ

21	You led Your people like a flock in the care of Moshe and Aharon.	*Nachita chatzon ammecha beyad-mosheh ve'aharon*

נָחִיתָ כַצֹּאן עַמֶּךָ בְּיַד־מֹשֶׁה וְאַהֲרֹן׃ כא

78

עֹזֵן

1	A maskil of Asaf. Give ear, my people, to my teaching, turn your ear to what I say.	*Maskil le'asaf ha'azinah ammi torati hattu azenechem le'imrei-fi*

מַשְׂכִּיל לְאָסָף הַאֲזִינָה עַמִּי תּוֹרָתִי הַטּוּ אָזְנְכֶם לְאִמְרֵי־פִי׃ א

2	I will expound a theme, hold forth on the lessons of the past,	*Eftechah vemashal pi abbi'ah chidot minni-kedem*

אֶפְתְּחָה בְמָשָׁל פִּי אַבִּיעָה חִידוֹת מִנִּי־קֶדֶם׃ ב

3	things we have heard and known, that our fathers have told us.	*Asher shama'nu vanneida'eim va'avoteinu sipperu-lanu*

אֲשֶׁר שָׁמַעְנוּ וַנֵּדָעֵם וַאֲבוֹתֵינוּ סִפְּרוּ־לָנוּ׃ ג

4	We will not withhold them from their children, telling the coming generation the praises of Hashem and His might, and the wonders He performed.	*Lo nechached mibbeneihem ledor acharon mesapperim tehillot Adonai ve'ezuzo venifle'otav asher asah*

לֹא נְכַחֵד מִבְּנֵיהֶם לְדוֹר אַחֲרוֹן מְסַפְּרִים תְּהִלּוֹת יְהֹוָה וֶעֱזוּזוֹ וְנִפְלְאוֹתָיו אֲשֶׁר עָשָׂה׃ ד

5 He established a decree in Yaakov, ordained a teaching in Yisrael, charging our fathers to make them known to their children,

Vayyakem edut beya'akov vetorah sam beyisra'el asher tzivvah et-avoteinu lehodi'am livneihem

וַיָּקֶם עֵדוּת בְּיַעֲקֹב וְתוֹרָה שָׂם בְּיִשְׂרָאֵל אֲשֶׁר צִוָּה אֶת־אֲבוֹתֵינוּ לְהוֹדִיעָם לִבְנֵיהֶם: ה

6 that a future generation might know —children yet to be born— and in turn tell their children

Lema'an yede'u dor acharon banim yivvaledu yakumu visapperu livneihem

לְמַעַן יֵדְעוּ דּוֹר אַחֲרוֹן בָּנִים יִוָּלֵדוּ יָקֻמוּ וִיסַפְּרוּ לִבְנֵיהֶם: ו

7 that they might put their confidence in Hashem, and not forget Hashem's great deeds, but observe His commandments,

Veyasimu velohim kislam velo yishkechu ma'allelei-el umitzvtav yintzoru

וְיָשִׂימוּ בֵאלֹהִים כִּסְלָם וְלֹא יִשְׁכְּחוּ מַעַלְלֵי־אֵל וּמִצְוֹתָיו יִנְצֹרוּ: ז

8 and not be like their fathers, a wayward and defiant generation, a generation whose heart was inconstant, whose spirit was not true to Hashem.

Velo yihyu ka'avotam dor sorer umoreh dor lo-heichin libbo velo-ne'emnah et-el rucho

וְלֹא יִהְיוּ כַּאֲבוֹתָם דּוֹר סוֹרֵר וּמֹרֶה דּוֹר לֹא־הֵכִין לִבּוֹ וְלֹא־נֶאֶמְנָה אֶת־אֵל רוּחוֹ: ח

9 Like the Ephraimite bowmen who played false in the day of battle,

Benei-efrayim noshekei romei-kashet hafechu beyom kerav

בְּנֵי־אֶפְרַיִם נוֹשְׁקֵי רוֹמֵי־קָשֶׁת הָפְכוּ בְּיוֹם קְרָב: ט

10 they did not keep Hashem's covenant, they refused to follow His instruction;

Lo shameru berit elohim uvetorato me'anu lalechet

לֹא שָׁמְרוּ בְּרִית אֱלֹהִים וּבְתוֹרָתוֹ מֵאֲנוּ לָלֶכֶת: י

11	they forgot His deeds and the wonders that He showed them.	*Vayyishkechu alilotav venifle'otav asher her'am*	וַיִּשְׁכְּחוּ עֲלִילוֹתָיו וְנִפְלְאוֹתָיו אֲשֶׁר הֶרְאָם:	יא

He performed marvels in the sight of their fathers, in the land of Egypt, the plain of Zoan.

neged avotam asah fele be'eretz mitzrayim sedeih-tzo'an

נֶגֶד אֲבוֹתָם עָשָׂה פֶלֶא בְּאֶרֶץ מִצְרַיִם שְׂדֵה־צֹעַן:

יב

12

He split the sea and took them through it; He made the waters stand like a wall.

Baka yam vayya'avirem vayyatzev-mayim kemo-neid

בָּקַע יָם וַיַּעֲבִירֵם וַיַּצֶּב־מַיִם כְּמוֹ־נֵד:

יג

13

He led them with a cloud by day, and throughout the night by the light of fire.

Vayyancheim be'anan yomam vechol-hallaylah be'or eish

וַיַּנְחֵם בֶּעָנָן יוֹמָם וְכָל־הַלַּיְלָה בְּאוֹר אֵשׁ:

יד

14

He split rocks in the wilderness and gave them drink as if from the great deep.

Yevakka tzurim bammidbar vayyashk kit'homot rabbah

יְבַקַּע צֻרִים בַּמִּדְבָּר וַיַּשְׁקְ כִּתְהֹמוֹת רַבָּה:

טו

15

He brought forth streams from a rock and made them flow down like a river.

Vayyotzi nozelim missala vayyored kanneharot mayim

וַיּוֹצִא נוֹזְלִים מִסָּלַע וַיּוֹרֶד כַּנְּהָרוֹת מָיִם:

טז

16

But they went on sinning against Him, defying the Most High in the parched land.

Vayyosifu od lachato-lo lamrot elyon batziyyah

וַיּוֹסִיפוּ עוֹד לַחֲטֹא־לוֹ לַמְרוֹת עֶלְיוֹן בַּצִּיָּה:

יז

17

To test Hashem was in their mind when they demanded food for themselves.

Vaynassu-el bilvavam lish'al-ochel lenafsham

וַיְנַסּוּ־אֵל בִּלְבָבָם לִשְׁאָל־אֹכֶל לְנַפְשָׁם:

יח

18

19	They spoke against Hashem, saying, "Can Hashem spread a feast in the wilderness?	*Vaydabberu beilohim ameru hayuchal el la'aroch shulchan bammidbar*	וַיְדַבְּרוּ בֵּאלֹהִים אָמְרוּ הֲיוּכַל אֵל לַעֲרֹךְ שֻׁלְחָן בַּמִּדְבָּר:	יט
20	True, He struck the rock and waters flowed, streams gushed forth; but can He provide bread? Can He supply His people with meat?"	*Hein hikkah-tzur vayyazuvu mayim unechalim yishtofu hagam-lechem yuchal teit im-yachin she'er le'ammo*	הֵן הִכָּה־צוּר וַיָּזוּבוּ מַיִם וּנְחָלִים יִשְׁטֹפוּ הֲגַם־לֶחֶם יוּכַל תֵּת אִם־יָכִין שְׁאֵר לְעַמּוֹ:	כ
21	Hashem heard and He raged; fire broke out against Yaakov, anger flared up at Yisrael,	*Lachein shama Adonai vayyit'abbar ve'eish nissekah veya'akov vegam-af alah veyisra'el*	לָכֵן שָׁמַע יְהֹוָה וַיִּתְעַבָּר וְאֵשׁ נִשְּׂקָה בְיַעֲקֹב וְגַם־אַף עָלָה בְיִשְׂרָאֵל:	כא
22	because they did not put their trust in Hashem, did not rely on His deliverance.	*Ki lo he'eminu beilohim velo vatechu bishu'ato*	כִּי לֹא הֶאֱמִינוּ בֵּאלֹהִים וְלֹא בָטְחוּ בִּישׁוּעָתוֹ:	כב
23	So He commanded the skies above, He opened the doors of heaven	*Vaytzav shechakim mimma'al vedaltei shamayim patach*	וַיְצַו שְׁחָקִים מִמָּעַל וְדַלְתֵי שָׁמַיִם פָּתָח:	כג
24	and rained manna upon them for food, giving them heavenly grain.	*Vayyamter aleihem mahn le'echol udegan-shamayim natan lamo*	וַיַּמְטֵר עֲלֵיהֶם מָן לֶאֱכֹל וּדְגַן־שָׁמַיִם נָתַן לָמוֹ:	כד
25	Each man ate a hero's meal; He sent them provision in plenty.	*lechem abbirim achal ish tzeidah shalach lahem lasova*	לֶחֶם אַבִּירִים אָכַל אִישׁ צֵידָה שָׁלַח לָהֶם לָשֹׂבַע:	כה
26	He set the east wind moving in heaven, and drove the south wind by His might.	*Yassa kadim bashamayim vaynaheig be'uzzo teiman*	יַסַּע קָדִים בַּשָּׁמָיִם וַיְנַהֵג בְּעֻזּוֹ תֵימָן:	כו

27	He rained meat on them like dust, winged birds like the sands of the sea,	*Vayyamter aleihem ke'afar she'er uchechol yammim ohf kanaf*	וַיַּמְטֵר עֲלֵיהֶם כֶּעָפָר שְׁאֵר וּכְחוֹל יַמִּים עוֹף כָּנָף:	כז
28	making them come down inside His camp, around His dwelling-place.	*Vayyappel bekerev machaneihu saviv lemishkenotav*	וַיַּפֵּל בְּקֶרֶב מַחֲנֵהוּ סָבִיב לְמִשְׁכְּנֹתָיו:	כח
29	They ate till they were sated; He gave them what they craved.	*Vayyochlu vayyisbe'u me'od veta'avatam yavi lahem*	וַיֹּאכְלוּ וַיִּשְׂבְּעוּ מְאֹד וְתַאֲוָתָם יָבִא לָהֶם:	כט
30	They had not yet wearied of what they craved, the food was still in their mouths	*Lo-zaru mitta'avatam od ochlam befihem*	לֹא־זָרוּ מִתַּאֲוָתָם עוֹד אָכְלָם בְּפִיהֶם:	ל
31	when Hashem's anger flared up at them. He slew their sturdiest, struck down the youth of Yisrael.	*Ve'af elohim alah vahem vayyaharog bemishmanneihem uvachurei yisra'el hichria'*	וְאַף אֱלֹהִים עָלָה בָהֶם וַיַּהֲרֹג בְּמִשְׁמַנֵּיהֶם וּבַחוּרֵי יִשְׂרָאֵל הִכְרִיעַ:	לא
32	Nonetheless, they went on sinning and had no faith in His wonders.	*Bechol-zot chate'u-od velo-he'eminu beniflc'otav*	בְּכָל־זֹאת חָטְאוּ־עוֹד וְלֹא־הֶאֱמִינוּ בְּנִפְלְאוֹתָיו:	לב
33	He made their days end in futility, their years in sudden death.	*Vaychal-bahevel yemeihem ushenotam babbehalah*	וַיְכַל־בַּהֶבֶל יְמֵיהֶם וּשְׁנוֹתָם בַּבֶּהָלָה:	לג
34	When He struck them, they turned to Him and sought Hashem once again.	*Im-haragam uderashuhu veshavu veshicharu-el*	אִם־הֲרָגָם וּדְרָשׁוּהוּ וְשָׁבוּ וְשִׁחֲרוּ־אֵל:	לד

35	They remembered that Hashem was their rock, Hashem Most High, their Redeemer.	*Vayyizkeru ki-elohim tzuram ve'el elyon go'alam*	וַיִּזְכְּרוּ כִּי־אֱלֹהִים צוּרָם וְאֵל עֶלְיוֹן גֹּאֲלָם:	לה
36	Yet they deceived Him with their speech, lied to Him with their words;	*Vayfattuhu befihem uvilshonam yechazzevu-lo*	וַיְפַתּוּהוּ בְּפִיהֶם וּבִלְשׁוֹנָם יְכַזְּבוּ־לוֹ:	לו
37	their hearts were inconstant toward Him; they were untrue to His covenant.	*Velibbam lo-nachon immo velo ne'emnu bivrito*	וְלִבָּם לֹא־נָכוֹן עִמּוֹ וְלֹא נֶאֶמְנוּ בִּבְרִיתוֹ:	לז
38	But He, being merciful, forgave iniquity and would not destroy; He restrained His wrath time and again and did not give full vent to His fury;	*Vehu rachum yechapper avon velo-yashchit vehirbah lehashiv appo velo-ya'ir kol-chamato*	וְהוּא רַחוּם יְכַפֵּר עָוֺן וְלֹא־יַשְׁחִית וְהִרְבָּה לְהָשִׁיב אַפּוֹ וְלֹא־יָעִיר כָּל־חֲמָתוֹ:	לח
39	for He remembered that they were but flesh, a passing breath that does not return.	*Vayyizkor ki-vasar heimmah ruach holeich velo yashuv*	וַיִּזְכֹּר כִּי־בָשָׂר הֵמָּה רוּחַ הוֹלֵךְ וְלֹא יָשׁוּב:	לט
40	How often did they defy Him in the wilderness, did they grieve Him in the wasteland!	*Kammah yamruhu vammidbar ya'atzivuhu bishimon*	כַּמָּה יַמְרוּהוּ בַמִּדְבָּר יַעֲצִיבוּהוּ בִּישִׁימוֹן:	מ
41	Again and again they tested Hashem, vexed the Holy One of Yisrael.	*Vayyashuvu vaynassu el ukedosh yisra'el hitvu*	וַיָּשׁוּבוּ וַיְנַסּוּ אֵל וּקְדוֹשׁ יִשְׂרָאֵל הִתְווּ:	מא

42	They did not remember His strength, or the day He redeemed them from the foe;	*Lo-zacheru et-yado yom asher-padam minni-tzar*	לֹא־זָכְרוּ אֶת־יָדוֹ יוֹם אֲשֶׁר־פָּדָם מִנִּי־צָר׃	מב
43	how He displayed His signs in Egypt, His wonders in the plain of Zoan.	*Asher-sam bemitzrayim ototav umofetav bisdeh-tzo'an*	אֲשֶׁר־שָׂם בְּמִצְרַיִם אֹתוֹתָיו וּמוֹפְתָיו בִּשְׂדֵה־צֹעַן׃	מג
44	He turned their rivers into blood; He made their waters undrinkable.	*Vayyahafoch ledam ye'oreihem venozeleihem bal-yishtayun*	וַיַּהֲפֹךְ לְדָם יְאֹרֵיהֶם וְנֹזְלֵיהֶם בַּל־יִשְׁתָּיוּן׃	מד
45	He inflicted upon them swarms of insects to devour them, frogs to destroy them.	*Yeshallach bahem arov vayyochlem utzefardea' vattash'chiteim*	יְשַׁלַּח בָּהֶם עָרֹב וַיֹּאכְלֵם וּצְפַרְדֵּעַ וַתַּשְׁחִיתֵם׃	מה
46	He gave their crops over to grubs, their produce to locusts.	*Vayyitten lechasil yevulam vigi'am la'arbeh*	וַיִּתֵּן לֶחָסִיל יְבוּלָם וִיגִיעָם לָאַרְבֶּה׃	מו
47	He killed their vines with hail, their sycamores with frost.	*Yaharog babbarad gafnam veshikmotam bachanamal*	יַהֲרֹג בַּבָּרָד גַּפְנָם וְשִׁקְמוֹתָם בַּחֲנָמַל׃	מז
48	He gave their beasts over to hail, their cattle to lightning bolts.	*Vayyasger labbarad be'iram umikneihem lareshafim*	וַיַּסְגֵּר לַבָּרָד בְּעִירָם וּמִקְנֵיהֶם לָרְשָׁפִים׃	מח
49	He inflicted His burning anger upon them, wrath, indignation, trouble, a band of deadly messengers.	*Yeshallach-bam charon appo evrah vaza'am vetzarah mishlachat mal'achei ra'im*	יְשַׁלַּח־בָּם חֲרוֹן אַפּוֹ עֶבְרָה וָזַעַם וְצָרָה מִשְׁלַחַת מַלְאֲכֵי רָעִים׃	מט

50	He cleared a path for His anger; He did not stop short of slaying them, but gave them over to pestilence.	*Yefalles nativ le'appo lo-chasach mimmavet nafsham vechayyatam laddever hisgir*	יְפַלֵּס נָתִיב לְאַפּוֹ לֹא־חָשַׂךְ מִמָּוֶת נַפְשָׁם וְחַיָּתָם לַדֶּבֶר הִסְגִּיר׃	נ
51	He struck every first-born in Egypt, the first fruits of their vigor in the tents of Ham.	*Vayyach kol-bechor bemitzrayim reshit onim be'oholei-cham*	וַיַּךְ כָּל־בְּכוֹר בְּמִצְרָיִם רֵאשִׁית אוֹנִים בְּאׇהֳלֵי־חָם׃	נא
52	He set His people moving like sheep, drove them like a flock in the wilderness.	*Vayyassa katzon ammo vaynahagem ka'eder bammidbar*	וַיַּסַּע כַּצֹּאן עַמּוֹ וַיְנַהֲגֵם כַּעֵדֶר בַּמִּדְבָּר׃	נב
53	He led them in safety; they were unafraid; as for their enemies, the sea covered them.	*Vayyancheim lavetach velo fachadu ve'et-oyeveihem kissah hayyam*	וַיַּנְחֵם לָבֶטַח וְלֹא פָחָדוּ וְאֶת־אוֹיְבֵיהֶם כִּסָּה הַיָּם׃	נג
54	He brought them to His holy realm the mountain His right hand had acquired.	*Vayvi'em el-gevul kodsho har-zeh kanetah yemino*	וַיְבִיאֵם אֶל־גְּבוּל קׇדְשׁוֹ הַר־זֶה קָנְתָה יְמִינוֹ׃	נד
55	He expelled nations before them, settled the tribes of Yisrael in their tents, allotting them their portion by the line.*	*Vaygaresh mippeneihem goyim vayyappilem bechevel nachalah vayyashken be'oholeihem shivtei yisra'el*	וַיְגָרֶשׁ מִפְּנֵיהֶם גּוֹיִם וַיַּפִּילֵם בְּחֶבֶל נַחֲלָה וַיַּשְׁכֵּן בְּאׇהֳלֵיהֶם שִׁבְטֵי יִשְׂרָאֵל׃	נה
56	Yet they defiantly tested Hashem Most High, and did not observe His decrees.	*Vaynassu vayyamru et-elohim elyon ve'edotav lo shamaru*	וַיְנַסּוּ וַיַּמְרוּ אֶת־אֱלֹהִים עֶלְיוֹן וְעֵדוֹתָיו לֹא שָׁמָרוּ׃	נו

57	They fell away, disloyal like their fathers; they played false like a treacherous bow.	*Vayyissogu vayyivgedu ka'avotam nehpechu kekeshet remiyyah*

וַיִּסֹּגוּ וַיִּבְגְּדוּ כַּאֲבוֹתָם נֶהְפְּכוּ כְּקֶשֶׁת רְמִיָּה: נז

58	They vexed Him with their high places; they incensed Him with their idols.	*Vayyach'isuhu bevamotam uvifsileihem yakni'uhu*

וַיַּכְעִיסוּהוּ בְּבָמוֹתָם וּבִפְסִילֵיהֶם יַקְנִיאוּהוּ: נח

59	Hashem heard it and was enraged; He utterly rejected Yisrael.	*Shama elohim vayyit'abbar vayyim'as me'od beyisra'el*

שָׁמַע אֱלֹהִים וַיִּתְעַבָּר וַיִּמְאַס מְאֹד בְּיִשְׂרָאֵל: נט

60	He forsook the Mishkan of Shilo, the tent He had set among men.	*Vayyittosh mishkan shilo ohel shikken ba'adam*

וַיִּטֹּשׁ מִשְׁכַּן שִׁלוֹ אֹהֶל שִׁכֵּן בָּאָדָם: ס

61	He let His might go into captivity, His glory into the hands of the foe.	*Vayyitten lashevi uzzo vetif'arto veyad-tzar*

וַיִּתֵּן לַשְּׁבִי עֻזּוֹ וְתִפְאַרְתּוֹ בְיַד־צָר: סא

62	He gave His people over to the sword; He was enraged at His very own.	*Vayyasger lacherev ammo uvenachalato hit'abbar*

וַיַּסְגֵּר לַחֶרֶב עַמּוֹ וּבְנַחֲלָתוֹ הִתְעַבָּר: סב

63	Fire consumed their young men, and their maidens remained unwed.	*Bachurav achelah-eish uvetulotav lo hullalu*

בַּחוּרָיו אָכְלָה־אֵשׁ וּבְתוּלֹתָיו לֹא הוּלָּלוּ: סג

64	Their Kohanim fell by the sword, and their widows could not weep.	*Kohanav bacherev nafalu ve'almenotav lo tivkenah*

כֹּהֲנָיו בַּחֶרֶב נָפָלוּ וְאַלְמְנֹתָיו לֹא תִבְכֶּינָה: סד

65	Hashem awoke as from sleep, like a warrior shaking off wine.	*Vayyikatz keyashein Adonai kegibbor mitronen miyyayin*	וַיִּקַץ כְּיָשֵׁן אֲדֹנָי כְּגִבּוֹר מִתְרוֹנֵן מִיָּיִן:	סה
66	He beat back His foes, dealing them lasting disgrace.	*Vayyach-tzarav achor cherpat olam natan lamo*	וַיַּךְ־צָרָיו אָחוֹר חֶרְפַּת עוֹלָם נָתַן לָמוֹ:	סו
67	He rejected the clan of Yosef; He did not choose the tribe of Efraim.	*Vayyim'as be'ohel yosef uveshevet efrayim lo vachar*	וַיִּמְאַס בְּאֹהֶל יוֹסֵף וּבְשֵׁבֶט אֶפְרַיִם לֹא בָחָר:	סז
68	He did choose the tribe of Yehuda, Mount Tzion, which He loved.	*Vayyivchar et-sheivet yehudah et-har tziyyon asher ahev*	וַיִּבְחַר אֶת־שֵׁבֶט יְהוּדָה אֶת־הַר צִיּוֹן אֲשֶׁר אָהֵב:	סח
69	He built His Sanctuary like the heavens, like the earth that He established forever.	*Vayyiven kemo-ramim mikdasho ke'eretz yesadah le'olam*	וַיִּבֶן כְּמוֹ־רָמִים מִקְדָּשׁוֹ כְּאֶרֶץ יְסָדָהּ לְעוֹלָם:	סט
70	He chose David, His servant, and took him from the sheepfolds.	*Vayyivchar bedavid avdo vayyikkachehu mimmichle'ot tzon*	וַיִּבְחַר בְּדָוִד עַבְדּוֹ וַיִּקָּחֵהוּ מִמִּכְלְאֹת צֹאן:	ע
71	He brought him from minding the nursing ewes to tend His people Yaakov, Yisrael, His very own.	*Me'achar alot hevi'o lir'ot beya'akov ammo uveyisra'el nachalato*	מֵאַחַר עָלוֹת הֱבִיאוֹ לִרְעוֹת בְּיַעֲקֹב עַמּוֹ וּבְיִשְׂרָאֵל נַחֲלָתוֹ:	עא
72	He tended them with blameless heart; with skillful hands he led them.	*Vayyir'em ketom levavo uvitvunot kappav yanchem*	וַיִּרְעֵם כְּתֹם לְבָבוֹ וּבִתְבוּנוֹת כַּפָּיו יַנְחֵם:	עב

79

1 A psalm of Asaf. O Hashem, heathens have entered Your domain, defiled Your holy temple, and turned Yerushalayim into ruins.

Mizmor le'asaf elohim ba'u goyim benachalatecha timme'u et-heichal kodshecha samu et-yerushala'im le'iyyim

מִזְמוֹר לְאָסָף אֱלֹהִים בָּאוּ גוֹיִם בְּנַחֲלָתֶךָ טִמְּאוּ אֶת־הֵיכַל קׇדְשֶׁךָ שָׂמוּ אֶת־יְרוּשָׁלַ͏ִם לְעִיִּים: א

2 They have left Your servants' corpses as food for the fowl of heaven, and the flesh of Your faithful for the wild beasts.

Natenu et-nivlat avadecha ma'achal le'of hashamayim besar chasidecha lechayto-aretz

נָתְנוּ אֶת־נִבְלַת עֲבָדֶיךָ מַאֲכָל לְעוֹף הַשָּׁמָיִם בְּשַׂר חֲסִידֶיךָ לְחַיְתוֹ־אָרֶץ: ב

3 Their blood was shed like water around Yerushalayim, with none to bury them.

Shafechu damam kammayim sevivot yerushala'im ve'ein kover

שָׁפְכוּ דָמָם כַּמַּיִם סְבִיבוֹת יְרוּשָׁלַ͏ִם וְאֵין קוֹבֵר: ג

4 We have become the butt of our neighbors, the scorn and derision of those around us.

Hayinu cherpah lishcheineinu la'ag vakeles lisvivoteinu

הָיִינוּ חֶרְפָּה לִשְׁכֵנֵינוּ לַעַג וָקֶלֶס לִסְבִיבוֹתֵינוּ: ד

5 How long, Hashem, will You be angry forever, will Your indignation blaze like fire?

Ad-mah Adonai te'enaf lanetzach tiv'ar kemo-eish kin'atecha

עַד־מָה יְהֹוָה תֶּאֱנַף לָנֶצַח תִּבְעַר כְּמוֹ־אֵשׁ קִנְאָתֶךָ: ה

6	Pour out Your fury on the nations that do not know You, upon the kingdoms that do not invoke Your name,	*Shefoch chamatecha el-haggoyim asher lo-yeda'ucha ve'al mamlachot asher beshimcha lo kara'u*	שְׁפֹךְ חֲמָתְךָ אֶל־הַגּוֹיִם אֲשֶׁר לֹא־יְדָעוּךָ וְעַל מַמְלָכוֹת אֲשֶׁר בְּשִׁמְךָ לֹא קָרָאוּ:	ו
7	for they have devoured Yaakov and desolated his home.	*Ki achal et-ya'akov ve'et-navehu heshammu*	כִּי אָכַל אֶת־יַעֲקֹב וְאֶת־נָוֵהוּ הֵשַׁמּוּ:	ז
8	Do not hold our former iniquities against us; let Your compassion come swiftly toward us, for we have sunk very low.	*Al-tizkar-lanu avnot rishonim maher yekaddemunu rachamecha ki dallonu me'od*	אַל־תִּזְכָּר־לָנוּ עֲוֺנֹת רִאשֹׁנִים מַהֵר יְקַדְּמוּנוּ רַחֲמֶיךָ כִּי דַלּוֹנוּ מְאֹד:	ח
9	Help us, O Hashem, our deliverer, for the sake of the glory of Your name. Save us and forgive our sin, for the sake of Your name.	*Azerenu elohei yish'enu al-devar kevod-shemecha vehatzilenu vechapper al-chattoteinu lema'an shemecha*	עָזְרֵנוּ אֱלֹהֵי יִשְׁעֵנוּ עַל־דְּבַר כְּבוֹד־שְׁמֶךָ וְהַצִּילֵנוּ וְכַפֵּר עַל־חַטֹּאתֵינוּ לְמַעַן שְׁמֶךָ:	ט
10	Let the nations not say, "Where is their God?" Before our eyes let it be known among the nations that You avenge the spilled blood of Your servants.	*lammah yomru haggoyim ayyeh eloheihem yivvada [baggoyim] le'eineinu nikmat dam-avadecha hashafuch*	לָמָּה יֹאמְרוּ הַגּוֹיִם אַיֵּה אֱלֹהֵיהֶם יִוָּדַע בַגיים [בַּגּוֹיִם] לְעֵינֵינוּ נִקְמַת דַּם־עֲבָדֶיךָ הַשָּׁפוּךְ:	י
11	Let the groans of the prisoners reach You; reprieve those condemned to death, as befits Your great strength.	*Tavo lefanecha enkat asir kegodel zero'acha hoter benei temutah*	תָּבוֹא לְפָנֶיךָ אֶנְקַת אָסִיר כְּגֹדֶל זְרוֹעֲךָ הוֹתֵר בְּנֵי תְמוּתָה:	יא

12	Pay back our neighbors sevenfold for the abuse they have flung at You, O Hashem.	*Vehashev lishcheineinu shiv'atayim el-cheikam cherpatam asher cherefucha Adonai*

וְהָשֵׁב לִשְׁכֵנֵינוּ שִׁבְעָתַיִם אֶל־חֵיקָם חֶרְפָּתָם אֲשֶׁר חֵרְפוּךָ אֲדֹנָי: יב

13	Then we, Your people, the flock You shepherd, shall glorify You forever; for all time we shall tell Your praises.	*Va'anachnu ammecha vetzon mar'itecha nodeh lecha le'olam ledor vador nesapper tehillatecha*

וַאֲנַחְנוּ עַמְּךָ וְצֹאן מַרְעִיתֶךָ נוֹדֶה לְּךָ לְעוֹלָם לְדֹר וָדֹר נְסַפֵּר תְּהִלָּתֶךָ: יג

80

—◦⟨◦⊛◦⟩◦—

פ

1	For the leader; on shoshannim, eduth. Of Asaf. A psalm.	*Lammenatzeach el-shoshannim edut le'asaf mizmor*

לַמְנַצֵּחַ אֶל־שֹׁשַׁנִּים עֵדוּת לְאָסָף מִזְמוֹר: א

2	Give ear, O shepherd of Yisrael who leads Yosef like a flock! Appear, You who are enthroned on the cherubim,	*Ro'eh yisra'el ha'azinah noheig katzon yosef yoshev hakkeruvim hofi'ah*

רֹעֵה יִשְׂרָאֵל הַאֲזִינָה נֹהֵג כַּצֹּאן יוֹסֵף יֹשֵׁב הַכְּרוּבִים הוֹפִיעָה: ב

3	at the head of Efraim, Binyamin, and Menashe! Rouse Your might and come to our help!	*Lifnei efrayim uvinyamin umenasheh orerah et-gevuratecha ulechah lishu'atah lanu*

לִפְנֵי אֶפְרַיִם וּבִנְיָמִן וּמְנַשֶּׁה עוֹרְרָה אֶת־גְּבוּרָתֶךָ וּלְכָה לִישֻׁעָתָה לָּנוּ: ג

4	Restore us, O Hashem; show Your favor that we may be delivered.	*Elohim hashivenu veha'er panecha venivvashei'ah*

אֱלֹהִים הֲשִׁיבֵנוּ וְהָאֵר פָּנֶיךָ וְנִוָּשֵׁעָה: ד

5	O Hashem, God of hosts, how long will You be wrathful toward the prayers of Your people?	*Adonai elohim tzeva'ot ad-matai ashanta bitfillat ammecha*	יְהֹוָה אֱלֹהִים צְבָאוֹת עַד־מָתַי עָשַׁנְתָּ בִּתְפִלַּת עַמֶּךָ:

ה

6	You have fed them tears as their daily bread, made them drink great measures of tears.	*He'echaltam lechem dim'ah vattashkeimo bidma'ot shalish*	הֶאֱכַלְתָּם לֶחֶם דִּמְעָה וַתַּשְׁקֵמוֹ בִּדְמָעוֹת שָׁלִישׁ:

ו

7	You set us at strife with our neighbors; our enemies mock us at will.	*Tesimenu madon lishcheineinu ve'oyeveinu yil'agu-lamo*	תְּשִׂימֵנוּ מָדוֹן לִשְׁכֵנֵינוּ וְאֹיְבֵינוּ יִלְעֲגוּ־לָמוֹ:

ז

8	O God of hosts, restore us; show Your favor that we may be delivered.	*Elohim tzeva'ot hashivenu veha'er panecha venivvashe'ah*	אֱלֹהִים צְבָאוֹת הֲשִׁיבֵנוּ וְהָאֵר פָּנֶיךָ וְנִוָּשֵׁעָה:

ח

9	You plucked up a vine from Egypt; You expelled nations and planted it.	*gefen mimmitzrayim tassia' tegareish goyim vattitta'eha*	גֶּפֶן מִמִּצְרַיִם תַּסִּיעַ תְּגָרֵשׁ גּוֹיִם וַתִּטָּעֶהָ:

ט

10	You cleared a place for it; it took deep root and filled the land.	*Pinnita lefaneha vattashreish sharasheha vattemallei-aretz*	פִּנִּיתָ לְפָנֶיהָ וַתַּשְׁרֵשׁ שָׁרָשֶׁיהָ וַתְּמַלֵּא־אָרֶץ:

י

11	The mountains were covered by its shade, mighty cedars by its boughs.	*Kassu harim tzillah va'anafeha arzei-el*	כָּסּוּ הָרִים צִלָּהּ וַעֲנָפֶיהָ אַרְזֵי־אֵל:

יא

12	Its branches reached the sea, its shoots, the river.	*Teshallach ketzireha ad-yam ve'el-nahar yonekoteiha*	תְּשַׁלַּח קְצִירֶהָ עַד־יָם וְאֶל־נָהָר יוֹנְקוֹתֶיהָ:

יב

13	Why did You breach its wall so that every passerby plucks its fruit,	*lammah paratzta gedeireha ve'aruha kol-overei darech*	לָמָּה פָּרַצְתָּ גְדֵרֶיהָ וְאָרוּהָ כׇּל־עֹבְרֵי דָרֶךְ: יג
14	wild boars gnaw at it, and creatures of the field feed on it?	*Yecharsemennah chazir miyya'ar veziz sadai yir'ennah*	יְכַרְסְמֶנָּה חֲזִיר מִיָּעַר וְזִיז שָׂדַי יִרְעֶנָּה: יד
15	O God of hosts, turn again, look down from heaven and see; take note of that vine,	*Elohim tzeva'ot shuv-na habbeit mishamayim ure'eh ufekod gefen zot*	אֱלֹהִים צְבָאוֹת שׁוּב־נָא הַבֵּט מִשָּׁמַיִם וּרְאֵה וּפְקֹד גֶּפֶן זֹאת: טו
16	the stock planted by Your right hand, the stem you have taken as Your own.	*Vechannah asher-nate'ah yeminecha ve'al-bein immatztah lach*	וְכַנָּה אֲשֶׁר־נָטְעָה יְמִינֶךָ וְעַל־בֵּן אִמַּצְתָּה לָּךְ: טז
17	For it is burned by fire and cut down, perishing before Your angry blast.	*Serufah va'eish kesuchah migga'arat panecha yovedu*	שְׂרֻפָה בָאֵשׁ כְּסוּחָה מִגַּעֲרַת פָּנֶיךָ יֹאבֵדוּ: יז
18	Grant Your help to the man at Your right hand, the one You have taken as Your own.	*Tehi-yadecha al-ish yeminecha al-ben-adam immatzta lach*	תְּהִי־יָדְךָ עַל־אִישׁ יְמִינֶךָ עַל־בֶּן־אָדָם אִמַּצְתָּ לָּךְ: יח
19	We will not turn away from You; preserve our life that we may invoke Your name.	*Velo-nasog mimmekka techayyeinu uveshimcha nikra*	וְלֹא־נָסוֹג מִמֶּךָּ תְּחַיֵּנוּ וּבְשִׁמְךָ נִקְרָא: יט
20	O Hashem, God of hosts, restore us; show Your favor that we may be delivered.	*Adonai elohim tzeva'ot hashivenu ha'er panecha venivvasheiah*	יְהֹוָה אֱלֹהִים צְבָאוֹת הֲשִׁיבֵנוּ הָאֵר פָּנֶיךָ וְנִוָּשֵׁעָה: כ

81

⊸०⟨∞⟩०⊶

פא

1	For the leader; on the gittith. Of Asaf.	*Lammenatzeach al-haggittit le'asaf*	לַמְנַצֵּחַ עַל־הַגִּתִּית לְאָסָף:	א
2	Sing joyously to Hashem, our strength; raise a shout for the God of Yaakov.	*Harninu lelohim uzzenu hari'u leilohei ya'akov*	הַרְנִינוּ לֵאלֹהִים עוּזֵּנוּ הָרִיעוּ לֵאלֹהֵי יַעֲקֹב:	ב
3	Take up the song, sound the timbrel, the melodious lyre and harp.	*Se'u-zimrah utenu-tof kinnor na'im im-navel*	שְׂאוּ־זִמְרָה וּתְנוּ־תֹף כִּנּוֹר נָעִים עִם־נָבֶל:	ג
4	Blow the shofar on the new moon, on the full moon for our feast day.	*Tik'u vachodesh shofar bakkeseh leyom chaggeinu*	תִּקְעוּ בַחֹדֶשׁ שׁוֹפָר בַּכֵּסֶה לְיוֹם חַגֵּנוּ:	ד
5	For it is a law for Yisrael, a ruling of the God of Yaakov;	*Ki chok leyisra'el hu mishpat leilohei ya'akov*	כִּי חֹק לְיִשְׂרָאֵל הוּא מִשְׁפָּט לֵאלֹהֵי יַעֲקֹב:	ה
6	He imposed it as a decree upon Yosef when he went forth from the land of Egypt; I heard a language that I knew not.	*Edut bihosef samo betzeito al-eretz mitzrayim sefat lo-yada'ti eshma*	עֵדוּת בִּיהוֹסֵף שָׂמוֹ בְּצֵאתוֹ עַל־אֶרֶץ מִצְרָיִם שְׂפַת לֹא־יָדַעְתִּי אֶשְׁמָע:	ו
7	I relieved his shoulder of the burden, his hands were freed from the basket.	*Hasiroti miseivel shichmo kappav middud ta'avorenah*	הֲסִירוֹתִי מִסֵּבֶל שִׁכְמוֹ כַּפָּיו מִדּוּד תַּעֲבֹרְנָה:	ז

8 In distress you called and I rescued you; I answered you from the secret place of thunder I tested you at the waters of Meribah. Selah.

Batzarah karata va'achalletzekka e'encha beseter ra'am evchanecha al-mei merivah selah

בַּצָּרָה קָרָאתָ וָאֲחַלְּצֶךָּ אֶעֶנְךָ בְּסֵתֶר רַעַם אֶבְחָנְךָ עַל־מֵי מְרִיבָה סֶלָה: ח

9 Hear, My people, and I will admonish you; Yisrael, if you would but listen to Me!

Shema ammi ve'a'idah bach yisra'el im-tishma-li

שְׁמַע עַמִּי וְאָעִידָה בָּךְ יִשְׂרָאֵל אִם־תִּשְׁמַע־לִי: ט

10 You shall have no foreign god, you shall not bow to an alien god.

Lo-yihyeh vecha el zar velo tishtachaveh le'el nechar

לֹא־יִהְיֶה בְךָ אֵל זָר וְלֹא תִשְׁתַּחֲוֶה לְאֵל נֵכָר: י

11 I Hashem am your God who brought you out of the land of Egypt; open your mouth wide and I will fill it.

Anochi Adonai elohecha hamma'alcha me'eretz mitzrayim harchev-picha va'amal'eihu

אָנֹכִי יְהֹוָה אֱלֹהֶיךָ הַמַּעַלְךָ מֵאֶרֶץ מִצְרָיִם הַרְחֶב־פִּיךָ וַאֲמַלְאֵהוּ: יא

12 But My people would not listen to Me, Yisrael would not obey Me.

Velo-shama ammi lekoli veyisra'el lo-avah li

וְלֹא־שָׁמַע עַמִּי לְקוֹלִי וְיִשְׂרָאֵל לֹא־אָבָה לִי: יב

13 So I let them go after their willful heart that they might follow their own devices.

Va'ashallechehu bishrirut libbam yeilechu bemo'atzoteihem

וָאֲשַׁלְּחֵהוּ בִּשְׁרִירוּת לִבָּם יֵלְכוּ בְּמוֹעֲצוֹתֵיהֶם: יג

14 If only My people would listen to Me, if Yisrael would follow My paths,

Lu ammi shomea' li yisra'el bidrachai yehalleichu

לוּ עַמִּי שֹׁמֵעַ לִי יִשְׂרָאֵל בִּדְרָכַי יְהַלֵּכוּ: יד

15	then would I subdue their enemies at once, strike their foes again and again.	*Kim'at oyeveihem achnia' ve'al tzareihem ashiv yadi*

כִּמְעַט אוֹיְבֵיהֶם אַכְנִיעַ
וְעַל צָרֵיהֶם אָשִׁיב יָדִי: טו

16	Those who hate Hashem shall cower before Him; their doom shall be eternal.	*Mesan'ei Adonai yechachashu-lo vihi ittam le'olam*

מְשַׂנְאֵי יְהֹוָה יְכַחֲשׁוּ־לוֹ
וִיהִי עִתָּם לְעוֹלָם: טז

17	He fed them the finest wheat; I sated you with honey from the rock.	*Vayya'achileihu meicheilev chittah umitzur devash asbi'echa*

וַיַּאֲכִילֵהוּ מֵחֵלֶב חִטָּה
וּמִצּוּר דְּבַשׁ אַשְׂבִּיעֶךָ: יז

82 — ◦⊙⧜⊙◦ — פב

1	A psalm of Asaf. Hashem stands in the divine assembly; among the divine beings He pronounces judgment.	*Mizmor le'asaf elohim nitzav ba'adat-el bekerev elohim yishpot*

מִזְמוֹר לְאָסָף אֱלֹהִים נִצָּב
בַּעֲדַת־אֵל בְּקֶרֶב אֱלֹהִים
יִשְׁפֹּט: א

2	How long will you judge perversely, showing favor to the wicked? Selah.	*Ad-matai tishpetu-avel ufenei resha'im tis'u-selah*

עַד־מָתַי תִּשְׁפְּטוּ־עָוֶל וּפְנֵי
רְשָׁעִים תִּשְׂאוּ־סֶלָה: ב

3	Judge the wretched and the orphan, vindicate the lowly and the poor,	*Shiftu-dal veyatom ani varash hatzdiku*

שִׁפְטוּ־דַל וְיָתוֹם עָנִי וָרָשׁ
הַצְדִּיקוּ: ג

4	rescue the wretched and the needy; save them from the hand of the wicked.	*Palletu-dal ve'evyon miyyad resha'im hatzilu*	פַּלְּטוּ־דַל וְאֶבְיוֹן מִיַּד רְשָׁעִים הַצִּילוּ: ד
5	They neither know nor understand, they go about in darkness; all the foundations of the earth totter.	*Lo yade'u velo yavinu bachasheichah yithallachu yimmotu kol-mosedei aretz*	לֹא יָדְעוּ וְלֹא יָבִינוּ בַּחֲשֵׁכָה יִתְהַלָּכוּ יִמּוֹטוּ כָּל־מוֹסְדֵי אָרֶץ: ה
6	I had taken you for divine beings, sons of the Most High, all of you;	*Ani-amarti elohim attem uvenei elyon kullechem*	אֲנִי־אָמַרְתִּי אֱלֹהִים אַתֶּם וּבְנֵי עֶלְיוֹן כֻּלְּכֶם: ו
7	but you shall die as men do, fall like any prince.	*Achen ke'adam temutun uche'achad hassarim tippolu*	אָכֵן כְּאָדָם תְּמוּתוּן וּכְאַחַד הַשָּׂרִים תִּפֹּלוּ: ז
8	Arise, O Hashem, judge the earth, for all the nations are Your possession.	*Kumah elohim shafetah ha'aretz ki-attah tinchal bechol-haggoyim*	קוּמָה אֱלֹהִים שָׁפְטָה הָאָרֶץ כִּי־אַתָּה תִנְחַל בְּכָל־הַגּוֹיִם: ח

83

—⚬⧉⚬—

פג

1	A song, a psalm of Asaf.	*Shir mizmor le'asaf*	שִׁיר מִזְמוֹר לְאָסָף: א
2	O Hashem, do not be silent; do not hold aloof; do not be quiet, O Hashem!	*Elohim al-domi-lach al-techerash ve'al-tishkot el*	אֱלֹהִים אַל־דֳּמִי־לָךְ אַל־תֶּחֱרַשׁ וְאַל־תִּשְׁקֹט אֵל: ב

3	For Your enemies rage, Your foes assert themselves.	*Ki-hinnei oyevecha yehemayun u'mesanecha nase'u rosh*	כִּי־הִנֵּה אוֹיְבֶיךָ יֶהֱמָיוּן וּמְשַׂנְאֶיךָ נָשְׂאוּ רֹאשׁ:	ג
4	They plot craftily against Your people, take counsel against Your treasured ones.	*Al-ammecha ya'arimu sod veyitya'atzu al-tzefunecha*	עַל־עַמְּךָ יַעֲרִימוּ סוֹד וְיִתְיָעֲצוּ עַל־צְפוּנֶיךָ:	ד
5	They say, "Let us wipe them out as a nation; Yisrael's name will be mentioned no more."	*Ameru lechu venach'chidem miggoy velo-yizzacher shem-yisra'el od*	אָמְרוּ לְכוּ וְנַכְחִידֵם מִגּוֹי וְלֹא־יִזָּכֵר שֵׁם־יִשְׂרָאֵל עוֹד:	ה
6	Unanimous in their counsel they have made an alliance against You—	*Ki no'atzu leiv yachdav alecha berit yichrotu*	כִּי נוֹעֲצוּ לֵב יַחְדָּו עָלֶיךָ בְּרִית יִכְרֹתוּ:	ו
7	the clans of Edom and the Ishmaelites, Moab and the Hagrites,	*Oholei edom veyishme'eilim mo'av vehagrim*	אָהֳלֵי אֱדוֹם וְיִשְׁמְעֵאלִים מוֹאָב וְהַגְרִים:	ז
8	Gebal, Ammon, and Amalek, Philistia with the inhabitants of Tyre;	*Geval ve'ammon va'amalek peleshet im-yoshevei tzor*	גְּבָל וְעַמּוֹן וַעֲמָלֵק פְּלֶשֶׁת עִם־יֹשְׁבֵי צוֹר:	ח
9	Assyria too joins forces with them; they give support to the sons of Lot. Selah.	*Gam-ashur nilvah immam hayu zeroa' livnei-lot selah*	גַּם־אַשּׁוּר נִלְוָה עִמָּם הָיוּ זְרוֹעַ לִבְנֵי־לוֹט סֶלָה:	ט
10	Deal with them as You did with Midian, with Sisera, with Jabin, at the brook Kishon—	*Aseih-lahem kemidyan kesisra cheyavin benachal kishon*	עֲשֵׂה־לָהֶם כְּמִדְיָן כְּסִיסְרָא כְיָבִין בְּנַחַל קִישׁוֹן:	י

11	who were destroyed at En-dor, who became dung for the field.	*Nishmedu ve'ein-dor hayu domen la'adamah*	נִשְׁמְדוּ בְעֵין־דֹּאר הָיוּ דֹּמֶן לָאֲדָמָה:
12	Treat their great men like Oreb and Zeeb, all their princes like Zebah and Zalmunna,	*Shitemo nediveimo ke'orev vechiz'ev uchezevach uchetzalmunna kol-nesicheimo*	שִׁיתֵמוֹ נְדִיבֵמוֹ כְּעֹרֵב וְכִזְאֵב וּכְזֶבַח וּכְצַלְמֻנָּע כָּל־נְסִיכֵמוֹ:
13	who said, "Let us take the meadows of Hashem as our possession."	*Asher ameru nirashah lanu et ne'ot elohim*	אֲשֶׁר אָמְרוּ נִירֲשָׁה לָּנוּ אֵת נְאוֹת אֱלֹהִים:
14	O my God, make them like thistledown, like stubble driven by the wind.	*Elohai shiteimo chaggalgal kekash lifnei-ruach*	אֱלֹהַי שִׁיתֵמוֹ כַגַּלְגַּל כְּקַשׁ לִפְנֵי־רוּחַ:
15	As a fire burns a forest, as flames scorch the hills,	*Ke'esh tiv'ar-ya'ar uchelehavah telaheit harim*	כְּאֵשׁ תִּבְעַר־יָעַר וּכְלֶהָבָה תְּלַהֵט הָרִים:
16	pursue them with Your tempest, terrify them with Your storm.	*Kein tirdefeim besa'arecha uvesufatecha tevahaleim*	כֵּן תִּרְדְּפֵם בְּסַעֲרֶךָ וּבְסוּפָתְךָ תְבַהֲלֵם:
17	Cover their faces with shame so that they seek Your name, Hashem.	*Malei feneihem kalon vivakshu shimcha Adonai*	מַלֵּא פְנֵיהֶם קָלוֹן וִיבַקְשׁוּ שִׁמְךָ יְהֹוָה:
18	May they be frustrated and terrified, disgraced and doomed forever.	*Yevoshu veyibbahalu adei-ad veyachperu veyoveidu*	יֵבֹשׁוּ וְיִבָּהֲלוּ עֲדֵי־עַד וְיַחְפְּרוּ וְיֹאבֵדוּ:

19	May they know that Your name, Yours alone, is Hashem, supreme over all the earth.	*Veyede'u ki-attah shimcha Adonai levaddecha elyon al-kol-ha'aretz*

וְיֵדְעוּ כִּי־אַתָּה שִׁמְךָ יְהֹוָה לְבַדֶּךָ עֶלְיוֹן עַל־כָּל־הָאָרֶץ: יט

84

פד

1	For the leader; on the gittith. Of the Korahites. A psalm.	*Lammenatzeach al-haggittit livnei-korach mizmor*

לַמְנַצֵּחַ עַל־הַגִּתִּית לִבְנֵי־קֹרַח מִזְמוֹר: א

2	How lovely is Your dwelling-place, LORD of hosts.	*Mah-yedidot mishkenotecha Adonai tzeva'ot*

מַה־יְּדִידוֹת מִשְׁכְּנוֹתֶיךָ יְהֹוָה צְבָאוֹת: ב

3	I long, I yearn for the courts of Hashem; my body and soul shout for joy to the living Hashem.	*Nichsefah vegam-kaletah nafshi lechatzrot Adonai libbi uvesari yerannenu el el-chai*

נִכְסְפָה וְגַם־כָּלְתָה נַפְשִׁי לְחַצְרוֹת יְהֹוָה לִבִּי וּבְשָׂרִי יְרַנְּנוּ אֶל אֵל־חָי: ג

4	Even the sparrow has found a home, and the swallow a nest for herself in which to set her young, near Your mizbayach, O lord of hosts, my king and my God.	*Gam-tzippor matze'ah vayit uderor kein lah asher-shatah efrocheha et-mizbechotecha Adonai tzeva'ot malki vei'lohai*

גַּם־צִפּוֹר מָצְאָה בַיִת וּדְרוֹר קֵן לָהּ אֲשֶׁר־שָׁתָה אֶפְרֹחֶיהָ אֶת־מִזְבְּחוֹתֶיךָ יְהֹוָה צְבָאוֹת מַלְכִּי וֵאלֹהָי: ד

5	Happy are those who dwell in Your house; they forever praise You. Selah.	*Ashrei yoshevei veitecha od yehallucha selah*

אַשְׁרֵי יוֹשְׁבֵי בֵיתֶךָ עוֹד יְהַלְלוּךָ סֶלָה: ה

6	Happy is the man who finds refuge in You, whose mind is on the [pilgrim] highways.	*Ashrei adam oz-lo vach mesillot bilvavam*	אַשְׁרֵי אָדָם עוֹז־לוֹ בָךְ מְסִלּוֹת בִּלְבָבָם:	ו
7	They pass through the Valley of Baca, regarding it as a place of springs, as if the early rain had covered it with blessing.	*Overei be'eimek habbacha ma'yan yeshituhu gam-berachot ya'teh moreh*	עֹבְרֵי בְּעֵמֶק הַבָּכָא מַעְיָן יְשִׁיתוּהוּ גַּם־בְּרָכוֹת יַעְטֶה מוֹרֶה:	ז
8	They go from rampart to rampart, appearing before Hashem in Tzion.	*Yelechu mei'chayil el-chayil yeira'eh el-elohim betziyyon*	יֵלְכוּ מֵחַיִל אֶל־חָיִל יֵרָאֶה אֶל־אֱלֹהִים בְּצִיּוֹן:	ח
9	O Hashem, God of hosts, hear my prayer; give ear, O God of Yaakov. Selah.	*Adonai elohim tzeva'ot shim'ah tefillati ha'azinah elohei ya'akov selah*	יְהֹוָה אֱלֹהִים צְבָאוֹת שִׁמְעָה תְפִלָּתִי הַאֲזִינָה אֱלֹהֵי יַעֲקֹב סֶלָה:	ט
10	O Hashem, behold our shield, look upon the face of Your anointed.	*Maginnenu re'eh elohim vehabbeit penei meshichecha*	מָגִנֵּנוּ רְאֵה אֱלֹהִים וְהַבֵּט פְּנֵי מְשִׁיחֶךָ:	י
11	Better one day in Your courts than a thousand [anywhere else]; I would rather stand at the threshold of Hashem's house than dwell in the tents of the wicked.	*Ki tov-yom bachatzeirecha me'alef bacharti histofeif beveit elohai middur be'oholei-resha*	כִּי טוֹב־יוֹם בַּחֲצֵרֶיךָ מֵאָלֶף בָּחַרְתִּי הִסְתּוֹפֵף בְּבֵית אֱלֹהַי מִדּוּר בְּאָהֳלֵי־רֶשַׁע:	יא

12   For Hashem is sun and shield; Hashem bestows grace and glory; He does not withhold His bounty from those who live without blame.

Ki shemesh u'magein Adonai elohim chein vechavod yitten Adonai lo yimna-tov laholechim betamim

כִּי שֶׁמֶשׁ וּמָגֵן יְהֹוָה אֱלֹהִים חֵן וְכָבוֹד יִתֵּן יְהֹוָה לֹא יִמְנַע־טוֹב לַהֹלְכִים בְּתָמִים: יב

13   O lord of hosts, happy is the man who trusts in You.

Adonai tzeva'ot ashrei adam botei'ach bach

יְהֹוָה צְבָאוֹת אַשְׁרֵי אָדָם בֹּטֵחַ בָּךְ: יג

85   —◦⦵⦵◦—   פה

1   For the leader. Of the Korahites. A psalm.

Lammenatzeach livnei-korach mizmor

לַמְנַצֵּחַ לִבְנֵי־קֹרַח מִזְמוֹר: א

2   Hashem, You will favor Your land, restore Yaakov's fortune;

Ratzita Adonai artzecha shavta [shevit] ya'akov

רָצִיתָ יְהֹוָה אַרְצֶךָ שַׁבְתָּ שְׁבוּת [שְׁבִית] יַעֲקֹב: ב

3   You will forgive Your people's iniquity, pardon all their sins; selah

Nasata avon ammecha kissita chol-chattatam selah

נָשָׂאתָ עֲוֹן עַמֶּךָ כִּסִּיתָ כָל־חַטָּאתָם סֶלָה: ג

4   You will withdraw all Your anger, turn away from Your rage.

Asafta chol-evratecha heshivota meicharon appecha

אָסַפְתָּ כָל־עֶבְרָתֶךָ הֱשִׁיבוֹתָ מֵחֲרוֹן אַפֶּךָ: ד

5   Turn again, O Hashem, our helper, revoke Your displeasure with us.

Shuvenu elohei yish'eini vehafer ka'ascha immanu

שׁוּבֵנוּ אֱלֹהֵי יִשְׁעֵנוּ וְהָפֵר כַּעַסְךָ עִמָּנוּ: ה

6	Will You be angry with us forever, prolong Your wrath for all generations?	*Hal'olam te'enaf-banu timshoch appecha ledor vador*	הַלְעוֹלָם תֶּאֱנַף־בָּנוּ תִּמְשֹׁךְ אַפְּךָ לְדֹר וָדֹר:
7	Surely You will revive us again, so that Your people may rejoice in You.	*Halo-attah tashuv techayyenu ve'ammecha yismechu-vach*	הֲלֹא־אַתָּה תָּשׁוּב תְּחַיֵּנוּ וְעַמְּךָ יִשְׂמְחוּ־בָךְ:
8	Show us, Hashem, Your faithfulness; grant us Your deliverance.	*Har'enu Adonai chasdecha veyesh'acha titten-lanu*	הַרְאֵנוּ יְהֹוָה חַסְדֶּךָ וְיֶשְׁעֲךָ תִּתֶּן־לָנוּ:
9	Let me hear what Hashem, Hashem, will speak; He will promise well-being to His people, His faithful ones; may they not turn to folly.	*Eshme'ah mah-yedabber ha'el Adonai ki yedabber shalom el-ammo ve'el-chasidav ve'al-yashuvu lechislah*	אֶשְׁמְעָה מַה־יְדַבֵּר הָאֵל יְהֹוָה כִּי יְדַבֵּר שָׁלוֹם אֶל־עַמּוֹ וְאֶל־חֲסִידָיו וְאַל־יָשׁוּבוּ לְכִסְלָה:
10	His help is very near those who fear Him, to make His glory dwell in our land.	*Ach karov lire'av yish'o lishkon kavod be'artzenu*	אַךְ קָרוֹב לִירֵאָיו יִשְׁעוֹ לִשְׁכֹּן כָּבוֹד בְּאַרְצֵנוּ:
11	Faithfulness and truth meet; justice and well-being kiss.	*chesed-ve'emet nifgashu tzedek veshalom nashaku*	חֶסֶד־וֶאֱמֶת נִפְגָּשׁוּ צֶדֶק וְשָׁלוֹם נָשָׁקוּ:
12	Truth springs up from the earth; justice looks down from heaven.	*Emet me'eretz titzmach vetzedek mishamayim nishkaf*	אֱמֶת מֵאֶרֶץ תִּצְמָח וְצֶדֶק מִשָּׁמַיִם נִשְׁקָף:
13	Hashem also bestows His bounty; our land yields its produce.	*Gam-Adonai yitein hattov ve'artzenu titten yevulah*	גַּם־יְהֹוָה יִתֵּן הַטּוֹב וְאַרְצֵנוּ תִּתֵּן יְבוּלָהּ:

14	Justice goes before Him as He sets out on His way.	*tzedek lefanav yehallech veyaseim lederech pe'amav*	צֶדֶק לְפָנָיו יְהַלֵּךְ וְיָשֵׂם לְדֶרֶךְ פְּעָמָיו:

86

—◦○◎○◦—

פו

1	A prayer of David. Incline Your ear, O Hashem, answer me, for I am poor and needy.	*Tefillah ledavid hatteh-Adonai oznecha aneni ki-ani ve'evyon ani*	תְּפִלָּה לְדָוִד הַטֵּה־יְהֹוָה אָזְנְךָ עֲנֵנִי כִּי־עָנִי וְאֶבְיוֹן אָנִי:	א
2	Preserve my life, for I am steadfast; O You, my God, deliver Your servant who trusts in You.	*Shamerah nafshi ki-chasid ani hosha avdecha attah elohai habboteach elecha*	שָׁמְרָה נַפְשִׁי כִּי־חָסִיד אָנִי הוֹשַׁע עַבְדְּךָ אַתָּה אֱלֹהַי הַבּוֹטֵחַ אֵלֶיךָ:	ב
3	Have mercy on me, O Hashem, for I call to You all day long;	*Channeni Adonai ki elecha ekra kol-hayyom*	חָנֵּנִי אֲדֹנָי כִּי אֵלֶיךָ אֶקְרָא כָּל־הַיּוֹם:	ג
4	bring joy to Your servant's life, for on You, Hashem, I set my hope.	*Sammeach nefesh avdecha ki elecha Adonai nafshi essa*	שַׂמֵּחַ נֶפֶשׁ עַבְדֶּךָ כִּי אֵלֶיךָ אֲדֹנָי נַפְשִׁי אֶשָּׂא:	ד
5	For You, Hashem, are good and forgiving, abounding in steadfast love to all who call on You.	*Ki-attah Adonai tov vesallach verav-chesed lechol-korecha*	כִּי־אַתָּה אֲדֹנָי טוֹב וְסַלָּח וְרַב־חֶסֶד לְכָל־קֹרְאֶיךָ:	ה

6	Give ear, Hashem, to my prayer; heed my plea for mercy.	*Ha'azinah Adonai tefillati vehakshivah bekol tachanunotai*	הַאֲזִינָה יְהֹוָה תְּפִלָּתִי וְהַקְשִׁיבָה בְּקוֹל תַּחֲנוּנוֹתָי:	ו
7	In my time of trouble I call You, for You will answer me.	*Beyom tzarati ekra'ekka ki ta'aneni*	בְּיוֹם צָרָתִי אֶקְרָאֶךָּ כִּי תַעֲנֵנִי:	ז
8	There is none like You among the gods, O Hashem, and there are no deeds like Yours.	*Ein-kamocha va'elohim Adonai ve'ein kema'asecha*	אֵין־כָּמוֹךָ בָאֱלֹהִים אֲדֹנָי וְאֵין כְּמַעֲשֶׂיךָ:	ח
9	All the nations You have made will come to bow down before You, O Hashem, and they will pay honor to Your name.	*Kol-goyim asher asita yavo'u veyishtachavu lefanecha Adonai vichabbedu lishmecha*	כָּל־גּוֹיִם אֲשֶׁר עָשִׂיתָ יָבוֹאוּ וְיִשְׁתַּחֲווּ לְפָנֶיךָ אֲדֹנָי וִיכַבְּדוּ לִשְׁמֶךָ:	ט
10	For You are great and perform wonders; You alone are God.	*Ki-gadol attah ve'oseih nifla'ot attah elohim levaddecha*	כִּי־גָדוֹל אַתָּה וְעֹשֵׂה נִפְלָאוֹת אַתָּה אֱלֹהִים לְבַדֶּךָ:	י
11	Teach me Your way, O Hashem; I will walk in Your truth; let my heart be undivided in reverence for Your name.	*Horeni Adonai darkecha ahalleich ba'amittecha yacheid levavi leyir'ah shemecha*	הוֹרֵנִי יְהֹוָה דַּרְכֶּךָ אֲהַלֵּךְ בַּאֲמִתֶּךָ יַחֵד לְבָבִי לְיִרְאָה שְׁמֶךָ:	יא
12	I will praise You, O Hashem, my God, with all my heart and pay honor to Your name forever.	*Odecha Adonai elohai bechol-levavi va'achabbedah shimcha le'olam*	אוֹדְךָ אֲדֹנָי אֱלֹהַי בְּכָל־לְבָבִי וַאֲכַבְּדָה שִׁמְךָ לְעוֹלָם:	יב

13	For Your steadfast love toward me is great; You have saved me from the depths of Sheol.	*Ki-chasdecha gadol alai vehitzalta nafshi mishe'ol tachtiyyah*	כִּי־חַסְדְּךָ גָּדוֹל עָלָי וְהִצַּלְתָּ נַפְשִׁי מִשְּׁאוֹל תַּחְתִּיָּה:	יג
14	O Hashem, arrogant men have risen against me; a band of ruthless men seek my life; they are not mindful of You.	*Elohim zeidim kamu-alai va'adat aritzim bikshu nafshi velo samucha lenegdam*	אֱלֹהִים זֵדִים קָמוּ־עָלַי וַעֲדַת עָרִיצִים בִּקְשׁוּ נַפְשִׁי וְלֹא שָׂמוּךָ לְנֶגְדָּם:	יד
15	But You, O Hashem, are a God compassionate and merciful, slow to anger, abounding in steadfast love and faithfulness.	*Ve'attah Adonai el-rachum vechannun erech appayim verav-chesed ve'emet*	וְאַתָּה אֲדֹנָי אֵל־רַחוּם וְחַנּוּן אֶרֶךְ אַפַּיִם וְרַב־חֶסֶד וֶאֱמֶת:	טו
16	Turn to me and have mercy on me; grant Your strength to Your servant and deliver the son of Your maidservant.	*Penei elai vechanneni tenah-uzzecha le'avdecha vehoshi'ah l'ven-amatecha*	פְּנֵה אֵלַי וְחָנֵּנִי תְּנָה־עֻזְּךָ לְעַבְדֶּךָ וְהוֹשִׁיעָה לְבֶן־אֲמָתֶךָ:	טז
17	Show me a sign of Your favor, that my enemies may see and be frustrated because You, Hashem, have given me aid and comfort.	*Asei-immi ot letovah veyir'u sone'ai veyeivosh ki-attah Adonai azartani venichamtani*	עֲשֵׂה־עִמִּי אוֹת לְטוֹבָה וְיִרְאוּ שֹׂנְאַי וְיֵבֹשׁוּ כִּי־אַתָּה יְהוָה עֲזַרְתַּנִי וְנִחַמְתָּנִי:	יז

87

פז

1	Of the Korahites. A psalm. A song. His foundation is on the holy mountains.	*Livnei-korach mizmor shir yesudato beharerei-kodesh*

לִבְנֵי־קֹרַח מִזְמוֹר שִׁיר יְסוּדָתוֹ בְּהַרְרֵי־קֹדֶשׁ: א

2 Hashem loves the gates of Tzion, more than all the dwellings of Yaakov.

Ohev Adonai sha'arei tziyyon mikkol mishkenot ya'akov

אֹהֵב יְהֹוָה שַׁעֲרֵי צִיּוֹן מִכֹּל מִשְׁכְּנוֹת יַעֲקֹב: ב

3 Glorious things are spoken of you, O city of Hashem. Selah.

Nichbadot medubbar bach ir ha'elohim selah

נִכְבָּדוֹת מְדֻבָּר בָּךְ עִיר הָאֱלֹהִים סֶלָה: ג

4 I mention Rahab and Babylon among those who acknowledge Me; Philistia, and Tyre, and Cush—each was born there.

Azkir rahav uvavel leyode'ai hinnei feleshet vetzor im-kush zeh yullad-sham

אַזְכִּיר רַהַב וּבָבֶל לְיֹדְעָי הִנֵּה פְלֶשֶׁת וְצוֹר עִם־כּוּשׁ זֶה יֻלַּד־שָׁם: ד

5 Indeed, it shall be said of Tzion, "Every man was born there." He, the Most High, will preserve it.

Ulatziyyon yei'amar ish ve'ish yullad-bah vehu yechoneneha elyon

וּלְצִיּוֹן יֵאָמַר אִישׁ וְאִישׁ יֻלַּד־בָּהּ וְהוּא יְכוֹנְנֶהָ עֶלְיוֹן: ה

6 Hashem will inscribe in the register of peoples that each was born there. Selah.

Adonai yispor bichtov ammim zeh yullad-sham selah

יְהֹוָה יִסְפֹּר בִּכְתוֹב עַמִּים זֶה יֻלַּד־שָׁם סֶלָה: ו

7 Singers and dancers alike [will say]: "All my roots are in You."

Vesharim kecholelim kol-ma'yanai bach

וְשָׁרִים כְּחֹלְלִים כָּל־מַעְיָנַי בָּךְ: ז

88

—o·⦿⦾⦿·o—

פח

1	A song. A psalm of the Korahites. For the leader; on mahalath leannoth. A maskil of Hayman the Ezrahite.	*Shir mizmor livnei korach lammenatzeach al-machalat le'annot maskil leheiman ha'ezrachi*	שִׁיר מִזְמוֹר לִבְנֵי קֹרַח לַמְנַצֵּחַ עַל־מָחֲלַת לְעַנּוֹת מַשְׂכִּיל לְהֵימָן הָאֶזְרָחִי: א
2	Hashem, God of my deliverance, when I cry out in the night before You,	*Adonai elohei yeshu'ati yom-tza'akti vallaylah negdecha*	יְהֹוָה אֱלֹהֵי יְשׁוּעָתִי יוֹם־צָעַקְתִּי בַלַּיְלָה נֶגְדֶּךָ: ב
3	let my prayer reach You; incline Your ear to my cry.	*Tavo lefanecha tefillati hattei-oznecha lerinnati*	תָּבוֹא לְפָנֶיךָ תְּפִלָּתִי הַטֵּה־אָזְנְךָ לְרִנָּתִי: ג
4	For I am sated with misfortune; I am at the brink of Sheol.	*Ki-save'ah vera'ot nafshi vechayyai lish'ol higgi'u*	כִּי־שָׂבְעָה בְרָעוֹת נַפְשִׁי וְחַיַּי לִשְׁאוֹל הִגִּיעוּ: ד
5	I am numbered with those who go down to the Pit; I am a helpless man	*Nechshavti im-yoredei vor hayiti kegever ein-eyal*	נֶחְשַׁבְתִּי עִם־יוֹרְדֵי בוֹר הָיִיתִי כְּגֶבֶר אֵין־אֱיָל: ה
6	abandoned among the dead, like bodies lying in the grave of whom You are mindful no more, and who are cut off from Your care.	*Bammetim chafeshi kemo chalalim shochevei kever asher lo zechartam od veheima miyyadecha nigzaru*	בַּמֵּתִים חָפְשִׁי כְּמוֹ חֲלָלִים שֹׁכְבֵי קֶבֶר אֲשֶׁר לֹא זְכַרְתָּם עוֹד וְהֵמָּה מִיָּדְךָ נִגְזָרוּ: ו

7	You have put me at the bottom of the Pit, in the darkest places, in the depths.	*Shattani bevor tachtiyyot bemachashakkim bimtzolot*	שַׁתַּנִי בְּבוֹר תַּחְתִּיּוֹת בְּמַחֲשַׁכִּים בִּמְצֹלוֹת׃	ז
8	Your fury lies heavy upon me; You afflict me with all Your breakers. Selah.	*Alai samechah chamatecha vechol-mishbarecha innita selah*	עָלַי סָמְכָה חֲמָתֶךָ וְכָל־מִשְׁבָּרֶיךָ עִנִּיתָ סֶּלָה׃	ח
9	You make my companions shun me; You make me abhorrent to them; I am shut in and do not go out.	*Hirchakta meyudda'ai mimmenni shattani to'evot lamo kalu velo etze*	הִרְחַקְתָּ מְיֻדָּעַי מִמֶּנִּי שַׁתַּנִי תוֹעֵבוֹת לָמוֹ כָּלֻא וְלֹא אֵצֵא׃	ט
10	My eyes pine away from affliction; I call to You, Hashem, each day; I stretch out my hands to You.	*Eini da'avah minni oni keraticha Adonai bechol-yom shittachti eleicha chappai*	עֵינִי דָאֲבָה מִנִּי עֹנִי קְרָאתִיךָ יְהֹוָה בְּכָל־יוֹם שִׁטַּחְתִּי אֵלֶיךָ כַפָּי׃	י
11	Do You work wonders for the dead? Do the shades rise to praise You? Selah.	*Halammetim ta'aseh-pele im-refa'im yakumu yoducha selah*	הֲלַמֵּתִים תַּעֲשֶׂה־פֶּלֶא אִם־רְפָאִים יָקוּמוּ יוֹדוּךָ סֶּלָה׃	יא
12	Is Your faithful care recounted in the grave, Your constancy in the place of perdition?	*Hayyesuppar bakkever chasdecha emunatecha ba'avaddon*	הַיְסֻפַּר בַּקֶּבֶר חַסְדֶּךָ אֱמוּנָתְךָ בָּאֲבַדּוֹן׃	יב
13	Are Your wonders made known in the netherworld, Your beneficent deeds in the land of oblivion?	*Hayivvada bachoshech pil'echa vetzidkatecha be'eretz neshiyyah*	הֲיִוָּדַע בַּחֹשֶׁךְ פִּלְאֶךָ וְצִדְקָתְךָ בְּאֶרֶץ נְשִׁיָּה׃	יג

14	As for me, I cry out to You, Hashem; each morning my prayer greets You.	*Va'ani eleicha Adonai shivva'ti uvabboker tefillati tekaddemekka*	וַאֲנִי אֵלֶיךָ יְהֹוָה שִׁוַּעְתִּי וּבַבֹּקֶר תְּפִלָּתִי תְקַדְּמֶךָּ׃	יד
15	Why, Hashem, do You reject me, do You hide Your face from me?	*Lamah Adonai tiznach nafshi tastir panecha mimmenni*	לָמָה יְהֹוָה תִּזְנַח נַפְשִׁי תַּסְתִּיר פָּנֶיךָ מִמֶּנִּי׃	טו
16	From my youth I have been afflicted and near death; I suffer Your terrors wherever I turn.	*Ani ani vegovea' minno'ar nasati eimecha afunah*	עָנִי אֲנִי וְגֹוֵעַ מִנֹּעַר נָשָׂאתִי אֵמֶיךָ אָפוּנָה׃	טז
17	Your fury overwhelms me; Your terrors destroy me.	*Alai averu charonecha bi'uteicha tzimmetutuni*	עָלַי עָבְרוּ חֲרוֹנֶיךָ בִּעוּתֶיךָ צִמְּתוּתֻנִי׃	יז
18	They swirl about me like water all day long; they encircle me on every side.	*Sabbuni chammayim kol-hayyom hikkifu alai yachad*	סַבּוּנִי כַמַּיִם כָּל־הַיּוֹם הִקִּיפוּ עָלַי יָחַד׃	יח
19	You have put friend and neighbor far from me and my companions out of my sight.	*Hirchakta mimmenni ohev varea' meyudda'ai machshach*	הִרְחַקְתָּ מִמֶּנִּי אֹהֵב וָרֵעַ מְיֻדָּעַי מַחְשָׁךְ׃	יט

89

—○⟨❈⟩○—

פט

1	A maskil of Ethan the Ezrahite.	*Maskil le'eitan ha'ezrachi*	מַשְׂכִּיל לְאֵיתָן הָאֶזְרָחִי׃	א

2   I will sing of Hashem's steadfast love forever; to all generations I will proclaim Your faithfulness with my mouth.

Chasdei Adonai olam ashirah ledor vador odia' emunatecha befi

חַסְדֵי יְהֹוָה עוֹלָם אָשִׁירָה לְדֹר וָדֹר אוֹדִיעַ אֱמוּנָתְךָ בְּפִי׃   ב

3   I declare, "Your steadfast love is confirmed forever; there in the heavens You establish Your faithfulness."

Ki-amarti olam chesed yibbaneh shamayim tachin emunatecha vahem

כִּי־אָמַרְתִּי עוֹלָם חֶסֶד יִבָּנֶה שָׁמַיִם תָּכִן אֱמוּנָתְךָ בָהֶם׃   ג

4   "I have made a covenant with My chosen one; I have sworn to My servant David:

Karatti verit livchiri nishba'ti ledavid avdi

כָּרַתִּי בְרִית לִבְחִירִי נִשְׁבַּעְתִּי לְדָוִד עַבְדִּי׃   ד

5   I will establish your offspring forever, I will confirm your throne for all generations." Selah.

Ad-olam achin zar'echa uvaniti ledor-vador kis'acha selah

עַד־עוֹלָם אָכִין זַרְעֶךָ וּבָנִיתִי לְדֹר־וָדוֹר כִּסְאֲךָ סֶלָה׃   ה

6   Your wonders, Hashem, are praised by the heavens, Your faithfulness, too, in the assembly of holy beings.

Veyodu shamayim pil'acha Adonai af-emunatecha bikhal kedoshim

וְיוֹדוּ שָׁמַיִם פִּלְאֲךָ יְהֹוָה אַף־אֱמוּנָתְךָ בִּקְהַל קְדֹשִׁים׃   ו

7   For who in the skies can equal Hashem, can compare with Hashem among the divine beings,

Ki mi vashachak ya'aroch lAdonai yidmeh lAdonai bivnei elim

כִּי מִי בַשַּׁחַק יַעֲרֹךְ לַיהֹוָה יִדְמֶה לַיהֹוָה בִּבְנֵי אֵלִים׃   ז

8	a Hashem greatly dreaded in the council of holy beings, held in awe by all around Him?	*El na'aratz besod-kedoshim rabbah venora al-kol-sevivav*	אֵל נַעֲרָץ בְּסוֹד־קְדֹשִׁים רַבָּה וְנוֹרָא עַל־כָּל־סְבִיבָיו:	ח
9	O Hashem, God of hosts, who is mighty like You, Hashem? Your faithfulness surrounds You;	*Adonai elohei tzeva'ot mi-chamocha chasin yah ve'emunatecha sevivotecha*	יְהֹוָה אֱלֹהֵי צְבָאוֹת מִי־כָמוֹךָ חֲסִין יָהּ וֶאֱמוּנָתְךָ סְבִיבוֹתֶיךָ:	ט
10	You rule the swelling of the sea; when its waves surge, You still them.	*Attah moshel bege'ut hayyam beso gallav attah teshabbechem*	אַתָּה מוֹשֵׁל בְּגֵאוּת הַיָּם בְּשׂוֹא גַלָּיו אַתָּה תְשַׁבְּחֵם:	י
11	You crushed Rahab; he was like a corpse; with Your powerful arm You scattered Your enemies.	*Attah dikkita chechalal rahav bizroa' uzzecha pizzarta oyevecha*	אַתָּה דִכִּאתָ כֶחָלָל רָהַב בִּזְרוֹעַ עֻזְּךָ פִּזַּרְתָּ אוֹיְבֶיךָ:	יא
12	The heaven is Yours, the earth too; the world and all it holds— You established them.	*Lecha shamayim af-lecha aretz teivel umelo'ah attah yesadtam*	לְךָ שָׁמַיִם אַף־לְךָ אָרֶץ תֵּבֵל וּמְלֹאָהּ אַתָּה יְסַדְתָּם:	יב
13	North and south— You created them; Tavor and Chermon sing forth Your name.	*Tzafon veyamin attah veratam tavor vechermon beshimcha yerannenu*	צָפוֹן וְיָמִין אַתָּה בְרָאתָם תָּבוֹר וְחֶרְמוֹן בְּשִׁמְךָ יְרַנֵּנוּ:	יג
14	Yours is an arm endowed with might; Your hand is strong; Your right hand, exalted.	*Lecha zeroa' im-gevurah ta'oz yadecha tarum yeminecha*	לְךָ זְרוֹעַ עִם־גְּבוּרָה תָּעֹז יָדְךָ תָּרוּם יְמִינֶךָ:	יד

15	Righteousness and justice are the base of Your throne; steadfast love and faithfulness stand before You.	*tzedek umishpat mechon kis'echa chesed ve'emet yekaddemu fanecha*	צֶדֶק וּמִשְׁפָּט מְכוֹן כִּסְאֶךָ חֶסֶד וֶאֱמֶת יְקַדְּמוּ פָנֶיךָ:	טו
16	Happy is the people who know the joyful shout; Hashem, they walk in the light of Your presence.	*Ashrei ha'am yode'ei teru'ah Adonai be'or-panecha yehallechun*	אַשְׁרֵי הָעָם יוֹדְעֵי תְרוּעָה יְהֹוָה בְּאוֹר־פָּנֶיךָ יְהַלֵּכוּן:	טז
17	They rejoice in Your name all day long; they are exalted through Your righteousness.	*Beshimcha yegilun kol-hayyom uvetzidkatecha yarumu*	בְּשִׁמְךָ יְגִילוּן כָּל־הַיּוֹם וּבְצִדְקָתְךָ יָרוּמוּ:	יז
18	For You are their strength in which they glory; our horn is exalted through Your favor.	*Ki-tif'eret uzzamo attah uvirtzonecha [tarum] karneinu*	כִּי־תִפְאֶרֶת עֻזָּמוֹ אָתָּה וּבִרְצֹנְךָ תרים [תָּרוּם] קַרְנֵנוּ:	יח
19	Truly our shield is of Hashem, our king, of the Holy One of Yisrael.	*Ki lAdonai magineinu velikdosh yisra'el malkeinu*	כִּי לַיהֹוָה מָגִנֵּנוּ וְלִקְדוֹשׁ יִשְׂרָאֵל מַלְכֵּנוּ:	יט
20	Then You spoke to Your faithful ones in a vision and said, "I have conferred power upon a warrior; I have exalted one chosen out of the people.	*Az dibbarta-vechazon lachasidecha vattomer shivviti eizer al-gibbor harimoti vachur me'am*	אָז דִּבַּרְתָּ־בְחָזוֹן לַחֲסִידֶיךָ וַתֹּאמֶר שִׁוִּיתִי עֵזֶר עַל־גִּבּוֹר הֲרִימוֹתִי בָחוּר מֵעָם:	כ
21	I have found David, My servant; anointed him with My sacred oil.	*Matzati david avdi beshemen kadeshi meshachtiv*	מָצָאתִי דָּוִד עַבְדִּי בְּשֶׁמֶן קָדְשִׁי מְשַׁחְתִּיו:	כא

22	My hand shall be constantly with him and My arm shall strengthen him.	*Asher yadi tikkon immo af-zero'i te'ammetzennu*	אֲשֶׁר יָדִי תִּכּוֹן עִמּוֹ אַף־זְרוֹעִי תְאַמְּצֶנּוּ:	כב
23	No enemy shall oppress him, no vile man afflict him.	*Lo-yashi oyeiv bo uven-avlah lo ye'annennu*	לֹא־יַשִּׁא אוֹיֵב בּוֹ וּבֶן־עַוְלָה לֹא יְעַנֶּנּוּ:	כג
24	I will crush his adversaries before him; I will strike down those who hate him.	*Vechattoti mippanav tzarav umesan'av eggof*	וְכַתּוֹתִי מִפָּנָיו צָרָיו וּמְשַׂנְאָיו אֶגּוֹף:	כד
25	My faithfulness and steadfast love shall be with him; his horn shall be exalted through My name.	*Ve'emunati vechasdi immo uvishmi tarum karno*	וֶאֱמוּנָתִי וְחַסְדִּי עִמּוֹ וּבִשְׁמִי תָּרוּם קַרְנוֹ:	כה
26	I will set his hand upon the sea, his right hand upon the rivers.	*Vesamti vayyam yado uvanneharot yemino*	וְשַׂמְתִּי בַיָּם יָדוֹ וּבַנְּהָרוֹת יְמִינוֹ:	כו
27	He shall say to Me, 'You are my father, my God, the rock of my deliverance.'	*Hu yikra'eni avi attah eili vetzur yeshu'ati*	הוּא יִקְרָאֵנִי אָבִי אָתָּה אֵלִי וְצוּר יְשׁוּעָתִי:	כז
28	I will appoint him first-born, highest of the kings of the earth.	*Af-ani bechor etteneihu elyon lemalchei-aretz*	אַף־אָנִי בְּכוֹר אֶתְּנֵהוּ עֶלְיוֹן לְמַלְכֵי־אָרֶץ:	כח
29	I will maintain My steadfast love for him always; My covenant with him shall endure.	*Le'olam [eshmar] lo chasdi uveriti ne'emenet lo*	לְעוֹלָם אשמור[אֶשְׁמָר־] לוֹ חַסְדִּי וּבְרִיתִי נֶאֱמֶנֶת לוֹ:	כט

30	I will establish his line forever, his throne, as long as the heavens last.	*Vesamti la'ad zar'o vechis'o kimei shamayim*	וְשַׂמְתִּי לָעַד זַרְעוֹ וְכִסְאוֹ כִּימֵי שָׁמָיִם:	ל
31	If his sons forsake My Teaching and do not live by My rules;	*Im-ya'azvu vanav torati uvemishpatai lo yeileichun*	אִם־יַעַזְבוּ בָנָיו תּוֹרָתִי וּבְמִשְׁפָּטַי לֹא יֵלֵכוּן:	לא
32	if they violate My laws, and do not observe My commands,	*Im-chukkotai yechalleilu umitzvotai lo yishmoru*	אִם־חֻקֹּתַי יְחַלֵּלוּ וּמִצְוֹתַי לֹא יִשְׁמֹרוּ:	לב
33	I will punish their transgression with the rod, their iniquity with plagues.	*Ufakadti vesheivet pish'am uvinga'im avonam*	וּפָקַדְתִּי בְשֵׁבֶט פִּשְׁעָם וּבִנְגָעִים עֲוֹנָם:	לג
34	But I will not take away My steadfast love from him; I will not betray My faithfulness.	*Vechasdi lo-afir me'immo velo-ashakker be'emunati*	וְחַסְדִּי לֹא־אָפִיר מֵעִמּוֹ וְלֹא־אֲשַׁקֵּר בֶּאֱמוּנָתִי:	לד
35	I will not violate My covenant, or change what I have uttered.	*Lo-achallel beriti umotza sefatai lo ashanneh*	לֹא־אֲחַלֵּל בְּרִיתִי וּמוֹצָא שְׂפָתַי לֹא אֲשַׁנֶּה:	לה
36	I have sworn by My holiness, once and for all; I will not be false to David.	*Achat nishba'ti vekadeshi im-ledavid achazzev*	אַחַת נִשְׁבַּעְתִּי בְקָדְשִׁי אִם־לְדָוִד אֲכַזֵּב:	לו
37	His line shall continue forever, his throne, as the sun before Me,	*Zar'o le'olam yihyeh vechis'o chashemesh negdi*	זַרְעוֹ לְעוֹלָם יִהְיֶה וְכִסְאוֹ כַשֶּׁמֶשׁ נֶגְדִּי:	לז

38	as the moon, established forever, an enduring witness in the sky." Selah.	*Keyareach yikkon olam ve'eid bashachak ne'eman selah*	כְּיָרֵחַ יִכּוֹן עוֹלָם וְעֵד בַּשַּׁחַק נֶאֱמָן סֶלָה:	לח
39	Yet You have rejected, spurned, and become enraged at Your anointed.	*Ve'attah zanachta vattim'as hit'abbarta im-meshichecha*	וְאַתָּה זָנַחְתָּ וַתִּמְאָס הִתְעַבַּרְתָּ עִם־מְשִׁיחֶךָ:	לט
40	You have repudiated the covenant with Your servant; You have dragged his dignity in the dust.	*Nei'artah berit avdecha chillalta la'aretz nizro*	נֵאַרְתָּה בְּרִית עַבְדֶּךָ חִלַּלְתָּ לָאָרֶץ נִזְרוֹ:	מ
41	You have breached all his defenses, shattered his strongholds.	*Paratzta chol-gedeirotav samta mivtzarav mechittah*	פָּרַצְתָּ כָל־גְּדֵרֹתָיו שַׂמְתָּ מִבְצָרָיו מְחִתָּה:	מא
42	All who pass by plunder him; he has become the butt of his neighbors.	*Shassuhu kol-overei darech hayah cherpah lishcheinav*	שַׁסֻּהוּ כָּל־עֹבְרֵי דָרֶךְ הָיָה חֶרְפָּה לִשְׁכֵנָיו:	מב
43	You have exalted the right hand of his adversaries, and made all his enemies rejoice.	*Harimota yemin tzarav hismachta kol-oyevav*	הֲרִימוֹתָ יְמִין צָרָיו הִשְׂמַחְתָּ כָּל־אוֹיְבָיו:	מג
44	You have turned back the blade of his sword, and have not sustained him in battle.	*Af-tashiv tzur charbo velo hakeimoto bammilchamah*	אַף־תָּשִׁיב צוּר חַרְבּוֹ וְלֹא הֲקֵימֹתוֹ בַּמִּלְחָמָה:	מד
45	You have brought his splendor to an end and have hurled his throne to the ground.	*Hishbatta mitteharo vechis'o la'aretz miggartah*	הִשְׁבַּתָּ מִטְּהָרוֹ וְכִסְאוֹ לָאָרֶץ מִגַּרְתָּה:	מה

46	You have cut short the days of his youth; You have covered him with shame. Selah.	*Hiktzarta yemei alumav he'etita alav bushah selah*	הִקְצַרְתָּ יְמֵי עֲלוּמָיו הֶעֱטִיתָ עָלָיו בּוּשָׁה סֶלָה:	מו
47	How long, Hashem; will You forever hide Your face, will Your fury blaze like fire?	*Ad-mah Adonai tissater lanetzach tiv'ar kemo-eish chamatecha*	עַד־מָה יְהֹוָה תִּסָּתֵר לָנֶצַח תִּבְעַר כְּמוֹ־אֵשׁ חֲמָתֶךָ:	מז
48	O remember how short my life is; why should You have created every man in vain?	*Zechar-ani meh-chaled al-mah-shav barata chol-benei-adam*	זְכָר־אֲנִי מֶה־חָלֶד עַל־מַה־שָּׁוְא בָּרָאתָ כָל־בְּנֵי־אָדָם:	מח
49	What man can live and not see death, can save himself from the clutches of Sheol? Selah.	*Mi gever yichyeh velo yir'eh-mavet yemallet nafsho miyyad-she'ol selah*	מִי גֶבֶר יִחְיֶה וְלֹא יִרְאֶה־מָּוֶת יְמַלֵּט נַפְשׁוֹ מִיַּד־שְׁאוֹל סֶלָה:	מט
50	O Hashem, where is Your steadfast love of old which You swore to David in Your faithfulness?	*Ayyei chasadecha harishonim Adonai nishba'ta ledavid be'emunatecha*	אַיֵּה חֲסָדֶיךָ הָרִאשֹׁנִים אֲדֹנָי נִשְׁבַּעְתָּ לְדָוִד בֶּאֱמוּנָתֶךָ:	נ
51	Remember, O Hashem, the abuse flung at Your servants that I have borne in my bosom [from] many peoples,	*Zechor Adonai cherpat avadecha se'eiti vecheiki kol-rabbim ammim*	זְכֹר אֲדֹנָי חֶרְפַּת עֲבָדֶיךָ שְׂאֵתִי בְחֵיקִי כָּל־רַבִּים עַמִּים:	נא
52	how Your enemies, Hashem, have flung abuse, abuse at Your anointed at every step.	*Asher cheirefu oyevecha Adonai asher cheirefu ikkevot meshichecha*	אֲשֶׁר חֵרְפוּ אוֹיְבֶיךָ יְהֹוָה אֲשֶׁר חֵרְפוּ עִקְּבוֹת מְשִׁיחֶךָ:	נב

53	Blessed is Hashem forever; Amen and Amen.	*Baruch Adonai le'olam amen ve'amen*	בָּרוּךְ יְהֹוָה לְעוֹלָם אָמֵן וְאָמֵן:	נג

90

1	A prayer of Moshe, the man of Hashem. O Hashem, You have been our refuge in every generation.	*Tefillah lemosheh ish-ha'elohim adonai ma'on attah hayita lanu bedor vador*	תְּפִלָּה לְמֹשֶׁה אִישׁ־הָאֱלֹהִים אֲדֹנָי מָעוֹן אַתָּה הָיִיתָ לָּנוּ בְּדֹר וָדֹר:	א
2	Before the mountains came into being, before You brought forth the earth and the world, from eternity to eternity You are Hashem.	*Beterem harim yulldu vattecholel eretz veteivel ume'olam ad-olam attah el*	בְּטֶרֶם הָרִים יֻלָּדוּ וַתְּחוֹלֵל אֶרֶץ וְתֵבֵל וּמֵעוֹלָם עַד־עוֹלָם אַתָּה אֵל:	ב
3	You return man to dust; You decreed, "Return you mortals!"	*Tashev enosh ad-dakka vattomer shuvu venei-adam*	תָּשֵׁב אֱנוֹשׁ עַד־דַּכָּא וַתֹּאמֶר שׁוּבוּ בְנֵי־אָדָם:	ג
4	For in Your sight a thousand years are like yesterday that has passed, like a watch of the night.	*Ki elef shanim be'eineicha keyom etmol ki ya'avor ve'ashmurah vallayelah*	כִּי אֶלֶף שָׁנִים בְּעֵינֶיךָ כְּיוֹם אֶתְמוֹל כִּי יַעֲבֹר וְאַשְׁמוּרָה בַלָּיְלָה:	ד
5	You engulf men in sleep; at daybreak they are like grass that renews itself;	*Zeramtam shenah yihyu babboker kechatzir yachalof*	זְרַמְתָּם שֵׁנָה יִהְיוּ בַּבֹּקֶר כֶּחָצִיר יַחֲלֹף:	ה

6	at daybreak it flourishes anew; by dusk it withers and dries up.	*Babboker yatzitz vechalaf la'erev yemolel veyavesh*	בַּבֹּקֶר יָצִיץ וְחָלָף לָעֶרֶב יְמוֹלֵל וְיָבֵשׁ:	ו
7	So we arc consumed by Your anger, terror-struck by Your fury.	*Ki-chalinu ve'appecha uvachamatecha nivhalenu*	כִּי־כָלִינוּ בְאַפֶּךָ וּבַחֲמָתְךָ נִבְהָלְנוּ:	ז
8	You have set our iniquities before You, our hidden sins in the light of Your face.	*Shattah avnoteinu lenegdecha alumenu lim'or panecha*	שַׁת [שַׁתָּה] עֲוֺנֹתֵינוּ לְנֶגְדֶּךָ עֲלֻמֵנוּ לִמְאוֹר פָּנֶיךָ:	ח
9	All our days pass away in Your wrath; we spend our years like a sigh.	*Ki chol-yameinu panu ve'evratecha killinu shaneinu chemo-hegeh*	כִּי כָל־יָמֵינוּ פָּנוּ בְעֶבְרָתֶךָ כִּלִּינוּ שָׁנֵינוּ כְמוֹ־הֶגֶה:	ט
10	The span of our life is seventy years, or, given the strength, eighty years; but the best of them are trouble and sorrow. They pass by speedily, and we are in darkness.	*Yemei-shenoteinu vahem shiv'im shanah ve'im bigvurot shemonim shanah verahebam amal va'aven ki-gaz chish vanna'ufah*	יְמֵי־שְׁנוֹתֵינוּ בָהֶם שִׁבְעִים שָׁנָה וְאִם בִּגְבוּרֹת שְׁמוֹנִים שָׁנָה וְרָהְבָּם עָמָל וָאָוֶן כִּי־גָז חִישׁ וַנָּעֻפָה:	י
11	Who can know Your furious anger? Your wrath matches the fear of You.	*Mi-yodea' oz appecha ucheyir'atecha evratecha*	מִי־יוֹדֵעַ עֹז אַפֶּךָ וּכְיִרְאָתְךָ עֶבְרָתֶךָ:	יא
12	Teach us to count our days rightly, that we may obtain a wise heart.	*Limnot yameinu kein hoda venavi levav chochmah*	לִמְנוֹת יָמֵינוּ כֵּן הוֹדַע וְנָבִא לְבַב חָכְמָה:	יב

13	Turn, Hashem! How long? Show mercy to Your servants.	*Shuvah Adonai ad-matai vehinnachem al-avadeicha*	שׁוּבָה יְהֹוָה עַד־מָתָי וְהִנָּחֵם עַל־עֲבָדֶיךָ:	יג
14	Satisfy us at daybreak with Your steadfast love that we may sing for joy all our days.	*Sabbe'enu vabboker chasdecha unerannenah venismechah bechol-yameinu*	שַׂבְּעֵנוּ בַבֹּקֶר חַסְדֶּךָ וּנְרַנְּנָה וְנִשְׂמְחָה בְּכָל־יָמֵינוּ:	יד
15	Give us joy for as long as You have afflicted us, for the years we have suffered misfortune.	*Sammechenu kimot innitanu shenot ra'inu ra'ah*	שַׂמְּחֵנוּ כִּימוֹת עִנִּיתָנוּ שְׁנוֹת רָאִינוּ רָעָה:	טו
16	Let Your deeds be seen by Your servants, Your glory by their children.	*Yera'eh el-avadeicha fo'olecha vahadarecha al-beneihem*	יֵרָאֶה אֶל־עֲבָדֶיךָ פָעֳלֶךָ וַהֲדָרְךָ עַל־בְּנֵיהֶם:	טז
17	May the favor of Hashem, our God, be upon us; let the work of our hands prosper, O prosper the work of our hands!	*Vihi no'am Adonai eloheinu aleinu uma'aseh yadeinu konenah aleinu uma'aseh yadeinu konenehu*	וִיהִי נֹעַם אֲדֹנָי אֱלֹהֵינוּ עָלֵינוּ וּמַעֲשֵׂה יָדֵינוּ כּוֹנְנָה עָלֵינוּ וּמַעֲשֵׂה יָדֵינוּ כּוֹנְנֵהוּ:	יז

91

⎯○⦅❈⦆○⎯

צֵא

1	O you who dwell in the shelter of the Most High and abide in the protection of Shaddai—	*Yoshev beseter elyon betzel shaddai yitlonan*	יֹשֵׁב בְּסֵתֶר עֶלְיוֹן בְּצֵל שַׁדַּי יִתְלוֹנָן:	א

2	I say of Hashem, my refuge and stronghold, my God in whom I trust,	*Omar lAdonai machsi umetzudati elohai evtach-bo*	אֹמַר לַיהֹוָה מַחְסִי וּמְצוּדָתִי אֱלֹהַי אֶבְטַח־בּוֹ:	ב
3	that He will save you from the fowler's trap, from the destructive plague.	*Ki hu yatzilcha mippach yakush middever havvvot*	כִּי הוּא יַצִּילְךָ מִפַּח יָקוּשׁ מִדֶּבֶר הַוּוֹת:	ג
4	He will cover you with His pinions; you will find refuge under His wings; His fidelity is an encircling shield.	*Be'evrato yasech lach vetachat-kenafav techseh tzinnah vesocherah amitto*	בְּאֶבְרָתוֹ יָסֶךְ לָךְ וְתַחַת־כְּנָפָיו תֶּחְסֶה צִנָּה וְסֹחֵרָה אֲמִתּוֹ:	ד
5	You need not fear the terror by night, or the arrow that flies by day,	*Lo-tira mippachad layelah mechetz ya'uf yomam*	לֹא־תִירָא מִפַּחַד לָיְלָה מֵחֵץ יָעוּף יוֹמָם:	ה
6	the plague that stalks in the darkness, or the scourge that ravages at noon.	*Middever ba'ofel yahaloch mikketev yashud tzohorayim*	מִדֶּבֶר בָּאֹפֶל יַהֲלֹךְ מִקֶּטֶב יָשׁוּד צָהֳרָיִם:	ו
7	A thousand may fall at your left side, ten thousand at your right, but it shall not reach you.	*Yippol mitziddecha elef urevavah miminecha eleicha lo yiggash*	יִפֹּל מִצִּדְּךָ אֶלֶף וּרְבָבָה מִימִינֶךָ אֵלֶיךָ לֹא יִגָּשׁ:	ז
8	You will see it with your eyes, you will witness the punishment of the wicked.	*Rak be'eineicha tabbit veshillumat resha'im tir'eh*	רַק בְּעֵינֶיךָ תַבִּיט וְשִׁלֻּמַת רְשָׁעִים תִּרְאֶה:	ח

9	Because you took Hashem—my refuge, the Most High—as your haven,	*Ki-attah Adonai machsi elyon samta me'onecha*	כִּי־אַתָּה יְהֹוָה מַחְסִי עֶלְיוֹן שַׂמְתָּ מְעוֹנֶךָ:	ט
10	no harm will befall you, no disease touch your tent.	*Lo-te'unneh eleicha ra'ah venega lo-yikrav be'oholecha*	לֹא־תְאֻנֶּה אֵלֶיךָ רָעָה וְנֶגַע לֹא־יִקְרַב בְּאׇהֳלֶךָ:	י
11	For He will order His angels to guard you wherever you go.	*Ki mal'achav yetzavveh-lach lishmarecha bechol-deracheicha*	כִּי מַלְאָכָיו יְצַוֶּה־לָּךְ לִשְׁמׇרְךָ בְּכׇל־דְּרָכֶיךָ:	יא
12	They will carry you in their hands lest you hurt your foot on a stone.	*Al-kappayim yissa'unecha pen-tiggof ba'even raglecha*	עַל־כַּפַּיִם יִשָּׂאוּנְךָ פֶּן־תִּגֹּף בָּאֶבֶן רַגְלֶךָ:	יב
13	You will tread on cubs and vipers; you will trample lions and asps.	*Al-shachal vafeten tidroch tirmos kefir vetannin*	עַל־שַׁחַל וָפֶתֶן תִּדְרֹךְ תִּרְמֹס כְּפִיר וְתַנִּין:	יג
14	"Because he is devoted to Me I will deliver him; I will keep him safe, for he knows My name.	*Ki vi chashak va'afalletehu asaggevehu ki-yada shemi*	כִּי בִי חָשַׁק וַאֲפַלְּטֵהוּ אֲשַׂגְּבֵהוּ כִּי־יָדַע שְׁמִי:	יד
15	When he calls on Me, I will answer him; I will be with him in distress; I will rescue him and make him honored;	*Yikra'eni ve'e'enehu immo-anochi vetzarah achalletzehu va'achabbedehu*	יִקְרָאֵנִי וְאֶעֱנֵהוּ עִמּוֹ־אָנֹכִי בְצָרָה אֲחַלְּצֵהוּ וַאֲכַבְּדֵהוּ:	טו
16	I will let him live to a ripe old age, and show him My salvation."	*Orech yamim asbi'ehu ve'ar'ehu bishu'ati*	אֹרֶךְ יָמִים אַשְׂבִּיעֵהוּ וְאַרְאֵהוּ בִּישׁוּעָתִי:	טז

92

1	A psalm. A song; for the Shabbat day.	*Mizmor shir leyom hashabbat*	מִזְמוֹר שִׁיר לְיוֹם הַשַּׁבָּת: א
2	It is good to praise Hashem, to sing hymns to Your name, O Most High,	*Tov lehodot lAdonai ulezammer leshimcha elyon*	טוֹב לְהֹדוֹת לַיהֹוָה וּלְזַמֵּר לְשִׁמְךָ עֶלְיוֹן: ב
3	To proclaim Your steadfast love at daybreak, Your faithfulness each night	*Lehaggid babboker chasdecha ve'emunatecha balleilot*	לְהַגִּיד בַּבֹּקֶר חַסְדֶּךָ וֶאֱמוּנָתְךָ בַּלֵּילוֹת: ג
4	With a ten-stringed harp, with voice and lyre together.	*Alei-asor va'alei-navel alei higgayon bechinnor*	עֲלֵי־עָשׂוֹר וַעֲלֵי־נָבֶל עֲלֵי הִגָּיוֹן בְּכִנּוֹר: ד
5	You have gladdened me by Your deeds, Hashem; I shout for joy at Your handiwork.	*Ki simmachtani Adonai befo'olecha bema'asei yadeicha arannen*	כִּי שִׂמַּחְתַּנִי יְהֹוָה בְּפָעֳלֶךָ בְּמַעֲשֵׂי יָדֶיךָ אֲרַנֵּן: ה
6	How great are Your works, Hashem, how very subtle Your designs!	*Mah-gadelu ma'aseicha Adonai me'od ameku machshevoteicha*	מַה־גָּדְלוּ מַעֲשֶׂיךָ יְהֹוָה מְאֹד עָמְקוּ מַחְשְׁבֹתֶיךָ: ו
7	A brutish man cannot know, a fool cannot understand this:	*Ish-ba'ar lo yeda uchesil lo-yavin et-zot*	אִישׁ־בַּעַר לֹא יֵדָע וּכְסִיל לֹא־יָבִין אֶת־זֹאת: ז

8	though the wicked sprout like grass, though all evildoers blossom, it is only that they may be destroyed forever.	*Bifroach resha'im kemo esev vayyatzitzu kol-po'alei aven lehishomdam adei-ad*	בִּפְרֹחַ רְשָׁעִים כְּמוֹ עֵשֶׂב וַיָּצִיצוּ כָּל־פֹּעֲלֵי אָוֶן לְהִשָּׁמְדָם עֲדֵי־עַד:	ח
9	But You are exalted, Hashem, for all time.	*Ve'attah marom le'olam Adonai*	וְאַתָּה מָרוֹם לְעֹלָם יְהֹוָה:	ט
10	Surely, Your enemies, Hashem, surely, Your enemies perish; all evildoers are scattered.	*Ki hinneh oyeveicha Adonai ki-hinneh oyeveicha yovedu yitparedu kol-po'alei aven*	כִּי הִנֵּה אֹיְבֶיךָ יְהֹוָה כִּי־הִנֵּה אֹיְבֶיךָ יֹאבֵדוּ יִתְפָּרְדוּ כָּל־פֹּעֲלֵי אָוֶן:	י
11	You raise my horn high like that of a wild ox; I am soaked in freshening oil.	*Vattarem kir'eim karni balloti beshemen ra'anan*	וַתָּרֶם כִּרְאֵים קַרְנִי בַּלֹּתִי בְּשֶׁמֶן רַעֲנָן:	יא
12	I shall see the defeat of my watchful foes, hear of the downfall of the wicked who beset me.	*Vattabbet eini beshurai bakkamim alai mere'im tishma'nah azenai*	וַתַּבֵּט עֵינִי בְּשׁוּרָי בַּקָּמִים עָלַי מְרֵעִים תִּשְׁמַעְנָה אָזְנָי:	יב
13	The righteous bloom like a date-palm; they thrive like a cedar in Lebanon;	*Tzaddik kattamar yifrach ke'erez ballevanon yisgeh*	צַדִּיק כַּתָּמָר יִפְרָח כְּאֶרֶז בַּלְּבָנוֹן יִשְׂגֶּה:	יג
14	planted in the house of Hashem, they flourish in the courts of our God.	*Shetulim beveit Adonai bechatzrot eloheinu yafrichu*	שְׁתוּלִים בְּבֵית יְהֹוָה בְּחַצְרוֹת אֱלֹהֵינוּ יַפְרִיחוּ:	יד
15	In old age they still produce fruit; they are full of sap and freshness,	*Od yenuvun beseivah deshenim vera'anannim yihyu*	עוֹד יְנוּבוּן בְּשֵׂיבָה דְּשֵׁנִים וְרַעֲנַנִּים יִהְיוּ:	טו

16 attesting that Hashem is upright, my rock, in whom there is no wrong.

Lehaggid ki-yashar Adonai tzuri velo-lth [avlatah] bo

לְהַגִּיד כִּי־יָשָׁר יְהֹוָה צוּרִי וְלֹא־עלתה [עַוְלָתָה] בּוֹ: טז

93

—o⟨✦⟩o—

צֵג

1 Hashem is king, He is robed in grandeur; Hashem is robed, He is girded with strength. The world stands firm; it cannot be shaken.

Adonai malach ge'ut lavesh lavesh Adonai oz hit'azzar af-tikkon tevel bal-timmot

יְהֹוָה מָלָךְ גֵּאוּת לָבֵשׁ לָבֵשׁ יְהֹוָה עֹז הִתְאַזָּר אַף־תִּכּוֹן תֵּבֵל בַּל־תִּמּוֹט: א

2 Your throne stands firm from of old; from eternity You have existed.

Nachon kis'acha me'az me'olam attah

נָכוֹן כִּסְאֲךָ מֵאָז מֵעוֹלָם אָתָּה: ב

3 The ocean sounds, Hashem, the ocean sounds its thunder, the ocean sounds its pounding.

Nase'u neharot Adonai nase'u neharot kolam yis'u neharot dochyam

נָשְׂאוּ נְהָרוֹת יְהֹוָה נָשְׂאוּ נְהָרוֹת קוֹלָם יִשְׂאוּ נְהָרוֹת דָּכְיָם: ג

4 Above the thunder of the mighty waters, more majestic than the breakers of the sea is Hashem, majestic on high.

Mikkolot mayim rabbim addirim mishberei-yam addir bammarom Adonai

מִקֹּלוֹת מַיִם רַבִּים אַדִּירִים מִשְׁבְּרֵי־יָם אַדִּיר בַּמָּרוֹם יְהֹוָה: ד

5 Your decrees are indeed enduring; holiness befits Your house, Hashem, for all times.

Edoteicha ne'emnu me'od leveitcha na'avah-kodesh Adonai le'orech yamim

עֵדֹתֶיךָ נֶאֶמְנוּ מְאֹד לְבֵיתְךָ נַאֲוָה־קֹדֶשׁ יְהֹוָה לְאֹרֶךְ יָמִים: ה

94

1	God of retribution, Hashem, God of retribution, appear!	*El-nekamot Adonai el nekamot hofiya*	אֵל־נְקָמוֹת יְהֹוָה אֵל נְקָמוֹת הוֹפִיעַ:	א
2	Rise up, judge of the earth, give the arrogant their deserts!	*Hinnase shofet ha'aretz hashev gemul al-ge'im*	הִנָּשֵׂא שֹׁפֵט הָאָרֶץ הָשֵׁב גְּמוּל עַל־גֵּאִים:	ב
3	How long shall the wicked, Hashem, how long shall the wicked exult,	*Ad-matai resha'im Adonai ad-matai resha'im ya'alozu*	עַד־מָתַי רְשָׁעִים יְהֹוָה עַד־מָתַי רְשָׁעִים יַעֲלֹזוּ:	ג
4	shall they utter insolent speech, shall all evildoers vaunt themselves?	*Yabbi'u yedabberu atak yit'ammeru kol-po'alei aven*	יַבִּיעוּ יְדַבְּרוּ עָתָק יִתְאַמְּרוּ כָּל־פֹּעֲלֵי אָוֶן:	ד
5	They crush Your people, Hashem, they afflict Your very own;	*Ammecha Adonai yedakke'u venachalatecha ye'annu*	עַמְּךָ יְהֹוָה יְדַכְּאוּ וְנַחֲלָתְךָ יְעַנּוּ:	ה
6	they kill the widow and the stranger; they murder the fatherless,	*Almanah veger yaharogu vitomim yeratzechu*	אַלְמָנָה וְגֵר יַהֲרֹגוּ וִיתוֹמִים יְרַצֵּחוּ:	ו
7	thinking, "Hashem does not see it, the God of Yaakov does not pay heed."	*Vayyomru lo yir'eh-yah velo-yavin elohei ya'akov*	וַיֹּאמְרוּ לֹא יִרְאֶה־יָּהּ וְלֹא־יָבִין אֱלֹהֵי יַעֲקֹב:	ז

8	Take heed, you most brutish people; fools, when will you get wisdom?	*binu bo'arim ba'am uchesilim matai taskilu*	בִּינוּ בֹּעֲרִים בָּעָם וּכְסִילִים מָתַי תַּשְׂכִּילוּ:	ח
9	Shall He who implants the ear not hear, He who forms the eye not see?	*Hanota ozen halo yishma im-yotzer ayin halo yabbit*	הֲנֹטַע אֹזֶן הֲלֹא יִשְׁמָע אִם־יֹצֵר עַיִן הֲלֹא יַבִּיט:	ט
10	Shall He who disciplines nations not punish, He who instructs men in knowledge?	*Hayoser goyim halo yochiach hammelammed adam da'at*	הֲיֹסֵר גּוֹיִם הֲלֹא יוֹכִיחַ הַמְלַמֵּד אָדָם דָּעַת:	י
11	Hashem knows the designs of men to be futile.	*Adonai yodea' machshevot adam ki-hemmah havel*	יְהֹוָה יֹדֵעַ מַחְשְׁבוֹת אָדָם כִּי־הֵמָּה הָבֶל:	יא
12	Happy is the man whom You discipline, Hashem, the man You instruct in Your teaching,	*Ashrei haggever asher-teyasserennu yah umittoratecha telammedennu*	אַשְׁרֵי הַגֶּבֶר אֲשֶׁר־תְּיַסְּרֶנּוּ יָּהּ וּמִתּוֹרָתְךָ תְלַמְּדֶנּוּ:	יב
13	to give him tranquillity in times of misfortune, until a pit be dug for the wicked.	*Lehashkit lo mimei ra ad yikhareh larasha shachat*	לְהַשְׁקִיט לוֹ מִימֵי רָע עַד יִכָּרֶה לָרָשָׁע שָׁחַת:	יג
14	For Hashem will not forsake His people; He will not abandon His very own.	*Ki lo-yittosh Adonai ammo venachalato lo ya'azov*	כִּי לֹא־יִטֹּשׁ יְהֹוָה עַמּוֹ וְנַחֲלָתוֹ לֹא יַעֲזֹב:	יד
15	Judgment shall again accord with justice and all the upright shall rally to it.	*Ki-ad-tzedek yashuv mishpat ve'acharav kol-yishrei-lev*	כִּי־עַד־צֶדֶק יָשׁוּב מִשְׁפָּט וְאַחֲרָיו כָּל־יִשְׁרֵי־לֵב:	טו

16	Who will take my part against evil men? Who will stand up for me against wrongdoers?	*Mi-yakum li im-mere'im mi-yityatzev li im-po'alei aven*	מִי־יָקוּם לִי עִם־מְרֵעִים מִי־יִתְיַצֵּב לִי עִם־פֹּעֲלֵי אָוֶן:	טז
17	Were not Hashem my help, I should soon dwell in silence.	*Lulei Adonai ezratah li kim'at shachenah dumah nafshi*	לוּלֵי יְהֹוָה עֶזְרָתָה לִּי כִּמְעַט שָׁכְנָה דוּמָה נַפְשִׁי:	יז
18	When I think my foot has given way, Your faithfulness, Hashem, supports me.	*Im-amarti matah ragli chasdecha Adonai yis'adeni*	אִם־אָמַרְתִּי מָטָה רַגְלִי חַסְדְּךָ יְהֹוָה יִסְעָדֵנִי:	יח
19	When I am filled with cares, Your assurance soothes my soul.	*Berov sar'appai bekirbi tanchumeicha yesha'ash'u nafshi*	בְּרֹב שַׂרְעַפַּי בְּקִרְבִּי תַּנְחוּמֶיךָ יְשַׁעַשְׁעוּ נַפְשִׁי:	יט
20	Shall the seat of injustice be Your partner, that frames mischief by statute?	*Hayyechovrecha kisse havvvot yotzer amal alei-chok*	הַיְחָבְרְךָ כִּסֵּא הַוּוֹת יֹצֵר עָמָל עֲלֵי־חֹק:	כ
21	They band together to do away with the righteous; they condemn the innocent to death.	*Yagoddu al-nefesh tzaddik vedam naki yarshi'u*	יָגוֹדּוּ עַל־נֶפֶשׁ צַדִּיק וְדָם נָקִי יַרְשִׁיעוּ:	כא
22	But Hashem is my haven; my God is my sheltering rock.	*Vayhi Adonai li lemisgav velohai letzur machsi*	וַיְהִי יְהֹוָה לִי לְמִשְׂגָּב וֵאלֹהַי לְצוּר מַחְסִי:	כב
23	He will make their evil recoil upon them, annihilate them through their own wickedness; Hashem our God will annihilate them.	*Vayyashev aleihem et-onam uvera'atam yatzmitem yatzmitem Adonai eloheinu*	וַיָּשֶׁב עֲלֵיהֶם אֶת־אוֹנָם וּבְרָעָתָם יַצְמִיתֵם יַצְמִיתֵם יְהֹוָה אֱלֹהֵינוּ:	כג

95

1	Come, let us sing joyously to Hashem, raise a shout for our rock and deliverer;	*Lechu nerannenah lAdonai nari'ah letzur yish'enu*	לְכוּ נְרַנְּנָה לַיהֹוָה נָרִיעָה לְצוּר יִשְׁעֵנוּ׃	א
2	let us come into His presence with praise; let us raise a shout for Him in song!	*Nekaddemah fanav betodah bizmirot naria' lo*	נְקַדְּמָה פָנָיו בְּתוֹדָה בִּזְמִרוֹת נָרִיעַ לוֹ׃	ב
3	For Hashem is a great Hashem, the great king of all divine beings.	*Ki el gadol Adonai umelech gadol al-kol-elohim*	כִּי אֵל גָּדוֹל יְהֹוָה וּמֶלֶךְ גָּדוֹל עַל־כָּל־אֱלֹהִים׃	ג
4	In His hand are the depths of the earth; the peaks of the mountains are His.	*Asher beyado mechkerei-aretz veto'afot harim lo*	אֲשֶׁר בְּיָדוֹ מֶחְקְרֵי־אָרֶץ וְתוֹעֲפוֹת הָרִים לוֹ׃	ד
5	His is the sea, He made it; and the land, which His hands fashioned.	*Asher-lo hayyam vehu asahu veyabbeshet yadav yatzaru*	אֲשֶׁר־לוֹ הַיָּם וְהוּא עָשָׂהוּ וְיַבֶּשֶׁת יָדָיו יָצָרוּ׃	ה
6	Come, let us bow down and kneel, bend the knee before Hashem our maker,	*bo'u nishtachaveh venichra'ah nivrechah lifnei-Adonai osenu*	בֹּאוּ נִשְׁתַּחֲוֶה וְנִכְרָעָה נִבְרְכָה לִפְנֵי־יְהֹוָה עֹשֵׂנוּ׃	ו

7	for He is our God, and we are the people He tends, the flock in His care. O, if you would but heed His charge this day:	*Ki hu eloheinu va'anachnu am mar'ito vetzon yado hayyom im-bekolo tishma'u*	כִּי הוּא אֱלֹהֵינוּ וַאֲנַחְנוּ עַם מַרְעִיתוֹ וְצֹאן יָדוֹ הַיּוֹם אִם־בְּקֹלוֹ תִשְׁמָעוּ:	ז
8	Do not be stubborn as at Meribah, as on the day of Massah, in the wilderness,	*Al-takshu levavchem kimrivah keyom massah bammidbar*	אַל־תַּקְשׁוּ לְבַבְכֶם כִּמְרִיבָה כְּיוֹם מַסָּה בַּמִּדְבָּר:	ח
9	when your fathers put Me to the test, tried Me, though they had seen My deeds.	*Asher nissuni avoteichem bechanuni gam-ra'u fo'oli*	אֲשֶׁר נִסּוּנִי אֲבוֹתֵיכֶם בְּחָנוּנִי גַּם־רָאוּ פָעֳלִי:	ט
10	Forty years I was provoked by that generation; I thought, "They are a senseless people; they would not know My ways."	*Arba'im shanah akut bedor va'omar am to'ei levav hem vehem lo-yade'u derachai*	אַרְבָּעִים שָׁנָה אָקוּט בְּדוֹר וָאֹמַר עַם תֹּעֵי לֵבָב הֵם וְהֵם לֹא־יָדְעוּ דְרָכָי:	י
11	Concerning them I swore in anger, "They shall never come to My resting-place!"	*Asher-nishba'ti ve'appi im-yevo'un el-menuchati*	אֲשֶׁר־נִשְׁבַּעְתִּי בְאַפִּי אִם־יְבֹאוּן אֶל־מְנוּחָתִי:	יא

96 —◦⦉⦊◦— צו

1	Sing to Hashem a new song, sing to Hashem, all the earth.	*Shiru lAdonai shir chadash shiru lAdonai kol-ha'aretz*	שִׁירוּ לַיהוָה שִׁיר חָדָשׁ שִׁירוּ לַיהוָה כָּל־הָאָרֶץ:	א

2	Sing to Hashem, bless His name, proclaim His victory day after day.	*Shiru lAdonai barachu shemo basseru miyyom-leyom yeshu'ato*	שִׁירוּ לַיהֹוָה בָּרֲכוּ שְׁמוֹ בַּשְּׂרוּ מִיּוֹם־לְיוֹם יְשׁוּעָתוֹ:	ב
3	Tell of His glory among the nations, His wondrous deeds, among all peoples.	*Sapperu vaggoyim kevodo bechol-ha'ammim nifle'otav*	סַפְּרוּ בַגּוֹיִם כְּבוֹדוֹ בְּכָל־הָעַמִּים נִפְלְאוֹתָיו:	ג
4	For Hashem is great and much acclaimed, He is held in awe by all divine beings.	*Ki gadol Adonai umehullal me'od nora hu al-kol-elohim*	כִּי גָדוֹל יְהֹוָה וּמְהֻלָּל מְאֹד נוֹרָא הוּא עַל־כָּל־אֱלֹהִים:	ד
5	All the gods of the peoples are mere idols, but Hashem made the heavens.	*Ki kol-elohei ha'ammim elilim vaihovah shamayim asah*	כִּי כָּל־אֱלֹהֵי הָעַמִּים אֱלִילִים וַיהֹוָה שָׁמַיִם עָשָׂה:	ה
6	Glory and majesty are before Him; strength and splendor are in His temple.	*Hod-vehadar lefanav oz vetif'eret bemikdasho*	הוֹד־וְהָדָר לְפָנָיו עֹז וְתִפְאֶרֶת בְּמִקְדָּשׁוֹ:	ו
7	Ascribe to Hashem, O families of the peoples, ascribe to Hashem glory and strength.	*Havu lAdonai mishpechot ammim havu lAdonai kavod va'oz*	הָבוּ לַיהֹוָה מִשְׁפְּחוֹת עַמִּים הָבוּ לַיהֹוָה כָּבוֹד וָעֹז:	ז
8	Ascribe to Hashem the glory of His name, bring tribute and enter His courts.	*Havu lAdonai kevod shemo se'u-minchah uvo'u lechatzrotav*	הָבוּ לַיהֹוָה כְּבוֹד שְׁמוֹ שְׂאוּ־מִנְחָה וּבֹאוּ לְחַצְרוֹתָיו:	ח

245

9	Bow down to Hashem majestic in holiness; tremble in His presence, all the earth!	*Hishtachavu lAdonai behadrat-kodesh chilu mippanav kol-ha'aretz*	הִשְׁתַּחֲווּ לַיהוָה בְּהַדְרַת־קֹדֶשׁ חִילוּ מִפָּנָיו כָּל־הָאָרֶץ: ט
10	Declare among the nations, "Hashem is king!" the world stands firm; it cannot be shaken; He judges the peoples with equity.	*Imru vaggoyim Adonai malach af-tikkon tevel bal-timmot yadin ammim bemeisharim*	אִמְרוּ בַגּוֹיִם יְהוָה מָלָךְ אַף־תִּכּוֹן תֵּבֵל בַּל־תִּמּוֹט יָדִין עַמִּים בְּמֵישָׁרִים: י
11	Let the heavens rejoice and the earth exult; let the sea and all within it thunder,	*Yismechu hashamayim vetagel ha'aretz yir'am hayyam umelo'o*	יִשְׂמְחוּ הַשָּׁמַיִם וְתָגֵל הָאָרֶץ יִרְעַם הַיָּם וּמְלֹאוֹ: יא
12	the fields and everything in them exult; then shall all the trees of the forest shout for joy	*Ya'aloz sadai vechol-asher-bo az yerannenu kol-atzei-ya'ar*	יַעֲלֹז שָׂדַי וְכָל־אֲשֶׁר־בּוֹ אָז יְרַנְּנוּ כָּל־עֲצֵי־יָעַר: יב
13	at the presence of Hashem, for He is coming, for He is coming to rule the earth; He will rule the world justly, and its peoples in faithfulness.	*Lifnei Adonai ki va ki va lishpot ha'aretz yishpot-tevel betzedek ve'ammim be'emunato*	לִפְנֵי יְהוָה כִּי בָא כִּי בָא לִשְׁפֹּט הָאָרֶץ יִשְׁפֹּט־תֵּבֵל בְּצֶדֶק וְעַמִּים בֶּאֱמוּנָתוֹ: יג

97

—◦⊰✦⊱◦—

צז

1	Hashem is king! Let the earth exult, the many islands rejoice!	*Adonai malach tagel ha'aretz yismechu iyyim rabbim*	יְהוָה מָלָךְ תָּגֵל הָאָרֶץ יִשְׂמְחוּ אִיִּים רַבִּים: א

2	Dense clouds are around Him, righteousness and justice are the base of His throne.	*Anan va'arafel sevivav tzedek umishpat mechon kis'o*	עָנָן וַעֲרָפֶל סְבִיבָיו צֶדֶק וּמִשְׁפָּט מְכוֹן כִּסְאוֹ: ב
3	Fire is His vanguard, burning His foes on every side.	*Esh lefanav telech utelahet saviv tzarav*	אֵשׁ לְפָנָיו תֵּלֵךְ וּתְלַהֵט סָבִיב צָרָיו: ג
4	His lightnings light up the world; the earth is convulsed at the sight;	*He'iru verakav tevel ra'atah vattachel ha'aretz*	הֵאִירוּ בְרָקָיו תֵּבֵל רָאֲתָה וַתָּחֵל הָאָרֶץ: ד
5	mountains melt like wax at Hashem's presence, at the presence of the Lord of all the earth.	*Harim kaddonag namassu millifnei Adonai millifnei adon kol-ha'aretz*	הָרִים כַּדּוֹנַג נָמַסּוּ מִלִּפְנֵי יְהֹוָה מִלִּפְנֵי אֲדוֹן כָּל־הָאָרֶץ: ה
6	The heavens proclaim His righteousness and all peoples see His glory.	*Higgidu hashamayim tzidko vera'u chol-ha'ammim kevodo*	הִגִּידוּ הַשָּׁמַיִם צִדְקוֹ וְרָאוּ כָל־הָעַמִּים כְּבוֹדוֹ: ו
7	All who worship images, who vaunt their idols, are dismayed; all divine beings bow down to Him.	*Yevoshu kol-ovedei fesel hammithallim ba'elilim hishtachavu-lo kol-elohim*	יֵבֹשׁוּ כָּל־עֹבְדֵי פֶסֶל הַמִּתְהַלְלִים בָּאֱלִילִים הִשְׁתַּחֲווּ־לוֹ כָּל־אֱלֹהִים: ז
8	Tzion, hearing it, rejoices, the towns of Yehuda exult, because of Your judgments, Hashem.	*Shame'ah vattismach tziyyon vattagelenah benot yehudah lema'an mishpateicha Adonai*	שָׁמְעָה וַתִּשְׂמַח צִיּוֹן וַתָּגֵלְנָה בְּנוֹת יְהוּדָה לְמַעַן מִשְׁפָּטֶיךָ יְהֹוָה: ח

9	For You, Hashem, are supreme over all the earth; You are exalted high above all divine beings.	*Ki-attah Adonai elyon al-kol-ha'aretz me'od na'aleita al-kol-elohim*

כִּי־אַתָּה יְהֹוָה עֶלְיוֹן עַל־כָּל־הָאָרֶץ מְאֹד נַעֲלֵיתָ עַל־כָּל־אֱלֹהִים: ט

10	O you who love Hashem, hate evil! He guards the lives of His loyal ones, saving them from the hand of the wicked.	*Ohavei Adonai sin'u ra shomer nafshot chasidav miyyad resha'im yatzilem*

אֹהֲבֵי יְהֹוָה שִׂנְאוּ רָע שֹׁמֵר נַפְשׁוֹת חֲסִידָיו מִיַּד רְשָׁעִים יַצִּילֵם: י

11	Light is sown for the righteous, radiance for the upright.	*Or zarua' latzaddik uleyishrei-lev simchah*

אוֹר זָרֻעַ לַצַּדִּיק וּלְיִשְׁרֵי־לֵב שִׂמְחָה: יא

12	O you righteous, rejoice in Hashem and acclaim His holy name!	*Simchu tzaddikim bAdonai vehodu lezecher kodsho*

שִׂמְחוּ צַדִּיקִים בַּיהֹוָה וְהוֹדוּ לְזֵכֶר קָדְשׁוֹ: יב

98

—o◯◯◯o—

צח

1	A psalm. Sing to Hashem a new song, for He has worked wonders; His right hand, His holy arm, has won Him victory.	*Mizmor shiru lAdonai shir chadash ki-nifla'ot asah hoshi'ah-lo yemino uzeroa' kodsho*

מִזְמוֹר שִׁירוּ לַיהֹוָה שִׁיר חָדָשׁ כִּי־נִפְלָאוֹת עָשָׂה הוֹשִׁיעָה־לּוֹ יְמִינוֹ וּזְרוֹעַ קָדְשׁוֹ: א

2	Hashem has manifested His victory, has displayed His triumph in the sight of the nations.	*Hodia' Adonai yeshu'ato le'einei haggoyim gillah tzidkato*

הוֹדִיעַ יְהֹוָה יְשׁוּעָתוֹ לְעֵינֵי הַגּוֹיִם גִּלָּה צִדְקָתוֹ: ב

3	He was mindful of His steadfast love and faithfulness toward the house of Yisrael; all the ends of the earth beheld the victory of our God.	*Zachar chasdo ve'emunato leveit yisra'el ra'u chol-afsei-aretz et yeshu'at eloheinu*	זָכַר חַסְדּוֹ וֶאֱמוּנָתוֹ לְבֵית יִשְׂרָאֵל רָאוּ כָל־אַפְסֵי־אָרֶץ אֵת יְשׁוּעַת אֱלֹהֵינוּ: ג
4	Raise a shout to Hashem, all the earth, break into joyous songs of praise!	*Hari'u lAdonai kol-ha'aretz pitzchu verannenu vezammeru*	הָרִיעוּ לַיהוָה כָּל־הָאָרֶץ פִּצְחוּ וְרַנְּנוּ וְזַמֵּרוּ: ד
5	Sing praise to Hashem with the lyre, with the lyre and melodious song.	*Zammeru lAdonai bechinnor bechinnor vekol zimrah*	זַמְּרוּ לַיהוָה בְּכִנּוֹר בְּכִנּוֹר וְקוֹל זִמְרָה: ה
6	With trumpets and the blast of the horn raise a shout before Hashem, the King.	*Bachatzotzerot vekol shofar hari'u lifnei hammelech Adonai*	בַּחֲצֹצְרוֹת וְקוֹל שׁוֹפָר הָרִיעוּ לִפְנֵי הַמֶּלֶךְ יְהוָה: ו
7	Let the sea and all within it thunder, the world and its inhabitants;	*Yir'am hayyam umelo'o tevel veyoshevei vah*	יִרְעַם הַיָּם וּמְלֹאוֹ תֵּבֵל וְיֹשְׁבֵי בָהּ: ז
8	let the rivers clap their hands, the mountains sing joyously together	*Neharot yimcha'u-chaf yachad harim yerannenu*	נְהָרוֹת יִמְחֲאוּ־כָף יַחַד הָרִים יְרַנֵּנוּ: ח
9	at the presence of Hashem, for He is coming to rule the earth; He will rule the world justly, and its peoples with equity.	*Lifnei-Adonai ki va lishpot ha'aretz yishpot-tevel betzedek ve'ammim bemeisharim*	לִפְנֵי־יְהוָה כִּי בָא לִשְׁפֹּט הָאָרֶץ יִשְׁפֹּט־תֵּבֵל בְּצֶדֶק וְעַמִּים בְּמֵישָׁרִים: ט

99

1	Hashem, enthroned on cherubim, is king, peoples tremble,* the earth quakes.	*Adonai malach yirgezu ammim yoshev keruvim tanut ha'aretz*	יְהֹוָה מָלָךְ יִרְגְּזוּ עַמִּים יֹשֵׁב כְּרוּבִים תָּנוּט הָאָרֶץ: א
2	Hashem is great in Tzion, and exalted above all peoples.	*Adonai betziyyon gadol veram hu al-kol-ha'ammim*	יְהֹוָה בְּצִיּוֹן גָּדוֹל וְרָם הוּא עַל־כָּל־הָעַמִּים: ב
3	They praise Your name as great and awesome; He is holy!	*yodu shimcha gadol venora kadosh hu*	יוֹדוּ שִׁמְךָ גָּדוֹל וְנוֹרָא קָדוֹשׁ הוּא: ג
4	Mighty king who loves justice, it was You who established equity, You who worked righteous judgment in Yaakov.	*Ve'oz melech mishpat ahev attah konanta meisharim mishpat utzedakah beya'akov attah asita*	וְעֹז מֶלֶךְ מִשְׁפָּט אָהֵב אַתָּה כּוֹנַנְתָּ מֵישָׁרִים מִשְׁפָּט וּצְדָקָה בְּיַעֲקֹב אַתָּה עָשִׂיתָ: ד
5	Exalt Hashem our God and bow down to His footstool; He is holy!	*Romemu Adonai eloheinu vehishtachavu lahadom raglav kadosh hu*	רוֹמְמוּ יְהֹוָה אֱלֹהֵינוּ וְהִשְׁתַּחֲווּ לַהֲדֹם רַגְלָיו קָדוֹשׁ הוּא: ה
6	Moshe and Aharon among His Kohanim, Shmuel, among those who call on His name— when they called to Hashem, He answered them.	*Mosheh ve'aharon bechohanav ushemu'el bekore'ei shemo korim el-Adonai vehu ya'anem*	מֹשֶׁה וְאַהֲרֹן בְּכֹהֲנָיו וּשְׁמוּאֵל בְּקֹרְאֵי שְׁמוֹ קֹרִאים אֶל־יְהֹוָה וְהוּא יַעֲנֵם: ו

7 He spoke to them in a pillar of cloud; they obeyed His decrees, the law He gave them.

Be'ammud anan yedabber aleihem shameru edotav vechok natan-lamo

בְּעַמּוּד עָנָן יְדַבֵּר אֲלֵיהֶם שָׁמְרוּ עֵדֹתָיו וְחֹק נָתַן־לָמוֹ: ז

8 Hashem our God, You answered them; You were a forgiving Hashem for them, but You exacted retribution for their misdeeds.

Adonai eloheinu attah anitam el nose hayita lahem venokem al-alilotam

יְהֹוָה אֱלֹהֵינוּ אַתָּה עֲנִיתָם אֵל נֹשֵׂא הָיִיתָ לָהֶם וְנֹקֵם עַל־עֲלִילוֹתָם: ח

9 Exalt Hashem our God, and bow toward His holy hill, for Hashem our God is holy.

Romemu Adonai eloheinu vehishtachavu lehar kodsho ki-kadosh Adonai eloheinu

רוֹמְמוּ יְהֹוָה אֱלֹהֵינוּ וְהִשְׁתַּחֲווּ לְהַר קׇדְשׁוֹ כִּי־קָדוֹשׁ יְהֹוָה אֱלֹהֵינוּ: ט

100

──◦⊙⧉⊙◦──

קן

1 A psalm for praise. Raise a shout for Hashem, all the earth;

Mizmor letodah hari'u lAdonai kol-ha'aretz

מִזְמוֹר לְתוֹדָה הָרִיעוּ לַיהֹוָה כׇּל־הָאָרֶץ: א

2 worship Hashem in gladness; come into His presence with shouts of joy.

Ivdu et-Adonai besimchah bo'u lefanav birnanah

עִבְדוּ אֶת־יְהֹוָה בְּשִׂמְחָה בֹּאוּ לְפָנָיו בִּרְנָנָה: ב

3 Acknowledge that Hashem is Hashem; He made us and we are His, His people, the flock He tends.

De'u ki-Adonai hu elohim hu-asanu vl [velo] anachnu ammo vetzon mar'ito

דְּעוּ כִּי־יְהֹוָה הוּא אֱלֹהִים הוּא־עָשָׂנוּ ולא [וְלוֹ] אֲנַחְנוּ עַמּוֹ וְצֹאן מַרְעִיתוֹ: ג

4　Enter His gates with praise, His courts with acclamation. Praise Him! Bless His name!

bo'u she'arav betodah chatzerotav bithillah hodu-lo barachu shemo

בֹּאוּ שְׁעָרָיו בְּתוֹדָה חֲצֵרֹתָיו בִּתְהִלָּה הוֹדוּ-לוֹ בָּרֲכוּ שְׁמוֹ: ד

5　For Hashem is good; His steadfast love is eternal; His faithfulness is for all generations.

Ki-tov Adonai le'olam chasdo ve'ad-dor vador emunato

כִּי-טוֹב יְהֹוָה לְעוֹלָם חַסְדּוֹ וְעַד-דֹּר וָדֹר אֱמוּנָתוֹ: ה

101

⊸∘⊸⧈⊸∘⊸

קא

1　Of David. A psalm. I will sing of faithfulness and justice; I will chant a hymn to You, Hashem.

Ledavid mizmor chesed-umishpat ashirah lecha Adonai azammerah

לְדָוִד מִזְמוֹר חֶסֶד-וּמִשְׁפָּט אָשִׁירָה לְךָ יְהֹוָה אֲזַמֵּרָה: א

2　I will study the way of the blameless; when shall I attain it? I will live without blame within my house.

Askilah bederech tamim matai tavo elai ethallech betam-levavi bekerev beiti

אַשְׂכִּילָה בְּדֶרֶךְ תָּמִים מָתַי תָּבוֹא אֵלָי אֶתְהַלֵּךְ בְּתָם-לְבָבִי בְּקֶרֶב בֵּיתִי: ב

3　I will not set before my eyes anything base; I hate crooked dealing; I will have none of it.

Lo-ashit leneged einai devar-beliyya'al asoh-setim saneti lo yidbak bi

לֹא-אָשִׁית לְנֶגֶד עֵינַי דְּבַר-בְּלִיָּעַל עֲשֹׂה-סֵטִים שָׂנֵאתִי לֹא יִדְבַּק בִּי: ג

4　Perverse thoughts will be far from me; I will know nothing of evil.

Levav ikkesh yasur mimmenni ra lo eda

לֵבָב עִקֵּשׁ יָסוּר מִמֶּנִּי רָע לֹא אֵדָע: ד

5 He who slanders his friend in secret I will destroy; I cannot endure the haughty and proud man.

Mlvshn [melasheni] vasseter re'ehu oto atzmit gevah-einayim urechav levav oto lo uchal

מלושני [מְלָשְׁנִי] בַסֵּתֶר רֵעֵהוּ אוֹתוֹ אַצְמִית גְּבַהּ־עֵינַיִם וּרְחַב לֵבָב אֹתוֹ לֹא אוּכָל: ה

6 My eyes are on the trusty men of the land, to have them at my side. He who follows the way of the blameless shall be in my service.

Einai bene'emnei-eretz lashevet immadi holech bederech tamim hu yeshareteni

עֵינַי בְּנֶאֶמְנֵי־אֶרֶץ לָשֶׁבֶת עִמָּדִי הֹלֵךְ בְּדֶרֶךְ תָּמִים הוּא יְשָׁרְתֵנִי: ו

7 He who deals deceitfully shall not live in my house; he who speaks untruth shall not stand before my eyes.

Lo-yeshev bekerev beiti oseh remiyyah dover shekarim lo-yikkon leneged einai

לֹא־יֵשֵׁב בְּקֶרֶב בֵּיתִי עֹשֵׂה רְמִיָּה דֹּבֵר שְׁקָרִים לֹא־יִכּוֹן לְנֶגֶד עֵינָי: ז

8 Each morning I will destroy all the wicked of the land, to rid the city of Hashem of all evildoers.

Labbekarim atzmit kol-rish'ei-aretz lehachrit me'ir-Adonai kol-po'alei aven

לַבְּקָרִים אַצְמִית כָּל־רִשְׁעֵי־אָרֶץ לְהַכְרִית מֵעִיר־יְהֹוָה כָּל־פֹּעֲלֵי אָוֶן: ח

102

1 A prayer of the lowly man when he is faint and pours forth his plea before Hashem.

Tefillah le'ani chi-ya'atof velifnei Adonai yishpoch sicho

תְּפִלָּה לְעָנִי כִי־יַעֲטֹף וְלִפְנֵי יְהֹוָה יִשְׁפֹּךְ שִׂיחוֹ: א

2	Hashem, hear my prayer; let my cry come before You.	*Adonai shim'ah tefillati veshav'ati eleicha tavo*	יְהֹוָה שִׁמְעָה תְפִלָּתִי וְשַׁוְעָתִי אֵלֶיךָ תָבוֹא:
3	Do not hide Your face from me in my time of trouble; turn Your ear to me; when I cry, answer me speedily.	*Al-taster panecha mimmenni beyom tzar li hatteh-elai oznecha beyom ekra maher aneni*	אַל־תַּסְתֵּר פָּנֶיךָ מִמֶּנִּי בְּיוֹם צַר לִי הַטֵּה־אֵלַי אָזְנֶךָ בְּיוֹם אֶקְרָא מַהֵר עֲנֵנִי:
4	For my days have vanished like smoke and my bones are charred like a hearth.	*Ki-chalu ve'ashan yamai ve'atzmotai kemo-ked nicharu*	כִּי־כָלוּ בְעָשָׁן יָמָי וְעַצְמוֹתַי כְּמוֹ־קֵד נִחָרוּ:
5	My body is stricken and withered like grass; too wasted to eat my food;	*Hukkah-cha'esev vayyivash libbi ki-shachachti me'achol lachmi*	הוּכָּה־כָעֵשֶׂב וַיִּבַשׁ לִבִּי כִּי־שָׁכַחְתִּי מֵאֲכֹל לַחְמִי:
6	on account of my vehement groaning my bones show through my skin.	*Mikkol anchati davekah atzmi livsari*	מִקּוֹל אַנְחָתִי דָּבְקָה עַצְמִי לִבְשָׂרִי:
7	I am like a great owl in the wilderness, an owl among the ruins.	*Damiti lik'at midbar hayiti kechos choravot*	דָּמִיתִי לִקְאַת מִדְבָּר הָיִיתִי כְּכוֹס חֳרָבוֹת:
8	I lie awake; I am like a lone bird upon a roof.	*Shakadti va'ehyeh ketzippor boded al-gag*	שָׁקַדְתִּי וָאֶהְיֶה כְּצִפּוֹר בּוֹדֵד עַל־גָּג:
9	All day long my enemies revile me; my deriders use my name to curse.	*Kol-hayyom cherefuni oyevai meholalai bi nishba'u*	כָּל־הַיּוֹם חֵרְפוּנִי אוֹיְבָי מְהוֹלָלַי בִּי נִשְׁבָּעוּ:

10	For I have eaten ashes like bread and mixed my drink with tears,	*Ki-efer kallechem achaleti veshikkuvai bivchi masacheti*	כִּי־אֵפֶר כַּלֶּחֶם אָכָלְתִּי וְשִׁקֻּוַי בִּבְכִי מָסָכְתִּי:	י
11	because of Your wrath and Your fury; for You have cast me far away.	*Mippenei-za'amcha vekitzpecha ki nesatani vattashlicheni*	מִפְּנֵי־זַעַמְךָ וְקִצְפֶּךָ כִּי נְשָׂאתַנִי וַתַּשְׁלִיכֵנִי:	יא
12	My days are like a lengthening shadow; I wither like grass.	*Yamai ketzel natui va'ani ka'esev ivash*	יָמַי כְּצֵל נָטוּי וַאֲנִי כָּעֵשֶׂב אִיבָשׁ:	יב
13	But You, Hashem, are enthroned forever; Your fame endures throughout the ages.	*Ve'attah Adonai le'olam teshev vezichrecha ledor vador*	וְאַתָּה יְהֹוָה לְעוֹלָם תֵּשֵׁב וְזִכְרְךָ לְדֹר וָדֹר:	יג
14	You will surely arise and take pity on Tzion, for it is time to be gracious to her; the appointed time has come.	*Attah takum terachem tziyyon ki-et lechennah ki-va mo'ed*	אַתָּה תָקוּם תְּרַחֵם צִיּוֹן כִּי־עֵת לְחֶנְנָהּ כִּי־בָא מוֹעֵד:	יד
15	Your servants take delight in its stones, and cherish its dust.	*Ki-ratzu avadeicha et-avaneiha ve'et-afarah yechonenu*	כִּי־רָצוּ עֲבָדֶיךָ אֶת־אֲבָנֶיהָ וְאֶת־עֲפָרָהּ יְחֹנֵנוּ:	טו
16	The nations will fear the name of Hashem, all the kings of the earth, Your glory.	*Veyir'u goyim et-shem Adonai vechol-malchei ha'aretz et-kevodecha*	וְיִירְאוּ גוֹיִם אֶת־שֵׁם יְהֹוָה וְכָל־מַלְכֵי הָאָרֶץ אֶת־כְּבוֹדֶךָ:	טז
17	For Hashem has built Tzion; He has appeared in all His glory.	*Ki-vanah Adonai tziyyon nir'ah bichvodo*	כִּי־בָנָה יְהֹוָה צִיּוֹן נִרְאָה בִּכְבוֹדוֹ:	יז

18	He has turned to the prayer of the destitute and has not spurned their prayer.	*Panah el-tefillat ha'ar'ar velo-vazah et-tefillatam*	פָּנָה אֶל־תְּפִלַּת הָעַרְעָר וְלֹא־בָזָה אֶת־תְּפִלָּתָם:	יח
19	May this be written down for a coming generation, that people yet to be created may praise Hashem.	*Tikkatev zot ledor acharon ve'am nivra yehallel-yah*	תִּכָּתֶב זֹאת לְדוֹר אַחֲרוֹן וְעַם נִבְרָא יְהַלֶּל־יָהּ:	יט
20	For He looks down from His holy height; Hashem beholds the earth from heaven	*Ki-hishkif mimmerom kodsho Adonai mishamayim el-eretz hibbit*	כִּי־הִשְׁקִיף מִמְּרוֹם קָדְשׁוֹ יְהֹוָה מִשָּׁמַיִם אֶל־אֶרֶץ הִבִּיט:	כ
21	to hear the groans of the prisoner, to release those condemned to death;	*Lishmoa' enkat asir lefatteach benei temutah*	לִשְׁמֹעַ אֶנְקַת אָסִיר לְפַתֵּחַ בְּנֵי תְמוּתָה:	כא
22	that the fame of Hashem may be recounted in Tzion, His praises in Yerushalayim,	*Lesapper betziyyon shem Adonai utehillato birushala im*	לְסַפֵּר בְּצִיּוֹן שֵׁם יְהֹוָה וּתְהִלָּתוֹ בִּירוּשָׁלָ͏ִם:	כב
23	when the nations gather together, the kingdoms, to serve Hashem.	*Behikkavetz ammim yachdav umamlachot la'avod et-Adonai*	בְּהִקָּבֵץ עַמִּים יַחְדָּו וּמַמְלָכוֹת לַעֲבֹד אֶת־יְהֹוָה:	כג
24	He drained my strength in mid-course, He shortened my days.	*Innah vadderech chchv [kochi] kitzar yamai*	עִנָּה בַדֶּרֶךְ כֹּחוֹ [כֹּחִי] קִצַּר יָמָי:	כד

25	I say, "O my God, do not take me away in the midst of my days, You whose years go on for generations on end.	*Omar eli al-ta'aleni bachatzi yamai bedor dorim shenoteicha*

אֹמַר אֵלִי אַל־תַּעֲלֵנִי בַּחֲצִי יָמָי בְּדוֹר דּוֹרִים שְׁנוֹתֶיךָ: כה

26	Of old You established the earth; the heavens are the work of Your hands.	*Lefanim ha'aretz yasadta uma'aseh yadeicha shamayim*

לְפָנִים הָאָרֶץ יָסַדְתָּ וּמַעֲשֵׂה יָדֶיךָ שָׁמָיִם: כו

27	They shall perish, but You shall endure; they shall all wear out like a garment; You change them like clothing and they pass away.	*hemmah yovedu ve'attah ta'amod vechullam kabbeged yivlu kallevush tachalifem veyachalofu*

הֵמָּה יֹאבֵדוּ וְאַתָּה תַעֲמֹד וְכֻלָּם כַּבֶּגֶד יִבְלוּ כַּלְּבוּשׁ תַּחֲלִיפֵם וְיַחֲלֹפוּ: כז

28	But You are the same, and Your years never end.	*Ve'attah-hu ushenoteicha lo yittammu*

וְאַתָּה־הוּא וּשְׁנוֹתֶיךָ לֹא יִתָּמּוּ: כח

29	May the children of Your servants dwell securely and their offspring endure in Your presence."	*Benei-avadeicha yishkonu vezar'am lefaneicha yikkon*

בְּנֵי־עֲבָדֶיךָ יִשְׁכּוֹנוּ וְזַרְעָם לְפָנֶיךָ יִכּוֹן: כט

103

—○⬡○—

קג

1	Of David. Bless Hashem, O my soul, all my being, His holy name.	*Ledavid barachi nafshi et-Adonai vechol-keravai et-shem kodsho*

לְדָוִד בָּרְכִי נַפְשִׁי אֶת־יְהֹוָה וְכָל־קְרָבַי אֶת־שֵׁם קָדְשׁוֹ: א

2	Bless Hashem, O my soul and do not forget all His bounties.	*Barachi nafshi et-Adonai ve'al-tishkechi kol-gemulav*	בָּרְכִי נַפְשִׁי אֶת־יְהֹוָה וְאַל־ תִּשְׁכְּחִי כָּל־גְּמוּלָיו:	ב
3	He forgives all your sins, heals all your diseases.	*Hassoleach lechol-avnechi harofe lechol-tachalu'ayechi*	הַסֹּלֵחַ לְכָל־עֲוֺנֵכִי הָרֹפֵא לְכָל־תַּחֲלֻאָיְכִי:	ג
4	He redeems your life from the Pit, surrounds you with steadfast love and mercy.	*Haggo'el mishachat chayyayechi hamme'atterechi chesed verachamim*	הַגּוֹאֵל מִשַּׁחַת חַיָּיְכִי הַמְעַטְּרֵכִי חֶסֶד וְרַחֲמִים:	ד
5	He satisfies you with good things in the prime of life, so that your youth is renewed like the eagle's.	*Hammasbiya battov edyech titchaddesh kannesher ne'urayechi*	הַמַּשְׂבִּיעַ בַּטּוֹב עֶדְיֵךְ תִּתְחַדֵּשׁ כַּנֶּשֶׁר נְעוּרָיְכִי:	ה
6	Hashem executes righteous acts and judgments for all who are wronged.	*Oseh tzedakot Adonai umishpatim lechol-ashukim*	עֹשֵׂה צְדָקוֹת יְהֹוָה וּמִשְׁפָּטִים לְכָל־עֲשׁוּקִים:	ו
7	He made known His ways to Moshe, His deeds to the children of Yisrael.	*Yodia' derachav lemosheh livnei yisra'el alilotav*	יוֹדִיעַ דְּרָכָיו לְמֹשֶׁה לִבְנֵי יִשְׂרָאֵל עֲלִילוֹתָיו:	ז
8	Hashem is compassionate and gracious, slow to anger, abounding in steadfast love.	*Rachum vechannun Adonai erech appayim verav-chased*	רַחוּם וְחַנּוּן יְהֹוָה אֶרֶךְ אַפַּיִם וְרַב־חָסֶד:	ח
9	He will not contend forever, or nurse His anger for all time.	*Lo-lanetzach yariv velo le'olam yittor*	לֹא־לָנֶצַח יָרִיב וְלֹא לְעוֹלָם יִטּוֹר:	ט

10	He has not dealt with us according to our sins, nor has He requited us according to our iniquities.	*Lo chachata'einu asah lanu velo cha'avnoteinu gamal aleinu*	לֹא כַחֲטָאֵינוּ עָשָׂה לָנוּ וְלֹא כַעֲוֹנֹתֵינוּ גָּמַל עָלֵינוּ:	י
11	For as the heavens are high above the earth, so great is His steadfast love toward those who fear Him.	*Ki chigvoah shamayim al-ha'aretz gavar chasdo al-yere'av*	כִּי כִגְבֹהַּ שָׁמַיִם עַל־הָאָרֶץ גָּבַר חַסְדּוֹ עַל־יְרֵאָיו:	יא
12	As east is far from west, so far has He removed our sins from us.	*Kirchok mizrach mimma'arav hirchik mimmennu et-pesha'einu*	כִּרְחֹק מִזְרָח מִמַּעֲרָב הִרְחִיק מִמֶּנּוּ אֶת־פְּשָׁעֵינוּ:	יב
13	As a father has compassion for his children, so Hashem has compassion for those who fear Him.	*Kerachem av al-banim richam Adonai al-yere'av*	כְּרַחֵם אָב עַל־בָּנִים רִחַם יְהֹוָה עַל־יְרֵאָיו:	יג
14	For He knows how we are formed; He is mindful that we are dust.	*Ki-hu yada yitzrenu zachur ki-afar anachenu*	כִּי־הוּא יָדַע יִצְרֵנוּ זָכוּר כִּי־עָפָר אֲנָחְנוּ:	יד
15	Man, his days are like those of grass; he blooms like a flower of the field;	*Enosh kechatzir yamav ketzitz hassadeh ken yatzitz*	אֱנוֹשׁ כֶּחָצִיר יָמָיו כְּצִיץ הַשָּׂדֶה כֵּן יָצִיץ:	טו
16	a wind passes by and it is no more, its own place no longer knows it.	*Ki ruach averah-bo ve'einennu velo-yakkirennu od mekomo*	כִּי רוּחַ עָבְרָה־בּוֹ וְאֵינֶנּוּ וְלֹא־יַכִּירֶנּוּ עוֹד מְקוֹמוֹ:	טז

259

17	But Hashem's steadfast love is for all eternity toward those who fear Him, and His beneficence is for the children's children	*Vechesed Adonai me'olam ve'ad-olam al-yere'av vetzidkato livnei vanim*

וְחֶסֶד יְהֹוָה מֵעוֹלָם וְעַד־עוֹלָם עַל־יְרֵאָיו וְצִדְקָתוֹ לִבְנֵי בָנִים: יז

18	of those who keep His covenant and remember to observe His precepts.	*Leshomerei verito ulezocherei fikkudav la'asotam*

לְשֹׁמְרֵי בְרִיתוֹ וּלְזֹכְרֵי פִקֻּדָיו לַעֲשׂוֹתָם: יח

19	Hashem has established His throne in heaven, and His sovereign rule is over all.	*Adonai bashamayim hechin kis'o umalchuto bakkol mashalah*

יְהֹוָה בַּשָּׁמַיִם הֵכִין כִּסְאוֹ וּמַלְכוּתוֹ בַּכֹּל מָשָׁלָה: יט

20	Bless Hashem, O His angels, mighty creatures who do His bidding, mever obedient to His bidding;	*Barachu Adonai mal'achav gibborei choach osei devaro lishmoa' bekol devaro*

בָּרְכוּ יְהֹוָה מַלְאָכָיו גִּבֹּרֵי כֹחַ עֹשֵׂי דְבָרוֹ לִשְׁמֹעַ בְּקוֹל דְּבָרוֹ: כ

21	bless Hashem, all His hosts, His servants who do His will;	*Barachu Adonai kol-tzeva'av mesharetav osei retzono*

בָּרְכוּ יְהֹוָה כָּל־צְבָאָיו מְשָׁרְתָיו עֹשֵׂי רְצוֹנוֹ: כא

22	bless Hashem, all His works, through the length and breadth of His realm; bless Hashem, O my soul.	*Barachu Adonai kol-ma'asav bechol-mekomot memshalto barachi nafshi et-Adonai*

בָּרְכוּ יְהֹוָה כָּל־מַעֲשָׂיו בְּכָל־מְקֹמוֹת מֶמְשַׁלְתּוֹ בָּרְכִי נַפְשִׁי אֶת־יְהֹוָה: כב

104

1	Bless Hashem, O my soul; Hashem, my God, You are very great; You are clothed in glory and majesty,	*Barachi nafshi et-Adonai Adonai elohai gadalta me'od hod vehadar lavasheta*	בָּרְכִי נַפְשִׁי אֶת־יְהֹוָה יְהֹוָה אֱלֹהַי גָּדַלְתָּ מְּאֹד הוֹד וְהָדָר לָבָשְׁתָּ: א
2	wrapped in a robe of light; You spread the heavens like a tent cloth.	*Oteh-or kassalmah noteh shamayim kayyeri'ah*	עֹטֶה־אוֹר כַּשַּׂלְמָה נוֹטֶה שָׁמַיִם כַּיְרִיעָה: ב
3	He sets the rafters of His lofts in the waters, makes the clouds His chariot, moves on the wings of the wind.	*Hamkareh vammayim aliyyotav hassam-avim rechuvo hammehallech al-kanfei-ruach*	הַמְקָרֶה בַמַּיִם עֲלִיּוֹתָיו הַשָּׂם־עָבִים רְכוּבוֹ הַמְהַלֵּךְ עַל־כַּנְפֵי־רוּחַ: ג
4	He makes the winds His messengers, fiery flames His servants.	*Oseh mal'achav ruchot mesharetav esh lohet*	עֹשֶׂה מַלְאָכָיו רוּחוֹת מְשָׁרְתָיו אֵשׁ לֹהֵט: ד
5	He established the earth on its foundations, so that it shall never totter.	*Yasad-eretz al-mechoneiha bal-timmot olam va'ed*	יָסַד־אֶרֶץ עַל־מְכוֹנֶיהָ בַּל־תִּמּוֹט עוֹלָם וָעֶד: ה
6	You made the deep cover it as a garment; the waters stood above the mountains.	*Tehom kallevush kissito al-harim ya'amdu-mayim*	תְּהוֹם כַּלְּבוּשׁ כִּסִּיתוֹ עַל־הָרִים יַעַמְדוּ־מָיִם: ו
7	They fled at Your blast, rushed away at the sound of Your thunder,	*Min-ga'aratecha yenusun min-kol ra'amcha yechafezun*	מִן־גַּעֲרָתְךָ יְנוּסוּן מִן־קוֹל רַעַמְךָ יֵחָפֵזוּן: ז

8	—mountains rising, valleys sinking— to the place You established for them.	*Ya'alu harim yeredu veka'ot el-mekom zeh yasadta lahem*	יַעֲלוּ הָרִים יֵרְדוּ בְקָעוֹת אֶל־מְקוֹם זֶה יָסַדְתָּ לָהֶם:	ח
9	You set bounds they must not pass so that they never again cover the earth.	*Gevul-samta bal-ya'avorun bal-yeshuvun lechassot ha'aretz*	גְּבוּל־שַׂמְתָּ בַּל־יַעֲבֹרוּן בַּל־יְשׁוּבוּן לְכַסּוֹת הָאָרֶץ:	ט
10	You make springs gush forth in torrents; they make their way between the hills,	*Hammeshalleach ma'yanim bannechalim bein harim yehallechun*	הַמְשַׁלֵּחַ מַעְיָנִים בַּנְּחָלִים בֵּין הָרִים יְהַלֵּכוּן:	י
11	giving drink to all the wild beasts; the wild asses slake their thirst.	*Yashku kol-chayto sadai yishberu fera'im tzema'am*	יַשְׁקוּ כָּל־חַיְתוֹ שָׂדָי יִשְׁבְּרוּ פְרָאִים צְמָאָם:	יא
12	The birds of the sky dwell beside them and sing among the foliage.	*Aleihem of-hashamayim yishkon mibbein ofayim yittenu-kol*	עֲלֵיהֶם עוֹף־הַשָּׁמַיִם יִשְׁכּוֹן מִבֵּין עֳפָאיִם יִתְּנוּ־קוֹל:	יב
13	You water the mountains from Your lofts; the earth is sated from the fruit of Your work.	*Mashkeh harim me'aliyyotav mipperi ma'aseicha tisba ha'aretz*	מַשְׁקֶה הָרִים מֵעֲלִיּוֹתָיו מִפְּרִי מַעֲשֶׂיךָ תִּשְׂבַּע הָאָרֶץ:	יג
14	You make the grass grow for the cattle, and herbage for man's labor that he may get food out of the earth—	*Matzmiach chatzir labbehemah ve'esev la'avodat ha'adam lehotzi lechem min-ha'aretz*	מַצְמִיחַ חָצִיר לַבְּהֵמָה וְעֵשֶׂב לַעֲבֹדַת הָאָדָם לְהוֹצִיא לֶחֶם מִן־הָאָרֶץ:	יד

15	wine that cheers the hearts of men oil that makes the face shine, and bread that sustains man's life.	*Veyayin yesammach levav-enosh lehatzhil panim mishamen velechem levav-enosh yis'ad*	וְיַ֤יִן ׀ יְשַׂמַּ֬ח לְֽבַב־אֱנ֗וֹשׁ לְהַצְהִ֣יל פָּנִ֣ים מִשָּׁ֑מֶן וְ֝לֶ֗חֶם לְֽבַב־אֱנ֥וֹשׁ יִסְעָֽד׃	טו
16	The trees of Hashem drink their fill, the cedars of Lebanon, His own planting,	*Yisbe'u atzei Adonai arzei levanon asher nata*	יִ֭שְׂבְּעוּ עֲצֵ֣י יְהֹוָ֑ה אַֽרְזֵ֥י לְ֝בָנ֗וֹן אֲשֶׁ֣ר נָטָֽע׃	טז
17	where birds make their nests; the stork has her home in the junipers.	*Asher-sham tzipporim yekannenu chasidah beroshim beitah*	אֲשֶׁר־שָׁ֭ם צִפֳּרִ֣ים יְקַנֵּ֑נוּ חֲ֝סִידָ֗ה בְּרוֹשִׁ֥ים בֵּיתָֽהּ׃	יז
18	The high mountains are for wild goats; the crags are a refuge for rock-badgers.	*Harim haggevohim layye'elim sela'im machseh lashfannim*	הָרִ֣ים הַ֭גְּבֹהִים לַיְּעֵלִ֑ים סְ֝לָעִ֗ים מַחְסֶ֥ה לַֽשְׁפַנִּֽים׃	יח
19	He made the moon to mark the seasons; the sun knows when to set.	*Asah yareach lemo'adim shemesh yada mevo'o*	עָשָׂ֣ה יָ֭רֵחַ לְמוֹעֲדִ֑ים שֶׁ֝֗מֶשׁ יָדַ֥ע מְבוֹאֽוֹ׃	יט
20	You bring on darkness and it is night, when all the beasts of the forests stir.	*tashet-choshech vihi layelah bo-tirmos kol-chayto-ya'ar*	תָּֽשֶׁת־חֹ֭שֶׁךְ וִ֣יהִי לָ֑יְלָה בּֽוֹ־תִ֝רְמֹ֗שׂ כָּל־חַיְתוֹ־יָֽעַר׃	כ
21	The lions roar for prey, seeking their food from Hashem.	*Hakkefirim sho'agim lattaref ulevakkesh me'el ochlam*	הַ֭כְּפִירִים שֹׁאֲגִ֣ים לַטָּ֑רֶף וּלְבַקֵּ֖שׁ מֵאֵ֣ל אָכְלָֽם׃	כא
22	When the sun rises, they come home and couch in their dens.	*Tizrach hashemesh ye'asefun ve'el-me'onotam yirbatzun*	תִּזְרַ֣ח הַ֭שֶּׁמֶשׁ יֵאָסֵפ֑וּן וְאֶל־מְ֝עוֹנֹתָ֗ם יִרְבָּצֽוּן׃	כב

23	Man then goes out to his work, to his labor until the evening.	*Yetze adam lefo'olo vela'avodato adei-arev*	יֵצֵא אָדָם לְפָעֳלוֹ וְלַעֲבֹדָתוֹ עֲדֵי־עָרֶב:	כג
24	How many are the things You have made, Hashem; You have made them all with wisdom; the earth is full of Your creations.	*Mah-rabbu ma'aseicha Adonai kullam bechochmah asita male'ah ha'aretz kinyanecha*	מָה־רַבּוּ מַעֲשֶׂיךָ יְהֹוָה כֻּלָּם בְּחָכְמָה עָשִׂיתָ מָלְאָה הָאָרֶץ קִנְיָנֶךָ:	כד
25	There is the sea, vast and wide, with its creatures beyond number, living things, small and great.	*Zeh hayyam gadol urechav yadayim sham-remes ve'ein mispar chayyot ketannot im-gedolot*	זֶה הַיָּם גָּדוֹל וּרְחַב יָדָיִם שָׁם־רֶמֶשׂ וְאֵין מִסְפָּר חַיּוֹת קְטַנּוֹת עִם־גְּדֹלוֹת:	כה
26	There go the ships, and Leviathan that You formed to sport with.	*Sham oniyyot yehallechun livyatan zeh-yatzarta lesachek-bo*	שָׁם אֳנִיּוֹת יְהַלֵּכוּן לִוְיָתָן זֶה־יָצַרְתָּ לְשַׂחֶק־בּוֹ:	כו
27	All of them look to You to give them their food when it is due.	*Kullam eleicha yesabberun latet ochlam be'itto*	כֻּלָּם אֵלֶיךָ יְשַׂבֵּרוּן לָתֵת אָכְלָם בְּעִתּוֹ:	כז
28	Give it to them, they gather it up; open Your hand, they are well satisfied;	*Titten lahem yilkotun tiftach yadecha yisbe'un tov*	תִּתֵּן לָהֶם יִלְקֹטוּן תִּפְתַּח יָדְךָ יִשְׂבְּעוּן טוֹב:	כח
29	hide Your face, they are terrified; take away their breath, they perish and turn again into dust;	*Tastir panecha yibbahelun tosef rucham yigva'un ve'el-afaram yeshuvun*	תַּסְתִּיר פָּנֶיךָ יִבָּהֵלוּן תֹּסֵף רוּחָם יִגְוָעוּן וְאֶל־עֲפָרָם יְשׁוּבוּן:	כט

30	send back Your breath, they are created, and You renew the face of the earth.	*Teshallach ruchacha yibbare'un utechaddesh penei adamah*	תְּשַׁלַּח רוּחֲךָ יִבָּרֵאוּן וּתְחַדֵּשׁ פְּנֵי אֲדָמָה:	ל

31	May the glory of Hashem endure forever; may Hashem rejoice in His works!	*Yehi chevod Adonai le'olam yismach Adonai bema'asav*	יְהִי כְבוֹד יְהוָה לְעוֹלָם יִשְׂמַח יְהוָה בְּמַעֲשָׂיו:	לא

32	He looks at the earth and it trembles; He touches the mountains and they smoke.	*Hammabbit la'aretz vattir'ad yigga beharim veye'eshanu*	הַמַּבִּיט לָאָרֶץ וַתִּרְעָד יִגַּע בֶּהָרִים וְיֶעֱשָׁנוּ:	לב

33	I will sing to Hashem as long as I live; all my life I will chant hymns to my God.	*Ashirah lAdonai bechayyai azammerah lelohai be'odi*	אָשִׁירָה לַיהוָה בְּחַיָּי אֲזַמְּרָה לֵאלֹהַי בְּעוֹדִי:	לג

34	May my prayer be pleasing to Him; I will rejoice in Hashem.	*Ye'erav alav sichi anochi esmach bAdonai*	יֶעֱרַב עָלָיו שִׂיחִי אָנֹכִי אֶשְׂמַח בַּיהוָה:	לד

35	May sinners disappear from the earth, and the wicked be no more. Bless Hashem, O my soul. Hallelujah.	*Yittammu chatta'im min-ha'aretz uresha'im od einam barachi nafshi et-Adonai hallu-yah*	יִתַּמּוּ חַטָּאִים מִן־הָאָרֶץ וּרְשָׁעִים עוֹד אֵינָם בָּרְכִי נַפְשִׁי אֶת־יְהוָה הַלְלוּ־יָהּ:	לה

105

—◦◦◦✦◦◦◦—

קה

1	Praise Hashem; call on His name; proclaim His deeds among the peoples.	*hodu lAdonai kir'u bishmo hodi'u va'ammim alilotav*	הוֹדוּ לַיהוָה קִרְאוּ בִשְׁמוֹ הוֹדִיעוּ בָעַמִּים עֲלִילוֹתָיו:	א

| 2 | Sing praises to Him; speak of all His wondrous acts. | *shiru-lo zammeru-lo sichu bechol-nifle'otav* | שִׁירוּ־לוֹ זַמְּרוּ־לוֹ שִׂיחוּ בְּכָל־נִפְלְאוֹתָיו: | ב |

| 3 | Exult in His holy name; let all who seek Hashem rejoice. | *Hithallu beshem kodsho yismach lev mevakshei Adonai* | הִתְהַלְלוּ בְּשֵׁם קָדְשׁוֹ יִשְׂמַח לֵב מְבַקְשֵׁי יְהֹוָה: | ג |

| 4 | Turn to Hashem, to His might; seek His presence constantly. | *Dirshu Adonai ve'uzzo bakkeshu fanav tamid* | דִּרְשׁוּ יְהֹוָה וְעֻזּוֹ בַּקְשׁוּ פָנָיו תָּמִיד: | ד |

| 5 | Remember the wonders He has done, His portents and the judgments He has pronounced, | *Zichru nifle'otav asher-asah mofetav umishpetei-fiv* | זִכְרוּ נִפְלְאוֹתָיו אֲשֶׁר־עָשָׂה מֹפְתָיו וּמִשְׁפְּטֵי־פִיו: | ה |

| 6 | O offspring of Avraham, His servant, O descendants of Yaakov, His chosen ones. | *zera avraham avdo benei ya'akov bechirav* | זֶרַע אַבְרָהָם עַבְדּוֹ בְּנֵי יַעֲקֹב בְּחִירָיו: | ו |

| 7 | He is Hashem our God; His judgments are throughout the earth. | *Hu Adonai eloheinu bechol-ha'aretz mishpatav* | הוּא יְהֹוָה אֱלֹהֵינוּ בְּכָל־הָאָרֶץ מִשְׁפָּטָיו: | ז |

| 8 | He is ever mindful of His covenant, the promise He gave for a thousand generations, | *Zachar le'olam berito davar tzivvah le'elef dor* | זָכַר לְעוֹלָם בְּרִיתוֹ דָּבָר צִוָּה לְאֶלֶף דּוֹר: | ח |

| 9 | that He made with Avraham, swore to Yitzchak, | *Asher karat et-avraham ushevu'ato leyischak* | אֲשֶׁר כָּרַת אֶת־אַבְרָהָם וּשְׁבוּעָתוֹ לְיִשְׂחָק: | ט |

10	and confirmed in a decree for Yaakov, for Yisrael, as an eternal covenant,	*Vayya'amideha leya'akov lechok leyisra'el berit olam*	וַיַּעֲמִידֶהָ לְיַעֲקֹב לְחֹק לְיִשְׂרָאֵל בְּרִית עוֹלָם:	י
11	saying, "To you I will give the land of Canaan as your allotted heritage."	*Lemor lecha etten et-eretz-kena'an chevel nachalatchem*	לֵאמֹר לְךָ אֶתֵּן אֶת־אֶרֶץ־כְּנָעַן חֶבֶל נַחֲלַתְכֶם:	יא
12	They were then few in number, a mere handful, sojourning there,	*Bihyotam metei mispar kim'at vegarim bah*	בִּהְיוֹתָם מְתֵי מִסְפָּר כִּמְעַט וְגָרִים בָּהּ:	יב
13	wandering from nation to nation, from one kingdom to another.	*Vayyithallechu miggoy el-goy mimmamlachah el-am acher*	וַיִּתְהַלְּכוּ מִגּוֹי אֶל־גּוֹי מִמַּמְלָכָה אֶל־עַם אַחֵר:	יג
14	He allowed no one to oppress them; He reproved kings on their account,	*Lo-hinniach adam le'oshkam vayyochach aleihem melachim*	לֹא־הִנִּיחַ אָדָם לְעָשְׁקָם וַיּוֹכַח עֲלֵיהֶם מְלָכִים:	יד
15	"Do not touch My anointed ones; do not harm My neviim."	*Al-tigge'u vimshichai velinvi'ai al-tare'u*	אַל־תִּגְּעוּ בִמְשִׁיחָי וְלִנְבִיאַי אַל־תָּרֵעוּ:	טו
16	He called down a famine on the land, destroyed every staff of bread.	*Vayyikra ra'av al-ha'aretz kol-matteh-lechem shavar*	וַיִּקְרָא רָעָב עַל־הָאָרֶץ כָּל־מַטֵּה־לֶחֶם שָׁבָר:	טז
17	He sent ahead of them a man, Yosef, sold into slavery.	*Shalach lifneihem ish le'eved nimkar yosef*	שָׁלַח לִפְנֵיהֶם אִישׁ לְעֶבֶד נִמְכַּר יוֹסֵף:	יז

18	His feet were subjected to fetters; an iron collar was put on his neck.	*Innu vakkevel rglv [raglo] barzel ba'ah nafsho*	עִנּוּ בַכֶּבֶל רגליו [רַגְלוֹ] בַּרְזֶל בָּאָה נַפְשׁוֹ:	יח
19	Until his prediction came true the decree of Hashem purged him.	*Ad-et bo-devaro imrat Adonai tzerafatehu*	עַד־עֵת בֹּא־דְבָרוֹ אִמְרַת יְהֹוָה צְרָפָתְהוּ:	יט
20	The king sent to have him freed; the ruler of nations released him.	*Shalach melech vayyattirehu moshel ammim vayfattechehu*	שָׁלַח מֶלֶךְ וַיַּתִּירֵהוּ מֹשֵׁל עַמִּים וַיְפַתְּחֵהוּ:	כ
21	He made him the lord of his household, empowered him over all his possessions,	*Samo adon leveito umoshel bechol-kinyano*	שָׂמוֹ אָדוֹן לְבֵיתוֹ וּמֹשֵׁל בְּכָל־קִנְיָנוֹ:	כא
22	to discipline his princes at will, to teach his elders wisdom.	*Le'sor sarav benafsho uzekenav yechakkem*	לֶאְסֹר שָׂרָיו בְּנַפְשׁוֹ וּזְקֵנָיו יְחַכֵּם:	כב
23	Then Yisrael came to Egypt; Yaakov sojourned in the land of Ham.	*Vayyavo yisra'el mitzrayim veya'akov gar be'eretz-cham*	וַיָּבֹא יִשְׂרָאֵל מִצְרָיִם וְיַעֲקֹב גָּר בְּאֶרֶץ־חָם:	כג
24	He made His people very fruitful, more numerous than their foes.	*Vayyefer et-ammo me'od vayya'atzimehu mitzarav*	וַיֶּפֶר אֶת־עַמּוֹ מְאֹד וַיַּעֲצִמֵהוּ מִצָּרָיו:	כד
25	He changed their heart to hate His people, to plot against His servants.	*Hafach libbam lisno ammo lehitnakkel ba'avadav*	הָפַךְ לִבָּם לִשְׂנֹא עַמּוֹ לְהִתְנַכֵּל בַּעֲבָדָיו:	כה

26	He sent His servant Moshe, and Aharon, whom He had chosen.	*Shalach mosheh avdo aharon asher bachar-bo*	שָׁלַח מֹשֶׁה עַבְדּוֹ אַהֲרֹן אֲשֶׁר בָּחַר־בּוֹ׃	כו
27	They performed His signs among them, His wonders, against the land of Ham.	*Samu-vam divrei ototav umofetim be'eretz cham*	שָׂמוּ־בָם דִּבְרֵי אֹתוֹתָיו וּמֹפְתִים בְּאֶרֶץ חָם׃	כז
28	He sent darkness; it was very dark; did they not defy His word?	*Shalach choshech vayyachshich velo-maru et-dvrvv [devaro]*	שָׁלַח חֹשֶׁךְ וַיַּחְשִׁךְ וְלֹא־מָרוּ אֶת־דבררו [דְּבָרוֹ]׃	כח
29	He turned their waters into blood and killed their fish.	*hafach et-meimeihem ledam vayyamet et-degatam*	הָפַךְ אֶת־מֵימֵיהֶם לְדָם וַיָּמֶת אֶת־דְּגָתָם׃	כט
30	Their land teemed with frogs, even the rooms of their king.	*Sharatz artzam tzefarde'im bechadrei malcheihem*	שָׁרַץ אַרְצָם צְפַרְדְּעִים בְּחַדְרֵי מַלְכֵיהֶם׃	ל
31	Swarms of insects came at His command, lice, throughout their country.	*Amar vayyavo arov kinnim bechol-gevulam*	אָמַר וַיָּבֹא עָרֹב כִּנִּים בְּכָל־גְּבוּלָם׃	לא
32	He gave them hail for rain, and flaming fire in their land.	*Natan gishmeihem barad esh lehavot be'artzam*	נָתַן גִּשְׁמֵיהֶם בָּרָד אֵשׁ לֶהָבוֹת בְּאַרְצָם׃	לב
33	He struck their vines and fig trees, broke down the trees of their country.	*Vayyach gafnam ute'enatam vayshabber etz gevulam*	וַיַּךְ גַּפְנָם וּתְאֵנָתָם וַיְשַׁבֵּר עֵץ גְּבוּלָם׃	לג
34	Locusts came at His command, grasshoppers without number.	*Amar vayyavo arbeh veyelek ve'ein mispar*	אָמַר וַיָּבֹא אַרְבֶּה וְיֶלֶק וְאֵין מִסְפָּר׃	לד

35	They devoured every green thing in the land; they consumed the produce of the soil.	*Vayyochal kol-esev be'artzam vayyochal peri admatam*	וַיֹּאכַל כָּל־עֵשֶׂב בְּאַרְצָם וַיֹּאכַל פְּרִי אַדְמָתָם:
36	He struck down every first-born in the land, the first fruit of their vigor.	*Vayyach kol-bechor be'artzam reshit lechol-onam*	וַיַּךְ כָּל־בְּכוֹר בְּאַרְצָם רֵאשִׁית לְכָל־אוֹנָם:
37	He led Yisrael out with silver and gold; none among their tribes faltered.	*Vayyotzi'em bechesef vezahav ve'ein bishvatav koshel*	וַיּוֹצִיאֵם בְּכֶסֶף וְזָהָב וְאֵין בִּשְׁבָטָיו כּוֹשֵׁל:
38	Egypt rejoiced when they left, for dread of Yisrael had fallen upon them.	*Samach mitzrayim betzetam ki-nafal pachdam aleihem*	שָׂמַח מִצְרַיִם בְּצֵאתָם כִּי־נָפַל פַּחְדָּם עֲלֵיהֶם:
39	He spread a cloud for a cover, and fire to light up the night.	*Paras anan lemasach ve'esh leha'ir layelah*	פָּרַשׂ עָנָן לְמָסָךְ וְאֵשׁ לְהָאִיר לָיְלָה:
40	They asked and He brought them quail, and satisfied them with food from heaven.	*Sha'al vayyave selav velechem shamayim yasbi'em*	שָׁאַל וַיָּבֵא שְׂלָו וְלֶחֶם שָׁמַיִם יַשְׂבִּיעֵם:
41	He opened a rock so that water gushed forth; it flowed as a stream in the parched land.	*Patach tzur vayyazuvu mayim halechu batziyyot nahar*	פָּתַח צוּר וַיָּזוּבוּ מָיִם הָלְכוּ בַּצִּיּוֹת נָהָר:
42	Mindful of His sacred promise to His servant Avraham,	*Ki-zachar et-devar kodsho et-avraham avdo*	כִּי־זָכַר אֶת־דְּבַר קָדְשׁוֹ אֶת־אַבְרָהָם עַבְדּוֹ:

| 43 | He led His people out in gladness, His chosen ones with joyous song. | *Vayyotzi ammo vesason berinnah et-bechirav* | וַיּוֹצִא עַמּוֹ בְשָׂשׂוֹן בְּרִנָּה אֶת־בְּחִירָיו: | מג |

| 44 | He gave them the lands of nations; they inherited the wealth of peoples, | *Vayyitten lahem artzot goyim va'amal le'ummim yirashu* | וַיִּתֵּן לָהֶם אַרְצוֹת גּוֹיִם וַעֲמַל לְאֻמִּים יִירָשׁוּ: | מד |

| 45 | that they might keep His laws and observe His teachings. Hallelujah. | *Ba'avur yishmeru chukkav vetorotav yintzoru hallu-yah* | בַּעֲבוּר יִשְׁמְרוּ חֻקָּיו וְתוֹרֹתָיו יִנְצֹרוּ הַלְלוּ־יָהּ: | מה |

106

קו

| 1 | Hallelujah. Praise Hashem for He is good; His steadfast love is eternal. | *Halluyah hodu lAdonai ki-tov ki le'olam chasdo* | הַלְלוּיָהּ הוֹדוּ לַיהֹוָה כִּי־ טוֹב כִּי לְעוֹלָם חַסְדּוֹ: | א |

| 2 | Who can tell the mighty acts of Hashem, proclaim all His praises? | *Mi yemallel gevurot Adonai yashmia' kol-tehillato* | מִי יְמַלֵּל גְּבוּרוֹת יְהֹוָה יַשְׁמִיעַ כָּל־תְּהִלָּתוֹ: | ב |

| 3 | Happy are those who act justly, who do right at all times. | *Ashrei shomerei mishpat oseh tzedakah vechol-et* | אַשְׁרֵי שֹׁמְרֵי מִשְׁפָּט עֹשֵׂה צְדָקָה בְכָל־עֵת: | ג |

| 4 | Be mindful of me, Hashem, when You favor Your people; take note of me when You deliver them, | *Zachereni Adonai birtzon ammecha pakedeni bishu'atecha* | זָכְרֵנִי יְהֹוָה בִּרְצוֹן עַמֶּךָ פָּקְדֵנִי בִּישׁוּעָתֶךָ: | ד |

5	that I may enjoy the prosperity of Your chosen ones, share the joy of Your nation, glory in Your very own people.	*Lir'ot betovat bechireicha lismoach besimchat goyecha lehithallel im-nachalatecha*	לִרְאוֹת בְּטוֹבַת בְּחִירֶיךָ לִשְׂמֹחַ בְּשִׂמְחַת גּוֹיֶךָ לְהִתְהַלֵּל עִם־נַחֲלָתֶךָ:	ה
6	We have sinned like our forefathers; we have gone astray, done evil.	*Chatanu im-avoteinu he'evinu hirsha'enu*	חָטָאנוּ עִם־אֲבוֹתֵינוּ הֶעֱוִינוּ הִרְשָׁעְנוּ:	ו
7	Our forefathers in Egypt did not perceive Your wonders; they did not remember Your abundant love, but rebelled at the sea, at the Sea of Reeds.	*Avoteinu vemitzrayim lo-hiskilu nifle'oteicha lo zacheru et-rov chasadeicha vayyamru al-yam beyam-suf*	אֲבוֹתֵינוּ בְמִצְרַיִם לֹא־הִשְׂכִּילוּ נִפְלְאוֹתֶיךָ לֹא זָכְרוּ אֶת־רֹב חֲסָדֶיךָ וַיַּמְרוּ עַל־יָם בְּיַם־סוּף:	ז
8	Yet He saved them, as befits His name, to make known His might.	*Vayyoshi'em lema'an shemo lehodia' et-gevurato*	וַיּוֹשִׁיעֵם לְמַעַן שְׁמוֹ לְהוֹדִיעַ אֶת־גְּבוּרָתוֹ:	ח
9	He sent His blast against the Sea of Reeds; it became dry; He led them through the deep as through a wilderness.	*Vayyig'ar beyam-suf vayyecherav vayyolichem battehomot kammidbar*	וַיִּגְעַר בְּיַם־סוּף וַיֶּחֱרָב וַיּוֹלִיכֵם בַּתְּהֹמוֹת כַּמִּדְבָּר:	ט
10	He delivered them from the foe, redeemed them from the enemy.	*Vayyoshi'em miyyad sone vayyig'alem miyyad oyev*	וַיּוֹשִׁיעֵם מִיַּד שׂוֹנֵא וַיִּגְאָלֵם מִיַּד אוֹיֵב:	י
11	Water covered their adversaries; not one of them was left.	*Vaychassu-mayim tzareihem echad mehem lo notar*	וַיְכַסּוּ־מַיִם צָרֵיהֶם אֶחָד מֵהֶם לֹא נוֹתָר:	יא

12	Then they believed His promise, and sang His praises.	*Vayya'aminu vidvarav yashiru tehillato*	וַיַּאֲמִינוּ בִדְבָרָיו יָשִׁירוּ תְּהִלָּתוֹ:	יב
13	But they soon forgot His deeds; they would not wait to learn His plan.	*Miharu shachechu ma'asav lo-chikku la'atzato*	מִהֲרוּ שָׁכְחוּ מַעֲשָׂיו לֹא־חִכּוּ לַעֲצָתוֹ:	יג
14	They were seized with craving in the wilderness, and put Hashem to the test in the wasteland.	*Vayyit'avvvv ta'avah bammidbar vaynassu-el bishimon*	וַיִּתְאַוּוּ תַאֲוָה בַּמִּדְבָּר וַיְנַסּוּ־אֵל בִּישִׁימוֹן:	יד
15	He gave them what they asked for, then made them waste away.	*Vayyitten lahem she'elatam vayshallach razon benafsham*	וַיִּתֵּן לָהֶם שֶׁאֱלָתָם וַיְשַׁלַּח רָזוֹן בְּנַפְשָׁם:	טו
16	There was envy of Moshe in the camp, and of Aharon, the holy one of Hashem.	*Vaykan'u lemosheh bammachaneh le'aharon kedosh Adonai*	וַיְקַנְאוּ לְמֹשֶׁה בַּמַּחֲנֶה לְאַהֲרֹן קְדוֹשׁ יְהֹוָה:	טז
17	The earth opened up and swallowed Datan, closed over the party of Aviram.	*Tiftach-eretz vattivla datan vattechas al-adat aviram*	תִּפְתַּח־אֶרֶץ וַתִּבְלַע דָּתָן וַתְּכַס עַל־עֲדַת אֲבִירָם:	יז
18	A fire blazed among their party, a flame that consumed the wicked.	*Vattiv'ar-esh ba'adatam lehavah telahet resha'im*	וַתִּבְעַר־אֵשׁ בַּעֲדָתָם לֶהָבָה תְּלַהֵט רְשָׁעִים:	יח
19	They made a calf at Horeb and bowed down to a molten image.	*Ya'asu-egel bechorev vayyishtachavu lemassechah*	יַעֲשׂוּ־עֵגֶל בְּחֹרֵב וַיִּשְׁתַּחֲווּ לְמַסֵּכָה:	יט

20	They exchanged their glory for the image of a bull that feeds on grass.	*Vayyamiru et-kevodam betavnit shor ochel esev*	וַיָּמִירוּ אֶת־כְּבוֹדָם בְּתַבְנִית שׁוֹר אֹכֵל עֵשֶׂב:	כ
21	They forgot Hashem who saved them, who performed great deeds in Egypt,	*Shachechu el moshi'am oseh gedolot bemitzrayim*	שָׁכְחוּ אֵל מוֹשִׁיעָם עֹשֶׂה גְדֹלוֹת בְּמִצְרָיִם:	כא
22	wondrous deeds in the land of Ham, awesome deeds at the Sea of Reeds.	*Nifla'ot be'eretz cham nora'ot al-yam-suf*	נִפְלָאוֹת בְּאֶרֶץ חָם נוֹרָאוֹת עַל־יַם־סוּף:	כב
23	He would have destroyed them had not Moshe His chosen one confronted Him in the breach to avert His destructive wrath.	*Vayyomer lehashmidam lulei mosheh vechiro amad bapperetz lefanav lehashiv chamato mehashchit*	וַיֹּאמֶר לְהַשְׁמִידָם לוּלֵי מֹשֶׁה בְחִירוֹ עָמַד בַּפֶּרֶץ לְפָנָיו לְהָשִׁיב חֲמָתוֹ מֵהַשְׁחִית:	כג
24	They rejected the desirable land, and put no faith in His promise.	*Vayyim'asu be'eretz chemdah lo-he'eminu lidvaro*	וַיִּמְאֲסוּ בְּאֶרֶץ חֶמְדָּה לֹא־הֶאֱמִינוּ לִדְבָרוֹ:	כד
25	They grumbled in their tents and disobeyed Hashem.	*Vayyeragenu ve'oholeihem lo shame'u bekol Adonai*	וַיֵּרָגְנוּ בְאָהֳלֵיהֶם לֹא שָׁמְעוּ בְּקוֹל יְהוָה:	כה
26	So He raised His hand in oath to make them fall in the wilderness,	*Vayyissa yado lahem lehappil otam bammidbar*	וַיִּשָּׂא יָדוֹ לָהֶם לְהַפִּיל אוֹתָם בַּמִּדְבָּר:	כו
27	to disperse their offspring among the nations and scatter them through the lands.	*Ulehappil zar'am baggoyim ulezarotam ba'aratzot*	וּלְהַפִּיל זַרְעָם בַּגּוֹיִם וּלְזָרוֹתָם בָּאֲרָצוֹת:	כז

28	They attached themselves to Baal Peor, ate sacrifices offered to the dead.	*Vayyitzamedu leva'al pe'or vayyochlu zivchei metim*	וַיִּצָּמְדוּ לְבַעַל פְּעוֹר וַיֹּאכְלוּ זִבְחֵי מֵתִים:	כח
29	They provoked anger by their deeds, and a plague broke out among them.	*Vayyach'isu bema'alleihem vattifratz-bam maggefah*	וַיַּכְעִיסוּ בְּמַעַלְלֵיהֶם וַתִּפְרָץ־בָּם מַגֵּפָה:	כט
30	Pinchas stepped forth and intervened, and the plague ceased.	*Vayya'amod pinchas vayfallel vatte'atzar hammaggefah*	וַיַּעֲמֹד פִּינְחָס וַיְפַלֵּל וַתֵּעָצַר הַמַּגֵּפָה:	ל
31	It was reckoned to his merit for all generations, to eternity.	*Vattechashev lo litzdakah ledor vador ad-olam*	וַתֵּחָשֶׁב לוֹ לִצְדָקָה לְדֹר וָדֹר עַד־עוֹלָם:	לא
32	They provoked wrath at the waters of Meribah and Moshe suffered on their account,	*Vayyaktzifu al-mei merivah vayyera lemosheh ba'avuram*	וַיַּקְצִיפוּ עַל־מֵי מְרִיבָה וַיֵּרַע לְמֹשֶׁה בַּעֲבוּרָם:	לב
33	because they rebelled against Him and he spoke rashly.	*Ki-himru et-rucho vayvatte bisfatav*	כִּי־הִמְרוּ אֶת־רוּחוֹ וַיְבַטֵּא בִּשְׂפָתָיו:	לג
34	They did not destroy the nations as Hashem had commanded them,	*Lo-hishmidu et-ha'ammim asher amar Adonai lahem*	לֹא־הִשְׁמִידוּ אֶת־הָעַמִּים אֲשֶׁר אָמַר יְהֹוָה לָהֶם:	לד
35	but mingled with the nations and learned their ways.	*Vayyit'arevu vaggoyim vayyilmedu ma'aseihem*	וַיִּתְעָרְבוּ בַגּוֹיִם וַיִּלְמְדוּ מַעֲשֵׂיהֶם:	לה
36	They worshiped their idols, which became a snare for them.	*Vayya'avdu et-atzabbeihem vayyihyu lahem lemokesh*	וַיַּעַבְדוּ אֶת־עֲצַבֵּיהֶם וַיִּהְיוּ לָהֶם לְמוֹקֵשׁ:	לו

37	Their own sons and daughters they sacrificed to demons.	*Vayyizbechu et-beneihem ve'et-benoteihem lashedim*	וַיִּזְבְּחוּ אֶת־בְּנֵיהֶם וְאֶת־בְּנוֹתֵיהֶם לַשֵּׁדִים:	לז
38	They shed innocent blood, the blood of their sons and daughters, whom they sacrificed to the idols of Canaan; so the land was polluted with bloodguilt.	*Vayyishpechu dam naki dam-beneihem uvenoteihem asher zibbechu la'atzabbei chena'an vattechenaf ha'aretz baddamim*	וַיִּשְׁפְּכוּ דָם נָקִי דַּם־בְּנֵיהֶם וּבְנוֹתֵיהֶם אֲשֶׁר זִבְּחוּ לַעֲצַבֵּי כְנָעַן וַתֶּחֱנַף הָאָרֶץ בַּדָּמִים:	לח
39	Thus they became defiled by their acts, debauched through their deeds.	*Vayyitme'u vema'aseihem vayyiznu bema'alleihem*	וַיִּטְמְאוּ בְמַעֲשֵׂיהֶם וַיִּזְנוּ בְּמַעַלְלֵיהֶם:	לט
40	Hashem was angry with His people and He abhorred His inheritance.	*Vayyichar-af Adonai be'ammo vayta'ev et-nachalato*	וַיִּחַר־אַף יְהוָה בְּעַמּוֹ וַיְתָעֵב אֶת־נַחֲלָתוֹ:	מ
41	He handed them over to the nations; their foes ruled them.	*Vayyittenem beyad-goyim vayyimshelu vahem sone'eihem*	וַיִּתְּנֵם בְּיַד־גּוֹיִם וַיִּמְשְׁלוּ בָהֶם שֹׂנְאֵיהֶם:	מא
42	Their enemies oppressed them and they were subject to their power.	*Vayyilchatzum oyeveihem vayyikkane'u tachat yadam*	וַיִּלְחָצוּם אוֹיְבֵיהֶם וַיִּכָּנְעוּ תַּחַת יָדָם:	מב
43	He saved them time and again, but they were deliberately rebellious, and so they were brought low by their iniquity.	*Pe'amim rabbot yatzilem vehemmah yamru va'atzatam vayyamokku ba'avnam*	פְּעָמִים רַבּוֹת יַצִּילֵם וְהֵמָּה יַמְרוּ בַעֲצָתָם וַיָּמֹכּוּ בַּעֲוֺנָם:	מג

44	When He saw that they were in distress, when He heard their cry,	*Vayyar batzar lahem beshom'o et-rinnatam*	וַיַּרְא בַּצַּר לָהֶם בְּשָׁמְעוֹ אֶת־רִנָּתָם:	מד
45	He was mindful of His covenant and in His great faithfulness relented.	*Vayyizkor lahem berito vayyinnachem kerov chsdv [chasadav]*	וַיִּזְכֹּר לָהֶם בְּרִיתוֹ וַיִּנָּחֵם כְּרֹב חסדו [חֲסָדָיו]:	מה
46	He made all their captors kindly disposed toward them.	*vayyitten otam lerachamim lifnei kol-shoveihem*	וַיִּתֵּן אוֹתָם לְרַחֲמִים לִפְנֵי כָּל־שׁוֹבֵיהֶם:	מו
47	Deliver us, Hashem our God, and gather us from among the nations, to acclaim Your holy name, to glory in Your praise.	*Hoshi'enu Adonai eloheinu vekabbetzenu min-haggoyim lehodot leshem kodshecha lehishtabbeach bithillatecha*	הוֹשִׁיעֵנוּ יְהֹוָה אֱלֹהֵינוּ וְקַבְּצֵנוּ מִן־הַגּוֹיִם לְהֹדוֹת לְשֵׁם קָדְשֶׁךָ לְהִשְׁתַּבֵּחַ בִּתְהִלָּתֶךָ:	מז
48	Blessed is Hashem, God of Yisrael, From eternity to eternity. Let all the people say "Amen." Hallelujah.	*Baruch-Adonai elohei yisra'el min-ha'olam ve'ad ha'olam ve'amar kol-ha'am amen hallu-yah*	בָּרוּךְ־יְהֹוָה אֱלֹהֵי יִשְׂרָאֵל מִן־הָעוֹלָם וְעַד הָעוֹלָם וְאָמַר כָּל־הָעָם אָמֵן הַלְלוּ־יָהּ:	מח

107

—◦⬡⬡⬡◦—

קז

1	"Praise Hashem, for He is good; His steadfast love is eternal!"	*Hodu laAdonai ki-tov ki le'olam chasdo*	הֹדוּ לַיהֹוָה כִּי־טוֹב כִּי לְעוֹלָם חַסְדּוֹ:	א

2	Thus let the redeemed of Hashem say, those He redeemed from adversity,	*Yomru ge'ulei Adonai asher ge'alam miyyad-tzar*	יֹאמְרוּ גְּאוּלֵי יְהֹוָה אֲשֶׁר גְּאָלָם מִיַּד־צָר:	ב
3	whom He gathered in from the lands, from east and west, from the north and from the sea.	*Ume'aratzot kibetzam mimmizrach umimma'arav mitzafon umiyyam*	וּמֵאֲרָצוֹת קִבְּצָם מִמִּזְרָח וּמִמַּעֲרָב מִצָּפוֹן וּמִיָּם:	ג
4	Some lost their way in the wilderness, in the wasteland; they found no settled place.	*Ta'u vammidbar bishimon darech ir moshav lo matza'u*	תָּעוּ בַמִּדְבָּר בִּישִׁימוֹן דָּרֶךְ עִיר מוֹשָׁב לֹא מָצָאוּ:	ד
5	Hungry and thirsty, their spirit failed.	*Re'ayvim gam-tzeme'im nafsham bahem tit'attaf*	רְעֵבִים גַּם־צְמֵאִים נַפְשָׁם בָּהֶם תִּתְעַטָּף:	ה
6	In their adversity they cried to Hashem, and He rescued them from their troubles.	*Vayyitz'aku el-Adonai batzar lahem mimmetzukoteihem yatzilem*	וַיִּצְעֲקוּ אֶל־יְהֹוָה בַּצַּר לָהֶם מִמְּצוּקוֹתֵיהֶם יַצִּילֵם:	ו
7	He showed them a direct way to reach a settled place.	*Vayyadrichem bederech yesharah lalechet el-ir moshav*	וַיַּדְרִיכֵם בְּדֶרֶךְ יְשָׁרָה לָלֶכֶת אֶל־עִיר מוֹשָׁב:	ז
8	Let them praise Hashem for His steadfast love, His wondrous deeds for mankind;	*Yodu laAdonai chasdo venifle'otav livnei adam*	יוֹדוּ לַיהֹוָה חַסְדּוֹ וְנִפְלְאוֹתָיו לִבְנֵי אָדָם:	ח
9	for He has satisfied the thirsty, filled the hungry with all good things.	*Ki-hisbia' nefesh shokekah venefesh re'evah milay-tov*	כִּי־הִשְׂבִּיעַ נֶפֶשׁ שֹׁקֵקָה וְנֶפֶשׁ רְעֵבָה מִלֵּא־טוֹב:	ט

10	Some lived in deepest darkness, bound in cruel irons,	*Yoshvei choshech vetzalmavet asirei oni uvarzel*	יֹשְׁבֵי חֹשֶׁךְ וְצַלְמָוֶת אֲסִירֵי עֳנִי וּבַרְזֶל:	י
11	because they defied the word of Hashem, spurned the counsel of the Most High.	*Ki-himru imrei-El va'atzat elyon na'atzu*	כִּי־הִמְרוּ אִמְרֵי־אֵל וַעֲצַת עֶלְיוֹן נָאָצוּ:	יא
12	He humbled their hearts through suffering; they stumbled with no one to help.	*Vayychna be'amal libbam kashlu ve'ein ozer*	וַיַּכְנַע בֶּעָמָל לִבָּם כָּשְׁלוּ וְאֵין עֹזֵר:	יב
13	In their adversity they cried to Hashem, and He rescued them from their troubles.	*Vayyiz'aku el-Adonai batzar lahem mimmetzukoteihem yoshi'em*	וַיִּזְעֲקוּ אֶל־יְהֹוָה בַּצַּר לָהֶם מִמְּצֻקוֹתֵיהֶם יוֹשִׁיעֵם:	יג
14	He brought them out of deepest darkness, broke their bonds asunder.	*Yotzi'em mechoshech vetzalmavet umosroteihem yenattek*	יוֹצִיאֵם מֵחֹשֶׁךְ וְצַלְמָוֶת וּמוֹסְרוֹתֵיהֶם יְנַתֵּק:	יד
15	Let them praise Hashem for His steadfast love, His wondrous deeds for mankind,	*Yodu laAdonai chasdo venifle'otav livnei adam*	יוֹדוּ לַיהֹוָה חַסְדּוֹ וְנִפְלְאוֹתָיו לִבְנֵי אָדָם:	טו
16	For He shattered gates of bronze, He broke their iron bars.	*Ki-shibbar daltot nechoshet uverichei varzel giddea'*	כִּי־שִׁבַּר דַּלְתוֹת נְחֹשֶׁת וּבְרִיחֵי בַרְזֶל גִּדֵּעַ:	טז
17	There were fools who suffered for their sinful way, and for their iniquities.	*Evilim midderech pish'am ume'avnoteihem yit'annu*	אֱוִלִים מִדֶּרֶךְ פִּשְׁעָם וּמֵעֲוֺנֹתֵיהֶם יִתְעַנּוּ:	יז

279

18	All food was loathsome to them; they reached the gates of death.	*Kol-ochel teta'ev nafsham vayyaggi'u ad-sha'arei mavet*	כָּל־אֹכֶל תְּתַעֵב נַפְשָׁם וַיַּגִּיעוּ עַד־שַׁעֲרֵי מָוֶת: יח
19	In their adversity they cried to Hashem and He saved them from their troubles.	*Vayyiz'aku el-Adonai batzar lahem mimmetzukoteihem yoshi'em*	וַיִּזְעֲקוּ אֶל־יְהֹוָה בַּצַּר לָהֶם מִמְּצֻקוֹתֵיהֶם יוֹשִׁיעֵם: יט
20	He gave an order and healed them; He delivered them from the pits.	*Yishlach devaro veyirpa'em vimallet mishechitotam*	יִשְׁלַח דְּבָרוֹ וְיִרְפָּאֵם וִימַלֵּט מִשְּׁחִיתוֹתָם: כ
21	Let them praise Hashem for His steadfast love, His wondrous deeds for mankind.	*Yodu laAdonai chasdo venifle'otav livnei adam*	יוֹדוּ לַיהֹוָה חַסְדּוֹ וְנִפְלְאוֹתָיו לִבְנֵי אָדָם: כא
22	Let them offer thanksgiving sacrifices, and tell His deeds in joyful song.	*Veyizbechu zivchei todah visapperu ma'asav berinnah*	וְיִזְבְּחוּ זִבְחֵי תוֹדָה וִיסַפְּרוּ מַעֲשָׂיו בְּרִנָּה: כב
23	Others go down to the sea in ships, ply their trade in the mighty waters;	*Yoredei hayyam bo'oniyyot osei melachah bemayim rabbim*	יוֹרְדֵי הַיָּם בָּאֳנִיּוֹת עֹשֵׂי מְלָאכָה בְּמַיִם רַבִּים: כג
24	they have seen the works of Hashem and His wonders in the deep.	*haymmah ra'u ma'asei Adonai venifle'otav bimtzulah*	הֵמָּה רָאוּ מַעֲשֵׂי יְהֹוָה וְנִפְלְאוֹתָיו בִּמְצוּלָה: כד
25	By His word He raised a storm wind that made the waves surge.	*Vayyomer vayya'amed ruach se'arah vatteromem gallav*	וַיֹּאמֶר וַיַּעֲמֵד רוּחַ סְעָרָה וַתְּרוֹמֵם גַּלָּיו: כה

26	Mounting up to the heaven, plunging down to the depths, disgorging in their misery,	*Ya'alu shamayim yerdu tehomot nafsham bera'ah titmogag*	יַעֲלוּ שָׁמַיִם יֵרְדוּ תְהוֹמוֹת נַפְשָׁם בְּרָעָה תִתְמוֹגָג:	כו
27	they reeled and staggered like a drunken man, all their skill to no avail.	*Yachoggu veyanu'u kashikkor vechol-chachematam titballa*	יָחוֹגּוּ וְיָנוּעוּ כַּשִּׁכּוֹר וְכָל־חָכְמָתָם תִּתְבַּלָּע:	כז
28	In their adversity they cried to Hashem, and He saved them from their troubles.	*Vayyitz'aku el-Adonai batzar lahem umimmetzukoteihem yotzi'em*	וַיִּצְעֲקוּ אֶל־יְהֹוָה בַּצַּר לָהֶם וּמִמְּצוּקֹתֵיהֶם יוֹצִיאֵם:	כח
29	He reduced the storm to a whisper; the waves were stilled.	*Yakem se'arah lidmamah vayyecheshu galleihem*	יָקֵם סְעָרָה לִדְמָמָה וַיֶּחֱשׁוּ גַּלֵּיהֶם:	כט
30	They rejoiced when all was quiet, and He brought them to the port they desired.	*Vayyismechu chi-yishtoku vayyanchem el-mechoz cheftzam*	וַיִּשְׂמְחוּ כִי־יִשְׁתֹּקוּ וַיַּנְחֵם אֶל־מְחוֹז חֶפְצָם:	ל
31	Let them praise Hashem for His steadfast love, His wondrous deeds for mankind.	*Yodu laAdonai chasdo venifle'otav livnei adam*	יוֹדוּ לַיהֹוָה חַסְדּוֹ וְנִפְלְאוֹתָיו לִבְנֵי אָדָם:	לא
32	Let them exalt Him in the congregation of the people, acclaim Him in the assembly of the elders.	*Viromemuhu bikhal-am uvemoshav zekenim yehalluhu*	וִירֹמְמוּהוּ בִּקְהַל־עָם וּבְמוֹשַׁב זְקֵנִים יְהַלְלוּהוּ:	לב

33	He turns the rivers into a wilderness, springs of water into thirsty land,	*Yasem neharot lemidbar umotza'ei mayim letzimma'on*	יָשֵׂם נְהָרוֹת לְמִדְבָּר וּמֹצָאֵי מַיִם לְצִמָּאוֹן׃	לג
34	fruitful land into a salt marsh, because of the wickedness of its inhabitants.	*Eretz peri limlayhah mayra'at yoshevei vah*	אֶרֶץ פְּרִי לִמְלֵחָה מֵרָעַת יֹשְׁבֵי בָהּ׃	לד
35	He turns the wilderness into pools, parched land into springs of water.	*Yasem midbar la'agam-mayim ve'eretz tziyyah lemotza'ei mayim*	יָשֵׂם מִדְבָּר לַאֲגַם־מַיִם וְאֶרֶץ צִיָּה לְמֹצָאֵי מָיִם׃	לה
36	There He settles the hungry; they build a place to settle in.	*Vayyoshev sham re'evim vaychonenu ir moshav*	וַיּוֹשֶׁב שָׁם רְעֵבִים וַיְכוֹנְנוּ עִיר מוֹשָׁב׃	לו
37	They sow fields and plant vineyards that yield a fruitful harvest.	*Vayyizre'u sadot vayyitte'u cheramim vayya'asu peri tevu'ah*	וַיִּזְרְעוּ שָׂדוֹת וַיִּטְּעוּ כְרָמִים וַיַּעֲשׂוּ פְּרִי תְבוּאָה׃	לז
38	He blesses them and they increase greatly; and He does not let their cattle decrease,	*Vayvarachem vayyirbu me'od uvehemtam lo yam'it*	וַיְבָרֲכֵם וַיִּרְבּוּ מְאֹד וּבְהֶמְתָּם לֹא יַמְעִיט׃	לח
39	after they had been few and crushed by oppression, misery, and sorrow.	*Vayyim'atu vayyashochu me'otzer ra'ah veyagon*	וַיִּמְעֲטוּ וַיָּשֹׁחוּ מֵעֹצֶר רָעָה וְיָגוֹן׃	לט
40	He pours contempt on great men and makes them lose their way in trackless deserts;	*Shofech buz al-nedivim vayyat'em betohu lo-darech*	שֹׁפֵךְ בּוּז עַל־נְדִיבִים וַיַּתְעֵם בְּתֹהוּ לֹא־דָרֶךְ׃	מ

41	but the needy He secures from suffering, and increases their families like flocks.	*Vaysaggev evyon me'oni vayyasem katzon mishpachot*	וַיְשַׂגֵּב אֶבְיוֹן מֵעוֹנִי וַיָּשֶׂם כַּצֹּאן מִשְׁפָּחוֹת: מא
42	The upright see it and rejoice; the mouth of all wrongdoers is stopped.	*Yir'u yesharim veyismachu vechol-avlah kaftzah piha*	יִרְאוּ יְשָׁרִים וְיִשְׂמָחוּ וְכָל־עַוְלָה קָפְצָה פִּיהָ: מב
43	The wise man will take note of these things; he will consider the steadfast love of Hashem.	*Mi-chacham veyishmar-elleh veyitbonenu chasdei Adonai*	מִי־חָכָם וְיִשְׁמָר־אֵלֶּה וְיִתְבּוֹנְנוּ חַסְדֵי יְהֹוָה: מג

108

–o◦✬◦o–

קח

1	A song. A psalm of David.	*Shir mizmor ledavid*	שִׁיר מִזְמוֹר לְדָוִד: א
2	My heart is firm, O Hashem; I will sing and chant a hymn with all my soul.	*Nachon libbi Elohim ashirah va'azammerah af-kevodi*	נָכוֹן לִבִּי אֱלֹהִים אָשִׁירָה וַאֲזַמְּרָה אַף־כְּבוֹדִי: ב
3	Awake, O harp and lyre! I will wake the dawn.	*Urah hannevel vechinnor a'irah shachar*	עוּרָה הַנֵּבֶל וְכִנּוֹר אָעִירָה שָּׁחַר: ג
4	I will praise You among the peoples, Hashem, sing a hymn to You among the nations;	*Odecha va'ammim Adonai va'azammercha bal-ummim*	אוֹדְךָ בָעַמִּים יְהֹוָה וַאֲזַמֶּרְךָ בַּל־אֻמִּים: ד

5	for Your faithfulness is higher than the heavens; Your steadfastness reaches to the sky.	*Ki-gadol me'al-shamayim chasdecha ve'ad-shechakim amittecha*	כִּי־גָדוֹל מֵעַל־שָׁמַיִם חַסְדֶּךָ וְעַד־שְׁחָקִים אֲמִתֶּךָ: ה
6	Exalt Yourself over the heavens, O Hashem; let Your glory be over all the earth!	*Rumah al-shamayim Elohim ve'al kol-ha'aretz kevodecha*	רוּמָה עַל־שָׁמַיִם אֱלֹהִים וְעַל כָּל־הָאָרֶץ כְּבוֹדֶךָ: ו
7	That those whom You love may be rescued, deliver with Your right hand and answer me.	*Lema'an yechalaytzun yedidecha hoshi'ah yemincha va'aneni*	לְמַעַן יֵחָלְצוּן יְדִידֶיךָ הוֹשִׁיעָה יְמִינְךָ וַעֲנֵנִי: ז
8	Hashem promised in His sanctuary that I would exultingly divide up Shechem, and measure the Valley of Sukkoth;	*Elohim dibber bekodsho e'lozah achallekah shechem ve'emek sukkot amadded*	אֱלֹהִים דִּבֶּר בְּקָדְשׁוֹ אֶעְלֹזָה אֲחַלְּקָה שְׁכֶם וְעֵמֶק סֻכּוֹת אֲמַדֵּד: ח
9	Gilad and Menashe would be mine, Efraim my chief stronghold, Yehuda my scepter;	*Li gil'ad li menasheh ve'efrayim ma'oz roshi yehudah mechokeki*	לִי גִלְעָד לִי מְנַשֶּׁה וְאֶפְרַיִם מָעוֹז רֹאשִׁי יְהוּדָה מְחֹקְקִי: ט
10	Moab would be my washbasin; on Edom I would cast my shoe; I would raise a shout over Philistia.	*Mo'av sir rachtzi al-edom ashlich na'ali alei-feleshet etro'a*	מוֹאָב סִיר רַחְצִי עַל־אֱדוֹם אַשְׁלִיךְ נַעֲלִי עָלֵי־פְּלֶשֶׁת אֶתְרוֹעָע: י
11	Would that I were brought to the bastion! Would that I were led to Edom!	*Mi yovileni ir mivtzar mi nachani ad-edom*	מִי יֹבִלֵנִי עִיר מִבְצָר מִי נָחַנִי עַד־אֱדוֹם: יא

12	But You have rejected us, O Hashem; Hashem, You do not march with our armies.	*Halo-Elohim zenachtanu velo-taytzay Elohim betziv'oteinu*	הֲלֹא־אֱלֹהִים זְנַחְתָּנוּ וְלֹא־ תֵצֵא אֱלֹהִים בְּצִבְאֹתֵינוּ: יב
13	Grant us Your aid against the foe, for the help of man is worthless.	*Havah-lanu ezrat mitzar veshov teshu'at adam*	הָבָה־לָּנוּ עֶזְרָת מִצָּר וְשָׁוְא תְּשׁוּעַת אָדָם: יג
14	With Hashem we shall triumph; He will trample our foes.	*B'Elohim na'aseh-chayil vehu yavus tzareinu*	בֵּאלֹהִים נַעֲשֶׂה־חָיִל וְהוּא יָבוּס צָרֵינוּ: יד

109

כ͏ט

1	For the leader. Of David. A psalm. O God of my praise, do not keep aloof,	*Lammenatzeach ledavid mizmor Elohei tehillati al-techerash*	לַמְנַצֵּחַ לְדָוִד מִזְמוֹר אֱלֹהֵי תְהִלָּתִי אַל־תֶּחֱרַשׁ: א
2	for the wicked and the deceitful open their mouth against me; they speak to me with lying tongue.	*Ki fi rasha ufi-mirmah alai patachu dibberu itti leshon shaker*	כִּי פִי רָשָׁע וּפִי־מִרְמָה עָלַי פָּתָחוּ דִּבְּרוּ אִתִּי לְשׁוֹן שָׁקֶר: ב
3	They encircle me with words of hate; they attack me without cause.	*Vedivrei sin'ah sevavuni vayyillachamuni chinnam*	וְדִבְרֵי שִׂנְאָה סְבָבוּנִי וַיִּלָּחֲמוּנִי חִנָּם: ג
4	They answer my love with accusation but I am all prayer	*Tachat-ahavati yistenuni va'ani tefillah*	תַּחַת־אַהֲבָתִי יִשְׂטְנוּנִי וַאֲנִי תְפִלָּה: ד

5	They repay me with evil for good, with hatred for my love.	*Vayyasimu alai ra'ah tachat tovah vesin'ah tachat ahavati*	וַיָּשִׂימוּ עָלַי רָעָה תַּחַת טוֹבָה וְשִׂנְאָה תַּחַת אַהֲבָתִי:	ה
6	Appoint a wicked man over him; may an accuser stand at his right side;	*Hafked alav rasha vesatan ya'amod al-yemino*	הַפְקֵד עָלָיו רָשָׁע וְשָׂטָן יַעֲמֹד עַל-יְמִינוֹ:	ו
7	may he be tried and convicted; may he be judged and found guilty.	*Behishofto yaytzay rasha utefillato tihyeh lachata'ah*	בְּהִשָּׁפְטוֹ יֵצֵא רָשָׁע וּתְפִלָּתוֹ תִּהְיֶה לַחֲטָאָה:	ז
8	May his days be few; may another take over his position.	*Yiheyu-yamav me'attim pekuddato yikkach acher*	יִהְיוּ-יָמָיו מְעַטִּים פְּקֻדָּתוֹ יִקַּח אַחֵר:	ח
9	May his children be orphans, his wife a widow.	*Yiheyu-vanav yetomim ve'ishto almanah*	יִהְיוּ-בָנָיו יְתוֹמִים וְאִשְׁתּוֹ אַלְמָנָה:	ט
10	May his children wander from their hovels, begging in search of [bread].	*Venoa' yanu'u vanav veshi'aylu vedarshu mecharevoteihem*	וְנוֹעַ יָנוּעוּ בָנָיו וְשִׁאֵלוּ וְדָרְשׁוּ מֵחָרְבוֹתֵיהֶם:	י
11	May his creditor seize all his possessions; may strangers plunder his wealth.	*Yenakkesh nosheh lechol-asher-lo veyavozzu zarim yegi'o*	יְנַקֵּשׁ נוֹשֶׁה לְכָל-אֲשֶׁר-לוֹ וְיָבֹזּוּ זָרִים יְגִיעוֹ:	יא
12	May no one show him mercy; may none pity his orphans;	*Al-yehi-lo moshech chesed ve'al-yehi chonen litomav*	אַל-יְהִי-לוֹ מֹשֵׁךְ חָסֶד וְאַל-יְהִי חוֹנֵן לִיתוֹמָיו:	יב

13	may his posterity be cut off; may their names be blotted out in the next generation.	*Yehi-acharito lehachrit bedor acher yimmach shemam*	יְהִי־אַחֲרִיתוֹ לְהַכְרִית בְּדוֹר אַחֵר יִמַּח שְׁמָם:	יג
14	May Hashem be ever mindful of his father's iniquity, and may the sin of his mother not be blotted out.	*Yizzacher avon avotav el-Adonai vechattat immo al-timmach*	יִזָּכֵר עֲוֹן אֲבֹתָיו אֶל־יְהֹוָה וְחַטַּאת אִמּוֹ אַל־תִּמָּח:	יד
15	May Hashem be aware of them always and cause their names to be cut off from the earth,	*Yiheyu neged-Adonai tamid veyachret me'eretz zichram*	יִהְיוּ נֶגֶד־יְהֹוָה תָּמִיד וְיַכְרֵת מֵאֶרֶץ זִכְרָם:	טו
16	because he was not minded to act kindly, and hounded to death the poor and needy man, one crushed in spirit.	*Ya'an asher lo zachar asot chased vayyirdof ish-ani ve'evyon venich'eh layvav lemotet*	יַעַן אֲשֶׁר לֹא זָכַר עֲשׂוֹת חָסֶד וַיִּרְדֹּף אִישׁ־עָנִי וְאֶבְיוֹן וְנִכְאֵה לֵבָב לְמוֹתֵת:	טז
17	He loved to curse—may a curse come upon him! He would not bless—may blessing be far from him!	*Vayye'ehav kelalah vattevo'ehu velo-chafetz bivrachah vattirchak mimmennu*	וַיֶּאֱהַב קְלָלָה וַתְּבוֹאֵהוּ וְלֹא־חָפֵץ בִּבְרָכָה וַתִּרְחַק מִמֶּנּוּ:	יז
18	May he be clothed in a curse like a garment, may it enter his body like water, his bones like oil.	*Vayyilbash kelalah kemaddo vattavo chammayim bekirbo vechashemen be'atzmotav*	וַיִּלְבַּשׁ קְלָלָה כְּמַדּוֹ וַתָּבֹא כַמַּיִם בְּקִרְבּוֹ וְכַשֶּׁמֶן בְּעַצְמוֹתָיו:	יח
19	Let it be like the cloak he wraps around him, like the belt he always wears.	*Tehi-lo keveged ya'teh ulemezach tamid yachgereha*	תְּהִי־לוֹ כְּבֶגֶד יַעְטֶה וּלְמֵזַח תָּמִיד יַחְגְּרֶהָ:	יט

20	May Hashem thus repay my accusers, all those who speak evil against me.	*Zot pe'ullat sotenai me'et Adonai vehaddoverim ra al-nafshi*	זֹאת פְּעֻלַּת שֹׂטְנַי מֵאֵת יְהֹוָה וְהַדֹּבְרִים רָע עַל־נַפְשִׁי:	כ
21	Now You, O Hashem, my Lord, act on my behalf as befits Your name. Good and faithful as You are, save me.	*Ve'attah Elohim Adonai aseh-itti lema'an shemecha ki-tov chasdecha hatzileni*	וְאַתָּה יְהֹוָה אֲדֹנָי עֲשֵׂה־אִתִּי לְמַעַן שְׁמֶךָ כִּי־טוֹב חַסְדְּךָ הַצִּילֵנִי:	כא
22	For I am poor and needy, and my heart is pierced within me.	*Ki-ani ve'evyon anochi velibbi chalal bekirbi*	כִּי־עָנִי וְאֶבְיוֹן אָנֹכִי וְלִבִּי חָלַל בְּקִרְבִּי:	כב
23	I fade away like a lengthening shadow; I am shaken off like locusts.	*Ketzel-kintoto nehelacheti nin'arti ka'arbeh*	כְּצֵל־כִּנְטוֹתוֹ נֶהֱלָכְתִּי נִנְעַרְתִּי כָּאַרְבֶּה:	כג
24	My knees give way from fasting; my flesh is lean, has lost its fat.	*Birkai kashlu mitzom uvesari kachash mishamen*	בִּרְכַּי כָּשְׁלוּ מִצּוֹם וּבְשָׂרִי כָּחַשׁ מִשָּׁמֶן:	כד
25	I am the object of their scorn; when they see me, they shake their head.	*Va'ani hayiti cherpah lahem yir'uni yeni'un rosham*	וַאֲנִי הָיִיתִי חֶרְפָּה לָהֶם יִרְאוּנִי יְנִיעוּן רֹאשָׁם:	כה
26	Help me, Hashem, my God; save me in accord with Your faithfulness,	*Azereni Adonai Elohai hoshi'eni chechasdecha*	עָזְרֵנִי יְהֹוָה אֱלֹהָי הוֹשִׁיעֵנִי כְחַסְדֶּךָ:	כו
27	that men may know that it is Your hand, that You, Hashem, have done it.	*Veyede'u ki-yadcha zot attah Adonai asitah*	וְיֵדְעוּ כִּי־יָדְךָ זֹּאת אַתָּה יְהֹוָה עֲשִׂיתָהּ:	כז

28	Let them curse, but You bless; let them rise up, but come to grief, while Your servant rejoices.	*Yekallu-haymmah ve'attah tevarech kamu vayyevoshu ve'avdecha yismach*	יְקַלְלוּ־הֵמָּה וְאַתָּה תְבָרֵךְ קָמוּ וַיֵּבֹשׁוּ וְעַבְדְּךָ יִשְׂמָח:	כח
29	My accusers shall be clothed in shame, wrapped in their disgrace as in a robe.	*Yilbeshu sotnai kelimmah veya'atu cham'il bashetam*	יִלְבְּשׁוּ שׂוֹטְנַי כְּלִמָּה וְיַעֲטוּ כַמְעִיל בָּשְׁתָּם:	כט
30	My mouth shall sing much praise to Hashem; I will acclaim Him in the midst of a throng,	*Odeh Adonai me'od befi uvetoch rabbim ahallennu*	אוֹדֶה יְהֹוָה מְאֹד בְּפִי וּבְתוֹךְ רַבִּים אֲהַלְלֶנּוּ:	ל
31	because He stands at the right hand of the needy, to save him from those who would condemn him.	*Ki-ya'amod limin evyon lehoshia' mishofetei nafsho*	כִּי־יַעֲמֹד לִימִין אֶבְיוֹן לְהוֹשִׁיעַ מִשֹּׁפְטֵי נַפְשׁוֹ:	לא

110

⎯⎯◦◦❈◦◦⎯⎯

קי

1	Of David. A psalm. Hashem said to my lord, "Sit at My right hand while I make your enemies your footstool."	*Ledavid mizmor ne'um Adonai laAdoni shev limini ad-ashit oyeveicha hadom leragleicha*	לְדָוִד מִזְמוֹר נְאֻם יְהֹוָה לַאדֹנִי שֵׁב לִימִינִי עַד־אָשִׁית אֹיְבֶיךָ הֲדֹם לְרַגְלֶיךָ:	א
2	Hashem will stretch forth from Tzion your mighty scepter; hold sway over your enemies!	*Matteh-uzzecha yishlach Adonai mitziyyon redeh bekerev oyeveicha*	מַטֵּה־עֻזְּךָ יִשְׁלַח יְהֹוָה מִצִּיּוֹן רְדֵה בְּקֶרֶב אֹיְבֶיךָ:	ב

3 Your people come forward willingly on your day of battle. In majestic holiness, from the womb, from the dawn, yours was the dew of youth.

Ammecha nedavot beyom cheilecha behadrei-kodesh merechem mishchar lecha tal yalduteicha

עַמְּךָ נְדָבֹת בְּיוֹם חֵילֶךָ בְּהַדְרֵי־קֹדֶשׁ מֵרֶחֶם מִשְׁחָר לְךָ טַל יַלְדֻתֶיךָ׃ ג

4 Hashem has sworn and will not relent, "You are a Kohen forever, after the manner of Melchizedek."

Nishba Adonai velo yinnachem attah-chohen le'olam al-divrati malki-tzedek

נִשְׁבַּע יְהֹוָה וְלֹא יִנָּחֵם אַתָּה־כֹהֵן לְעוֹלָם עַל־דִּבְרָתִי מַלְכִּי־צֶדֶק׃ ד

5 Hashem is at your right hand. He crushes kings in the day of His anger.

Adonai al-yemincha machatz beyom-appo melachim

אֲדֹנָי עַל־יְמִינְךָ מָחַץ בְּיוֹם־אַפּוֹ מְלָכִים׃ ה

6 He works judgment upon the nations, heaping up bodies, crushing heads far and wide.

Yadin baggoyim malay geviyyot machatz rosh al-eretz rabbah

יָדִין בַּגּוֹיִם מָלֵא גְוִיּוֹת מָחַץ רֹאשׁ עַל־אֶרֶץ רַבָּה׃ ו

7 He drinks from the stream on his way; therefore he holds his head high.

Minnachal badderech yishteh al-kayn yarim rosh

מִנַּחַל בַּדֶּרֶךְ יִשְׁתֶּה עַל־כֵּן יָרִים רֹאשׁ׃ ז

111

קיא

1 Hallelujah. I praise Hashem with all my heart in the assembled congregation of the upright.

Hallu yah odeh Adonai bechol-levav besod yesharim ve'edah

הַלְלוּ יָהּ אוֹדֶה יְהֹוָה בְּכָל־לֵבָב בְּסוֹד יְשָׁרִים וְעֵדָה׃ א

2	The works of Hashem are great, within reach of all who desire them.	*Gedolim ma'asei Adonai derushim lechol-cheftzeihem*	גְּדֹלִים מַעֲשֵׂי יְהֹוָה דְּרוּשִׁים לְכָל־חֶפְצֵיהֶם: ב
3	His deeds are splendid and glorious; His beneficence is everlasting;	*Hod-vehadar po'olo vetzidkato omedet la'ad*	הוֹד־וְהָדָר פׇּעֳלוֹ וְצִדְקָתוֹ עֹמֶדֶת לָעַד: ג
4	He has won renown for His wonders. Hashem is gracious and compassionate;	*Zecher asah lenifle'otav channun verachum Adonai*	זֵכֶר עָשָׂה לְנִפְלְאֹתָיו חַנּוּן וְרַחוּם יְהֹוָה: ד
5	He gives food to those who fear Him; He is ever mindful of His covenant.	*Teref natan lire'av yizkor le'olam berito*	טֶרֶף נָתַן לִירֵאָיו יִזְכֹּר לְעוֹלָם בְּרִיתוֹ: ה
6	He revealed to His people His powerful works, in giving them the heritage of nations.	*Koach ma'asav higgid le'ammo latet lahem nachalat goyim*	כֹּחַ מַעֲשָׂיו הִגִּיד לְעַמּוֹ לָתֵת לָהֶם נַחֲלַת גּוֹיִם: ו
7	His handiwork is truth and justice; all His precepts are enduring,	*Ma'asei yadav emet umishpat ne'emanim kol-pikkudav*	מַעֲשֵׂי יָדָיו אֱמֶת וּמִשְׁפָּט נֶאֱמָנִים כׇּל־פִּקּוּדָיו: ז
8	well-founded for all eternity, wrought of truth and equity.	*Semuchim la'ad le'olam asuyim be'emet veyashar*	סְמוּכִים לָעַד לְעוֹלָם עֲשׂוּיִם בֶּאֱמֶת וְיָשָׁר: ח
9	He sent redemption to His people; He ordained His covenant for all time; His name is holy and awesome.	*Pedut shalach le'ammo tzivvah-le'olam berito kadosh venora shemo*	פְּדוּת שָׁלַח לְעַמּוֹ צִוָּה־לְעוֹלָם בְּרִיתוֹ קָדוֹשׁ וְנוֹרָא שְׁמוֹ: ט

10 The beginning of wisdom is the fear of Hashem; all who practice it gain sound understanding. Praise of Him is everlasting.

Reshit chochmah yir'at Adonai sechel tov lechol-oseihem tehillato omedet la'ad

רֵאשִׁית חָכְמָה יִרְאַת יְהֹוָה שֵׂכֶל טוֹב לְכָל־עֹשֵׂיהֶם תְּהִלָּתוֹ עֹמֶדֶת לָעַד:

י

112

כ"ב

1 Hallelujah. Happy is the man who fears Hashem, who is ardently devoted to His commandments.

Hallu yah ashrei-ish yaray et-Adonai bemitzvtav chafetz me'od

הַלְלוּ יָהּ אַשְׁרֵי־אִישׁ יָרֵא אֶת־יְהֹוָה בְּמִצְוֹתָיו חָפֵץ מְאֹד:

א

2 His descendants will be mighty in the land, a blessed generation of upright men.

Gibbor ba'aretz yihyeh zar'o dor yesharim yevorach

גִּבּוֹר בָּאָרֶץ יִהְיֶה זַרְעוֹ דּוֹר יְשָׁרִים יְבֹרָךְ:

ב

3 Wealth and riches are in his house, and his beneficence lasts forever.

Hon-va'osher beveito vetzidkato omedet la'ad

הוֹן־וָעֹשֶׁר בְּבֵיתוֹ וְצִדְקָתוֹ עֹמֶדֶת לָעַד:

ג

4 A light shines for the upright in the darkness; he is gracious, compassionate, and beneficent.

Zarach bachoshech or layyesharim channun verachum vetzaddik

זָרַח בַּחֹשֶׁךְ אוֹר לַיְשָׁרִים חַנּוּן וְרַחוּם וְצַדִּיק:

ד

5 All goes well with the man who lends generously, who conducts his affairs with equity.

Tov-ish chonen umalveh yechalkel devarav bemishpat

טוֹב־אִישׁ חוֹנֵן וּמַלְוֶה יְכַלְכֵּל דְּבָרָיו בְּמִשְׁפָּט:

ה

6 He shall never be shaken; the beneficent man will be remembered forever.

Ki-le'olam lo-yimmot lezecher olam yihyeh tzaddik

כִּי־לְעוֹלָם לֹא־יִמּוֹט לְזֵכֶר עוֹלָם יִהְיֶה צַדִּיק: ו

7 He is not afraid of evil tidings; his heart is firm, he trusts in Hashem.

Mishemu'ah ra'ah lo yira nachon libbo batuach bAdonai

מִשְּׁמוּעָה רָעָה לֹא יִירָא נָכוֹן לִבּוֹ בָּטֻחַ בַּיהֹוָה: ז

8 His heart is resolute, he is unafraid; in the end he will see the fall of his foes.

Samuch libbo lo yira ad asher-yir'eh vetzarav

סָמוּךְ לִבּוֹ לֹא יִירָא עַד אֲשֶׁר־יִרְאֶה בְצָרָיו: ח

9 He gives freely to the poor; his beneficence lasts forever; his horn is exalted in honor.

Pizzar natan la'evyonim tzidkato omedet la'ad karno tarum bechavod

פִּזַּר נָתַן לָאֶבְיוֹנִים צִדְקָתוֹ עֹמֶדֶת לָעַד קַרְנוֹ תָּרוּם בְּכָבוֹד: ט

10 The wicked man shall see it and be vexed; he shall gnash his teeth; his courage shall fail. The desire of the wicked shall come to nothing.

Rasha yir'eh vecha'as shinnav yacharok venamas ta'avat resha'im toved

רָשָׁע יִרְאֶה וְכָעָס שִׁנָּיו יַחֲרֹק וְנָמָס תַּאֲוַת רְשָׁעִים תֹּאבֵד: י

113

—◦⟨❈⟩◦—

קי״ג

1 Hallelujah. O servants of Hashem, give praise; praise the name of Hashem.

Hallu yah hallu avdei Adonai hallu et-shem Adonai

הַלְלוּ יָהּ הַלְלוּ עַבְדֵי יְהֹוָה הַלְלוּ אֶת־שֵׁם יְהֹוָה: א

293

2	Let the name of Hashem be blessed now and forever.	*Yehi shem Adonai mevorach me'attah ve'ad-olam*

יְהִי שֵׁם יְהֹוָה מְבֹרָךְ מֵעַתָּה וְעַד־עוֹלָם: ב

3	From east to west the name of Hashem is praised.	*Mimmizrach-shemesh ad-mevo'o mehullal shem Adonai*

מִמִּזְרַח־שֶׁמֶשׁ עַד־מְבוֹאוֹ מְהֻלָּל שֵׁם יְהֹוָה: ג

4	Hashem is exalted above all nations; His glory is above the heavens.	*Ram al-kol-goyim Adonai al hashamayim kevodo*

רָם עַל־כָּל־גּוֹיִם יְהֹוָה עַל הַשָּׁמַיִם כְּבוֹדוֹ: ד

5	Who is like Hashem our God, who, enthroned on high,	*Mi kAdonai Eloheinu hammagbihi lashavet*

מִי כַּיהֹוָה אֱלֹהֵינוּ הַמַּגְבִּיהִי לָשָׁבֶת: ה

6	sees what is below, in heaven and on earth?	*Hammashpili lir'ot bashamayim uva'aretz*

הַמַּשְׁפִּילִי לִרְאוֹת בַּשָּׁמַיִם וּבָאָרֶץ: ו

7	He raises the poor from the dust, lifts up the needy from the refuse heap	*Mekimi me'afar dal me'ashpot yarim evyon*

מְקִימִי מֵעָפָר דָּל מֵאַשְׁפֹּת יָרִים אֶבְיוֹן: ז

8	to set them with the great, with the great men of His people.	*Lehoshivi im-nedivim im nedivei ammo*

לְהוֹשִׁיבִי עִם־נְדִיבִים עִם נְדִיבֵי עַמּוֹ: ח

9	He sets the childless woman among her household as a happy mother of children. Hallelujah.	*Moshivi akeret habbayit em-habbanim semechah hallu-yah*

מוֹשִׁיבִי עֲקֶרֶת הַבַּיִת אֵם־הַבָּנִים שְׂמֵחָה הַלְלוּ־יָהּ: ט

114

קי״ד

1	When Yisrael went forth from Egypt, the house of Yaakov from a people of strange speech,	*Betzet yisra'el mimmitzrayim beit ya'akov me'am lo'ez*	בְּצֵאת יִשְׂרָאֵל מִמִּצְרָיִם בֵּית יַעֲקֹב מֵעַם לֹעֵז:	א
2	Yehuda became His holy one, Yisrael, His dominion.	*Hayetah yehudah lekodsho yisra'el mamshelotav*	הָיְתָה יְהוּדָה לְקׇדְשׁוֹ יִשְׂרָאֵל מַמְשְׁלוֹתָיו:	ב
3	The sea saw them and fled, Yarden ran backward,	*Hayyam ra'ah vayyanos hayyarden yissov le'achor*	הַיָּם רָאָה וַיָּנֹס הַיַּרְדֵּן יִסֹּב לְאָחוֹר:	ג
4	mountains skipped like rams, hills like sheep.	*Heharim rakedu che'eilim geva'ot kivnei-tzon*	הֶהָרִים רָקְדוּ כְאֵילִים גְּבָעוֹת כִּבְנֵי־צֹאן:	ד
5	What alarmed you, O sea, that you fled, Yarden, that you ran backward,	*Mah-lecha hayyam ki tanus hayyarden tissov le'achor*	מַה־לְּךָ הַיָּם כִּי תָנוּס הַיַּרְדֵּן תִּסֹּב לְאָחוֹר:	ה
6	mountains, that you skipped like rams, hills, like sheep?	*Heharim tirkedu che'eilim geva'ot kivnei-tzon*	הֶהָרִים תִּרְקְדוּ כְאֵילִים גְּבָעוֹת כִּבְנֵי־צֹאן:	ו
7	Tremble, O earth, at the presence of Hashem, at the presence of the God of Yaakov,	*Millifnei adon chuli aretz millifnei eloah ya'akov*	מִלִּפְנֵי אָדוֹן חוּלִי אָרֶץ מִלִּפְנֵי אֱלוֹהַּ יַעֲקֹב:	ז

8	who turned the rock into a pool of water, the flinty rock into a fountain.	*Hahofechi hatzur agam-mayim challamish lema'yeno-mayim*	הַהֹפְכִי הַצּוּר אֲגַם־מָיִם חַלָּמִישׁ לְמַעְיְנוֹ־מָיִם: ח

115

⊸–◦⊗◦–⊶

קטו

1	Not to us, Hashem, not to us but to Your name bring glory for the sake of Your love and Your faithfulness.	*Lo lanu Adonai lo lanu ki-leshimcha ten kavod al-chasdecha al-amittecha*	לֹא לָנוּ יְהֹוָה לֹא לָנוּ כִּי־לְשִׁמְךָ תֵּן כָּבוֹד עַל־חַסְדְּךָ עַל־אֲמִתֶּךָ: א
2	Let the nations not say, "Where, now, is their God?"	*Lammah yomru haggoyim ayyeh-na Eloheihem*	לָמָּה יֹאמְרוּ הַגּוֹיִם אַיֵּה־נָא אֱלֹהֵיהֶם: ב
3	when our God is in heaven and all that He wills He accomplishes.	*VEloheinu vashamayim kol asher-chafetz asah*	וֵאלֹהֵינוּ בַשָּׁמָיִם כֹּל אֲשֶׁר־חָפֵץ עָשָׂה: ג
4	Their idols are silver and gold, the work of men's hands.	*Atzabbeihem kesef vezahav ma'aseh yedei adam*	עֲצַבֵּיהֶם כֶּסֶף וְזָהָב מַעֲשֵׂה יְדֵי אָדָם: ד
5	They have mouths, but cannot speak, eyes, but cannot see;	*Peh-lahem velo yedabberu einayim lahem velo yir'u*	פֶּה־לָהֶם וְלֹא יְדַבֵּרוּ עֵינַיִם לָהֶם וְלֹא יִרְאוּ: ה
6	they have ears, but cannot hear, noses, but cannot smell;	*Oznayim lahem velo yishma'u af lahem velo yerichun*	אָזְנַיִם לָהֶם וְלֹא יִשְׁמָעוּ אַף לָהֶם וְלֹא יְרִיחוּן: ו

7	they have hands, but cannot touch, feet, but cannot walk; they can make no sound in their throats.	*Yedeihem velo yemishun ragleihem velo yehallechu lo-yehgu bigronam*	יְדֵיהֶם וְלֹא יְמִישׁוּן רַגְלֵיהֶם וְלֹא יְהַלֵּכוּ לֹא־יֶהְגּוּ בִּגְרוֹנָם: ז
8	Those who fashion them, all who trust in them, shall become like them.	*Kemohem yihyu oseihem kol asher-boteach bahem*	כְּמוֹהֶם יִהְיוּ עֹשֵׂיהֶם כֹּל אֲשֶׁר־בֹּטֵחַ בָּהֶם: ח
9	O Yisrael, trust in Hashem! He is their help and shield.	*Yisra'el betach baAdonai ezram umaginnam hu*	יִשְׂרָאֵל בְּטַח בַּיהוָה עֶזְרָם וּמָגִנָּם הוּא: ט
10	O house of Aharon, trust in Hashem! He is their help and shield.	*Beit aharon bitchu baAdonai ezram umaginnam hu*	בֵּית אַהֲרֹן בִּטְחוּ בַיהוָה עֶזְרָם וּמָגִנָּם הוּא: י
11	O you who fear Hashem, trust in Hashem! He is their help and shield.	*Yir'ei Adonai bitchu baAdonai ezram umaginnam hu*	יִרְאֵי יְהוָה בִּטְחוּ בַיהוָה עֶזְרָם וּמָגִנָּם הוּא: יא
12	Hashem is mindful of us. He will bless us; He will bless the house of Yisrael; He will bless the house of Aharon;	*Adonai zecharanu yevarech yevarech et-beit yisra'el yevarech et-beit aharon*	יְהוָה זְכָרָנוּ יְבָרֵךְ יְבָרֵךְ אֶת־בֵּית יִשְׂרָאֵל יְבָרֵךְ אֶת־בֵּית אַהֲרֹן: יב
13	He will bless those who fear Hashem, small and great alike.	*Yevarech yir'ei Adonai hakketannim im-haggedolim*	יְבָרֵךְ יִרְאֵי יְהוָה הַקְּטַנִּים עִם־הַגְּדֹלִים: יג
14	May Hashem increase your numbers, yours and your children's also.	*Yosef Adonai aleichem aleichem ve'al-beneichem*	יֹסֵף יְהוָה עֲלֵיכֶם עֲלֵיכֶם וְעַל־בְּנֵיכֶם: יד

15	May you be blessed by Hashem, Maker of heaven and earth.	*Beruchim attem laAdonai oseh shamayim va'aretz*	בְּרוּכִים אַתֶּם לַיהֹוָה עֹשֵׂה שָׁמַיִם וָאָרֶץ: טו
16	The heavens belong to Hashem, but the earth He gave over to man.	*Hashamayim shamayim laAdonai veha'aretz natan livnei-adam*	הַשָּׁמַיִם שָׁמַיִם לַיהֹוָה וְהָאָרֶץ נָתַן לִבְנֵי־אָדָם: טז
17	The dead cannot praise Hashem, nor any who go down into silence.	*Lo hammetim yehallu-yah velo kol-yoredei dumah*	לֹא הַמֵּתִים יְהַלְלוּ־יָהּ וְלֹא כָּל־יֹרְדֵי דוּמָה: יז
18	But we will bless Hashem now and forever. Hallelujah.	*Va'anachnu nevarech yah me'attah ve'ad-olam hallu-yah*	וַאֲנַחְנוּ נְבָרֵךְ יָהּ מֵעַתָּה וְעַד־עוֹלָם הַלְלוּ־יָהּ: יח

116   —◦◦⟨⬦⟩◦◦—   קטז

1	I love Hashem* for He hears my voice, my pleas;	*Ahavti ki-yishma Adonai et-koli tachanunai*	אָהַבְתִּי כִּי־יִשְׁמַע יְהֹוָה אֶת־קוֹלִי תַּחֲנוּנָי: א
2	for He turns His ear to me whenever I call.	*Ki-hittah ozno li uveyamai ekra*	כִּי־הִטָּה אָזְנוֹ לִי וּבְיָמַי אֶקְרָא: ב
3	The bonds of death encompassed me; the torments of Sheol overtook me. I came upon trouble and sorrow	*Afafuni chevlei-mavet umetzarei she'ol metza'uni tzarah veyagon emtza*	אֲפָפוּנִי חֶבְלֵי־מָוֶת וּמְצָרֵי שְׁאוֹל מְצָאוּנִי צָרָה וְיָגוֹן אֶמְצָא: ג

4	and I invoked the name of Hashem, "Hashem, save my life!"	*Uveshem-Adonai ekra annah Adonai malletah nafshi*	וּבְשֵׁם־יְהֹוָה אֶקְרָא אָנָּה יְהֹוָה מַלְּטָה נַפְשִׁי:	ד
5	Hashem is gracious and beneficent; our God is compassionate.	*Channun Adonai vetzaddik vEloheinu merachem*	חַנּוּן יְהֹוָה וְצַדִּיק וֵאלֹהֵינוּ מְרַחֵם:	ה
6	Hashem protects the simple; I was brought low and He saved me.	*Shomer petayim Adonai dalloti velee yehoshia'*	שֹׁמֵר פְּתָאִים יְהֹוָה דַּלּוֹתִי וְלִי יְהוֹשִׁיעַ:	ו
7	Be at rest, once again, O my soul, for Hashem has been good to you.	*Shuvi nafshi limnuchayechi ki-Adonai gamal alayechi*	שׁוּבִי נַפְשִׁי לִמְנוּחָיְכִי כִּי־יְהֹוָה גָּמַל עָלָיְכִי:	ז
8	You have delivered me from death, my eyes from tears, my feet from stumbling.	*Ki chillatzta nafshi mimmavet et-eini min-dim'ah et-ragli middechi*	כִּי חִלַּצְתָּ נַפְשִׁי מִמָּוֶת אֶת־עֵינִי מִן־דִּמְעָה אֶת־רַגְלִי מִדֶּחִי:	ח
9	I shall walk before Hashem in the lands of the living.	*Ethallech lifnei Adonai be'artzot hachayyim*	אֶתְהַלֵּךְ לִפְנֵי יְהֹוָה בְּאַרְצוֹת הַחַיִּים:	ט
10	I trust [in Hashem]; out of great suffering I spoke	*He'emanti ki adabber ani aniti me'od*	הֶאֱמַנְתִּי כִּי אֲדַבֵּר אֲנִי עָנִיתִי מְאֹד:	י
11	and said rashly, "All men are false."	*Ani amarti vechafezi kol-ha'adam kozev*	אֲנִי אָמַרְתִּי בְחָפְזִי כָּל־הָאָדָם כֹּזֵב:	יא
12	How can I repay Hashem for all His bounties to me?	*Mah-ashiv laAdonai kol-tagmulohi alai*	מָה־אָשִׁיב לַיהֹוָה כָּל־תַּגְמוּלוֹהִי עָלָי:	יב

13 | I raise the cup of deliverance and invoke the name of Hashem. | *Kos-yeshu'ot essa uveshem Adonai ekra* | כּוֹס־יְשׁוּעוֹת אֶשָּׂא וּבְשֵׁם יְהֹוָה אֶקְרָא: | יג

14 | I will pay my vows to Hashem in the presence of all His people. | *Nedarai laAdonai ashallem negdah-na lechol-ammo* | נְדָרַי לַיהֹוָה אֲשַׁלֵּם נֶגְדָה־נָּא לְכָל־עַמּוֹ: | יד

15 | The death of His faithful ones is grievous in Hashem's sight. | *Yakar be'einei Adonai hammavetah lachasidav* | יָקָר בְּעֵינֵי יְהֹוָה הַמָּוְתָה לַחֲסִידָיו: | טו

16 | Hashem, I am Your servant, Your servant, the son of Your maidservant; You have undone the cords that bound me. | *Annah Adonai ki-ani avdecha ani-avdecha ben-amatecha pittachta lemoserai* | אָנָּה יְהֹוָה כִּי־אֲנִי עַבְדֶּךָ אֲנִי־עַבְדְּךָ בֶּן־אֲמָתֶךָ פִּתַּחְתָּ לְמוֹסֵרָי: | טז

17 | I will sacrifice a thank offering to You and invoke the name of Hashem. | *Lecha-ezbach zevach todah uveshem Adonai ekra* | לְךָ־אֶזְבַּח זֶבַח תּוֹדָה וּבְשֵׁם יְהֹוָה אֶקְרָא: | יז

18 | I will pay my vows to Hashem in the presence of all His people, | *Nedarai laAdonai ashallem negdah-na lechol-ammo* | נְדָרַי לַיהֹוָה אֲשַׁלֵּם נֶגְדָה־נָּא לְכָל־עַמּוֹ: | יח

19 | in the courts of the house of Hashem, in the midst of Yerushalayim. Hallelujah. | *Bechatzrot beit Adonai betochechi yerushala im hallu-yah* | בְּחַצְרוֹת בֵּית יְהֹוָה בְּתוֹכֵכִי יְרוּשָׁלָ͏ִם הַלְלוּ־יָהּ: | יט

117

1 Praise Hashem, all you nations; extol Him, all you peoples,

Hallu et-Adonai kol-goyim shabbechuhu kol-ha'ummim

הַלְלוּ אֶת־יְהֹוָה כָּל־גּוֹיִם שַׁבְּחוּהוּ כָּל־הָאֻמִּים׃

2 for great is His steadfast love toward us; the faithfulness of Hashem endures forever. Hallelujah.

Ki gavar aleinu chasdo ve'emet-Adonai le'olam hallu-yah

כִּי גָבַר עָלֵינוּ חַסְדּוֹ וֶאֱמֶת־יְהֹוָה לְעוֹלָם הַלְלוּ־יָהּ׃

118

1 Praise Hashem, for He is good, His steadfast love is eternal.

hodu lAdonai ki-tov ki le'olam chasdo

הוֹדוּ לַיהֹוָה כִּי־טוֹב כִּי לְעוֹלָם חַסְדּוֹ׃

2 Let Yisrael declare, "His steadfast love is eternal."

Yomar-na yisra'el ki le'olam chasdo

יֹאמַר־נָא יִשְׂרָאֵל כִּי לְעוֹלָם חַסְדּוֹ׃

3 Let the house of Aharon declare, "His steadfast love is eternal."

Yomru-na veit-aharon ki le'olam chasdo

יֹאמְרוּ־נָא בֵית־אַהֲרֹן כִּי לְעוֹלָם חַסְדּוֹ׃

4 Let those who fear Hashem declare, "His steadfast love is eternal."

Yomru-na yir'ei Adonai ki le'olam chasdo

יֹאמְרוּ־נָא יִרְאֵי יְהֹוָה כִּי לְעוֹלָם חַסְדּוֹ׃

5	In distress I called on Hashem; Hashem answered me and brought me relief.	*Min-hammetzar karati yah anani vammerchav yah*

מִן־הַמֵּצַר קָרָאתִי יָּהּ עָנָנִי בַמֶּרְחָב יָהּ׃ ה

6	Hashem is on my side, I have no fear; what can man do to me?	*Adonai li lo ira mah-ya'aseh li adam*

יְהֹוָה לִי לֹא אִירָא מַה־יַּעֲשֶׂה לִי אָדָם׃ ו

7	With Hashem on my side as my helper, I will see the downfall of my foes.	*Adonai li be'ozerai va'ani er'eh vesone'ai*

יְהֹוָה לִי בְּעֹזְרָי וַאֲנִי אֶרְאֶה בְשֹׂנְאָי׃ ז

8	It is better to take refuge in Hashem than to trust in mortals;	*Tov lachasot bAdonai mibbetoach ba'adam*

טוֹב לַחֲסוֹת בַּיהֹוָה מִבְּטֹחַ בָּאָדָם׃ ח

9	it is better to take refuge in Hashem than to trust in the great.	*Tov lachasot bAdonai mibbetoach bindivim*

טוֹב לַחֲסוֹת בַּיהֹוָה מִבְּטֹחַ בִּנְדִיבִים׃ ט

10	All nations have beset me; by the name of Hashem I will surely cut them down.	*Kol-goyim sevavuni beshem Adonai ki amilam*

כׇּל־גּוֹיִם סְבָבוּנִי בְּשֵׁם יְהֹוָה כִּי אֲמִילַם׃ י

11	They beset me, they surround me; by the name of Hashem I will surely cut them down.	*Sabbuni gam-sevavuni beshem Adonai ki amilam*

סַבּוּנִי גַם־סְבָבוּנִי בְּשֵׁם יְהֹוָה כִּי אֲמִילַם׃ יא

12	They have beset me like bees; they shall be extinguished like burning thorns; by the name of Hashem I will surely cut them down.	*Sabbuni chidvorim do'achu ke'esh kotzim beshem Adonai ki amilam*

סַבּוּנִי כִדְבוֹרִים דֹּעֲכוּ כְּאֵשׁ קוֹצִים בְּשֵׁם יְהֹוָה כִּי אֲמִילַם׃ יב

13	You pressed me hard, I nearly fell; but Hashem helped me.	*Dachoh dechitani linpol vaihovah azarani*	דָּחֹה דְחִיתַנִי לִנְפֹּל וַיהֹוָה עֲזָרָנִי:	יג
14	Hashem is my strength and might; He has become my deliverance.	*Azzi vezimrat yah vayhi-li lishu'ah*	עׇזִּי וְזִמְרָת יָהּ וַיְהִי־לִי לִישׁוּעָה:	יד
15	The tents of the victorious resound with joyous shouts of deliverance, "The right hand of Hashem is triumphant!	*Kol rinnah vishu'ah be'oholei tzaddikim yemin Adonai osah chayil*	קוֹל רִנָּה וִישׁוּעָה בְּאׇהֳלֵי צַדִּיקִים יְמִין יְהֹוָה עֹשָׂה חָיִל:	טו
16	The right hand of Hashem is exalted! The right hand of Hashem is triumphant!"	*Yemin Adonai romemah yemin Adonai osah chayil*	יְמִין יְהֹוָה רוֹמֵמָה יְמִין יְהֹוָה עֹשָׂה חָיִל:	טז
17	I shall not die but live and proclaim the works of Hashem.	*Lo amut ki-echyeh va'asapper ma'asei yah*	לֹא אָמוּת כִּי־אֶחְיֶה וַאֲסַפֵּר מַעֲשֵׂי יָהּ:	יז
18	Hashem punished me severely, but did not hand me over to death.	*Yassor yisseranni yah velammavet lo netanani*	יַסֹּר יִסְּרַנִּי יָּהּ וְלַמָּוֶת לֹא נְתָנָנִי:	יח
19	Open the gates of victory for me that I may enter them and praise Hashem.	*Pitchu-li sha'arei-tzedek avo-vam odeh yah*	פִּתְחוּ־לִי שַׁעֲרֵי־צֶדֶק אָבֹא־בָם אוֹדֶה יָהּ:	יט
20	This is the gateway to Hashem— the victorious shall enter through it.	*Zeh-hasha'ar lAdonai tzaddikim yavo'u vo*	זֶה־הַשַּׁעַר לַיהֹוָה צַדִּיקִים יָבֹאוּ בוֹ:	כ

21	I praise You, for You have answered me, and have become my deliverance.	*Odcha ki anitani vattehi-li lishu'ah*	אוֹדְךָ כִּי עֲנִיתָנִי וַתְּהִי־לִי לִישׁוּעָה׃	כא
22	The stone that the builders rejected has become the chief cornerstone.	*Even ma'asu habbonim hayetah lerosh pinnah*	אֶבֶן מָאֲסוּ הַבּוֹנִים הָיְתָה לְרֹאשׁ פִּנָּה׃	כב
23	This is Hashem's doing; it is marvelous in our sight.	*Me'et Adonai hayetah zot hi niflat be'eineinu*	מֵאֵת יְהֹוָה הָיְתָה זֹּאת הִיא נִפְלָאת בְּעֵינֵינוּ׃	כג
24	This is the day that Hashem has made— let us exult and rejoice on it.	*Zeh-hayyom asah Adonai nagilah venismechah vo*	זֶה־הַיּוֹם עָשָׂה יְהֹוָה נָגִילָה וְנִשְׂמְחָה בוֹ׃	כד
25	Hashem, deliver us! Hashem, let us prosper!	*Anna Adonai hoshi'ah na anna Adonai hatzlichah na*	אָנָּא יְהֹוָה הוֹשִׁיעָה נָּא אָנָּא יְהֹוָה הַצְלִיחָה נָּא׃	כה
26	May he who enters be blessed in the name of Hashem; we bless you from the House of Hashem.	*Baruch habba beshem Adonai berachnuchem mibbeit Adonai*	בָּרוּךְ הַבָּא בְּשֵׁם יְהֹוָה בֵּרַכְנוּכֶם מִבֵּית יְהֹוָה׃	כו
27	Hashem is Hashem; He has given us light; bind the festal offering to the horns of the mizbayach with cords.	*El Adonai vayya'er lanu isru-chag ba'avotim ad-karnot hammizbeach*	אֵל יְהֹוָה וַיָּאֶר לָנוּ אִסְרוּ־חַג בַּעֲבֹתִים עַד־קַרְנוֹת הַמִּזְבֵּחַ׃	כז
28	You are my God and I will praise You; You are my God and I will extol You.	*Eli attah ve'odekka Elohai aromemekka*	אֵלִי אַתָּה וְאוֹדֶךָּ אֱלֹהַי אֲרוֹמְמֶךָּ׃	כח

29	Praise Hashem for He is good, His steadfast love is eternal.	*hodu lAdonai ki-tov ki le'olam chasdo*	הוֹדוּ לַיהֹוָה כִּי־טוֹב כִּי לְעוֹלָם חַסְדּוֹ:	כט

119

—o◦⧜◦o—

כיט

1	Happy are those whose way is blameless, who follow the teaching of Hashem.	*Ashrei temimei-darech haholechim betorat Adonai*	אַשְׁרֵי תְמִימֵי־דָרֶךְ הַהֹלְכִים בְּתוֹרַת יְהֹוָה:	א
2	Happy are those who observe His decrees, who turn to Him wholeheartedly.	*Ashrei notzerei edotav bechol-lev yidreshuhu*	אַשְׁרֵי נֹצְרֵי עֵדֹתָיו בְּכָל־לֵב יִדְרְשׁוּהוּ:	ב
3	They have done no wrong, but have followed His ways.	*Af lo-fa'alu avlah bidrachav halachu*	אַף לֹא־פָעֲלוּ עַוְלָה בִּדְרָכָיו הָלָכוּ:	ג
4	You have commanded that Your precepts be kept diligently.	*Attah tzivvitah fikkudeicha lishmor me'od*	אַתָּה צִוִּיתָה פִקֻּדֶיךָ לִשְׁמֹר מְאֹד:	ד
5	Would that my ways were firm in keeping Your laws;	*Achalai yikkonu derachai lishmor chukkeicha*	אַחֲלַי יִכֹּנוּ דְרָכָי לִשְׁמֹר חֻקֶּיךָ:	ה
6	then I would not be ashamed when I regard all Your commandments.	*Az lo-evosh behabbiti el-kol-mitzvteicha*	אָז לֹא־אֵבוֹשׁ בְּהַבִּיטִי אֶל־כָּל־מִצְוֹתֶיךָ:	ו

7	I will praise You with a sincere heart as I learn Your just rules.	*Odcha beyosher levav belamedi mishpetei tzidkecha*	אוֹדְךָ בְּיֹשֶׁר לֵבָב בְּלָמְדִי מִשְׁפְּטֵי צִדְקֶךָ:	ז
8	I will keep Your laws; do not utterly forsake me.	*Et-chukkeicha eshmor al-ta'azveni ad-me'od*	אֶת־חֻקֶּיךָ אֶשְׁמֹר אַל־תַּעַזְבֵנִי עַד־מְאֹד:	ח
9	How can a young man keep his way pure?— by holding to Your word.	*Bammeh yezakkeh-na'ar et-orcho lishmor kidvarecha*	בַּמֶּה יְזַכֶּה־נַּעַר אֶת־אָרְחוֹ לִשְׁמֹר כִּדְבָרֶךָ:	ט
10	I have turned to You with all my heart; do not let me stray from Your commandments.	*Bechol-libbi derashticha al-tashgeni mimmitzvteicha*	בְּכָל־לִבִּי דְרַשְׁתִּיךָ אַל־תַּשְׁגֵּנִי מִמִּצְוֹתֶיךָ:	י
11	In my heart I treasure Your promise; therefore I do not sin against You.	*Belibbi tzafanti imratecha lema'an lo echeta-lach*	בְּלִבִּי צָפַנְתִּי אִמְרָתֶךָ לְמַעַן לֹא אֶחֱטָא־לָךְ:	יא
12	Blessed are You, Hashem; train me in Your laws.	*Baruch attah Adonai lammedeni chukkeicha*	בָּרוּךְ אַתָּה יְהֹוָה לַמְּדֵנִי חֻקֶּיךָ:	יב
13	With my lips I rehearse all the rules You proclaimed.	*Bisfatai sipparti kol mishpetei-ficha*	בִּשְׂפָתַי סִפַּרְתִּי כֹּל מִשְׁפְּטֵי־פִיךָ:	יג
14	I rejoice over the way of Your decrees as over all riches.	*Bederech edevteicha sasti ke'al kol-hon*	בְּדֶרֶךְ עֵדְוֹתֶיךָ שַׂשְׂתִּי כְּעַל כָּל־הוֹן:	יד
15	I study Your precepts; I regard Your ways;	*Befikkudecha asichah ve'abbitah orchoteicha*	בְּפִקֻּדֶיךָ אָשִׂיחָה וְאַבִּיטָה אֹרְחֹתֶיךָ:	טו

16	I take delight in Your laws; I will not neglect Your word.	*Bechukkotecha eshta'asha lo eshkach devarecha*	בְּחֻקֹּתֶיךָ אֶשְׁתַּעֲשָׁע לֹא אֶשְׁכַּח דְּבָרֶךָ:	טז
17	Deal kindly with Your servant, that I may live to keep Your word.	*Gemol al-avdecha echyeh ve'eshmerah devarecha*	גְּמֹל עַל־עַבְדְּךָ אֶחְיֶה וְאֶשְׁמְרָה דְּבָרֶךָ:	יז
18	Open my eyes, that I may perceive the wonders of Your teaching.	*Gal-einai ve'abbitah nifla'ot mittoratecha*	גַּל־עֵינַי וְאַבִּיטָה נִפְלָאוֹת מִתּוֹרָתֶךָ:	יח
19	I am only a sojourner in the land; do not hide Your commandments from me.	*Ger anochi va'aretz al-taster mimmenni mitzvotecha*	גֵּר אָנֹכִי בָאָרֶץ אַל־תַּסְתֵּר מִמֶּנִּי מִצְוֹתֶיךָ:	יט
20	My soul is consumed with longing for Your rules at all times.	*Garesah nafshi leta'avah el-mishpatecha vechol-et*	גָּרְסָה נַפְשִׁי לְתַאֲבָה אֶל־מִשְׁפָּטֶיךָ בְכָל־עֵת:	כ
21	You blast the accursed insolent ones who stray from Your commandments.	*Ga'arta zedim arurim hashogim mimmitzvotecha*	גָּעַרְתָּ זֵדִים אֲרוּרִים הַשֹּׁגִים מִמִּצְוֹתֶיךָ:	כא
22	Take away from me taunt and abuse, because I observe Your decrees.	*Gal me'alai cherpah vavuz ki edotecha natzareti*	גַּל מֵעָלַי חֶרְפָּה וָבוּז כִּי עֵדֹתֶיךָ נָצָרְתִּי:	כב
23	Though princes meet and speak against me, Your servant studies Your laws.	*Gam yashvu sarim bi nidbaru avdecha yasiach bechukkecha*	גַּם יָשְׁבוּ שָׂרִים בִּי נִדְבָּרוּ עַבְדְּךָ יָשִׂיחַ בְּחֻקֶּיךָ:	כג

24	For Your decrees are my delight, my intimate companions.	*Gam-edotecha sha'ashu'ai anshei atzati*	גַּם־עֵדֹתֶיךָ שַׁעֲשֻׁעָי אַנְשֵׁי עֲצָתִי:	כד
25	My soul clings to the dust; revive me in accordance with Your word.	*Davk'ah le'afar nafshi chayyeni kidvarecha*	דָּבְקָה לֶעָפָר נַפְשִׁי חַיֵּנִי כִּדְבָרֶךָ:	כה
26	I have declared my way, and You have answered me; train me in Your laws.	*Derachai sipparti vatta'aneni lammdeni chukkeicha*	דְּרָכַי סִפַּרְתִּי וַתַּעֲנֵנִי לַמְּדֵנִי חֻקֶּיךָ:	כו
27	Make me understand the way of Your precepts, that I may study Your wondrous acts.	*Derech-pikkudeicha havineni ve'asichah benifle'otecha*	דֶּרֶךְ־פִּקּוּדֶיךָ הֲבִינֵנִי וְאָשִׂיחָה בְּנִפְלְאוֹתֶיךָ:	כז
28	I am racked with grief; sustain me in accordance with Your word.	*Dalfah nafshi mittugah kayyemeni kidvarecha*	דָּלְפָה נַפְשִׁי מִתּוּגָה קַיְּמֵנִי כִּדְבָרֶךָ:	כח
29	Remove all false ways from me; favor me with Your teaching.	*Derech-sheker haser mimmenni vetoratcha channeni*	דֶּרֶךְ־שֶׁקֶר הָסֵר מִמֶּנִּי וְתוֹרָתְךָ חָנֵּנִי:	כט
30	I have chosen the way of faithfulness; I have set Your rules before me.	*Derech-emunah vachareti mishpateicha shivviti*	דֶּרֶךְ־אֱמוּנָה בָחָרְתִּי מִשְׁפָּטֶיךָ שִׁוִּיתִי:	ל
31	I cling to Your decrees; Hashem, do not put me to shame.	*Davakti ve'edevotecha Adonai al-tevisheni*	דָּבַקְתִּי בְעֵדְוֹתֶיךָ יְהוָה אַל־תְּבִישֵׁנִי:	לא

32	I eagerly pursue Your commandments, for You broaden my understanding.	*Derech-mitzvotecha arutz ki tarchiv libbi*	דֶּרֶךְ־מִצְוֹתֶיךָ אָרוּץ כִּי תַרְחִיב לִבִּי:	לב
33	Teach me, Hashem, the way of Your laws; I will observe them to the utmost.	*Horeni Adonai derech chukkeicha ve'etzrennah aykev*	הוֹרֵנִי יְהֹוָה דֶּרֶךְ חֻקֶּיךָ וְאֶצְּרֶנָּה עֵקֶב:	לג
34	Give me understanding, that I may observe Your teaching and keep it wholeheartedly.	*Havineni ve'etzerah toratecha ve'eshmerennah vechol-lev*	הֲבִינֵנִי וְאֶצְּרָה תוֹרָתֶךָ וְאֶשְׁמְרֶנָּה בְכָל־לֵב:	לד
35	Lead me in the path of Your commandments, for that is my concern.	*Hadricheni bintiv mitzvotecha ki-vo chafatzeti*	הַדְרִיכֵנִי בִּנְתִיב מִצְוֹתֶיךָ כִּי־בוֹ חָפָצְתִּי:	לה
36	Turn my heart to Your decrees and not to love of gain.	*Hat-libbi el-edevotecha ve'al el-batza*	הַט־לִבִּי אֶל־עֵדְוֹתֶיךָ וְאַל אֶל־בָּצַע:	לו
37	Avert my eyes from seeing falsehood; by Your ways preserve me.	*Ha'aver einai mere'ot shov bidrachecha chayyeni*	הַעֲבֵר עֵינַי מֵרְאוֹת שָׁוְא בִּדְרָכֶךָ חַיֵּנִי:	לז
38	Fulfill Your promise to Your servant, which is for those who worship You.	*Hakem le'avdecha imratecha asher leyir'atecha*	הָקֵם לְעַבְדְּךָ אִמְרָתֶךָ אֲשֶׁר לְיִרְאָתֶךָ:	לח
39	Remove the taunt that I dread, for Your rules are good.	*Ha'aver cherpati asher yagoreti ki mishpateicha tovim*	הַעֲבֵר חֶרְפָּתִי אֲשֶׁר יָגֹרְתִּי כִּי מִשְׁפָּטֶיךָ טוֹבִים:	לט

40	See, I have longed for Your precepts; by Your righteousness preserve me.	*Hinneh ta'avti lefikkudeicha betzidkatcha chayyeni*	הִנֵּה תָּאַבְתִּי לְפִקֻּדֶיךָ בְּצִדְקָתְךָ חַיֵּנִי׃	מ
41	May Your steadfast love reach me, Hashem, Your deliverance, as You have promised.	*Vivo'uni chasadecha Adonai teshu'atecha ke'imratecha*	וִיבֹאֻנִי חֲסָדֶךָ יְהֹוָה תְּשׁוּעָתְךָ כְּאִמְרָתֶךָ׃	מא
42	I shall have an answer for those who taunt me, for I have put my trust in Your word.	*Ve'e'eneh chorefi davar ki-vatachti bidvarecha*	וְאֶעֱנֶה חֹרְפִי דָבָר כִּי־בָטַחְתִּי בִּדְבָרֶךָ׃	מב
43	Do not utterly take the truth away from my mouth, for I have put my hope in Your rules.	*Ve'al-tatzel mippi devar-emet ad-me'od ki lemishpatecha yichaleti*	וְאַל־תַּצֵּל מִפִּי דְבַר־אֱמֶת עַד־מְאֹד כִּי לְמִשְׁפָּטֶךָ יִחָלְתִּי׃	מג
44	I will always obey Your teaching, forever and ever.	*Ve'eshmerah toratcha tamid le'olam va'ed*	וְאֶשְׁמְרָה תוֹרָתְךָ תָמִיד לְעוֹלָם וָעֶד׃	מד
45	I will walk about at ease, for I have turned to Your precepts.	*Ve'ethallechah varechavah ki fikkudeicha darasheti*	וְאֶתְהַלְּכָה בָרְחָבָה כִּי פִקֻּדֶיךָ דָרָשְׁתִּי׃	מה
46	I will speak of Your decrees, and not be ashamed in the presence of kings.	*Va'adabberah ve'edoteicha neged melachim velo evosh*	וַאֲדַבְּרָה בְעֵדֹתֶיךָ נֶגֶד מְלָכִים וְלֹא אֵבוֹשׁ׃	מו
47	I will delight in Your commandments, which I love.	*Ve'eshta'asha bemitzvotecha asher ahaveti*	וְאֶשְׁתַּעֲשַׁע בְּמִצְוֺתֶיךָ אֲשֶׁר אָהָבְתִּי׃	מז

48	I reach out for Your commandments, which I love; I study Your laws.	*Ve'essa-chappai el-mitzvotecha asher ahaveti ve'asichah vechukkeicha*	וְאֶשָּׂא־כַפַּי אֶל־מִצְוֺתֶיךָ אֲשֶׁר אָהָבְתִּי וְאָשִׂיחָה בְחֻקֶּיךָ:	מח
49	Remember Your word to Your servant through which You have given me hope.	*Zechor-davar le'avdecha al asher yichaltani*	זְכֹר־דָּבָר לְעַבְדֶּךָ עַל אֲשֶׁר יִחַלְתָּנִי:	מט
50	This is my comfort in my affliction, that Your promise has preserved me.	*Zot nechamati ve'aneyi ki imratcha chiyyateni*	זֹאת נֶחָמָתִי בְעָנְיִי כִּי אִמְרָתְךָ חִיָּתְנִי:	נ
51	Though the arrogant have cruelly mocked me, I have not swerved from Your teaching.	*Zaydim helitzuni ad-me'od mittoratcha lo natiti*	זֵדִים הֱלִיצֻנִי עַד־מְאֹד מִתּוֹרָתְךָ לֹא נָטִיתִי:	נא
52	I remember Your rules of old, Hashem, and find comfort in them.	*Zacharti mishpatecha me'olam Adonai va'etnecham*	זָכַרְתִּי מִשְׁפָּטֶיךָ מֵעוֹלָם יְהֹוָה וָאֶתְנֶחָם:	נב
53	I am seized with rage because of the wicked who forsake Your teaching.	*Zal'afah achazatni meresha'im ozevei toratecha*	זַלְעָפָה אֲחָזַתְנִי מֵרְשָׁעִים עֹזְבֵי תוֹרָתֶךָ:	נג
54	Your laws are a source of strength to me wherever I may dwell.	*Zemirot hayu-li chukkeicha beveit megurai*	זְמִרוֹת הָיוּ־לִי חֻקֶּיךָ בְּבֵית מְגוּרָי:	נד
55	I remember Your name at night, Hashem, and obey Your teaching.	*Zacharti vallaylah shimcha Adonai va'eshmerah toratecha*	זָכַרְתִּי בַלַּיְלָה שִׁמְךָ יְהֹוָה וָאֶשְׁמְרָה תּוֹרָתֶךָ:	נה

56	This has been my lot, for I have observed Your precepts.	*Zot hayetah-li ki fikkudeicha natzareti*	זֹאת הָיְתָה־לִּי כִּי פִקֻּדֶיךָ נָצָרְתִּי:	נו
57	Hashem is my portion; I have resolved to keep Your words.	*Chelki Adonai amarti lishmor devareicha*	חֶלְקִי יְהֹוָה אָמַרְתִּי לִשְׁמֹר דְּבָרֶיךָ:	נז
58	I have implored You with all my heart; have mercy on me, in accordance with Your promise.	*Chilliti fanecha vechol-lev channeni ke'imratecha*	חִלִּיתִי פָנֶיךָ בְכָל־לֵב חָנֵּנִי כְּאִמְרָתֶךָ:	נח
59	I have considered my ways, and have turned back to Your decrees.	*Chishavti derachai va'ashivah raglai el-edotecha*	חִשַּׁבְתִּי דְרָכָי וָאָשִׁיבָה רַגְלַי אֶל־עֵדֹתֶיךָ:	נט
60	I have hurried and not delayed to keep Your commandments.	*Chashti velo hitmahmaheti lishmor mitzvotecha*	חַשְׁתִּי וְלֹא הִתְמַהְמָהְתִּי לִשְׁמֹר מִצְוֺתֶיךָ:	ס
61	Though the bonds of the wicked are coiled round me, I have not neglected Your teaching.	*Chevlei resha'im ivveduni toratecha lo shachacheti*	חֶבְלֵי רְשָׁעִים עִוְּדֻנִי תּוֹרָתְךָ לֹא שָׁכָחְתִּי:	סא
62	I arise at midnight to praise You for Your just rules.	*Chatzot-layyelah akum lehodot lach al mishpetei tzidkecha*	חֲצוֹת־לַיְלָה אָקוּם לְהוֹדוֹת לָךְ עַל מִשְׁפְּטֵי צִדְקֶךָ:	סב
63	I am a companion to all who fear You, to those who keep Your precepts.	*Chaver ani lechol-asher yere'ucha uleshomerei pikkudecha*	חָבֵר אָנִי לְכָל־אֲשֶׁר יְרֵאוּךָ וּלְשֹׁמְרֵי פִּקּוּדֶיךָ:	סג

64	Your steadfast love, Hashem, fills the earth; teach me Your laws.	*Chasdecha Adonai mal'ah ha'aretz chukkecha lammedeni*	חַסְדְּךָ יְהֹוָה מָלְאָה הָאָרֶץ חֻקֶּיךָ לַמְּדֵנִי:	סד
65	You have treated Your servant well, according to Your word, Hashem.	*Tov asita im-avdecha Adonai kidvarecha*	טוֹב עָשִׂיתָ עִם־עַבְדְּךָ יְהֹוָה כִּדְבָרֶךָ:	סה
66	Teach me good sense and knowledge, for I have put my trust in Your commandments.	*Tuv ta'am vada'at lammedeni ki vemitzvotecha he'emaneti*	טוּב טַעַם וָדַעַת לַמְּדֵנִי כִּי בְמִצְוֺתֶיךָ הֶאֱמָנְתִּי:	סו
67	Before I was humbled I went astray, but now I keep Your word.	*Terem e'eneh ani shogeg ve'attah imratecha shamareti*	טֶרֶם אֶעֱנֶה אֲנִי שֹׁגֵג וְעַתָּה אִמְרָתְךָ שָׁמָרְתִּי:	סז
68	You are good and beneficent; teach me Your laws.	*Tov-attah umetiv lammedeni chukkecha*	טוֹב־אַתָּה וּמֵטִיב לַמְּדֵנִי חֻקֶּיךָ:	סח
69	Though the arrogant have accused me falsely, I observe Your precepts wholeheartedly.	*Taflu alai sheker zaydim ani bechol-lev etzor pikkudecha*	טָפְלוּ עָלַי שֶׁקֶר זֵדִים אֲנִי בְּכָל־לֵב אֶצֹּר פִּקּוּדֶיךָ:	סט
70	Their minds are thick like fat; as for me, Your teaching is my delight.	*Tafash kachelev libbam ani toratcha shi'asha'eti*	טָפַשׁ כַּחֵלֶב לִבָּם אֲנִי תוֹרָתְךָ שִׁעֲשָׁעְתִּי:	ע
71	It was good for me that I was humbled, so that I might learn Your laws.	*Tov-li chi-unneiti lema'an elmad chukkecha*	טוֹב־לִי כִי־עֻנֵּיתִי לְמַעַן אֶלְמַד חֻקֶּיךָ:	עא
72	I prefer the teaching You proclaimed to thousands of gold and silver pieces.	*Tov-li torat-picha me'alfei zahav vachasef*	טוֹב־לִי תוֹרַת־פִּיךָ מֵאַלְפֵי זָהָב וָכָסֶף:	עב

73	Your hands made me and fashioned me; give me understanding that I may learn Your commandments.	*Yadecha asuni vaychonenuni havineni ve'elmedah mitzvotecha*	יָדֶיךָ עָשׂוּנִי וַיְכוֹנְנוּנִי הֲבִינֵנִי וְאֶלְמְדָה מִצְוֺתֶיךָ׃	עג
74	Those who fear You will see me and rejoice, for I have put my hope in Your word.	*Yere'eicha yir'uni veyismachu ki lidvarecha yichaleti*	יְרֵאֶיךָ יִרְאוּנִי וְיִשְׂמָחוּ כִּי לִדְבָרְךָ יִחָלְתִּי׃	עד
75	I know, Hashem, that Your rulings are just; rightly have You humbled me.	*Yada'ti Adonai ki-tzedek mishpatecha ve'emunah innitani*	יָדַעְתִּי יְהֹוָה כִּי־צֶדֶק מִשְׁפָּטֶיךָ וֶאֱמוּנָה עִנִּיתָנִי׃	עה
76	May Your steadfast love comfort me in accordance with Your promise to Your servant.	*Yehi-na chasdecha lenachameni ke'imratecha le'avdecha*	יְהִי־נָא חַסְדְּךָ לְנַחֲמֵנִי כְּאִמְרָתְךָ לְעַבְדֶּךָ׃	עו
77	May Your mercy reach me, that I might live, for Your teaching is my delight.	*Yevo'uni rachamecha ve'echyeh ki-toratecha sha'ashu'ai*	יְבֹאוּנִי רַחֲמֶיךָ וְאֶחְיֶה כִּי־תוֹרָתְךָ שַׁעֲשֻׁעָי׃	עז
78	Let the insolent be dismayed, for they have wronged me without cause; I will study Your precepts.	*Yevoshu zedim ki-sheker ivvetuni ani asiach befikkudecha*	יֵבֹשׁוּ זֵדִים כִּי־שֶׁקֶר עִוְּתוּנִי אֲנִי אָשִׂיחַ בְּפִקּוּדֶיךָ׃	עח
79	May those who fear You, those who know Your decrees, turn again to me.	*Yashuvu li yere'eicha veyode'ei edotecha*	יָשׁוּבוּ לִי יְרֵאֶיךָ וידעו [וְיֹדְעֵי] עֵדֹתֶיךָ׃	עט

80	May I wholeheartedly follow Your laws so that I do not come to grief.	*Yehi-libbi tamim bechukkecha lema'an lo evosh*	יְהִי־לִבִּי תָמִים בְּחֻקֶּיךָ לְמַעַן לֹא אֵבוֹשׁ:	פ
81	I long for Your deliverance; I hope for Your word.	*Kaltah litshu'atcha nafshi lidvarcha yichaleti*	כָּלְתָה לִתְשׁוּעָתְךָ נַפְשִׁי לִדְבָרְךָ יִחָלְתִּי:	פא
82	My eyes pine away for Your promise; I say, "When will You comfort me?"	*Kalu einai le'imratecha laymor matai tenachamayni*	כָּלוּ עֵינַי לְאִמְרָתֶךָ לֵאמֹר מָתַי תְּנַחֲמֵנִי:	פב
83	Though I have become like a water-skin dried in smoke, I have not neglected Your laws.	*Ki-hayiti kenod bekitor chukkeicha lo shachachti*	כִּי־הָיִיתִי כְּנֹאד בְּקִיטוֹר חֻקֶּיךָ לֹא שָׁכָחְתִּי:	פג
84	How long has Your servant to live? when will You bring my persecutors to judgment?	*Kammah yemei-avdecha matai ta'aseh verodefai mishpat*	כַּמָּה יְמֵי־עַבְדֶּךָ מָתַי תַּעֲשֶׂה בְרֹדְפַי מִשְׁפָּט:	פד
85	The insolent have dug pits for me, flouting Your teaching.	*Karu-li zaydim shichot asher lo chetoratecha*	כָּרוּ־לִי זֵדִים שִׁיחוֹת אֲשֶׁר לֹא כְתוֹרָתֶךָ:	פה
86	All Your commandments are enduring; I am persecuted without cause; help me!	*Kol-mitzvotecha emunah sheker redafuni azereni*	כָּל־מִצְוֹתֶיךָ אֱמוּנָה שֶׁקֶר רְדָפוּנִי עָזְרֵנִי:	פו
87	Though they almost wiped me off the earth, I did not abandon Your precepts.	*Kim'at killuni va'aretz va'ani lo-azavti fikkuvdeicha*	כִּמְעַט כִּלּוּנִי בָאָרֶץ וַאֲנִי לֹא־עָזַבְתִּי פִקּוּדֶיךָ:	פז

315

88	As befits Your steadfast love, preserve me, so that I may keep the decree You proclaimed.	*Kechasdecha chayyeni ve'eshmerah edut picha*	כְּחַסְדְּךָ חַיֵּנִי וְאֶשְׁמְרָה עֵדוּת פִּיךָ:	פח
89	Hashem exists forever; Your word stands firm in heaven.	*Le'olam Adonai devarecha nitzav bashamayim*	לְעוֹלָם יְהֹוָה דְּבָרְךָ נִצָּב בַּשָּׁמָיִם:	פט
90	Your faithfulness is for all generations; You have established the earth, and it stands.	*Ledor vador emunatecha konanta eretz vatta'amod*	לְדֹר וָדֹר אֱמוּנָתֶךָ כּוֹנַנְתָּ אֶרֶץ וַתַּעֲמֹד:	צ
91	They stand this day to [carry out] Your rulings, for all are Your servants.	*Lemishpateicha amedu hayyom ki hakkol avadeicha*	לְמִשְׁפָּטֶיךָ עָמְדוּ הַיּוֹם כִּי הַכֹּל עֲבָדֶיךָ:	צא
92	Were not Your teaching my delight I would have perished in my affliction.	*Lulei toratecha sha'ashu'ai az avadti ve'aneyi*	לוּלֵי תוֹרָתְךָ שַׁעֲשֻׁעָי אָז אָבַדְתִּי בְעָנְיִי:	צב
93	I will never neglect Your precepts, for You have preserved my life through them.	*Le'olam lo-eshkach pikkudecha ki vam chiyyitani*	לְעוֹלָם לֹא־אֶשְׁכַּח פִּקּוּדֶיךָ כִּי בָם חִיִּיתָנִי:	צג
94	I am Yours; save me! For I have turned to Your precepts.	*Lecha-ani hoshi'eni ki fikkudecha darasheti*	לְךָ־אֲנִי הוֹשִׁיעֵנִי כִּי פִקּוּדֶיךָ דָרָשְׁתִּי:	צד
95	The wicked hope to destroy me, but I ponder Your decrees.	*Li kioo resha'im le'abbedeni edotecha etbonan*	לִי קִוּוּ רְשָׁעִים לְאַבְּדֵנִי עֵדֹתֶיךָ אֶתְבּוֹנָן:	צה

96	I have seen that all things have their limit, but Your commandment is broad beyond measure.	*Lechol tichlah ra'iti ketz rechavah mitzvatecha me'od*	לְכָל תִּכְלָה רָאִיתִי קֵץ רְחָבָה מִצְוָתְךָ מְאֹד:	צו
97	O how I love Your teaching! It is my study all day long.	*Mah-ahavti toratecha kol-hayyom hi sichati*	מָה־אָהַבְתִּי תוֹרָתֶךָ כָּל־הַיּוֹם הִיא שִׂיחָתִי:	צז
98	Your commandments make me wiser than my enemies; they always stand by me.	*Me'oyevai techakkemeni mitzvotecha ki le'olam hi-li*	מֵאֹיְבַי תְּחַכְּמֵנִי מִצְוֹתֶךָ כִּי לְעוֹלָם הִיא־לִי:	צח
99	I have gained more insight than all my teachers, for Your decrees are my study.	*Mikkol-melammedai hiskalti ki edevotecha sichah li*	מִכָּל־מְלַמְּדַי הִשְׂכַּלְתִּי כִּי עֵדְוֹתֶיךָ שִׂיחָה לִי:	צט
100	I have gained more understanding than my elders, for I observe Your precepts.	*Mizzkaynim etbonan ki fikkudecha natzareti*	מִזְּקֵנִים אֶתְבּוֹנָן כִּי פִקּוּדֶיךָ נָצָרְתִּי:	ק
101	I have avoided every evil way so that I may keep Your word.	*Mikkol-orach ra kaliti raglai lema'an eshmor devarecha*	מִכָּל־אֹרַח רָע כָּלִאתִי רַגְלָי לְמַעַן אֶשְׁמֹר דְּבָרֶךָ:	קא
102	I have not departed from Your rules, for You have instructed me.	*Mimmishpatecha lo-sarti ki-attah horetani*	מִמִּשְׁפָּטֶיךָ לֹא־סָרְתִּי כִּי־אַתָּה הוֹרֵתָנִי:	קב
103	How pleasing is Your word to my palate, sweeter than honey.	*Mah-nimletzu lechikki imratecha middevash lefi*	מַה־נִּמְלְצוּ לְחִכִּי אִמְרָתֶךָ מִדְּבַשׁ לְפִי:	קג

104	I ponder Your precepts; therefore I hate every false way.	*Mippikkudeicha etbonan al-ken saneti kol-orach shaker*	מִפִּקּוּדֶיךָ אֶתְבּוֹנָן עַל־כֵּן שָׂנֵאתִי כָּל־אֹרַח שָׁקֶר:	קד
105	Your word is a lamp to my feet, a light for my path.	*Ner-leragli devarecha ve'or lintivati*	נֵר־לְרַגְלִי דְבָרֶךָ וְאוֹר לִנְתִיבָתִי:	קה
106	I have firmly sworn to keep Your just rules.	*Nishba'ti va'akayyemah lishmor mishpetei tzidkecha*	נִשְׁבַּעְתִּי וָאֲקַיֵּמָה לִשְׁמֹר מִשְׁפְּטֵי צִדְקֶךָ:	קו
107	I am very much afflicted; Hashem, preserve me in accordance with Your word.	*Na'aneiti ad-me'od Adonai chayyeni chidvarecha*	נַעֲנֵיתִי עַד־מְאֹד יְהֹוָה חַיֵּנִי כִדְבָרֶךָ:	קז
108	Accept, Hashem, my freewill offerings; teach me Your rules.	*Nidvot pi retzay-na Adonai umishpateicha lammedeni*	נִדְבוֹת פִּי רְצֵה־נָא יְהֹוָה וּמִשְׁפָּטֶיךָ לַמְּדֵנִי:	קח
109	Though my life is always in danger, I do not neglect Your teaching.	*Nafshi vechappi tamid vetoratecha lo shachacheti*	נַפְשִׁי בְכַפִּי תָמִיד וְתוֹרָתְךָ לֹא שָׁכָחְתִּי:	קט
110	Though the wicked have set a trap for me, I have not strayed from Your precepts.	*Natnu resha'im pach li umippikkudecha lo ta'iti*	נָתְנוּ רְשָׁעִים פַּח לִי וּמִפִּקּוּדֶיךָ לֹא תָעִיתִי:	קי
111	Your decrees are my eternal heritage; they are my heart's delight.	*Nachalti edevotecha le'olam ki-seson libbi hemmah*	נָחַלְתִּי עֵדְוֹתֶיךָ לְעוֹלָם כִּי־שְׂשׂוֹן לִבִּי הֵמָּה:	קיא
112	I am resolved to follow Your laws to the utmost forever.	*Natiti libbi la'asot chukkecha le'olam ekev*	נָטִיתִי לִבִּי לַעֲשׂוֹת חֻקֶּיךָ לְעוֹלָם עֵקֶב:	קיב

113	I hate men of divided heart, but I love Your teaching.	*Se'afim saneti vetoratcha ahaveti*	סֵעֲפִים שָׂנֵאתִי וְתוֹרָתְךָ אָהָבְתִּי:	קיג
114	You are my protection and my shield; I hope for Your word.	*Sitri umaginni attah lidvarecha yichaleti*	סִתְרִי וּמָגִנִּי אָתָּה לִדְבָרְךָ יִחָלְתִּי:	קיד
115	Keep away from me, you evildoers, that I may observe the commandments of my God.	*Suru-mimmenni mere'im ve'etzerah mitzvot Elohai*	סוּרוּ־מִמֶּנִּי מְרֵעִים וְאֶצְּרָה מִצְוֹת אֱלֹהָי:	קטו
116	Support me as You promised, so that I may live; do not thwart my expectation.	*Samecheni che'imratcha ve'echyeh ve'al-tevisheni missivri*	סָמְכֵנִי כְאִמְרָתְךָ וְאֶחְיֶה וְאַל־תְּבִישֵׁנִי מִשִּׂבְרִי:	קטז
117	Sustain me that I may be saved, and I will always muse upon Your laws.	*Se'adeni ve'ivvashe'ah ve'esh'ah vechukkeicha tamid*	סְעָדֵנִי וְאִוָּשֵׁעָה וְאֶשְׁעָה בְחֻקֶּיךָ תָמִיד:	קיז
118	You reject all who stray from Your laws, for they are false and deceitful.	*Salita kol-shogim mechukkecha ki-sheker tarmitam*	סָלִיתָ כָּל־שׁוֹגִים מֵחֻקֶּיךָ כִּי־שֶׁקֶר תַּרְמִיתָם:	קיח
119	You do away with the wicked as if they were dross; rightly do I love Your decrees.	*Sigim hishbatta chol-rish'ei-aretz lachen ahavti edotecha*	סִגִים הִשְׁבַּתָּ כָל־רִשְׁעֵי־אָרֶץ לָכֵן אָהַבְתִּי עֵדֹתֶיךָ:	קיט
120	My flesh creeps from fear of You; I am in awe of Your rulings.	*Samar mippachdecha vesari umimmishpatecha yareti*	סָמַר מִפַּחְדְּךָ בְשָׂרִי וּמִמִּשְׁפָּטֶיךָ יָרֵאתִי:	קכ

319

121	I have done what is just and right; do not abandon me to those who would wrong me.	*Asiti mishpat vatzedek bal-tannicheni le'oshekai*	עָשִׂיתִי מִשְׁפָּט וָצֶדֶק בַּל־תַּנִּיחֵנִי לְעֹשְׁקָי:	קכא
122	Guarantee Your servant's well-being; do not let the arrogant wrong me.	*Arov avdecha letov al-ya'ashkuni zaydim*	עֲרֹב עַבְדְּךָ לְטוֹב אַל־יַעַשְׁקֻנִי זֵדִים:	קכב
123	My eyes pine away for Your deliverance, for Your promise of victory.	*Einai kalu lishu'atecha ule'imrat tzidkecha*	עֵינַי כָּלוּ לִישׁוּעָתֶךָ וּלְאִמְרַת צִדְקֶךָ:	קכג
124	Deal with Your servant as befits Your steadfast love; teach me Your laws.	*Aseh im-avdecha chechasdecha vechukkeicha lammedeni*	עֲשֵׂה עִם־עַבְדְּךָ כְחַסְדֶּךָ וְחֻקֶּיךָ לַמְּדֵנִי:	קכד
125	I am Your servant; give me understanding, that I might know Your decrees.	*Avdecha-ani havineni ve'ede'ah edotecha*	עַבְדְּךָ־אָנִי הֲבִינֵנִי וְאֵדְעָה עֵדֹתֶיךָ:	קכה
126	It is a time to act for Hashem, for they have violated Your teaching.	*Et la'asot lAdonai heferu toratecha*	עֵת לַעֲשׂוֹת לַיהֹוָה הֵפֵרוּ תּוֹרָתֶךָ:	קכו
127	Rightly do I love Your commandments more than gold, even fine gold.	*Al-ken ahavti mitzvotecha mizzahav umippaz*	עַל־כֵּן אָהַבְתִּי מִצְוֹתֶיךָ מִזָּהָב וּמִפָּז:	קכז
128	Truly by all [Your] precepts I walk straight; I hate every false way.	*Al-ken kol-pikkudei chol yishareti kol-orach sheker saneti*	עַל־כֵּן כָּל־פִּקּוּדֵי כֹל יִשָּׁרְתִּי כָּל־אֹרַח שֶׁקֶר שָׂנֵאתִי:	קכח

129	Your decrees are wondrous; rightly do I observe them.	*Pela'ot edevotecha al-ken netzaratam nafshi*	פְּלָאוֹת עֵדְוֺתֶיךָ עַל־כֵּן נְצָרָתַם נַפְשִׁי׃	קכט
130	The words You inscribed give light, and grant understanding to the simple.	*Petach devareicha ya'ir mevin petayim*	פֵּתַח דְּבָרֶיךָ יָאִיר מֵבִין פְּתָיִים׃	קל
131	I open my mouth wide, I pant, longing for Your commandments.	*Pi-fa'arti va'esh'afah ki lemitzvotecha ya'avti*	פִּי־פָעַרְתִּי וָאֶשְׁאָפָה כִּי לְמִצְוֺתֶיךָ יָאָבְתִּי׃	קלא
132	Turn to me and be gracious to me, as is Your rule with those who love Your name.	*Peneh-elai vechanneni kemishpat le'ohavei shemecha*	פְּנֵה־אֵלַי וְחׇנֵּנִי כְּמִשְׁפָּט לְאֹהֲבֵי שְׁמֶךָ׃	קלב
133	Make my feet firm through Your promise; do not let iniquity dominate me.	*Pe'amai hachen be'imratecha ve'al-tashlet-bi chol-aven*	פְּעָמַי הָכֵן בְּאִמְרָתֶךָ וְאַל־תַּשְׁלֶט־בִּי כָל־אָוֶן׃	קלג
134	Redeem me from being wronged by man, that I may keep Your precepts.	*Pedeni me'oshek adam ve'eshmerah pikkudecha*	פְּדֵנִי מֵעֹשֶׁק אָדָם וְאֶשְׁמְרָה פִּקּוּדֶיךָ׃	קלד
135	Show favor to Your servant, and teach me Your laws.	*panecha ha'er be'avdecha velammedeni et-chukkecha*	פָּנֶיךָ הָאֵר בְּעַבְדֶּךָ וְלַמְּדֵנִי אֶת־חֻקֶּיךָ׃	קלה
136	My eyes shed streams of water because men do not obey Your teaching.	*Palgei-mayim yaredu einai al lo-shamru toratecha*	פַּלְגֵי־מַיִם יָרְדוּ עֵינָי עַל לֹא־שָׁמְרוּ תוֹרָתֶךָ׃	קלו

137	You are righteous, Hashem; Your rulings are just.	*Tzaddik attah Adonai veyashar mishpatecha*	צַדִּיק אַתָּה יְהֹוָה וְיָשָׁר מִשְׁפָּטֶיךָ:	קלז
138	You have ordained righteous decrees they are firmly enduring.	*Tzivvita tzedek edotecha ve'emunah me'od*	צִוִּיתָ צֶדֶק עֵדֹתֶיךָ וֶאֱמוּנָה מְאֹד:	קלח
139	I am consumed with rage over my foes' neglect of Your words.	*Tzimmetatni kin'ati ki-shachechu devarecha tzarai*	צִמְּתַתְנִי קִנְאָתִי כִּי־שָׁכְחוּ דְבָרֶיךָ צָרָי:	קלט
140	Your word is exceedingly pure, and Your servant loves it.	*Tzerufah imratecha me'od ve'avdecha ahevah*	צְרוּפָה אִמְרָתְךָ מְאֹד וְעַבְדְּךָ אֲהֵבָהּ:	קמ
141	Though I am belittled and despised, I have not neglected Your precepts.	*Tza'ir anochi venivzeh pikkudecha lo shachacheti*	צָעִיר אָנֹכִי וְנִבְזֶה פִּקֻּדֶיךָ לֹא שָׁכָחְתִּי:	קמא
142	Your righteousness is eternal; Your teaching is true.	*Tzidkatcha tzedek le'olam vetoratcha emet*	צִדְקָתְךָ צֶדֶק לְעוֹלָם וְתוֹרָתְךָ אֱמֶת:	קמב
143	Though anguish and distress come upon me, Your commandments are my delight.	*Tzar-umatzok metza'uni mitzvotecha sha'ashu'ai*	צַר־וּמָצוֹק מְצָאוּנִי מִצְוֹתֶיךָ שַׁעֲשֻׁעָי:	קמג
144	Your righteous decrees are eternal; give me understanding, that I might live.	*tzedek edevteicha le'olam havineni ve'echyeh*	צֶדֶק עֵדְוֹתֶיךָ לְעוֹלָם הֲבִינֵנִי וְאֶחְיֶה:	קמד
145	I call with all my heart; answer me, Hashem, that I may observe Your laws.	*Karati vechol-lev aneni Adonai chukkeicha etzorah*	קָרָאתִי בְכָל־לֵב עֲנֵנִי יְהֹוָה חֻקֶּיךָ אֶצֹּרָה:	קמה

146	I call upon You; save me, that I may keep Your decrees.	*Keraticha hoshi'eni ve'eshmerah edoteicha*	קְרָאתִיךָ הוֹשִׁיעֵנִי וְאֶשְׁמְרָה עֵדֹתֶיךָ:	קמו
147	I rise before dawn and cry for help; I hope for Your word.	*Kiddamti vanneshef va'ashavve'ah lidvarecha yichaleti*	קִדַּמְתִּי בַנֶּשֶׁף וָאֲשַׁוֵּעָה לדבריך [לִדְבָרְךָ] יִחָלְתִּי:	קמז
148	My eyes greet each watch of the night, as I meditate on Your promise.	*Kiddemu einai ashmurot lasiach be'imratecha*	קִדְּמוּ עֵינַי אַשְׁמֻרוֹת לָשִׂיחַ בְּאִמְרָתֶךָ:	קמח
149	Hear my voice as befits Your steadfast love; Hashem, preserve me, as is Your rule.	*Koli shim'ah chechasdecha Adonai kemishpatecha chayyeni*	קוֹלִי שִׁמְעָה כְחַסְדֶּךָ יְהֹוָה כְּמִשְׁפָּטֶךָ חַיֵּנִי:	קמט
150	Those who pursue intrigue draw near; they are far from Your teaching.	*Karvu rodefei zimmah mittoratcha rachaku*	קָרְבוּ רֹדְפֵי זִמָּה מִתּוֹרָתְךָ רָחָקוּ:	קנ
151	You, Hashem, are near, and all Your commandments are true.	*Karov attah Adonai vechol-mitzvotecha emet*	קָרוֹב אַתָּה יְהֹוָה וְכָל־מִצְוֺתֶיךָ אֱמֶת:	קנא
152	I know from Your decrees of old that You have established them forever.	*Kedem yada'ti me'edotecha ki le'olam yesadtam*	קֶדֶם יָדַעְתִּי מֵעֵדֹתֶיךָ כִּי לְעוֹלָם יְסַדְתָּם:	קנב
153	See my affliction and rescue me, for I have not neglected Your teaching.	*Re'eh-aneyi vechalletzeni ki-toratcha lo shachacheti*	רְאֵה־עָנְיִי וְחַלְּצֵנִי כִּי־תוֹרָתְךָ לֹא שָׁכָחְתִּי:	קנג

154	Champion my cause and redeem me; preserve me according to Your promise.	*Rivah rivi uge'aleni le'imratecha chayyeni*	רִיבָה רִיבִי וּגְאָלֵנִי לְאִמְרָתְךָ חַיֵּנִי׃	קנד
155	Deliverance is far from the wicked, for they have not turned to Your laws.	*Rachok meresha'im yeshu'ah ki-chukkecha lo darashu*	רָחוֹק מֵרְשָׁעִים יְשׁוּעָה כִּי־חֻקֶּיךָ לֹא דָרָשׁוּ׃	קנה
156	Your mercies are great, Hashem; as is Your rule, preserve me.	*Rachamecha rabbim Adonai kemishpatecha chayyeni*	רַחֲמֶיךָ רַבִּים יְהוָה כְּמִשְׁפָּטֶיךָ חַיֵּנִי׃	קנו
157	Many are my persecutors and foes; I have not swerved from Your decrees.	*Rabbim rodfai vetzarai me'edevotecha lo natiti*	רַבִּים רֹדְפַי וְצָרָי מֵעֵדְוֹתֶיךָ לֹא נָטִיתִי׃	קנז
158	I have seen traitors and loathed them, because they did not keep Your word in mind.	*Ra'iti vogdim va'etkotatah asher imratecha lo shamaru*	רָאִיתִי בֹגְדִים וָאֶתְקוֹטָטָה אֲשֶׁר אִמְרָתְךָ לֹא שָׁמָרוּ׃	קנח
159	See that I have loved Your precepts; Hashem, preserve me, as befits Your steadfast love.	*Re'eh ki-fikkudecha ahaveti Adonai kechasdecha chayyeni*	רְאֵה כִּי־פִקּוּדֶיךָ אָהָבְתִּי יְהוָה כְּחַסְדְּךָ חַיֵּנִי׃	קנט
160	Truth is the essence of Your word; Your just rules are eternal.	*Rosh-devarecha emet ule'olam kol-mishpat tzidkecha*	רֹאשׁ־דְּבָרְךָ אֱמֶת וּלְעוֹלָם כָּל־מִשְׁפַּט צִדְקֶךָ׃	קס
161	Princes have persecuted me without reason; my heart thrills at Your word.	*Sarim redafuni chinnam umiddevarecha pachad libbi*	שָׂרִים רְדָפוּנִי חִנָּם וּמִדְּבָרֶיךָ [וּמִדְּבָרְךָ] פָּחַד לִבִּי׃	קסא

162	I rejoice over Your promise as one who obtains great spoil.	*Sas anochi al-imratecha kemotze shalal rav*	שָׂשׂ אָנֹכִי עַל־אִמְרָתֶךָ כְּמוֹצֵא שָׁלָל רָב:	קסב
163	I hate and abhor falsehood; I love Your teaching.	*Sheker saneti va'ata'evah toratecha ahaveti*	שֶׁקֶר שָׂנֵאתִי וַאֲתַעֵבָה תּוֹרָתְךָ אָהָבְתִּי:	קסג
164	I praise You seven times each day for Your just rules.	*Sheva bayyom hillalticha al mishpetei tzidkecha*	שֶׁבַע בַּיּוֹם הִלַּלְתִּיךָ עַל מִשְׁפְּטֵי צִדְקֶךָ:	
165	Those who love Your teaching enjoy wellbeing; they encounter no adversity.	*Shalom rav le'ohavei toratecha ve'ein-lamo michshol*	שָׁלוֹם רָב לְאֹהֲבֵי תוֹרָתֶךָ וְאֵין־לָמוֹ מִכְשׁוֹל:	קסד
166	I hope for Your deliverance, Hashem; I observe Your commandments.	*Sibbarti lishu'atcha Adonai umitzvotecha asiti*	שִׂבַּרְתִּי לִישׁוּעָתְךָ יְהֹוָה וּמִצְוֺתֶיךָ עָשִׂיתִי:	קסה
167	I obey Your decrees and love them greatly.	*Shamerah nafshi edotecha va'ohavem me'od*	שָׁמְרָה נַפְשִׁי עֵדֹתֶיךָ וָאֹהֲבֵם מְאֹד:	קסו
168	I obey Your precepts and decrees; all my ways are before You.	*Shamarti fikkudecha ve'edotecha ki chol-derachai negdecha*	שָׁמַרְתִּי פִקּוּדֶיךָ וְעֵדֹתֶיךָ כִּי כָל־דְּרָכַי נֶגְדֶּךָ:	קסז
169	May my plea reach You, Hashem; grant me understanding according to Your word.	*Tikrav rinnati lefanecha Adonai kidvarecha havineni*	תִּקְרַב רִנָּתִי לְפָנֶיךָ יְהֹוָה כִּדְבָרְךָ הֲבִינֵנִי:	קסח

170	May my petition come before You; save me in accordance with Your promise.	*Tavo techinnati lefaneicha ke'imratecha hatzileni*	תָּבוֹא תְחִנָּתִי לְפָנֶיךָ כְּאִמְרָתְךָ הַצִּילֵנִי:	קסט
171	My lips shall pour forth praise, for You teach me Your laws.	*Tabba'nah sefatai tehillah ki telammedeni chukkecha*	תַּבַּעְנָה שְׂפָתַי תְּהִלָּה כִּי תְלַמְּדֵנִי חֻקֶּיךָ:	קע
172	My tongue shall declare Your promise, for all Your commandments are just.	*Ta'an leshoni imratecha ki chol-mitzvteicha tzedek*	תַּעַן לְשׁוֹנִי אִמְרָתֶךָ כִּי כָל־מִצְוֹתֶיךָ צֶּדֶק:	קעא
173	Lend Your hand to help me, for I have chosen Your precepts.	*Tehi-yadcha le'azereni ki fikkudecha vachareti*	תְּהִי־יָדְךָ לְעָזְרֵנִי כִּי פִקּוּדֶיךָ בָחָרְתִּי:	קעב
174	I have longed for Your deliverance, Hashem; Your teaching is my delight.	*Ta'avti lishu'atcha Adonai vetoratcha sha'ashu'ai*	תָּאַבְתִּי לִישׁוּעָתְךָ יְהֹוָה וְתוֹרָתְךָ שַׁעֲשֻׁעָי:	קעג
175	Let me live, that I may praise You; may Your rules be my help;	*Techi-nafshi utehallekka umishpatecha ya'azruni*	תְּחִי־נַפְשִׁי וּתְהַלְלֶךָּ וּמִשְׁפָּטֶךָ יַעֲזְרֻנִי:	קעד
176	I have strayed like a lost sheep; search for Your servant, for I have not neglected Your commandments.	*Ta'iti keseh oved bakkesh avdecha ki mitzvotecha lo shachachti*	תָּעִיתִי כְּשֶׂה אֹבֵד בַּקֵּשׁ עַבְדֶּךָ כִּי מִצְוֹתֶיךָ לֹא שָׁכָחְתִּי:	קעה

120

1	A song of ascents. In my distress I called to Hashem and He answered me.	*Shir hamma'alot el-Adonai batzaratah li karati vayya'aneni*	שִׁיר הַמַּעֲלוֹת אֶל־יְהֹוָה בַּצָּרָתָה לִּי קָרָאתִי וַיַּעֲנֵנִי׃
2	Hashem, save me from treacherous lips, from a deceitful tongue!	*Adonai hatzilah nafshi missefat-sheker millashon remiyyah*	יְהֹוָה הַצִּילָה נַפְשִׁי מִשְּׂפַת־שֶׁקֶר מִלָּשׁוֹן רְמִיָּה׃
3	What can you profit, what can you gain, O deceitful tongue?	*Mah-yitten lecha umah-yosif lach lashon remiyyah*	מַה־יִּתֵּן לְךָ וּמַה־יֹּסִיף לָךְ לָשׁוֹן רְמִיָּה׃
4	A warrior's sharp arrows, with hot coals of broom-wood.	*Chitzei gibbor shenunim im gachalei retamim*	חִצֵּי גִבּוֹר שְׁנוּנִים עִם גַּחֲלֵי רְתָמִים׃
5	Woe is me, that I live with Meshech, that I dwell among the clans of Kedar.	*Oyah-li ki-garti meshech shachanti im-oholei kedar*	אוֹיָה־לִי כִּי־גַרְתִּי מֶשֶׁךְ שָׁכַנְתִּי עִם־אׇהֳלֵי קֵדָר׃
6	Too long have I dwelt with those who hate peace.	*Rabbat shachenah-lah nafshi im sonei shalom*	רַבַּת שָׁכְנָה־לָּהּ נַפְשִׁי עִם שׂוֹנֵא שָׁלוֹם׃
7	I am all peace; but when I speak, they are for war.	*Ani-shalom vechi adabber hemmah lammilchamah*	אֲנִי־שָׁלוֹם וְכִי אֲדַבֵּר הֵמָּה לַמִּלְחָמָה׃

121

1 A song for ascents. I turn my eyes to the mountains; from where will my help come?

Shir lamma'alot essa einai el-heharim me'ayin yavo ezri

שִׁיר לַמַּעֲלוֹת אֶשָּׂא עֵינַי אֶל־הֶהָרִים מֵאַיִן יָבֹא עֶזְרִי׃ א

2 My help comes from Hashem, maker of heaven and earth.

Ezri me'im Adonai oseh shamayim va'aretz

עֶזְרִי מֵעִם יְהֹוָה עֹשֵׂה שָׁמַיִם וָאָרֶץ׃ ב

3 He will not let your foot give way; your guardian will not slumber;

Al-yitten lammot raglecha al-yanum shomerecha

אַל־יִתֵּן לַמּוֹט רַגְלֶךָ אַל־יָנוּם שֹׁמְרֶךָ׃ ג

4 See, the guardian of Yisrael neither slumbers nor sleeps!

Hinneh lo-yanum velo yishan shomer yisra'el

הִנֵּה לֹא־יָנוּם וְלֹא יִישָׁן שׁוֹמֵר יִשְׂרָאֵל׃ ד

5 Hashem is your guardian, Hashem is your protection at your right hand.

Adonai shomerecha Adonai tzillecha al-yad yeminecha

יְהֹוָה שֹׁמְרֶךָ יְהֹוָה צִלְּךָ עַל־יַד יְמִינֶךָ׃ ה

6 By day the sun will not strike you, nor the moon by night.

Yomam hashemesh lo-yakkekkah veyareach ballayelah

יוֹמָם הַשֶּׁמֶשׁ לֹא־יַכֶּכָּה וְיָרֵחַ בַּלָּיְלָה׃ ו

7 Hashem will guard you from all harm; He will guard your life.

Adonai yishmarecha mikkol-ra yishmor et-nafshecha

יְהֹוָה יִשְׁמָרְךָ מִכָּל־רָע יִשְׁמֹר אֶת־נַפְשֶׁךָ׃ ז

8	Hashem will guard your going and coming now and forever.	*Adonai yishmar-tzetcha uvo'echa me'attah ve'ad-olam*

יְהֹוָה יִשְׁמׇר־צֵאתְךָ וּבוֹאֶךָ מֵעַתָּה וְעַד־עוֹלָם: ח

122

–o⬭⬤⬭o–

כב

1	A song of ascents. Of David. I rejoiced when they said to me, "We are going to the House of Hashem."	*Shir hamma'alot ledavid samachti be'omerim li beit Adonai nelech*	שִׁיר הַמַּעֲלוֹת לְדָוִד שָׂמַחְתִּי בְּאֹמְרִים לִי בֵּית יְהֹוָה נֵלֵךְ: א
2	Our feet stood inside your gates, O Yerushalayim,	*Omedot hayu ragleinu bish'arayich yerushalayim*	עֹמְדוֹת הָיוּ רַגְלֵינוּ בִּשְׁעָרַיִךְ יְרוּשָׁלָ͏ִם: ב
3	Yerushalayim built up, a city knit together,	*Yerushalayim habbenuyah ke'ir shechubberah-lah yachdav*	יְרוּשָׁלַ͏ִם הַבְּנוּיָה כְּעִיר שֶׁחֻבְּרָה־לָּהּ יַחְדָּו: ג
4	to which tribes would make pilgrimage, the tribes of Hashem, —as was enjoined upon Yisrael— to praise the name of Hashem.	*Shesham alu shevatim shivtei-yah edut leyisra'el lehodot leshem Adonai*	שֶׁשָּׁם עָלוּ שְׁבָטִים שִׁבְטֵי־יָהּ עֵדוּת לְיִשְׂרָאֵל לְהֹדוֹת לְשֵׁם יְהֹוָה: ד
5	There the thrones of judgment stood, thrones of the house of David.	*Ki shammah yashevu chis'ot lemishpat kis'ot leveit david*	כִּי שָׁמָּה יָשְׁבוּ כִסְאוֹת לְמִשְׁפָּט כִּסְאוֹת לְבֵית דָּוִיד: ה

6	Pray for the well-being of Yerushalayim; "May those who love you be at peace.	*Sha'alu shelom yerushalayim yishlayu ohavayich*	שַׁאֲלוּ שְׁלוֹם יְרוּשָׁלָם יִשְׁלָיוּ אֹהֲבָיִךְ:

ו

7	May there be well-being within your ramparts, peace in your citadels."	*Yehi-shalom becheilech shalvah be'armenotayich*	יְהִי־שָׁלוֹם בְּחֵילֵךְ שַׁלְוָה בְּאַרְמְנוֹתָיִךְ:

ז

8	For the sake of my kin and friends, I pray for your well-being;	*Lema'an achai vere'ai adabberah-na shalom bach*	לְמַעַן אַחַי וְרֵעָי אֲדַבְּרָה־נָּא שָׁלוֹם בָּךְ:

ח

9	for the sake of the house of Hashem our God, I seek your good.	*Lema'an beit-Adonai eloheinu avakshah tov lach*	לְמַעַן בֵּית־יְהֹוָה אֱלֹהֵינוּ אֲבַקְשָׁה טוֹב לָךְ:

ט

123

1	A song of ascents. To You, enthroned in heaven, I turn my eyes.	*Shir hamma'alot eleicha nasati et-einai hayyoshevi bashamayim*	שִׁיר הַמַּעֲלוֹת אֵלֶיךָ נָשָׂאתִי אֶת־עֵינַי הַיֹּשְׁבִי בַּשָּׁמָיִם:

א

2	As the eyes of slaves follow their master's hand, as the eyes of a slave-girl follow the hand of her mistress, so our eyes are toward Hashem our God, awaiting His favor.	*Hinneh che'einei avadim el-yad adoneihem ke'einei shifchah el-yad gevirtah ken eineinu el-Adonai eloheinu ad sheyyechonnenu*	הִנֵּה כְעֵינֵי עֲבָדִים אֶל־יַד אֲדוֹנֵיהֶם כְּעֵינֵי שִׁפְחָה אֶל־יַד גְּבִרְתָּהּ כֵּן עֵינֵינוּ אֶל־יְהֹוָה אֱלֹהֵינוּ עַד שֶׁיְּחָנֵּנוּ:

יא

3	Show us favor, Hashem, show us favor! We have had more than enough of contempt.	*Chonnenu Adonai chonnenu ki-rav sava'nu vuz*	חׇנֵּנוּ יְהֹוָה חׇנֵּנוּ כִּי־רַב שָׂבַעְנוּ בוּז:	יב
4	Long enough have we endured the scorn of the complacent, the contempt of th haughty.	*Rabbat save'ah-lah nafshenu halla'ag hasha'anannim habbuz lig'eyonim*	רַבַּת שָׂבְעָה־לָּהּ נַפְשֵׁנוּ הַלַּעַג הַשַּׁאֲנַנִּים הַבּוּז לִגְאֵיוֹנִים:	יג

124

—◦⬡◦—

קכד

1	A song of ascents. Of David. Were it not for Hashem, who was on our side, let Yisrael now declare,	*Shir hamma'alot ledavid lulei Adonai shehayah lanu yomar-na yisra'el*	שִׁיר הַמַּעֲלוֹת לְדָוִד לוּלֵי יְהֹוָה שֶׁהָיָה לָנוּ יֹאמַר־נָא יִשְׂרָאֵל:	א
2	were it not for Hashem, who was on our side when men assailed us,	*Lulei Adonai shehayah lanu bekum aleinu adam*	לוּלֵי יְהֹוָה שֶׁהָיָה לָנוּ בְּקוּם עָלֵינוּ אָדָם:	ב
3	they would have swallowed us alive in their burning rage against us;	*Azai chayyim bela'unu bacharot appam banu*	אֲזַי חַיִּים בְּלָעוּנוּ בַּחֲרוֹת אַפָּם בָּנוּ:	ג
4	the waters would have carried us off, the torrent would have swept over us;	*Azai hammayim shetafunu nachlah avar al-nafshenu*	אֲזַי הַמַּיִם שְׁטָפוּנוּ נַחְלָה עָבַר עַל־נַפְשֵׁנוּ:	ד
5	over us would have swept the seething waters.	*Azai avar al-nafshenu hammayim hazzeidonim*	אֲזַי עָבַר עַל־נַפְשֵׁנוּ הַמַּיִם הַזֵּידוֹנִים:	ה

6   Blessed is Hashem, who did not let us be ripped apart by their teeth.   *Baruch Adonai shello netananu teref leshinneihem*   בָּרוּךְ יְהֹוָה שֶׁלֹּא נְתָנָנוּ טֶרֶף לְשִׁנֵּיהֶם: ו

7   We are like a bird escaped from the fowler's trap; the trap broke and we escaped.   *Nafshenu ketzippor nimletah mippach yokeshim happach nishbar va'anachnu nimlatenu*   נַפְשֵׁנוּ כְּצִפּוֹר נִמְלְטָה מִפַּח יוֹקְשִׁים הַפַּח נִשְׁבָּר וַאֲנַחְנוּ נִמְלָטְנוּ:   ז

8   Our help is the name of Hashem, maker of heaven and earth.   *Ezrenu beshem Adonai oseh shamayim va'aretz*   עֶזְרֵנוּ בְּשֵׁם יְהֹוָה עֹשֵׂה שָׁמַיִם וָאָרֶץ: ח

125   —◦❈◦—   כה

1   A song of ascents. Those who trust in Hashem are like Mount Tzion that cannot be moved, enduring forever.   *Shir hamma'alot habbotechim bAdonai kehar-tziyyon lo-yimmot le'olam yeshev*   שִׁיר הַמַּעֲלוֹת הַבֹּטְחִים בַּיהֹוָה כְּהַר־צִיּוֹן לֹא־יִמּוֹט לְעוֹלָם יֵשֵׁב: א

2   Yerushalayim, hills enfold it, and Hashem enfolds His people now and forever.   *Yerushalayim harim saviv lah v'Adonai saviv le'ammo me'attah ve'ad-olam*   יְרוּשָׁלַ͏ִם הָרִים סָבִיב לָהּ וַיהֹוָה סָבִיב לְעַמּוֹ מֵעַתָּה וְעַד־עוֹלָם: ב

3   The scepter of the wicked shall never rest upon the land allotted to the righteous, that the righteous not set their hand to wrongdoing.   *Ki lo yanuach shevet haresha al goral hatzaddikim lema'an lo-yishlechu hatzaddikim be'avlatah yedeihem*   כִּי לֹא יָנוּחַ שֵׁבֶט הָרֶשַׁע עַל גּוֹרַל הַצַּדִּיקִים לְמַעַן לֹא־יִשְׁלְחוּ הַצַּדִּיקִים בְּעַוְלָתָה יְדֵיהֶם: ג

4 Do good, Hashem, to the good, to the upright in heart.

Heitivah Adonai lattovim velisharim belibbotam

הֵיטִיבָה יְהֹוָה לַטּוֹבִים
וְלִישָׁרִים בְּלִבּוֹתָם: ד

5 But those who in their crookedness act corruptly, let Hashem make them go the way of evildoers. May it be well with Yisrael!

Vehammattim akalkallotam yolichem Adonai et-po'alei ha'aven shalom al-yisra'el

וְהַמַּטִּים עֲקַלְקַלּוֹתָם
יוֹלִיכֵם יְהֹוָה אֶת־פֹּעֲלֵי
הָאָוֶן שָׁלוֹם עַל־יִשְׂרָאֵל: ה

126

—◦⊖◈◈◈⊖◦—

קכו

1 A song of ascents. When Hashem restores the fortunes of Tzion —we see it as in a dream—

Shir hamma'alot beshuv Adonai et-shivat tziyyon hayinu kecholemim

שִׁיר הַמַּעֲלוֹת בְּשׁוּב יְהֹוָה
אֶת־שִׁיבַת צִיּוֹן הָיִינוּ
כְּחֹלְמִים: א

2 our mouths shall be filled with laughter, our tongues, with songs of joy. Then shall they say among the nations, "Hashem has done great things for them!"

Az yimmale sechok pinu uleshonenu rinnah az yomru vaggoyim higdil Adonai la'asot im-elleh

אָז יִמָּלֵא שְׂחוֹק פִּינוּ
וּלְשׁוֹנֵנוּ רִנָּה אָז יֹאמְרוּ
בַגּוֹיִם הִגְדִּיל יְהֹוָה
לַעֲשׂוֹת עִם־אֵלֶּה: ב

3 Hashem will do great things for us and we shall rejoice.

Higdil Adonai la'asot immanu hayinu semechim

הִגְדִּיל יְהֹוָה לַעֲשׂוֹת עִמָּנוּ
הָיִינוּ שְׂמֵחִים: ג

4 Restore our fortunes, Hashem, like watercourses in the Negev.

Shuvah Adonai et-shevitenu ka'afikim bannegev

שׁוּבָה יְהֹוָה אֶת־שְׁבוּתֵנוּ
[שְׁבִיתֵנוּ] כַּאֲפִיקִים בַּנֶּגֶב: ד

	English	Transliteration	Hebrew

5 They who sow in tears shall reap with songs of joy.

Hazzore'im bedim'ah berinnah yiktzoru

הַזֹּרְעִים בְּדִמְעָה בְּרִנָּה יִקְצֹרוּ: ה

6 Though he goes along weeping, carrying the seed-bag, he shall come back with songs of joy, carrying his sheaves.

Haloch yelech uvachoh nosei meshech-hazzara bo-yavo verinnah nosei alummotav

הָלוֹךְ יֵלֵךְ וּבָכֹה נֹשֵׂא מֶשֶׁךְ־הַזָּרַע בֹּא־יָבוֹא בְרִנָּה נֹשֵׂא אֲלֻמֹּתָיו: ו

127

כז

1 A song of ascents. Of Shlomo. Unless Hashem builds the house, its builders labor in vain on it; unless Hashem watches over the city, the watchman keeps vigil in vain.

Shir hamma'alot lishlomoh im-Adonai lo-yivneh vayit shav amelu vonav bo im-Adonai lo-yishmar-ir shav shakad shomer

שִׁיר הַמַּעֲלוֹת לִשְׁלֹמֹה אִם־יְהֹוָה לֹא־יִבְנֶה בַיִת שָׁוְא עָמְלוּ בוֹנָיו בּוֹ אִם־יְהֹוָה לֹא־יִשְׁמָר־עִיר שָׁוְא שָׁקַד שׁוֹמֵר: א

2 In vain do you rise early and stay up late, you who toil for the bread you eat; He provides as much for His loved ones while they sleep.

Shave lachem mashkimei kum me'acharei-shevet ochelei lechem ha'atzavim ken yitten lidido sheina

שָׁוְא לָכֶם מַשְׁכִּימֵי קוּם מְאַחֲרֵי־שֶׁבֶת אֹכְלֵי לֶחֶם הָעֲצָבִים כֵּן יִתֵּן לִידִידוֹ שֵׁנָא: ב

3 Sons are the provision of Hashem; the fruit of the womb, His reward.

Hinneh nachalat Adonai banim sachar peri habbaten

הִנֵּה נַחֲלַת יְהֹוָה בָּנִים שָׂכָר פְּרִי הַבָּטֶן: ג

4	Like arrows in the hand of a warrior are sons born to a man in his youth.	*Kechitzim beyad-gibbor ken benei hanne'urim*

כְּחִצִּים בְּיַד־גִּבּוֹר כֵּן בְּנֵי הַנְּעוּרִים: ד

5	Happy is the man who fills his quiver with them; they shall not be put to shame when they contend with the enemy in the gate.	*Ashrei haggever asher millei et-ashpato mehem lo-yevoshu ki-yedabberu et-oyevim basha'ar*

אַשְׁרֵי הַגֶּבֶר אֲשֶׁר מִלֵּא אֶת־אַשְׁפָּתוֹ מֵהֶם לֹא־יֵבֹשׁוּ כִּי־יְדַבְּרוּ אֶת־אוֹיְבִים בַּשָּׁעַר: ה

128

קכח

1	A song of ascents. Happy are all who fear Hashem, who follow His ways.	*Shir hamma'alot ashrei kol-yerei Adonai haholech bidrachav*

שִׁיר הַמַּעֲלוֹת אַשְׁרֵי כָּל־יְרֵא יְהוָה הַהֹלֵךְ בִּדְרָכָיו: א

2	You shall enjoy the fruit of your labors; you shall be happy and you shall prosper.	*Yegia' kappecha ki tochel ashrecha vetov lach*

יְגִיעַ כַּפֶּיךָ כִּי תֹאכֵל אַשְׁרֶיךָ וְטוֹב לָךְ: ב

3	Your wife shall be like a fruitful vine within your house; your sons, like olive saplings around your table.	*Eshtecha kegefen poriyyah beyarketei veitecha banecha kishtilei zeitim saviv leshulchanecha*

אֶשְׁתְּךָ כְּגֶפֶן פֹּרִיָּה בְּיַרְכְּתֵי בֵיתֶךָ בָּנֶיךָ כִּשְׁתִלֵי זֵיתִים סָבִיב לְשֻׁלְחָנֶךָ: ג

4	So shall the man who fears Hashem be blessed.	*Hinneh chi-chen yevorach gaver yere Adonai*

הִנֵּה כִי־כֵן יְבֹרַךְ גָּבֶר יְרֵא יְהוָה: ד

5	May Hashem bless you from Tzion; may you share the prosperity of Yerushalayim all the days of your life,	*Yevarechcha Adonai mitziyyon ure'eh betuv yerushalayim kol yemei chayyeicha*	יְבָרֶכְךָ יְהוָה מִצִּיּוֹן וּרְאֵה בְּטוּב יְרוּשָׁלָ͏ִם כֹּל יְמֵי חַיֶּיךָ:
6	and live to see your children's children. May all be well with Yisrael!	*Ure'eh-vanim levanecha shalom al-yisra'el*	וּרְאֵה־בָנִים לְבָנֶיךָ שָׁלוֹם עַל־יִשְׂרָאֵל:

129

—◦⣇⣿⣸◦— קכט

1	A song of ascents. Since my youth they have often assailed me, let Yisrael now declare,	*Shir hamma'alot rabbat tzeraruni minne'urai yomar-na yisra'el*	שִׁיר הַמַּעֲלוֹת רַבַּת צְרָרוּנִי מִנְּעוּרַי יֹאמַר־נָא יִשְׂרָאֵל:
2	since my youth they have often assailed me, but they have never overcome me.	*Rabbat tzeraruni minne'urai gam lo-yachelu li*	רַבַּת צְרָרוּנִי מִנְּעוּרָי גַּם לֹא־יָכְלוּ לִי:
3	Plowmen plowed across my back; they made long furrows.	*Al-gabbi chareshu choreshim he'erichu lm'nvtm [lema'anitam]*	עַל־גַּבִּי חָרְשׁוּ חֹרְשִׁים הֶאֱרִיכוּ למענותם [לְמַעֲנִיתָם:]
4	Hashem, the righteous one, has snapped the cords of the wicked.	*Adonai tzaddik kitzetz avot resha'im*	יְהוָה צַדִּיק קִצֵּץ עֲבוֹת רְשָׁעִים:
5	Let all who hate Tzion fall back in disgrace.	*Yevoshu veyissogu achor kol sone'ei tziyyon*	יֵבֹשׁוּ וְיִסֹּגוּ אָחוֹר כֹּל שֹׂנְאֵי צִיּוֹן:

6	Let them be like grass on roofs that fades before it can be pulled up,	*Yihyu kachatzir gaggot shekkadmat shalaf yavesh*

יִהְיוּ כַּחֲצִיר גַּגּוֹת שֶׁקַּדְמַת שָׁלַף יָבֵשׁ: ו

7	that affords no handful for the reaper, no armful for the gatherer of sheaves,	*Shello millei chappo kotzer vechitzno me'ammer*

שֶׁלֹּא מִלֵּא כַפּוֹ קוֹצֵר וְחִצְנוֹ מְעַמֵּר: ז

8	no exchange with passersby: "The blessing of Hashem be upon you." "We bless you by the name of Hashem."	*Velo ameru ha'overim birkat-Adonai aleichem berachnu etchem beshem Adonai*

וְלֹא אָמְרוּ הָעֹבְרִים בִּרְכַּת־יְהֹוָה אֲלֵיכֶם בֵּרַכְנוּ אֶתְכֶם בְּשֵׁם יְהֹוָה: ח

130

—◦⧖◦—

קל

1	A song of ascents. Out of the depths I call You, Hashem.	*Shir hamma'alot mimma'amakkim keraticha Adonai*

שִׁיר הַמַּעֲלוֹת מִמַּעֲמַקִּים קְרָאתִיךָ יְהֹוָה: א

2	O Hashem, listen to my cry; let Your ears be attentive to my plea for mercy.	*Adonai shim'ah vekoli tihyenah azeneicha kashuvot lekol tachanunai*

אֲדֹנָי שִׁמְעָה בְקוֹלִי תִּהְיֶינָה אָזְנֶיךָ קַשֻּׁבוֹת לְקוֹל תַּחֲנוּנָי: ב

3	If You keep account of sins, Hashem, Lord, who will survive?	*Im-avonot tishmar-yah Adonai mi ya'amod*

אִם־עֲוֹנוֹת תִּשְׁמָר־יָהּ אֲדֹנָי מִי יַעֲמֹד: ג

4	Yours is the power to forgive so that You may be held in awe.	*Ki-immecha hasselichah lema'an tivvarei*

כִּי־עִמְּךָ הַסְּלִיחָה לְמַעַן תִּוָּרֵא: ד

5	I look to Hashem; I look to Him; I await His word.	*Kivviti Adonai kivvetah nafshi velidvaro hochaleti*	קִוִּיתִי יְהֹוָה קִוְּתָה נַפְשִׁי וְלִדְבָרוֹ הוֹחָלְתִּי:	ה
6	I am more eager for Hashem than watchmen for the morning, watchmen for the morning.	*Nafshi lAdonai mishomerim labboker shomerim labboker*	נַפְשִׁי לַאדֹנָי מִשֹּׁמְרִים לַבֹּקֶר שֹׁמְרִים לַבֹּקֶר:	ו
7	O Yisrael, wait for Hashem; for with Hashem is steadfast love and great power to redeem.	*Yachel yisra'el el-Adonai ki-im-Adonai hachesed veharbeh immo fedut*	יַחֵל יִשְׂרָאֵל אֶל-יְהֹוָה כִּי-עִם-יְהֹוָה הַחֶסֶד וְהַרְבֵּה עִמּוֹ פְדוּת:	ז
8	It is He who will redeem Yisrael from all their iniquities.	*Vehu yifdeh et-yisra'el mikkol avnotav*	וְהוּא יִפְדֶּה אֶת-יִשְׂרָאֵל מִכֹּל עֲוֹנֹתָיו:	ח

131

קלא

1	A song of ascents. Of David. Hashem, my heart is not proud nor my look haughty; I do not aspire to great things or to what is beyond me;	*Shir hamma'alot ledavid Adonai lo-gavah libbi velo-ramu einai velo-hillachti bigdolot uvenifla'ot mimmenni*	שִׁיר הַמַּעֲלוֹת לְדָוִד יְהֹוָה לֹא-גָבַהּ לִבִּי וְלֹא-רָמוּ עֵינַי וְלֹא-הִלַּכְתִּי בִּגְדֹלוֹת וּבְנִפְלָאוֹת מִמֶּנִּי:	א
2	but I have taught myself to be contented like a weaned child with its mother; like a weaned child am I in my mind.	*Im-lo shivviti vedomamti nafshi kegamul alei immo kaggamul alai nafshi*	אִם-לֹא שִׁוִּיתִי וְדוֹמַמְתִּי נַפְשִׁי כְּגָמֻל עֲלֵי אִמּוֹ כַּגָּמֻל עָלַי נַפְשִׁי:	ב

3 | O Yisrael, wait for Hashem now and forever. | *Yachel yisra'el el-Adonai me'attah ve'ad-olam* | יַחֵל יִשְׂרָאֵל אֶל־יְהֹוָה מֵעַתָּה וְעַד־עוֹלָם: | ג

132

⎯○⟨⟨⊗⟩⟩○⎯

קלב

1 | A song of ascents. Hashem, remember in David's favor his extreme self-denial, | *Shir hamma'alot zechor-Adonai ledavid et kol-unnoto* | שִׁיר הַמַּעֲלוֹת זְכוֹר־יְהֹוָה לְדָוִד אֵת כָּל־עֻנּוֹתוֹ: | א

2 | how he swore to Hashem, vowed to the Mighty One of Yaakov, | *Asher nishba lAdonai nadar la'avir ya'akov* | אֲשֶׁר נִשְׁבַּע לַיהֹוָה נָדַר לַאֲבִיר יַעֲקֹב: | ב

3 | "I will not enter my house, nor will I mount my bed, | *Im-avo be'ohel beiti im-e'eleh al-eres yetzu'ai* | אִם־אָבֹא בְּאֹהֶל בֵּיתִי אִם־אֶעֱלֶה עַל־עֶרֶשׂ יְצוּעָי: | ג

4 | I will not give sleep to my eyes, or slumber to my eyelids | *Im-etten shenat le'einai le'afappai tenumah* | אִם־אֶתֵּן שְׁנַת לְעֵינָי לְעַפְעַפַּי תְּנוּמָה: | ד

5 | until I find a place for Hashem, an abode for the Mighty One of Yaakov." | *Ad-emtza mukom lAdonai mishkanot la'avir ya'akov* | עַד־אֶמְצָא מָקוֹם לַיהֹוָה מִשְׁכָּנוֹת לַאֲבִיר יַעֲקֹב: | ה

6 | We heard it was in Efrat; we came upon it in the region of Jaar. | *Hinneh-shema'anuha ve'efratah metzanuha bisdei-ya'ar* | הִנֵּה־שְׁמַעֲנוּהָ בְאֶפְרָתָה מְצָאנוּהָ בִּשְׂדֵי־יָעַר: | ו

7 | Let us enter His abode, bow at His footstool. | *Navo'ah lemishkenotav nishtachaveh lahadom raglav* | נָבוֹאָה לְמִשְׁכְּנוֹתָיו נִשְׁתַּחֲוֶה לַהֲדֹם רַגְלָיו: | ז

8	Advance, Hashem, to Your resting-place, You and Your mighty Aron!	*Kumah Adonai limnuchatecha attah va'aron uzzecha*	קוּמָה יְהֹוָה לִמְנוּחָתֶךָ אַתָּה וַאֲרוֹן עֻזֶּךָ: ח
9	Your Kohanim are clothed in triumph; Your loyal ones sing for joy.	*Kohanecha yilbeshu-tzedek vachasidecha yerannenu*	כֹּהֲנֶיךָ יִלְבְּשׁוּ־צֶדֶק וַחֲסִידֶיךָ יְרַנֵּנוּ: ט
10	For the sake of Your servant David do not reject Your anointed one.	*Ba'avur david avdecha al-tashev penei meshichecha*	בַּעֲבוּר דָּוִד עַבְדֶּךָ אַל־תָּשֵׁב פְּנֵי מְשִׁיחֶךָ: י
11	Hashem swore to David a firm oath that He will not renounce, "One of your own issue I will set upon your throne.	*Nishba-Adonai ledavid emet lo-yashuv mimmennah mipperi vitnecha ashit lechissei-lach*	נִשְׁבַּע־יְהֹוָה לְדָוִד אֱמֶת לֹא־יָשׁוּב מִמֶּנָּה מִפְּרִי בִטְנְךָ אָשִׁית לְכִסֵּא־לָךְ: יא
12	If your sons keep My covenant and My decrees that I teach them, then their sons also, to the end of time, shall sit upon your throne."	*Im-yishmeru vanecha beriti ve'edoti zo alammedem gam-beneihem adei-ad yeishevu lechisse-lach*	אִם־יִשְׁמְרוּ בָנֶיךָ בְּרִיתִי וְעֵדֹתִי זוֹ אֲלַמְּדֵם גַּם־בְּנֵיהֶם עֲדֵי־עַד יֵשְׁבוּ לְכִסֵּא־לָךְ: יב
13	For Hashem has chosen Tzion; He has desired it for His seat.	*Ki-vachar Adonai betziyyon ivvah lemoshav lo*	כִּי־בָחַר יְהֹוָה בְּצִיּוֹן אִוָּהּ לְמוֹשָׁב לוֹ: יג
14	"This is my resting-place for all time; here I will dwell, for I desire it.	*Zot-menuchati adei-ad poh-eshev ki ivvitiha*	זֹאת־מְנוּחָתִי עֲדֵי־עַד פֹּה אֵשֵׁב כִּי אִוִּתִיהָ: יד

15 I will amply bless its store of food, give its needy their fill of bread.

Tzeidah barech avarech evyoneha asbia' lachem

צֵידָהּ בָּרֵךְ אֲבָרֵךְ אֶבְיוֹנֶיהָ אַשְׂבִּיעַ לָחֶם: טו

16 I will clothe its Kohanim in victory, its loyal ones shall sing for joy.

Vechohaneha albish yesha vachasideha rannen yerannenu

וְכֹהֲנֶיהָ אַלְבִּישׁ יֶשַׁע וַחֲסִידֶיהָ רַנֵּן יְרַנֵּנוּ: טז

17 There I will make a horn sprout for David; I have prepared a lamp for My anointed one.

Sham atzmiach keren ledavid arachti ner limshichi

שָׁם אַצְמִיחַ קֶרֶן לְדָוִד עָרַכְתִּי נֵר לִמְשִׁיחִי: יז

18 I will clothe his enemies in disgrace, while on him his crown shall sparkle."

Oyevav albish boshet ve'alav yatzitz nizro

אוֹיְבָיו אַלְבִּישׁ בֹּשֶׁת וְעָלָיו יָצִיץ נִזְרוֹ: יח

133

⎯○⊗⊗⊗○⎯

קלג

1 A song of ascents. Of David. How good and how pleasant it is that brothers dwell together.

Shir hamma'alot ledavid hinneh mah-tov umah-na'im shevet achim gam-yachad

שִׁיר הַמַּעֲלוֹת לְדָוִד הִנֵּה מַה־טּוֹב וּמַה־נָּעִים שֶׁבֶת אַחִים גַּם־יָחַד: א

2 It is like fine oil on the head running down onto the beard, the beard of Aharon, that comes down over the collar of his robe;

Kashemen hattov al-harosh yored al-hazzakan zekan-aharon sheyyored al-pi middotav

כַּשֶּׁמֶן הַטּוֹב עַל־הָרֹאשׁ יֹרֵד עַל־הַזָּקָן זְקַן־אַהֲרֹן שֶׁיֹּרֵד עַל־פִּי מִדּוֹתָיו: ב

3	like the dew of Chermon that falls upon the mountains of Tzion. There Hashe ordained blessing, everlasting life.	*Ketal-chermon sheyyored al-harerei tziyyon ki sham tzivvah Adonai et-habberachah chayyim ad-ha'olam*	כְּטַל־חֶרְמוֹן שֶׁיֹּרֵד עַל־הַרְרֵי צִיּוֹן כִּי שָׁם צִוָּה יְהֹוָה אֶת־הַבְּרָכָה חַיִּים עַד־הָעוֹלָם: ג

134

כְלד

1	A song of ascents. Now bless Hashem, all you servants of Hashem who stand nightly in the house of Hashem.	*Shir hamma'alot hinneh barachu et-Adonai kol-avdei Adonai ha'omedim beveit-Adonai balleilot*	שִׁיר הַמַּעֲלוֹת הִנֵּה בָּרֲכוּ אֶת־יְהֹוָה כָּל־עַבְדֵי יְהֹוָה הָעֹמְדִים בְּבֵית־יְהֹוָה בַּלֵּילוֹת: א
2	Lift your hands toward the sanctuary and bless Hashem.	*Se'u-yedechem kodesh uvarachu et-Adonai*	שְׂאוּ־יְדֵכֶם קֹדֶשׁ וּבָרֲכוּ אֶת־יְהֹוָה: ב
3	May Hashem, maker of heaven and earth, bless you from Tzion.	*Yevarechecha Adonai mitziyyon oseh shamayim va'aretz*	יְבָרֶכְךָ יְהֹוָה מִצִּיּוֹן עֹשֵׂה שָׁמַיִם וָאָרֶץ: ג

135

כלה

1	Hallelujah. Praise the name of Hashem; give praise, you servants of Hashem	*Hallu yah hallu et-shem Adonai hallu avdei Adonai*	הַלְלוּ יָהּ הַלְלוּ אֶת־שֵׁם יְהֹוָה הַלְלוּ עַבְדֵי יְהֹוָה: א

2	who stand in the house of Hashem, in the courts of the house of our God.	*She'omedim beveit Adonai bechatzrot beit eloheinu*

שֶׁעֹמְדִים בְּבֵית יְהֹוָה בְּחַצְרוֹת בֵּית אֱלֹהֵינוּ׃ ב

| 3 | Praise Hashem, for Hashem is good; sing hymns to His name, for it is pleasant. | *Hallu-yah ki-tov Adonai zammeru lishmo ki na'im* |

הַלְלוּיָהּ כִּי־טוֹב יְהֹוָה זַמְּרוּ לִשְׁמוֹ כִּי נָעִים׃ ג

| 4 | For Hashem has chosen Yaakov for Himself, Yisrael, as His treasured possession. | *Ki-ya'akov bachar lo yah yisra'el lisgullato* |

כִּי־יַעֲקֹב בָּחַר לוֹ יָהּ יִשְׂרָאֵל לִסְגֻלָּתוֹ׃ ד

| 5 | For I know that Hashem is great, that our Lord is greater than all gods. | *Ki ani yada'ti ki-gadol Adonai va'adoneinu mikkol-elohim* |

כִּי אֲנִי יָדַעְתִּי כִּי־גָדוֹל יְהֹוָה וַאֲדֹנֵינוּ מִכָּל־אֱלֹהִים׃ ה

| 6 | Whatever Hashem desires He does in heaven and earth, in the seas and all the depths. | *Kol asher-chafetz Adonai asah bashamayim uva'aretz bayyammim vechol-tehomot* |

כֹּל אֲשֶׁר־חָפֵץ יְהֹוָה עָשָׂה בַּשָּׁמַיִם וּבָאָרֶץ בַּיַּמִּים וְכָל־תְּהוֹמוֹת׃ ו

| 7 | He makes clouds rise from the end of the earth; He makes lightning for the rain; He releases the wind from His vaults. | *Ma'aleh nesi'im miktzeh ha'aretz berakim lammatar asah motze-ruach me'otzerotav* |

מַעֲלֶה נְשִׂאִים מִקְצֵה הָאָרֶץ בְּרָקִים לַמָּטָר עָשָׂה מוֹצֵא־רוּחַ מֵאוֹצְרוֹתָיו׃ ז

| 8 | He struck down the first-born of Egypt, man and beast alike; | *Shehikkah bechorei mitzrayim me'adam ad-behemah* |

שֶׁהִכָּה בְּכוֹרֵי מִצְרָיִם מֵאָדָם עַד־בְּהֵמָה׃ ח

9	He sent signs and portents against Egypt, against Pharaoh and all his servants;	*Shalach otot umofetim betochechi mitzrayim befar'oh uvechol-avadav*	שָׁלַח אֹתֹת וּמֹפְתִים בְּתוֹכֵכִי מִצְרָיִם בְּפַרְעֹה וּבְכָל־עֲבָדָיו:	ט
10	He struck down many nations and slew numerous kings—	*Shehikkah goyim rabbim veharag melachim atzumim*	שֶׁהִכָּה גּוֹיִם רַבִּים וְהָרַג מְלָכִים עֲצוּמִים:	י
11	Sihon, king of the Amorites, Og, king of Bashan, and all the royalty of Canaan—	*Lesichon melech ha'emori ule'og melech habbashan ulechol mamlechot kena'an*	לְסִיחוֹן מֶלֶךְ הָאֱמֹרִי וּלְעוֹג מֶלֶךְ הַבָּשָׁן וּלְכֹל מַמְלְכוֹת כְּנָעַן:	יא
12	and gave their lands as a heritage, as a heritage to His people Yisrael.	*Venatan artzam nachalah nachalah leyisra'el ammo*	וְנָתַן אַרְצָם נַחֲלָה נַחֲלָה לְיִשְׂרָאֵל עַמּוֹ:	יב
13	Hashem, Your name endures forever, Your fame, Hashem, through all generations;	*Adonai shimcha le'olam Adonai zichrecha ledor-vador*	יְהֹוָה שִׁמְךָ לְעוֹלָם יְהֹוָה זִכְרְךָ לְדֹר־וָדֹר:	יג
14	for Hashem will Champion His people, and obtain satisfaction for His servants.	*Ki-yadin Adonai ammo ve'al-avadav yitnecham*	כִּי־יָדִין יְהֹוָה עַמּוֹ וְעַל־עֲבָדָיו יִתְנֶחָם:	יד
15	The idols of the nations are silver and gold, the work of men's hands.	*Atzabbei haggoyim kesef vezahav ma'aseh yedei adam*	עֲצַבֵּי הַגּוֹיִם כֶּסֶף וְזָהָב מַעֲשֵׂה יְדֵי אָדָם:	טו

16	They have mouths, but cannot speak; they have eyes, but cannot see;	*Peh-lahem velo yedabberu einayim lahem velo yir'u*	פֶּה־לָהֶם וְלֹא יְדַבֵּרוּ עֵינַיִם לָהֶם וְלֹא יִרְאוּ׃ טז
17	they have ears, but cannot hear, nor is there breath in their mouths.	*Oznayim lahem velo ya'azinu af ein-yesh-ruach befihem*	אָזְנַיִם לָהֶם וְלֹא יַאֲזִינוּ אַף אֵין־יֶשׁ־רוּחַ בְּפִיהֶם׃ יז
18	Those who fashion them, all who trust in them, shall become like them.	*Kemohem yihyu oseihem kol asher-boteach bahem*	כְּמוֹהֶם יִהְיוּ עֹשֵׂיהֶם כֹּל אֲשֶׁר־בֹּטֵחַ בָּהֶם׃ יח
19	O house of Yisrael, bless Hashem; O house of Aharon, bless Hashem;	*Beit yisra'el barachu et-Adonai beit aharon barachu et-Adonai*	בֵּית יִשְׂרָאֵל בָּרְכוּ אֶת־יְהֹוָה בֵּית אַהֲרֹן בָּרְכוּ אֶת־יְהֹוָה׃ יט
20	O house of Levi, bless Hashem; you who fear Hashem, bless Hashem.	*Beit hallevi barachu et-Adonai yir'ei Adonai barachu et-Adonai*	בֵּית הַלֵּוִי בָּרְכוּ אֶת־יְהֹוָה יִרְאֵי יְהֹוָה בָּרְכוּ אֶת־יְהֹוָה׃ כ
21	Blessed is Hashem from Tzion, He who dwells in Yerushalayim. Hallelujah.	*Baruch Adonai mitziyyon shochen yerushalayim hallu-yah*	בָּרוּךְ יְהֹוָה מִצִּיּוֹן שֹׁכֵן יְרוּשָׁלָ͏ִם הַלְלוּ־יָהּ׃ כא

136

֎ קלו

1	Praise Hashem; for He is good, His steadfast love is eternal.	*hodu lAdonai ki-tov ki le'olam chasdo*	הוֹדוּ לַיהֹוָה כִּי־טוֹב כִּי לְעוֹלָם חַסְדּוֹ׃ א

2	Praise the God of gods, His steadfast love is eternal.	*hodu lelohei ha'elohim ki le'olam chasdo*	הוֹדוּ לֵאלֹהֵי הָאֱלֹהִים כִּי לְעוֹלָם חַסְדּוֹ: ב
3	Praise the Lord of lords, His steadfast love is eternal;	*hodu la'adonei ha'adonim ki le'olam chasdo*	הוֹדוּ לַאֲדֹנֵי הָאֲדֹנִים כִּי לְעוֹלָם חַסְדּוֹ: ג
4	Who alone works great marvels, His steadfast love is eternal;	*Le'oseh nifla'ot gedolot levaddo ki le'olam chasdo*	לְעֹשֵׂה נִפְלָאוֹת גְּדֹלוֹת לְבַדּוֹ כִּי לְעוֹלָם חַסְדּוֹ: ד
5	Who made the heavens with wisdom, His steadfast love is eternal;	*Le'oseh hashamayim bitvunah ki le'olam chasdo*	לְעֹשֵׂה הַשָּׁמַיִם בִּתְבוּנָה כִּי לְעוֹלָם חַסְדּוֹ: ה
6	Who spread the earth over the water, His steadfast love is eternal;	*Leroka ha'aretz al-hammayim ki le'olam chasdo*	לְרֹקַע הָאָרֶץ עַל־הַמָּיִם כִּי לְעוֹלָם חַסְדּוֹ: ו
7	Who made the great lights, His steadfast love is eternal;	*Le'oseh orim gedolim ki le'olam chasdo*	לְעֹשֵׂה אוֹרִים גְּדֹלִים כִּי לְעוֹלָם חַסְדּוֹ: ז
8	the sun to dominate the day, His steadfast love is eternal;	*Et-hashemesh lememshelet bayyom ki le'olam chasdo*	אֶת־הַשֶּׁמֶשׁ לְמֶמְשֶׁלֶת בַּיּוֹם כִּי לְעוֹלָם חַסְדּוֹ: ח
9	the moon and the stars to dominate the night, His steadfast love is eternal;	*Et-hayyareach vechochavim lememshelot ballayelah ki le'olam chasdo*	אֶת־הַיָּרֵחַ וְכוֹכָבִים לְמֶמְשָׁלוֹת בַּלָּיְלָה כִּי לְעוֹלָם חַסְדּוֹ: ט

10	Who struck Egypt through their first-born, His steadfast love is eternal;	*Lemakkeh mitzrayim bivchoreihem ki le'olam chasdo*	לְמַכֵּה מִצְרַיִם בִּבְכוֹרֵיהֶם כִּי לְעוֹלָם חַסְדּוֹ:	י
11	and brought Yisrael out of their midst, His steadfast love is eternal;	*Vayyotze yisra'el mittocham ki le'olam chasdo*	וַיּוֹצֵא יִשְׂרָאֵל מִתּוֹכָם כִּי לְעוֹלָם חַסְדּוֹ:	יא
12	with a strong hand and outstretched arm, His steadfast love is eternal;	*Beyad chazakah uvizroa' netuyah ki le'olam chasdo*	בְּיָד חֲזָקָה וּבִזְרוֹעַ נְטוּיָה כִּי לְעוֹלָם חַסְדּוֹ:	יב
13	Who split apart the Sea of Reeds, His steadfast love is eternal;	*Legozer yam-suf ligzarim ki le'olam chasdo*	לְגֹזֵר יַם־סוּף לִגְזָרִים כִּי לְעוֹלָם חַסְדּוֹ:	יג
14	and made Yisrael pass through it, His steadfast love is eternal;	*Vehe'evir yisra'el betocho ki le'olam chasdo*	וְהֶעֱבִיר יִשְׂרָאֵל בְּתוֹכוֹ כִּי לְעוֹלָם חַסְדּוֹ:	יד
15	Who hurled Pharaoh and his army into the Sea of Reeds, His steadfast love is eternal;	*Veni'er par'oh vecheilo veyam-suf ki le'olam chasdo*	וְנִעֵר פַּרְעֹה וְחֵילוֹ בְיַם־סוּף כִּי לְעוֹלָם חַסְדּוֹ:	טו
16	Who led His people through the wilderness, His steadfast love is eternal;	*Lemolich ammo bammidbar ki le'olam chasdo*	לְמוֹלִיךְ עַמּוֹ בַּמִּדְבָּר כִּי לְעוֹלָם חַסְדּוֹ:	טז
17	Who struck down great kings, His steadfast love is eternal;	*Lemakkeh melachim gedolim ki le'olam chasdo*	לְמַכֵּה מְלָכִים גְּדֹלִים כִּי לְעוֹלָם חַסְדּוֹ:	יז
18	and slew mighty kings— His steadfast love is eternal;	*Vayyaharog melachim addirim ki le'olam chasdo*	וַיַּהֲרֹג מְלָכִים אַדִּירִים כִּי לְעוֹלָם חַסְדּוֹ:	יח

19	Sihon, king of the Amorites, His steadfast love is eternal;	*Lesichon melech ha'emori ki le'olam chasdo*	לְסִיחוֹן מֶלֶךְ הָאֱמֹרִי כִּי לְעוֹלָם חַסְדּוֹ:	יט
20	Og, king of Bashan— His steadfast love is eternal;	*Ule'og melech habbashan ki le'olam chasdo*	וּלְעוֹג מֶלֶךְ הַבָּשָׁן כִּי לְעוֹלָם חַסְדּוֹ:	כ
21	and gave their land as a heritage, His steadfast love is eternal;	*Venatan artzam lenachalah ki le'olam chasdo*	וְנָתַן אַרְצָם לְנַחֲלָה כִּי לְעוֹלָם חַסְדּוֹ:	כא
22	a heritage to His servant Yisrael, His steadfast love is eternal;	*Nachalah leyisra'el avdo ki le'olam chasdo*	נַחֲלָה לְיִשְׂרָאֵל עַבְדּוֹ כִּי לְעוֹלָם חַסְדּוֹ:	כב
23	Who took note of us in our degradation, His steadfast love is eternal;	*Shebbeshiflenu zachar lanu ki le'olam chasdo*	שֶׁבְּשִׁפְלֵנוּ זָכַר לָנוּ כִּי לְעוֹלָם חַסְדּוֹ:	כג
24	and rescued us from our enemies, His steadfast love is eternal;	*Vayyifrekenu mitzareinu ki le'olam chasdo*	וַיִּפְרְקֵנוּ מִצָּרֵינוּ כִּי לְעוֹלָם חַסְדּוֹ:	כד
25	Who gives food to all flesh, His steadfast love is eternal.	*Noten lechem lechol-basar ki le'olam chasdo*	נֹתֵן לֶחֶם לְכָל־בָּשָׂר כִּי לְעוֹלָם חַסְדּוֹ:	כה
26	Praise the God of heaven, His steadfast love is eternal.	*hodu le'el hashamayim ki le'olam chasdo*	הוֹדוּ לְאֵל הַשָּׁמָיִם כִּי לְעוֹלָם חַסְדּוֹ:	כו

137

קלז

	English	Transliteration	Hebrew	

1   By the rivers of Babylon, there we sat, sat and wept, as we thought of Tzion.

Al naharot bavel sham yashavnu gam-bachinu bezacherenu et-tziyyon

עַל נַהֲרוֹת בָּבֶל שָׁם יָשַׁבְנוּ גַּם־בָּכִינוּ בְּזָכְרֵנוּ אֶת־צִיּוֹן׃   א

2   There on the poplars we hung up our lyres,

Al-aravim betochah talinu kinnoroteinu

עַל־עֲרָבִים בְּתוֹכָהּ תָּלִינוּ כִּנֹּרוֹתֵינוּ׃   ב

3   for our captors asked us there for songs, our tormentors, for amusement, "Sing us one of the songs of Tzion."

Ki sham she'elunu shoveinu divrei-shir vetolaleinu simchah shiru lanu mishir tziyyon

כִּי שָׁם שְׁאֵלוּנוּ שׁוֹבֵינוּ דִּבְרֵי־שִׁיר וְתוֹלָלֵינוּ שִׂמְחָה שִׁירוּ לָנוּ מִשִּׁיר צִיּוֹן׃   ג

4   How can we sing a song of Hashem on alien soil?

Eich nashir et-shir-Adonai al admat nechar

אֵיךְ נָשִׁיר אֶת־שִׁיר־יְהֹוָה עַל אַדְמַת נֵכָר׃   ד

5   If I forget you, O Yerushalayim, let my right hand wither;

Im-eshkachech yerushalayim tishkach yemini

אִם־אֶשְׁכָּחֵךְ יְרוּשָׁלָ͏ִם תִּשְׁכַּח יְמִינִי׃   ה

6   let my tongue stick to my palate if I cease to think of you, if I do not keep Yerushalayim in memory even at my happiest hour.

Tidbak-leshoni lechikki im-lo ezkerechi im-lo a'aleh et-yerushalayim al rosh simchati

תִּדְבַּק־לְשׁוֹנִי לְחִכִּי אִם־לֹא אֶזְכְּרֵכִי אִם־לֹא אַעֲלֶה אֶת־יְרוּשָׁלַ͏ִם עַל רֹאשׁ שִׂמְחָתִי׃   ו

7

Remember, Hashem, against the Edomites the day of Yerushalayim's fall; how they cried, "Strip her, strip her to her very foundations!"

Zechor Adonai livnei edom et yom yerushalayim ha'omerim aru aru ad hayyesod bah

זְכֹר יְהֹוָה לִבְנֵי אֱדוֹם אֵת יוֹם יְרוּשָׁלָ͏ִם הָאֹמְרִים עָרוּ עָרוּ עַד הַיְסוֹד בָּהּ׃ ז

8

Fair Babylon, you predator, a blessing on him who repays you in kind what you have inflicted on us;

Bat-bavel hashedudah ashrei sheyshallem-lach et-gemulech sheggamalt lanu

בַּת־בָּבֶל הַשְּׁדוּדָה אַשְׁרֵי שֶׁיְשַׁלֶּם־לָךְ אֶת־גְּמוּלֵךְ שֶׁגָּמַלְתְּ לָנוּ׃ ח

9

a blessing on him who seizes your babies and dashes them against the rocks!

Ashrei sheyyochez venippetz et-olalayich el-hassala

אַשְׁרֵי שֶׁיֹּאחֵז וְנִפֵּץ אֶת־עֹלָלַיִךְ אֶל־הַסָּלַע׃ ט

138

קלח

1

Of David. I praise You with all my heart, sing a hymn to You before the divine beings;

Ledavid odecha vechol-libbi neged elohim azammerekka

לְדָוִד אוֹדְךָ בְכָל־לִבִּי נֶגֶד אֱלֹהִים אֲזַמְּרֶךָּ׃ א

2

I bow toward Your holy temple and praise Your name for Your steadfast love and faithfulness, because You have exalted Your name, Your word, above all.

Eshtachaveh el-heichal kodshecha ve'odeh et-shemecha al-chasdecha ve'al-amittecha ki-higdalta al-kol-shimcha imratecha

אֶשְׁתַּחֲוֶה אֶל־הֵיכַל קָדְשְׁךָ וְאוֹדֶה אֶת־שְׁמֶךָ עַל־חַסְדְּךָ וְעַל־אֲמִתֶּךָ כִּי־הִגְדַּלְתָּ עַל־כָּל־שִׁמְךָ אִמְרָתֶךָ׃ ב

3
When I called, You answered me, You inspired me with courage.

Beyom karati vatta'aneni tarhiveni venafshi oz

בְּיוֹם קָרָאתִי וַתַּעֲנֵנִי תַּרְהִבֵנִי בְנַפְשִׁי עֹז׃

ג

4
All the kings of the earth shall praise You, Hashem, for they have heard the words You spoke.

Yoducha Adonai kol-malchei-aretz ki shame'u imrei-ficha

יוֹדוּךָ יְהֹוָה כָּל־מַלְכֵי־אָרֶץ כִּי שָׁמְעוּ אִמְרֵי־פִיךָ׃

ד

5
They shall sing of the ways of Hashem, "Great is the majesty of Hashem!"

Veyashiru bedarchei Adonai ki gadol kevod Adonai

וְיָשִׁירוּ בְּדַרְכֵי יְהֹוָה כִּי גָדוֹל כְּבוֹד יְהֹוָה׃

ה

6
High though Hashem is, He sees the lowly; lofty, He perceives from afar.

Ki-ram Adonai veshafal yir'eh vegavoah mimmerchak yeyeda

כִּי־רָם יְהֹוָה וְשָׁפָל יִרְאֶה וְגָבֹהַּ מִמֶּרְחָק יְיֵדָע׃

ו

7
Though I walk among enemies, You preserve me in the face of my foes; You extend Your hand; with Your right hand You deliver me.

Im-elech bekerev tzarah techayyeni al af oyevai tishlach yadecha vetoshi'eni yeminecha

אִם־אֵלֵךְ בְּקֶרֶב צָרָה תְּחַיֵּנִי עַל אַף אֹיְבַי תִּשְׁלַח יָדֶךָ וְתוֹשִׁיעֵנִי יְמִינֶךָ׃

ז

8
Hashem will settle accounts for me. Hashem, Your steadfast love is eternal; do not forsake the work of Your hands.

Adonai yigmor bu'adi Adonai chasdecha le'olam ma'asei yadecha al-teref

יְהֹוָה יִגְמֹר בַּעֲדִי יְהֹוָה חַסְדְּךָ לְעוֹלָם מַעֲשֵׂי יָדֶיךָ אַל־תֶּרֶף׃

ח

139

	English	Transliteration	Hebrew
1	For the leader. Of David. A psalm. Hashem, You have examined me and know me.	*Lammenatzeach ledavid mizmor Adonai chakartani vatteda*	לַמְנַצֵּחַ לְדָוִד מִזְמוֹר יְהֹוָה חֲקַרְתַּנִי וַתֵּדָע: א
2	When I sit down or stand up You know it; You discern my thoughts from afar.	*Attah yada'ta shivti vekumi bantah lere'i merachok*	אַתָּה יָדַעְתָּ שִׁבְתִּי וְקוּמִי בַּנְתָּה לְרֵעִי מֵרָחוֹק: ב
3	You observe my walking and reclining, and are familiar with all my ways.	*Arechi veriv'i zerita vechol-derachai hiskantah*	אָרְחִי וְרִבְעִי זֵרִיתָ וְכׇל־דְּרָכַי הִסְכַּנְתָּה: ג
4	There is not a word on my tongue but that You, Hashem, know it well.	*Ki ein millah bilshoni hen Adonai yada'ta chullah*	כִּי אֵין מִלָּה בִּלְשׁוֹנִי הֵן יְהֹוָה יָדַעְתָּ כֻלָּהּ: ד
5	You hedge me before and behind; You lay Your hand upon me.	*Achor vakedem tzartani vattashet alai kappechah*	אָחוֹר וָקֶדֶם צַרְתָּנִי וַתָּשֶׁת עָלַי כַּפֶּכָה: ה
6	It is beyond my knowledge; it is a mystery; I cannot fathom it.	*Peli'ah da'at mimmenni nisgevah lo-uchal lah*	פְּלִיאָה [פְּלִאָה] דַעַת מִמֶּנִּי נִשְׂגְּבָה לֹא־אוּכַל לָהּ: ו
7	Where can I escape from Your spirit? Where can I flee from Your presence?	*Anah elech meruchecha ve'anah mippanecha evrach*	אָנָה אֵלֵךְ מֵרוּחֶךָ וְאָנָה מִפָּנֶיךָ אֶבְרָח: ז

8	If I ascend to heaven, You are there; if I descend to Sheol, You are there too.	*Im-essak shamayim sham attah ve'atzi'ah she'ol hinnekka*	אִם־אֶסַּק שָׁמַיִם שָׁם אָתָּה וְאַצִּיעָה שְּׁאוֹל הִנֶּךָּ׃	ח
9	If I take wing with the dawn to come to rest on the western horizon,	*Essa chanfei-shachar eshkenah be'acharit yam*	אֶשָּׂא כַנְפֵי־שָׁחַר אֶשְׁכְּנָה בְּאַחֲרִית יָם׃	ט
10	even there Your hand will be guiding me, Your right hand will be holding me fast.	*Gam-sham yadecha tancheni vetochazeni yeminecha*	גַּם־שָׁם יָדְךָ תַנְחֵנִי וְתֹאחֲזֵנִי יְמִינֶךָ׃	י
11	If I say, "Surely darkness will conceal me, night will provide me with cover,"	*Va'omar ach-choshech yeshufeni velayyelah or ba'adeni*	וָאֹמַר אַךְ־חֹשֶׁךְ יְשׁוּפֵנִי וְלַיְלָה אוֹר בַּעֲדֵנִי׃	יא
12	darkness is not dark for You; night is as light as day; darkness and light are the same.	*Gam-choshech lo-yachshich mimmecha velayyelah kayyom ya'ir kachasheichah ka'orah*	גַּם־חֹשֶׁךְ לֹא־יַחְשִׁיךְ מִמֶּךָ וְלַיְלָה כַּיּוֹם יָאִיר כַּחֲשֵׁיכָה כָּאוֹרָה׃	יב
13	It was You who created my conscience; You fashioned me in my mother's womb.	*Ki-attah kanita chilyotai tesukkeni beveten immi*	כִּי־אַתָּה קָנִיתָ כִלְיֹתָי תְּסֻכֵּנִי בְּבֶטֶן אִמִּי׃	יג
14	I praise You, for I am awesomely, wondrously made; Your work is wonderful; I know it very well.	*Odecha al ki nora'ot nifleiti nifla'im ma'asecha venafshi yoda'at me'od*	אוֹדְךָ עַל כִּי נוֹרָאוֹת נִפְלֵיתִי נִפְלָאִים מַעֲשֶׂיךָ וְנַפְשִׁי יֹדַעַת מְאֹד׃	יד

15	My frame was not concealed from You when I was shaped in a hidden place, knit together in the recesses of the earth.	*Lo-nichchad atzemi mimmekka asher-usseiti vasseter rukkamti betachtiyyot aretz*	לֹא־נִכְחַד עׇצְמִי מִמֶּךָּ אֲשֶׁר־עֻשֵּׂיתִי בַסֵּתֶר רֻקַּמְתִּי בְּתַחְתִּיּוֹת אָרֶץ:	טו
16	Your eyes saw my unformed limbs; they were all recorded in Your book; in due time they were formed, to the very last one of them.	*Galemi ra'u einecha ve'al-sifrecha kullam yikkatevu yamim yutzaru velo echad bahem*	גׇּלְמִי רָאוּ עֵינֶיךָ וְעַל־סִפְרְךָ כֻּלָּם יִכָּתֵבוּ יָמִים יֻצָּרוּ וְלֹא [וְלוֹ] אֶחָד בָּהֶם:	טז
17	How weighty Your thoughts seem to me, O Hashem, how great their number!	*Veli mah-yakeru re'eicha el meh atzemu rasheihem*	וְלִי מַה־יָּקְרוּ רֵעֶיךָ אֵל מֶה עָצְמוּ רָאשֵׁיהֶם:	יז
18	I count them—they exceed the grains of sand; I end—but am still with You.	*Esperem mechol yirbun hekitzoti ve'odi immach*	אֶסְפְּרֵם מֵחוֹל יִרְבּוּן הֱקִיצֹתִי וְעוֹדִי עִמָּךְ:	יח
19	O Hashem, if You would only slay the wicked— you murderers, away from me!—	*Im-tiktol eloah rasha ve'anshei damim suru menni*	אִם־תִּקְטֹל אֱלוֹהַּ רָשָׁע וְאַנְשֵׁי דָמִים סוּרוּ מֶנִּי:	יט
20	who invoke You for intrigue, Your enemies who swear by You falsely.	*Asher yomrucha limzimmah nasu lashav arecha*	אֲשֶׁר יֹאמְרֻךָ לִמְזִמָּה נָשֻׂא לַשָּׁוְא עָרֶיךָ:	כ
21	Hashem, You know I hate those who hate You, and loathe Your adversaries.	*Halo-mesan'echa Adonai esna uvitkomemecha etkotat*	הֲלוֹא־מְשַׂנְאֶיךָ יְהֹוָה אֶשְׂנָא וּבִתְקוֹמְמֶיךָ אֶתְקוֹטָט:	כא

22	I feel a perfect hatred toward them; I count them my enemies.	*Tachlit sin'ah senetim le'oyevim hayu li*

תַּכְלִית שִׂנְאָה שְׂנֵאתִים לְאוֹיְבִים הָיוּ לִי: כב

23	Examine me, O Hashem, and know my mind; probe me and know my thoughts.	*Chakereni el veda levavi bechaneni veda sar'appai*

חָקְרֵנִי אֵל וְדַע לְבָבִי בְּחָנֵנִי וְדַע שַׂרְעַפָּי: כג

24	See if I have vexatious ways, and guide me in ways everlasting.	*Ure'eh im-derech-otzev bi unecheni bederech olam*

וּרְאֵה אִם־דֶּרֶךְ־עֹצֶב בִּי וּנְחֵנִי בְּדֶרֶךְ עוֹלָם: כד

140

—◦◦⬡◦◦—

קמ

1	For the leader. A psalm of David.	*Lammenatzeach mizmor ledavid*

לַמְנַצֵּחַ מִזְמוֹר לְדָוִד: א

2	Rescue me, Hashem, from evil men; save me from the lawless,	*Challetzeni Adonai me'adam ra me'ish chamasim tintzereni*

חַלְּצֵנִי יְהֹוָה מֵאָדָם רָע מֵאִישׁ חֲמָסִים תִּנְצְרֵנִי: ב

3	whose minds are full of evil schemes, who plot war every day.	*Asher chashevu ra'ot belev kol-yom yaguru milchamot*

אֲשֶׁר חָשְׁבוּ רָעוֹת בְּלֵב כָּל־יוֹם יָגוּרוּ מִלְחָמוֹת: ג

4	They sharpen their tongues like serpents; spiders' poison is on their lips. Selah.	*Shananu leshonam kemo-nachash chamat achshuv tachat sefateimo selah*

שָׁנְנוּ לְשׁוֹנָם כְּמוֹ־נָחָשׁ חֲמַת עַכְשׁוּב תַּחַת שְׂפָתֵימוֹ סֶלָה: ד

5	Hashem, keep me out of the clutches of the wicked; save me from lawless men who scheme to make me fall.	*Shamereni Adonai midei rasha me'ish chamasim tintzereni asher chashevu lidchot pe'amai*	שָׁמְרֵנִי יְהֹוָה מִידֵי רָשָׁע מֵאִישׁ חֲמָסִים תִּנְצְרֵנִי אֲשֶׁר חָשְׁבוּ לִדְחוֹת פְּעָמָי:	א
6	Arrogant men laid traps with ropes for me; they spread out a net along the way; they set snares for me. Selah.	*Tamenu-ge'im pach li vachavalim paresu reshet leyad-ma'gal mokeshim shatu-li selah*	טָמְנוּ־גֵאִים פַּח לִי וַחֲבָלִים פָּרְשׂוּ רֶשֶׁת לְיַד־מַעְגָּל מֹקְשִׁים שָׁתוּ־לִי סֶלָה:	ב
7	I said to Hashem: You are my God; give ear, Hashem, to my pleas for mercy.	*Amarti lAdonai eli attah ha'azinah Adonai kol tachanunai*	אָמַרְתִּי לַיהֹוָה אֵלִי אָתָּה הַאֲזִינָה יְהֹוָה קוֹל תַּחֲנוּנָי:	ג
8	O Hashem, my Lord, the strength of my deliverance, You protected my head on the day of battle.	*Adonai Adonai oz yeshu'ati sakkotah leroshi beyom nashek*	יְהֹוָה אֲדֹנָי עֹז יְשׁוּעָתִי סַכֹּתָה לְרֹאשִׁי בְּיוֹם נָשֶׁק:	ד
9	Hashem, do not grant the desires of the wicked; do not let their plan succeed, else they be exalted. Selah.	*Al-titten Adonai ma'avayyei rasha zemamo al-tafek yarumu selah*	אַל־תִּתֵּן יְהֹוָה מַאֲוַיֵּי רָשָׁע זְמָמוֹ אַל־תָּפֵק יָרוּמוּ סֶלָה:	ה
10	May the heads of those who beset me be covered with the mischief of their lips.	*Rosh mesibbai amal sefateimo yechassemo*	רֹאשׁ מְסִבָּי עֲמַל שְׂפָתֵימוֹ יכסומו [יְכַסֵּמוֹ:]	ו
11	may coals of fire drop down upon them, and they be cast into pits, never to rise again.	*Yimmotu aleihem gechalim ba'esh yappilem bemahamorot bal-yakumu*	ימיטו [יִמּוֹטוּ] עֲלֵיהֶם גֶּחָלִים בָּאֵשׁ יַפִּלֵם בְּמַהֲמֹרוֹת בַּל־יָקוּמוּ:	ז

12	Let slanderers have no place in the land; let the evil of the lawless man drive him into corrals.	*Ish lashon bal-yikkon ba'aretz ish-chamas ra yetzudennu lemadchefot*	אִישׁ לָשׁוֹן בַּל־יִכּוֹן בָּאָרֶץ אִישׁ־חָמָס רָע יְצוּדֶנּוּ לְמַדְחֵפֹת:	ח
13	I know that Hashem will Champion the cause of the poor, the right of the needy.	*Yada'ti ki-ya'aseh Adonai din ani mishpat evyonim*	ידעת [יָדַעְתִּי] כִּי־יַעֲשֶׂה יְהֹוָה דִּין עָנִי מִשְׁפַּט אֶבְיֹנִים:	ט
14	Righteous men shall surely praise Your name; the upright shall dwell in Your presence.	*Ach tzaddikim yodu lishmecha yeshevu yesharim et-panecha*	אַךְ צַדִּיקִים יוֹדוּ לִשְׁמֶךָ יֵשְׁבוּ יְשָׁרִים אֶת־פָּנֶיךָ:	י

141

—◦⟨⊗⟩◦—

קמ״א

1	A psalm of David. I call You, Hashem, hasten to me; give ear to my cry when I call You.	*Mizmor ledavid Adonai keraticha chushah li ha'azinah koli bekare'i-lach*	מִזְמוֹר לְדָוִד יְהֹוָה קְרָאתִיךָ חוּשָׁה לִּי הַאֲזִינָה קוֹלִי בְּקָרְאִי־לָךְ:	א
2	Take my prayer as an offering of incense, my upraised hands as an evening sacrifice.	*Tikkon tefillati ketoret lefanecha mas'at kappai minchat-arev*	תִּכּוֹן תְּפִלָּתִי קְטֹרֶת לְפָנֶיךָ מַשְׂאַת כַּפַּי מִנְחַת־עָרֶב:	ב
3	Hashem, set a guard over my mouth, a watch at the door of my lips;	*Shitah Adonai shamerah lefi nitzerah al-dal sefatai*	שִׁיתָה יְהֹוָה שָׁמְרָה לְפִי נִצְּרָה עַל־דַּל שְׂפָתָי:	ג

4 let my mind not turn to an evil thing, to practice deeds of wickedness with men who are evildoers; let me not feast on their dainties.

Al-tat-libbi ledavar ra lehit'olel alilot beresha et-ishim po'alei-aven uval-elcham beman'ammeihem

אַל־תַּט־לִבִּי לְדָבָר רָע לְהִתְעוֹלֵל עֲלִלוֹת בְּרֶשַׁע אֶת־אִישִׁים פֹּעֲלֵי־אָוֶן וּבַל־אֶלְחַם בְּמַנְעַמֵּיהֶם: ד

5 Let the righteous man strike me in loyalty, let him reprove me; let my head not refuse such choice oil. My prayers are still against their evil deeds.

Yehelmeni-tzaddik chesed veyochicheni shemen rosh al-yani roshi ki-od utefillati bera'oteihem

יֶהֶלְמֵנִי־צַדִּיק חֶסֶד וְיוֹכִיחֵנִי שֶׁמֶן רֹאשׁ אַל־יָנִי רֹאשִׁי כִּי־עוֹד וּתְפִלָּתִי בְּרָעוֹתֵיהֶם: ה

6 May their judges slip on the rock, but let my words be heard, for they are sweet.

Nishmetu videi-sela shofeteihem veshame'u amarai ki na'emu

נִשְׁמְטוּ בִידֵי־סֶלַע שֹׁפְטֵיהֶם וְשָׁמְעוּ אֲמָרַי כִּי נָעֵמוּ: ו

7 As when the earth is cleft and broken up our bones are scattered at the mouth of Sheol.

Kemo foleach uvokea' ba'aretz nifzeru atzameinu lefi she'ol

כְּמוֹ פֹלֵחַ וּבֹקֵעַ בָּאָרֶץ נִפְזְרוּ עֲצָמֵינוּ לְפִי שְׁאוֹל: ז

8 My eyes are fixed upon You, O Hashem my Lord; I seek refuge in You, do not put me in jeopardy.

Ki eleicha Adonai Adonai einai bechah chasiti al-te'ar nafshi

כִּי אֵלֶיךָ יְהֹוָה אֲדֹנָי עֵינָי בְּכָה חָסִיתִי אַל־תְּעַר נַפְשִׁי: ח

9 Keep me from the trap laid for me, and from the snares of evildoers.

Shamereni midei fach yakeshu li umokeshot po'alei aven

שָׁמְרֵנִי מִידֵי פַח יָקְשׁוּ לִי וּמֹקְשׁוֹת פֹּעֲלֵי אָוֶן: ט

10 Let the wicked fall into their nets while I alone come through.

Yippelu vemachmorav resha'im yachad anochi ad-e'evor

יִפְּלוּ בְמַכְמֹרָיו רְשָׁעִים יַחַד אָנֹכִי עַד־אֶעֱבוֹר: י

142

1	A maskil of David, while he was in the cave. A prayer.	*Maskil ledavid bihyoto vamme'arah tefillah*	מַשְׂכִּיל לְדָוִד בִּהְיוֹתוֹ בַמְּעָרָה תְפִלָּה:	א
2	I cry aloud to Hashem; I appeal to Hashem loudly for mercy.	*Koli el-Adonai ez'ak koli el-Adonai etchannan*	קוֹלִי אֶל־יְהֹוָה אֶזְעָק קוֹלִי אֶל־יְהֹוָה אֶתְחַנָּן:	ב
3	I pour out my complaint before Him; I lay my trouble before Him	*Eshpoch lefanav sichi tzarati lefanav aggid*	אֶשְׁפֹּךְ לְפָנָיו שִׂיחִי צָרָתִי לְפָנָיו אַגִּיד:	ג
4	when my spirit fails within me. You know my course; they have laid a trap in the path I walk.	*Behit'attef alai ruchi ve'attah yada'ta netivati be'orach-zu ahallech tamenu fach li*	בְּהִתְעַטֵּף עָלַי רוּחִי וְאַתָּה יָדַעְתָּ נְתִיבָתִי בְּאֹרַח־זוּ אֲהַלֵּךְ טָמְנוּ פַח לִי:	ד
5	Look at my right and see— I have no friend; there is nowhere I can flee, no one cares about me.	*Habbeit yamin ure'eh ve'ein-li makkir avad manos mimmenni ein doresh lenafshi*	הַבֵּיט יָמִין וּרְאֵה וְאֵין־לִי מַכִּיר אָבַד מָנוֹס מִמֶּנִּי אֵין דּוֹרֵשׁ לְנַפְשִׁי:	ה
6	So I cry to You, Hashem; I say, "You are my refuge, all I have in the land of the living."	*Za'akti eleicha Adonai amarti attah machsi chelki be'eretz hachayyim*	זָעַקְתִּי אֵלֶיךָ יְהֹוָה אָמַרְתִּי אַתָּה מַחְסִי חֶלְקִי בְּאֶרֶץ הַחַיִּים:	ו

7
Listen to my cry, for I have been brought very low; save me from my pursuers, for they are too strong for me.

Hakshivah el-rinnati ki-dalloti me'od hatzileni merodefai ki ametzu mimmenni

הַקְשִׁיבָה אֶל־רִנָּתִי כִּי־דַלּוֹתִי מְאֹד הַצִּילֵנִי מֵרֹדְפַי כִּי אָמְצוּ מִמֶּנִּי:
ז

8
Free me from prison, that I may praise Your name. The righteous shall glory in me for Your gracious dealings with me.

Hotzi'ah mimmasger nafshi lehodot et-shemecha bi yachtiru tzaddikim ki tigmol alai

הוֹצִיאָה מִמַּסְגֵּר נַפְשִׁי לְהוֹדוֹת אֶת־שְׁמֶךָ בִּי יַכְתִּרוּ צַדִּיקִים כִּי תִגְמֹל עָלָי:
ח

143

קמג

1
A psalm of David. Hashem, hear my prayer; give ear to my plea, as You are faithful; answer me, as You are beneficent.

Mizmor ledavid Adonai shema tefillati ha'azinah el-tachanunai be'emunatecha aneni betzidkatecha

מִזְמוֹר לְדָוִד יְהוָה שְׁמַע תְּפִלָּתִי הַאֲזִינָה אֶל־תַּחֲנוּנַי בֶּאֱמֻנָתְךָ עֲנֵנִי בְּצִדְקָתֶךָ:
א

2
Do not enter into judgment with Your servant, for before You no creature is in the right.

Ve'al-tavo vemishpat et-avdecha ki lo-yitzdak lefanecha chol-chai

וְאַל־תָּבוֹא בְמִשְׁפָּט אֶת־עַבְדֶּךָ כִּי לֹא־יִצְדַּק לְפָנֶיךָ כָל־חָי:
ב

3
My foe hounded me; he crushed me to the ground; he made me dwell in darkness like those long dead.

Ki radaf oyev nafshi dikka la'aretz chayyati hoshivani vemachashakkim kemetei olam

כִּי רָדַף אוֹיֵב נַפְשִׁי דִּכָּא לָאָרֶץ חַיָּתִי הוֹשִׁיבַנִי בְמַחֲשַׁכִּים כְּמֵתֵי עוֹלָם:
ג

4 | My spirit failed within me; my mind was numbed with horror. | *Vattit'attef alai ruchi betochi yishtomem libbi* | וַתִּתְעַטֵּף עָלַי רוּחִי בְּתוֹכִי יִשְׁתּוֹמֵם לִבִּי: | ד

5 | Then I thought of the days of old; I rehearsed all Your deeds, recounted the work of Your hands. | *Zacharti yamim mikkedem hagiti vechol-po'olecha bema'aseh yadecha asocheach* | זָכַרְתִּי יָמִים מִקֶּדֶם הָגִיתִי בְכָל־פָּעֳלֶךָ בְּמַעֲשֵׂה יָדֶיךָ אֲשׂוֹחֵחַ: | ה

6 | I stretched out my hands to You, longing for You like thirsty earth. Selah. | *Perasti yadai eleicha nafshi ke'eretz-ayefah lecha selah* | פֵּרַשְׂתִּי יָדַי אֵלֶיךָ נַפְשִׁי כְּאֶרֶץ־עֲיֵפָה לְךָ סֶלָה: | ו

7 | Answer me quickly, Hashem; my spirit can endure no more. Do not hide Your face from me, or I shall become like those who descend into the Pit. | *Maher aneni Adonai kaletah ruchi al-taster panecha mimmenni venimshalti im-yoredei vor* | מַהֵר עֲנֵנִי יְהֹוָה כָּלְתָה רוּחִי אַל־תַּסְתֵּר פָּנֶיךָ מִמֶּנִּי וְנִמְשַׁלְתִּי עִם־יֹרְדֵי בוֹר: | ז

8 | Let me learn of Your faithfulness by daybreak, for in You I trust; let me know the road I must take, for on You I have set my hope. | *Hashmi'eni vabboker chasdecha ki-vecha vatacheti hodi'eni derech-zu elech ki-eleicha nasati nafshi* | הַשְׁמִיעֵנִי בַבֹּקֶר חַסְדֶּךָ כִּי־בְךָ בָטָחְתִּי הוֹדִיעֵנִי דֶּרֶךְ־זוּ אֵלֵךְ כִּי־אֵלֶיךָ נָשָׂאתִי נַפְשִׁי: | ח

9 | Save me from my foes, Hashem; to You I look for cover. | *Hatzileni me'oyevai Adonai eleicha chissiti* | הַצִּילֵנִי מֵאֹיְבַי יְהֹוָה אֵלֶיךָ כִסִּתִי: | ט

10 | Teach me to do Your will, for You are my God. Let Your gracious spirit lead me on level ground. | *Lammedeni la'asot retzonecha ki-attah elohai ruchacha tovah tancheni be'eretz mishor* | לַמְּדֵנִי לַעֲשׂוֹת רְצוֹנֶךָ כִּי־אַתָּה אֱלוֹהָי רוּחֲךָ טוֹבָה תַנְחֵנִי בְּאֶרֶץ מִישׁוֹר: | י

11 For the sake of Your name, Hashem, preserve me; as You are beneficent, free me from distress.

Lema'an-shimcha Adonai techayyeni betzidkatecha totzi mitzarah nafshi

לְמַעַן־שִׁמְךָ יְהֹוָה תְּחַיֵּנִי בְּצִדְקָתְךָ תוֹצִיא מִצָּרָה נַפְשִׁי:

יא

12 As You are faithful, put an end to my foes; destroy all my mortal enemies, for I am Your servant.

Uvechasdecha tatzmit oyevai veha'avadta kol-tzorarei nafshi ki ani avdecha

וּבְחַסְדְּךָ תַּצְמִית אֹיְבָי וְהַאֲבַדְתָּ כָּל־צֹרְרֵי נַפְשִׁי כִּי אֲנִי עַבְדֶּךָ:

יב

144

קמד

1 Of David. Blessed is Hashem, my rock, who trains my hands for battle, my fingers for warfare;

Ledavid baruch Adonai tzuri hammelammed yadai lakrav etzbe'otai lammilchamah

לְדָוִד בָּרוּךְ יְהֹוָה צוּרִי הַמְלַמֵּד יָדַי לַקְרָב אֶצְבְּעוֹתַי לַמִּלְחָמָה:

א

2 my faithful one, my fortress, my haven and my deliverer, my shield, in whom I take shelter, who makes peoples subject to me.

Chasdi umetzudati misgabbi umefalti li maginni uvo chasiti haroded ammi tachtai

חַסְדִּי וּמְצוּדָתִי מִשְׂגַּבִּי וּמְפַלְטִי לִי מָגִנִּי וּבוֹ חָסִיתִי הָרוֹדֵד עַמִּי תַחְתָּי:

ב

3 Hashem, what is man that You should care about him, mortal man, that You should think of him?

Adonai mah-adam vatteda'ehu ben-enosh vattechashevehu

יְהֹוָה מָה־אָדָם וַתֵּדָעֵהוּ בֶּן־אֱנוֹשׁ וַתְּחַשְּׁבֵהוּ:

ג

4 Man is like a breath; his days are like a passing shadow.

Adam lahevel damah yamav ketzel over

אָדָם לַהֶבֶל דָּמָה יָמָיו כְּצֵל עוֹבֵר:

ד

5	Hashem, bend Your sky and come down; touch the mountains and they will smoke.	*Adonai hat-shamecha vetered ga beharim veye'eshanu*

יְהֹוָה הַט־שָׁמֶיךָ וְתֵרֵד גַּע בֶּהָרִים וְיֶעֱשָׁנוּ: ה

6	Make lightning flash and scatter them; shoot Your arrows and rout them.	*Berok barak utefitzem shelach chitzecha utehummem*

בְּרוֹק בָּרָק וּתְפִיצֵם שְׁלַח חִצֶּיךָ וּתְהֻמֵּם: ו

7	Reach Your hand down from on high; rescue me, save me from the mighty waters, from the hands of foreigners,	*Shelach yadecha mimmarom petzeni vehatzileni mimmayim rabbim miyyad benei nechar*

שְׁלַח יָדֶיךָ מִמָּרוֹם פְּצֵנִי וְהַצִּילֵנִי מִמַּיִם רַבִּים מִיַּד בְּנֵי נֵכָר: ז

8	whose mouths speak lies, and whose oaths are false.	*Asher pihem dibber-shav viminam yemin shaker*

אֲשֶׁר פִּיהֶם דִּבֶּר־שָׁוְא וִימִינָם יְמִין שָׁקֶר: ח

9	O Hashem, I will sing You a new song, sing a hymn to You with a ten-stringed harp,	*Elohim shir chadash ashirah lach benevel asor azammerah-lach*

אֱלֹהִים שִׁיר חָדָשׁ אָשִׁירָה לָּךְ בְּנֵבֶל עָשׂוֹר אֲזַמְּרָה־לָּךְ: ט

10	to You who give victory to kings, who rescue His servant David from the deadly sword.	*Hannoten teshu'ah lammelachim happotzeh et-david avdo mecherev ra'ah*

הַנּוֹתֵן תְּשׁוּעָה לַמְּלָכִים הַפּוֹצֶה אֶת־דָּוִד עַבְדּוֹ מֵחֶרֶב רָעָה: י

11	Rescue me, save me from the hands of foreigners, whose mouths speak lies, and whose oaths are false.	*Petzeni vehatzileni miyyad benei-nechar asher pihem dibber-shav viminam yemin shaker*

פְּצֵנִי וְהַצִּילֵנִי מִיַּד בְּנֵי־נֵכָר אֲשֶׁר פִּיהֶם דִּבֶּר־שָׁוְא וִימִינָם יְמִין שָׁקֶר: יא

12 For our sons are like saplings, well-tended in their youth; our daughters are like cornerstones trimmed to give shape to a palace.

Asher baneinu kinti'im meguddalim bin'ureihem benoteinu chezaviyyot mechuttavot tavnit heichal

אֲשֶׁר בָּנֵינוּ כִּנְטִעִים מְגֻדָּלִים בִּנְעוּרֵיהֶם בְּנוֹתֵינוּ כְזָוִיֹּת מְחֻטָּבוֹת תַּבְנִית הֵיכָל: יב

13 Our storehouses are full, supplying produce of all kinds; our flocks number thousands, even myriads, in our fields;

Mezaveinu mele'im mefikim mizzan el-zan tzovnenu ma'alifot merubbavot bechutzoteinu

מְזָוֵינוּ מְלֵאִים מְפִיקִים מִזַּן אֶל־זַן צֹאונֵנוּ מַאֲלִיפוֹת מְרֻבָּבוֹת בְּחוּצוֹתֵינוּ: יג

14 our cattle are well cared for There is no breaching and no sortie, and no wailing in our streets.

Allufeinu mesubbalim ein-peretz ve'ein yotzet ve'ein tzevachah birchovoteinu

אַלּוּפֵינוּ מְסֻבָּלִים אֵין־פֶּרֶץ וְאֵין יוֹצֵאת וְאֵין צְוָחָה בִּרְחֹבֹתֵינוּ: יד

15 Happy the people who have it so; happy the people whose God is Hashem.

Ashrei ha'am shekkachah lo ashrei ha'am She'Adonai elohav

אַשְׁרֵי הָעָם שֶׁכָּכָה לּוֹ אַשְׁרֵי הָעָם שֶׁיֲהוָה אֱלֹהָיו: טו

145

קמה

1 A song of praise. Of David. I will extol You, my God and king, and bless Your name forever and ever.

Tehillah ledavid aromimcha elohai hammelech va'avarachah shimcha le'olam va'ed

תְּהִלָּה לְדָוִד אֲרוֹמִמְךָ אֱלוֹהַי הַמֶּלֶךְ וַאֲבָרְכָה שִׁמְךָ לְעוֹלָם וָעֶד: א

364

2	Every day will I bless You and praise Your name forever and ever.	*Bechol-yom avarachekka va'ahallah shimcha le'olam va'ed*	בְּכָל־יוֹם אֲבָרְכֶךָּ וַאֲהַלְלָה שִׁמְךָ לְעוֹלָם וָעֶד:	ב
3	Great is Hashem and much acclaimed; His greatness cannot be fathomed.	*Gadol Adonai umehullal me'od veligdullato ein cheker*	גָּדוֹל יְהֹוָה וּמְהֻלָּל מְאֹד וְלִגְדֻלָּתוֹ אֵין חֵקֶר:	ג
4	One generation shall laud Your works to another and declare Your mighty acts.	*Dor ledor yeshabbach ma'asecha ugevurotecha yaggidu*	דּוֹר לְדוֹר יְשַׁבַּח מַעֲשֶׂיךָ וּגְבוּרֹתֶיךָ יַגִּידוּ:	ד
5	The glorious majesty of Your splendor and Your wondrous acts will I recite.	*Hadar kevod hodecha vedivrei nifle'otecha asichah*	הֲדַר כְּבוֹד הוֹדֶךָ וְדִבְרֵי נִפְלְאֹתֶיךָ אָשִׂיחָה:	ה
6	Men shall talk of the might of Your awesome deeds, and I will recount Your greatness.	*Ve'ezuz nore'otecha yomeru ugedullatecha asapperennah*	וֶעֱזוּז נוֹרְאֹתֶיךָ יֹאמֵרוּ וגדולתיך [וּגְדוּלָּתְךָ] אֲסַפְּרֶנָּה:	ו
7	They shall celebrate Your abundant goodness, and sing joyously of Your beneficence.	*zecher rav-tuvecha yabbi'u vetzidkatecha yerannenu*	זֵכֶר רַב־טוּבְךָ יַבִּיעוּ וְצִדְקָתְךָ יְרַנֵּנוּ:	ז
8	Hashem is gracious and compassionate, slow to anger and abounding in kindness.	*Channun verachum Adonai erech appayim ugedal-chased*	חַנּוּן וְרַחוּם יְהֹוָה אֶרֶךְ אַפַּיִם וּגְדָל־חָסֶד:	ח
9	Hashem is good to all, and His mercy is upon all His works.	*Tov-Adonai lakkol verachamav al-kol-ma'asav*	טוֹב־יְהֹוָה לַכֹּל וְרַחֲמָיו עַל־כָּל־מַעֲשָׂיו:	ט

10	All Your works shall praise You, Hashem, and Your faithful ones shall bless You.	*Yoducha Adonai kol-ma'asecha vachasidecha yevarachuchah*	יוֹדוּךָ יְהֹוָה כָּל־מַעֲשֶׂיךָ וַחֲסִידֶיךָ יְבָרֲכוּכָה׃	י
11	They shall talk of the majesty of Your kingship, and speak of Your might,	*Kevod malchutecha yomeru ugevuratecha yedabberu*	כְּבוֹד מַלְכוּתְךָ יֹאמֵרוּ וּגְבוּרָתְךָ יְדַבֵּרוּ׃	יא
12	to make His mighty acts known among men and the majestic glory of His kingship.	*Lehodia' livnei ha'adam gevurotav uchevod hadar malchuto*	לְהוֹדִיעַ לִבְנֵי הָאָדָם גְּבוּרֹתָיו וּכְבוֹד הֲדַר מַלְכוּתוֹ׃	יב
13	Your kingship is an eternal kingship; Your dominion is for all generations.	*Malchutecha malchut kol-olamim umemsheltecha bechol-dor vador*	מַלְכוּתְךָ מַלְכוּת כָּל־עֹלָמִים וּמֶמְשַׁלְתְּךָ בְּכָל־דּוֹר וָדוֹר׃	יג
14	Hashem supports all who stumble, and makes all who are bent stand straight.	*Somech Adonai lechol-hannofelim vezokef lechol-hakkefufim*	סוֹמֵךְ יְהֹוָה לְכָל־הַנֹּפְלִים וְזוֹקֵף לְכָל־הַכְּפוּפִים׃	יד
15	The eyes of all look to You expectantly, and You give them their food when it is due.	*Einei-chol eleicha yesabberu ve'attah noten-lahem et-ochlam be'itto*	עֵינֵי־כֹל אֵלֶיךָ יְשַׂבֵּרוּ וְאַתָּה נוֹתֵן־לָהֶם אֶת־אָכְלָם בְּעִתּוֹ׃	טו
16	You give it openhandedly, feeding every creature to its heart's content.	*Poteach et-yadecha umasbia' lechol-chai ratzon*	פּוֹתֵחַ אֶת־יָדֶךָ וּמַשְׂבִּיעַ לְכָל־חַי רָצוֹן׃	טז
17	Hashem is beneficent in all His ways and faithful in all His works.	*Tzaddik Adonai bechol-derachav vechasid bechol-ma'asav*	צַדִּיק יְהֹוָה בְּכָל־דְּרָכָיו וְחָסִיד בְּכָל־מַעֲשָׂיו׃	יז

18	Hashem is near to all who call Him, to all who call Him with sincerity.	*Karov Adonai lechol-kore'av lechol asher yikra'uhu ve'emet*	קָרוֹב יְהֹוָה לְכָל־קֹרְאָיו לְכֹל אֲשֶׁר יִקְרָאֻהוּ בֶאֱמֶת:	יח
19	He fulfills the wishes of those who fear Him; He hears their cry and delivers them.	*Retzon-yere'av ya'aseh ve'et-shav'atam yishma veyoshi'em*	רְצוֹן־יְרֵאָיו יַעֲשֶׂה וְאֶת־שַׁוְעָתָם יִשְׁמַע וְיוֹשִׁיעֵם:	יט
20	Hashem watches over all who love Him, but all the wicked He will destroy.	*Shomer Adonai et-kol-ohavav ve'et kol-haresha'im yashmid*	שׁוֹמֵר יְהֹוָה אֶת־כָּל־אֹהֲבָיו וְאֵת כָּל־הָרְשָׁעִים יַשְׁמִיד:	כ
21	My mouth shall utter the praise of Hashem, and all creatures shall bless His holy name forever and ever.	*Tehillat Adonai yedabber-pi vivarech kol-basar shem kodsho le'olam va'ed*	תְּהִלַּת יְהֹוָה יְדַבֶּר־פִּי וִיבָרֵךְ כָּל־בָּשָׂר שֵׁם קָדְשׁוֹ לְעוֹלָם וָעֶד:	כא

146 ──◦⊗◦── קמו

1	Hallelujah. Praise Hashem, O my soul!	*Hallu-yah halli nafshi et-Adonai*	הַלְלוּ־יָהּ הַלְלִי נַפְשִׁי אֶת־יְהֹוָה:	א
2	I will praise Hashem all my life, sing hymns to my God while I exist.	*Ahallah Adonai bechayyai azammerah lelohai be'odi*	אֲהַלְלָה יְהֹוָה בְּחַיָּי אֲזַמְּרָה לֵאלֹהַי בְּעוֹדִי:	ב
3	Put not your trust in the great, in mortal man who cannot save.	*Al-tivtechu vindivim beven-adam she'ein lo teshu'ah*	אַל־תִּבְטְחוּ בִנְדִיבִים בְּבֶן־אָדָם שֶׁאֵין לוֹ תְשׁוּעָה:	ג

4	His breath departs; he returns to the dust; on that day his plans come to nothing.	*Tetze rucho yashuv le'admato bayyom hahu avedu eshtonotav*	תֵּצֵא רוּחוֹ יָשֻׁב לְאַדְמָתוֹ בַּיּוֹם הַהוּא אָבְדוּ עֶשְׁתֹּנֹתָיו: ד
5	Happy is he who has the God of Yaakov for his help, whose hope is in Hashem his God,	*Ashrei she'el ya'akov be'ezro sivro al-Adonai elohav*	אַשְׁרֵי שֶׁאֵל יַעֲקֹב בְּעֶזְרוֹ שִׂבְרוֹ עַל־יְהֹוָה אֱלֹהָיו: ה
6	maker of heaven and earth, the sea and all that is in them; who keeps faith forever;	*Oseh shamayim va'aretz et-hayyam ve'et-kol-asher-bam hashomer emet le'olam*	עֹשֶׂה שָׁמַיִם וָאָרֶץ אֶת־הַיָּם וְאֶת־כָּל־אֲשֶׁר־בָּם הַשֹּׁמֵר אֱמֶת לְעוֹלָם: ו
7	who secures justice for those who are wronged, gives food to the hungry. Hashem sets prisoners free;	*Oseh mishpat la'ashukim noten lechem lare'evim Adonai mattir asurim*	עֹשֶׂה מִשְׁפָּט לָעֲשׁוּקִים נֹתֵן לֶחֶם לָרְעֵבִים יְהֹוָה מַתִּיר אֲסוּרִים: ז
8	Hashem restores sight to the blind; Hashem makes those who are bent stand straight; Hashem loves the righteous;	*Adonai pokeach ivrim Adonai zokef kefufim Adonai ohev tzaddikim*	יְהֹוָה פֹּקֵחַ עִוְרִים יְהֹוָה זֹקֵף כְּפוּפִים יְהֹוָה אֹהֵב צַדִּיקִים: ח
9	Hashem watches over the stranger; He gives courage to the orphan and widow, but makes the path of the wicked tortuous.	*Adonai shomer et-gerim yatom ve'almanah ye'oded vederech resha'im ye'avvet*	יְהֹוָה שֹׁמֵר אֶת־גֵּרִים יָתוֹם וְאַלְמָנָה יְעוֹדֵד וְדֶרֶךְ רְשָׁעִים יְעַוֵּת: ט
10	Hashem shall reign forever, your God, O Tzion, for all generations. Hallelujah.	*Yimloch Adonai le'olam elohayich tziyyon ledor vador hallu-yah*	יִמְלֹךְ יְהֹוָה לְעוֹלָם אֱלֹהַיִךְ צִיּוֹן לְדֹר וָדֹר הַלְלוּ־יָהּ: י

147

1	Hallelujah. It is good to chant hymns to our God; it is pleasant to sing glorious praise.	*Hallu yah ki-tov zammerah eloheinu ki-na'im navah tehillah*	הַלְלוּ יָהּ כִּי־טוֹב זַמְּרָה אֱלֹהֵינוּ כִּי־נָעִים נָאוָה תְהִלָּה: א
2	Hashem rebuilds Yerushalayim; He gathers in the exiles of Yisrael.	*Boneh yerushalayim Adonai nidchei yisra'el yechannes*	בּוֹנֵה יְרוּשָׁלַ͏ִם יְהֹוָה נִדְחֵי יִשְׂרָאֵל יְכַנֵּס: ב
3	He heals their broken hearts, and binds up their wounds.	*Harofe lishvurei lev umechabbesh le'atzevotam*	הָרֹפֵא לִשְׁבוּרֵי לֵב וּמְחַבֵּשׁ לְעַצְּבוֹתָם: ג
4	He reckoned the number of the stars; to each He gave its name.	*Moneh mispar lakkochavim lechullam shemot yikra*	מוֹנֶה מִסְפָּר לַכּוֹכָבִים לְכֻלָּם שֵׁמוֹת יִקְרָא: ד
5	Great is our Lord and full of power; His wisdom is beyond reckoning.	*Gadol adoneinu verav-koach litvunato ein mispar*	גָּדוֹל אֲדוֹנֵינוּ וְרַב־כֹּחַ לִתְבוּנָתוֹ אֵין מִסְפָּר: ה
6	Hashem gives courage to the lowly, and brings the wicked down to the dust.	*Me'oded anavim Adonai mashpil resha'im adei-aretz*	מְעוֹדֵד עֲנָוִים יְהֹוָה מַשְׁפִּיל רְשָׁעִים עֲדֵי־אָרֶץ: ו
7	Sing to Hashem a song of praise, chant a hymn with a lyre to our God,	*Enu lAdonai betodah zammeru leloheinu vechinnor*	עֱנוּ לַיהֹוָה בְּתוֹדָה זַמְּרוּ לֵאלֹהֵינוּ בְכִנּוֹר: ז

8	who covers the heavens with clouds, provides rain for the earth, makes mountains put forth grass;	*Hammechasseh shamayim be'avim hammechin la'aretz matar hammatzmiach harim chatzir*	הַמְכַסֶּה שָׁמַיִם בְּעָבִים הַמֵּכִין לָאָרֶץ מָטָר הַמַּצְמִיחַ הָרִים חָצִיר: ח
9	who gives the beasts their food, to the raven's brood what they cry for.	*Noten livhemah lachmah livnei orev asher yikra'u*	נוֹתֵן לִבְהֵמָה לַחְמָהּ לִבְנֵי עֹרֵב אֲשֶׁר יִקְרָאוּ: ט
10	He does not prize the strength of horses, nor value the fleetness of men;	*Lo vigvurat hassus yechpatz lo-veshokei ha'ish yirtzeh*	לֹא בִגְבוּרַת הַסּוּס יֶחְפָּץ לֹא־בְשׁוֹקֵי הָאִישׁ יִרְצֶה: י
11	but Hashem values those who fear Him, those who depend on His faithful care.	*Rotzeh Adonai et-yere'av et-hammeyachalim lechasdo*	רוֹצֶה יְהוָה אֶת־יְרֵאָיו אֶת־הַמְיַחֲלִים לְחַסְדּוֹ: יא
12	O Yerushalayim, glorify Hashem; praise your God, O Tzion!	*Shabbechi yerushalayim et-Adonai halli elohayich tziyyon*	שַׁבְּחִי יְרוּשָׁלַ͏ִם אֶת־יְהוָה הַלְלִי אֱלֹהַיִךְ צִיּוֹן: יב
13	For He made the bars of your gates strong, and blessed your children within you.	*Ki-chizzak berichei she'arayich berach banayich bekirbech*	כִּי־חִזַּק בְּרִיחֵי שְׁעָרָיִךְ בֵּרַךְ בָּנַיִךְ בְּקִרְבֵּךְ: יג
14	He endows your realm with well-being, and satisfies you with choice wheat.	*Hassam-gevulech shalom chelev chittim yasbi'ech*	הַשָּׂם־גְּבוּלֵךְ שָׁלוֹם חֵלֶב חִטִּים יַשְׂבִּיעֵךְ: יד
15	He sends forth His word to the earth; His command runs swiftly.	*Hasholeach imrato aretz ad-meherah yarutz devaro*	הַשֹּׁלֵחַ אִמְרָתוֹ אָרֶץ עַד־מְהֵרָה יָרוּץ דְּבָרוֹ: טו

16	He lays down snow like fleece, scatters frost like ashes.	*Hannoten sheleg katzamer kefor ka'efer yefazzer*

הַנֹּתֵן שֶׁלֶג כַּצָּמֶר כְּפוֹר כָּאֵפֶר יְפַזֵּר: טז

17	He tosses down hail like crumbs— who can endure His icy cold?	*Mashlich karcho chefittim lifnei karato mi ya'amod*

מַשְׁלִיךְ קַרְחוֹ כְפִתִּים לִפְנֵי קָרָתוֹ מִי יַעֲמֹד: יז

18	He issues a command—it melts them; He breathes— the waters flow.	*Yishlach devaro veyamsem yashev rucho yizzelu-mayim*

יִשְׁלַח דְּבָרוֹ וְיַמְסֵם יַשֵּׁב רוּחוֹ יִזְּלוּ־מָיִם: יח

19	He issued His commands to Yaakov, His statutes and rules to Yisrael.	*Maggid devarav leya'akov chukkav umishpatav leyisra'el*

מַגִּיד דברו [דְּבָרָיו] לְיַעֲקֹב חֻקָּיו וּמִשְׁפָּטָיו לְיִשְׂרָאֵל: יט

20	He did not do so for any other nation; of such rules they know nothing. Hallelujah.	*Lo asah chen lechol-goy umishpatim bal-yeda'um hallu-yah*

לֹא עָשָׂה כֵן לְכָל־גּוֹי וּמִשְׁפָּטִים בַּל־יְדָעוּם הַלְלוּ־יָהּ: כ

148

⊸-◦⦿⬡⦿◦-⊷

קמ״ח

1	Hallelujah. Praise Hashem from the heavens; praise Him on high.	*Hallu yah hallu et-Adonai min-hashamayim halluhu bammeromim*

הַלְלוּ יָהּ הַלְלוּ אֶת־יְהֹוָה מִן־הַשָּׁמַיִם הַלְלוּהוּ בַּמְּרוֹמִים: א

2	Praise Him, all His angels, praise Him, all His hosts.	*Halluhu chol-mal'achav halluhu kol-tzeva'av*

הַלְלוּהוּ כָל־מַלְאָכָיו הַלְלוּהוּ כָּל־צבאו [צְבָאָיו]: ב

3	Praise Him, sun and moon, praise Him, all bright stars.	*halluhu shemesh veyareach halluhu kol-kochevei or*	הַלְלוּהוּ שֶׁמֶשׁ וְיָרֵחַ הַלְלוּהוּ כָּל־כּוֹכְבֵי אוֹר:	ג
4	Praise Him, highest heavens, and you waters that are above the heavens.	*Halluhu shemei hashamayim vehammayim asher me'al hashamayim*	הַלְלוּהוּ שְׁמֵי הַשָּׁמָיִם וְהַמַּיִם אֲשֶׁר מֵעַל הַשָּׁמָיִם:	ד
5	Let them praise the name of Hashem, for it was He who commanded that they be created.	*Yehallu et-shem Adonai ki hu tzivvah venivra'u*	יְהַלְלוּ אֶת־שֵׁם יְהֹוָה כִּי הוּא צִוָּה וְנִבְרָאוּ:	ה
6	He made them endure forever, establishing an order that shall never change.	*Vayya'amidem la'ad le'olam chak-natan velo ya'avor*	וַיַּעֲמִידֵם לָעַד לְעוֹלָם חָק־נָתַן וְלֹא יַעֲבוֹר:	ו
7	Praise Hashem, O you who are on earth, all sea monsters and ocean depths,	*Hallu et-Adonai min-ha'aretz tanninim vechol-tehomot*	הַלְלוּ אֶת־יְהֹוָה מִן־הָאָרֶץ תַּנִּינִים וְכָל־תְּהֹמוֹת:	ז
8	fire and hail, snow and smoke, storm wind that executes His command,	*Esh uvarad sheleg vekitor ruach se'arah osah devaro*	אֵשׁ וּבָרָד שֶׁלֶג וְקִיטוֹר רוּחַ סְעָרָה עֹשָׂה דְבָרוֹ:	ח
9	all mountains and hills, all fruit trees and cedars,	*Heharim vechol-geva'ot etz peri vechol-arazim*	הֶהָרִים וְכָל־גְּבָעוֹת עֵץ פְּרִי וְכָל־אֲרָזִים:	ט
10	all wild and tamed beasts, creeping things and winged birds,	*Hachayyah vechol-behemah remes vetzippor kanaf*	הַחַיָּה וְכָל־בְּהֵמָה רֶמֶשׂ וְצִפּוֹר כָּנָף:	י

11	all kings and peoples of the earth, all princes of the earth and its judges,	*Malchei-eretz vechol-le'ummim sarim vechol-shofetei aretz*

מַלְכֵי־אֶרֶץ וְכָל־לְאֻמִּים שָׂרִים וְכָל־שֹׁפְטֵי אָרֶץ: יא

| 12 | youths and maidens alike, old and young together. | *Bachurim vegam-betulot zekenim im-ne'arim* |

בַּחוּרִים וְגַם־בְּתוּלוֹת זְקֵנִים עִם־נְעָרִים: יב

| 13 | Let them praise the name of Hashem, for His name, His alone, is sublime; His splendor covers heaven and earth. | *Yehallu et-shem Adonai ki-nisgav shemo levaddo hodo al-eretz veshamayim* |

יְהַלְלוּ אֶת־שֵׁם יְהֹוָה כִּי־נִשְׂגָּב שְׁמוֹ לְבַדּוֹ הוֹדוֹ עַל־אֶרֶץ וְשָׁמָיִם: יג

| 14 | He has exalted the horn of His people for the glory of all His faithful ones, Yisrael, the people close to Him. Hallelujah. | *Vayyarem keren le'ammo tehillah lechol-chasidav livnei yisra'el am-kerovo hallu-yah* |

וַיָּרֶם קֶרֶן לְעַמּוֹ תְּהִלָּה לְכָל־חֲסִידָיו לִבְנֵי יִשְׂרָאֵל עַם־קְרֹבוֹ הַלְלוּיָהּ: יד

149

◦─○◦⬡◦○─◦

קמ״ט

| 1 | Hallelujah. Sing to Hashem a new song, His praises in the congregation of the faithful. | *Hallu yah shiru lAdonai shir chadash tehillato bikhal chasidim* |

הַלְלוּ יָהּ שִׁירוּ לַיהֹוָה שִׁיר חָדָשׁ תְּהִלָּתוֹ בִּקְהַל חֲסִידִים: א

2	Let Yisrael rejoice in its maker; let the children of Tzion exult in their king.	*Yismach yisra'el be'osav benei-tziyyon yagilu vemalkam*	יִשְׂמַח יִשְׂרָאֵל בְּעֹשָׂיו בְּנֵי־צִיּוֹן יָגִילוּ בְמַלְכָּם: ב
3	Let them praise His name in dance; with timbrel and lyre let them chant His praises.	*Yehal'lu shemo vemachol betof vechinnor yezammeru-lo*	יְהַלְלוּ שְׁמוֹ בְמָחוֹל בְּתֹף וְכִנּוֹר יְזַמְּרוּ־לוֹ: ג
4	For Hashem delights in His people; He adorns the lowly with victory.	*Ki-rotzeh Adonai be'ammo yefa'er anavim bishu'ah*	כִּי־רוֹצֶה יְהֹוָה בְּעַמּוֹ יְפָאֵר עֲנָוִים בִּישׁוּעָה: ד
5	Let the faithful exult in glory; let them shout for joy upon their couches,	*Ya'lezu chasidim bechavod yerannenu al-mishkevotam*	יַעְלְזוּ חֲסִידִים בְּכָבוֹד יְרַנְּנוּ עַל־מִשְׁכְּבוֹתָם: ה
6	with paeans to Hashem in their throats and two-edged swords in their hands,	*Romemot el bigronam vecherev pifiyyot beyadam*	רוֹמְמוֹת אֵל בִּגְרוֹנָם וְחֶרֶב פִּיפִיּוֹת בְּיָדָם: ו
7	to impose retribution upon the nations, punishment upon the peoples,	*La'asot nekamah baggoyim tochechot bal-ummim*	לַעֲשׂוֹת נְקָמָה בַּגּוֹיִם תּוֹכֵחֹת בַּלְאֻמִּים: ז
8	binding their kings with shackles, their nobles with chains of iron,	*Le'sor malcheihem bezikkim venichbedeihem bechavlei varzel*	לֶאְסֹר מַלְכֵיהֶם בְּזִקִּים וְנִכְבְּדֵיהֶם בְּכַבְלֵי בַרְזֶל: ח

150

1	Hallelujah. Praise Hashem in His sanctuary; praise Him in the sky, His stronghold.	*Hallu yah hallu-el bekodsho halluhu birkia' uzzo*	הַלְלוּ יָהּ הַלְלוּ־אֵל בְּקָדְשׁוֹ הַלְלוּהוּ בִּרְקִיעַ עֻזּוֹ׃	א
2	Praise Him for His mighty acts; praise Him for His exceeding greatness.	*Halluhu vigvurotav halluhu kerov gudlo*	הַלְלוּהוּ בִגְבוּרֹתָיו הַלְלוּהוּ כְּרֹב גֻּדְלוֹ׃	ב
3	Praise Him with blasts of the shofar; praise Him with harp and lyre.	*Halluhu beteka shofar halluhu benevel vechinnor*	הַלְלוּהוּ בְּתֵקַע שׁוֹפָר הַלְלוּהוּ בְּנֵבֶל וְכִנּוֹר׃	ג
4	Praise Him with timbrel and dance; praise Him with lute and pipe.	*Halluhu vetof umachol halluhu beminnim ve'ugav*	הַלְלוּהוּ בְתֹף וּמָחוֹל הַלְלוּהוּ בְּמִנִּים וְעוּגָב׃	ד
5	Praise Him with resounding cymbals; praise Him with loud-clashing cymbals.	*Halluhu vetziltzelei-shama halluhu betziltzelei teru'ah*	הַלְלוּהוּ בְצִלְצְלֵי־שָׁמַע הַלְלוּהוּ בְּצִלְצְלֵי תְרוּעָה׃	ה
6	Let all that breathes praise Hashem. Hallelujah.	*Kol hanneshamah tehallel yah hallu-yah*	כֹּל הַנְּשָׁמָה תְּהַלֵּל יָהּ הַלְלוּ־יָהּ׃	ו

For more inspiring
commentary, interactive maps,
educational videos, vivid
photographs and more,
please visit our website

www.TheIsraelBible.com

THE
ISRAEL
BIBLE